THE RATIONAL CHOICE CONTROVERSY

The Rational Choice Controversy

Economic Models of Politics Reconsidered

Edited by
Jeffrey Friedman

Yale University Press
New Haven & London

Originally published 1995 (as *Critical Review*, Vol. 9, Nos. 1–2) by Critical Review
Foundation. Revised paperbound edition published 1996 by Yale University Press.
Published by arrangement with Critical Review Foundation.

Printed in the United States of America.

Library of Congress Cataloging-in-Publication Data
The rational choice controversy: economic models of politics reconsidered / edited by
    Jeffrey Friedman.
        p.   cm.
    Includes bibliographical references and index.
    ISBN 0–300–06821–2 (pbk.: alk. paper)
    1. Political science—Methodology.   2. Rational choice theory.
    I. Friedman, Jeffrey.
JA71. R295   1996
320'.01—DC20   96–17325
                    CIP

A catalogue record for this book is available from the British Library.

The paper in this book meets the guidelines for permanence and durability of the
Committee on Production Guidelines for Book Longevity of the Council on Library
Resources.

10   9   8   7   6   5   4   3   2   1

CONTENTS

Jeffrey Friedman

INTRODUCTION:
ECONOMIC APPROACHES
TO POLITICS

The debate over Green and Shapiro's Pathologies of Rational Choice Theory sustains their contention that rational choice theory has not produced novel, empirically sustainable findings about politics—if one accepts their definition of empirically sustainable findings. Green and Shapiro show that rational choice research often resembles the empirically vacuous practices in which economists engage under the aegis of instrumentalism. Yet Green and Shapiro's insistence that theoretical constructs should produce accurate predictions may itself lead to instrumentalism. Some of Green and Shapiro's critics hint at a better approach, which would eschew predictively "testing the validity" of rational choice theory in favor of testing the applicability *of the theory to particular cases. For this approach to work, however, the theory cannot be assumed* to apply to any particular case.

Politics has often been portrayed as a preeminent arena of the accidental, the emotional, the ideological, the habitual, and the traditional. Yet in recent years, growing numbers of scholars have attempted to apply to politics the postulates of rational choice theory. How can politics and, by implication, history be regarded as products of "rational choice"?

Public Choice Theory and Empirical Reality

To answer that question, a distinction should first be drawn between two

Jeffrey Friedman, Department of Political Science, Yale University, thanks Joseph Agassi, Peter J. Boettke, James M. Buchanan, Bruce Caldwell, Dennis Chong, Tyler Cowen, Donald P. Green, Daniel M. Hausman, James Bernard Murphy, Mancur Olson, Norman Schofield, Ian Shapiro, and Juliet Williams for their comments on earlier drafts.

terms that are often used imprecisely or synonymously: *rational choice* and *public choice*. One understanding of the difference holds that public choice theory applies economic analysis to political (i.e., "public") decision making, while rational choice theory goes even farther, applying economics to other nonmarket realms, such as family life. This distinction, to adopt John Ferejohn's (1991) terminology, attributes to both public and rational choice theory a "thin" understanding of the economists' rationality postulate: individuals are assumed to have only the inclination to satisfy their stable and ordered preferences, whether these are selfish or not. But outside the academy, public choice theory has a decidedly "thick" connotation, referring to the alleged propensity of political actors to pursue their material self-interest. This understanding of public choice theory, associated with its "Virginia school," is used here.[1] Accordingly, I mean by "rational choice theory" the much broader claim that, regardless of what sort of ends people pursue, they do so through strategic, instrumentally rational behavior. If public choice theory is false or its applicability is restricted, rational choice theory may yet be completely vindicated; but if rational choice theory fails, public choice theory goes down with it.

By systematically examining whether political actors are primarily motivated by selfish ends, public choice theory has raised crucial questions about the advisability of previously accepted policies, institutions, and political systems. Not only does public choice theory forcefully remind empirical scholars of Machiavelli's and Hobbes's suggestion that self-interest may animate putatively public-spirited policies, but it impels normative scholars to ask if any given substitution of political for market processes depends unrealistically on selfless voters, legislators, or bureaucrats.

Like most important ideas, however, public choice theory is liable to polemical oversimplification. The main danger is that the *possibility* that people are as self-interested in their political as their economic behavior may be treated as the *assumption* that self-interest is always and everywhere the real fountainhead of politics. This tendency is present even in the work of one of the most careful public choice scholars, James Buchanan, who writes, for example, that "the burden of proof should rest with those who suggest that wholly different models of man apply in the political and the economic realms of behavior" (1984, 13-14; cf. Buchanan and Tullock 1962, 19). The validity of Buchanan's argument is far from obvious. Scientifically speaking, the notion that people are as selfish in politics as in their economic dealings should be treated as skeptically as any other "model." That is, it should be treated as a hypothesis—even if it has *always* turned out to be true—simply because no claim about empirical reality can be assumed to be true a priori.

As a practical matter, of course, one may want to treat *as if* it were true, a priori, a theory that seems to explain an empirical regularity; that is, one may want to use such a theory as a rule of thumb (cf. Ordeshook below, 187) to guide one's future actions—but always with the caveat that new circumstances may alter the applicability of the "rule." Rules of thumb are not laws, and while, in a given time and place, one may cautiously generalize from observed self-interest, neither the prevalence of self-interest nor its magnitude when compared to other causal factors is an ahistorical given. Therefore, while political actors (as opposed to scholars) may justifiably treat past regularities as starting points for future predictions, such predictions remain hypothetical, and in the consideration of new cases, competing hypotheses—while perhaps less initially plausible—should bear no greater *evidentiary* burdens than old regularities. To insist on a double standard here would be dogmatic.

It is easy to see why public choice scholars may view their theory as self-evident rather than contingent. Most public choice scholars are economists, and the thick-rational picture of human beings as members of the species *Homo economicus*, while supposedly hypothetical even in economics textbooks, is, in the practice of economics, taken for granted as an obvious truth. We should be cognizant, however, of Buchanan and Gordon Tullock's admonition that "the ultimate defense of the economic-individualist behavioral assumption must be empirical. . . . The only final test of a model lies in its ability to assist in understanding real phenomena" (Buchanan and Tullock 1962, 28; cf. ibid., 21). Otherwise, models are likely to be mistaken for real-world phenomena even when there is little evidence that the models actually apply. And empirical researchers are liable to take for granted that finding a correlation between private interests and the adoption of a given public policy—which establishes the mere *possibility* that the public choice explanation is valid—actually demonstrates causality, and, moreover, causality of universal scope.

Perhaps for those reasons, the effort of comparing public choice hypotheses against alternatives frequently falls to non-public choice scholars. One such effort is Leif Lewin's *Self-Interest and Public Interest in Western Democracies*, published by Oxford University Press in 1991. Reviewing in detail the empirical literature on a variety of public choice claims—almost all of which was written by non-public choice researchers—Lewin found that in no case does public choice theory withstand scrutiny as a general hypothesis about the ubiquity of self-interest in politics. Thus, voters usually fail to "vote their pocketbooks"; when economic concerns are salient (which is not always the case; cf. Wattenberg 1991, 27), they tend to vote not egoistically, as public choice theory predicts, but "sociotropically," favoring the candidate or party they think likeliest to benefit the economy of their society as a whole (Lewin 1991, ch. 2; cf. Kiewiet 1983; Kinder and

Kiewiet 1981; Fiorina 1981; but see Nannestad and Paldam 1994). Nor is there plausible evidence for the allegedly pervasive "political business cycle": for the most part, politicians appear to have primed the pump before election day only in the mid-twentieth-century United States (Lewin 1991, ch. 3). And the growth of the public sector cannot be convincingly attributed to bureaucrats who maximize their agencies' budgets for personal gain; even if bureaucrats are assumed to be primarily self-seeking—an assumption persuasively disputed by Mark Kelman (1988, 218–20)—it is unclear how budget maximization would, even in theory, serve their selfish ends (see Blais and Dion 1991). Not surprisingly, then, little empirical evidence supporting the budget-maximization claim has been unearthed (Lewin 1991, ch. 4).

The evidence adduced by Lewin (and Kelman) suggests that there is, in fact, a disjunction between the prevalence of self-interest in the economy and in other spheres, contrary to the public choice assumption. A plausible reason for this finding is not hard to come by. In the modern West, it is widely assumed that personal gain is the legitimate goal of economic activity, while it is thought to be illegitimate in other spheres, such as political and personal life. Indeed, the economic realm could be *defined* as the arena in which selfishness is considered legitimate. It is only to be expected, then, that—to some extent—people will internalize and be guided by unselfish norms in noneconomic realms (cf. Steven Kelman 1987, 244–45; Green 1992). The extent of self-interestedness is therefore likely to vary historically as perceptions of appropriate behavior change. It would be foolish to deny the *possibility* that public choice theory will be applicable in a given instance, but it is equally unwise to assert in advance that it *must* apply in all cases merely because it applies in some.

Green and Shapiro's Critique of Rational Choice Theory

Since the claim that people are instrumentally rational seems to be even more "obvious" than the claim that they are selfish, it is impressive that rational choice scholars tend to take more seriously than their public choice colleagues the need to test their claim against empirical data. That they do is shown by the attention they have paid to a work that questions whether rational choice theory succeeds in explaining real-world phenomena: Donald P. Green and Ian Shapiro's *Pathologies of Rational Choice Theory: A Critique of Applications in Political Science* (Yale University Press, 1994).[2] While Lewin's *Self-Interest and Public Interest* made barely a ripple in public choice circles, Green and Shapiro's book was the subject of well-attended panels at successive meetings of the American Political Science Association and heated debates at dozens of American, Canadian, British, and Australian universities. In response to the controversy and to the important issues it raised, not only concerning rational choice and public choice theory but social science methodology, *Critical Review: An Interdisciplinary Journal of Politics and Society* published a double issue on Green and Shapiro's book in 1995, republished here.

Most of the contributors to the present volume agree that rational choice theory should be empirically tested rather than treated as an a priori truth. While some contributors applaud *Pathologies* or urge more uncompromising criticisms of rational choice theory (Abelson, Lane, Murphy, and Taylor below), others argue that Green and Shapiro misunderstand the theory (Lohmann, Schofield below), overlook its achievements (Fiorina, Kelley, Ordeshook, Shepsle below), or adhere to naive methodological standards (Chong, Diermeier, Ferejohn and Satz below). If a debate this complex can be summarized briefly, perhaps it can be said that most of their critics concede Green and Shapiro's main contention: that the applicability of nonobvious rational choice hypotheses to real-world political phenomena has yet to be demonstrated empirically   but only if we accept Green and Shapiro's view of what counts as an empirical demonstration. For the most part, then, the debate below tends to focus on the approach to empirical science that underpins Green and Shapiro's list of methodological "pathologies."

The first of these pathologies is "post hoc theory development" (*Pathologies*, 34–35)—known to statisticians as "curve fitting." Green and Shapiro contend that rather than formulating bold predictions that are falsifiable by empirical evidence, rational choice theorists tend first to look at the empirical evidence, then design a rational choice model that fits it. If disconfirming data should later come in, a new version of rational choice theory is concocted to redescribe the anomaly as "rational." A related vice, according to Green and Shapiro, is the tendency to compare rational choice theories against "either untenable alternatives or none at all" (ibid., 37)—as is often the case in public choice scholarship.

Second, Green and Shapiro contend that those rational choice predictions that are not amended post hoc are spared modification only because they rely on unmeasurable ("unobservable") entities, such as "equilibrium," making it difficult to detect whether the antecedent or "initial" conditions from which a predicted result should be expected to follow did, in fact, obtain.

Third, rational choice theorists allegedly engage in "arbitrary domain restriction." It is one thing, Green and Shapiro contend, to specify in advance *particular* reasons why a theory may not explain a certain class of phenomena. It is another thing, however, to suggest that rational choice theory is applicable "wherever the theory seems to work" (*Pathologies*,

45)—that is, that rational choice theory is valid *ceteris paribus,* where the scope of the caveat is unspecified by the theory.

Fourth, Green and Shapiro charge that rational choice predictions often only vaguely specify the magnitude of the effects being predicted.

Finally, they argue that rational choice theorists frequently search for confirming rather than falsifying evidence—or misconstrue the latter as the former.

The first three chapters of *Pathologies* and its conclusion, where Green and Shapiro describe rational choice theory and the methodological basis of their critique of it, may be the most important parts of the book. While there is insufficient space to reproduce the subtleties of those chapters here, we can illustrate the "pathologies" by surveying the middle chapters of the book, where Green and Shapiro substantiate their indictments by examining the best-developed applications of rational choice theory to American politics. A summary of their conclusions in these chapters may be useful to readers unfamiliar with the empirical issues to which many of the essays in this volume refer. Readers interested in the detailed argumentation and evidence for Green and Shapiro's conclusions, however, must consult *Pathologies* itself.

In Chapter 4, Green and Shapiro examine the phenomenon of voting— a major paradox for rational choice theory. In a real-world election with a large electorate, it is instrumentally irrational for anyone to cast a ballot, since no single vote has more than an infinitesimal chance of deciding the outcome. Whether one favors selfish or selfless ends, virtually any activity in pursuit of those ends would be more effective than the time spent on voting (and on educating oneself about candidates and issues). Yet hundreds of millions of people do vote. For rational choice theory, this would appear to be a gigantic anomaly.

Green and Shapiro point out that the usual response of rational choice theorists has been to modify their theory, post hoc, such that the "selective incentives" to vote come to encompass not only the material benefits that might flow to a voter from the election of a friendly candidate, but also, for instance, the psychic benefits public-spirited citizens feel when doing their duty by voting—regardless of the chance that their votes will affect the outcome. Hence the rational choice "point prediction" changes from no turnout to massive turnout. Another approach Green and Shapiro condemn is to declare that rational choice theory does not apply to cases (such as mass elections) where an individual's action is so inefficacious that instrumental considerations should not be expected to predominate in the first place. In Green and Shapiro's estimation, then, rational choice theory only avoids falsification by the phenomenon of voting by being either arbitrarily restricted to other domains or modified beyond recognition.

In Chapter 5 Green and Shapiro turn to other cases of "free riding." Voting in mass elections is but one instance of a larger problem for rational choice theory: why should anyone—again, irrespective of whether or not the goals she pursues are self-interested—devote resources of time or money to causes she favors, but has little chance of decisively assisting? Why not, instead, catch a free ride on the efforts of others to help the cause succeed? Rational choice theory would seem to be refuted not only by people who vote, but by those who contribute small amounts of money to political campaigns, attend rallies, and engage in other forms of collective action designed to secure goals whose achievement is independent of the efforts of any single participant.

According to Green and Shapiro, rational choice scholars avoid this problem by discussing only confirming evidence for their theory or by comparing it only to unchallenging null hypotheses. Oftentimes, rational choice accounts of collective action also "expand what counts as a selective incentive in order to evade problematic evidence" (*Pathologies*, 87), interpreting collective action as benefitting individual participants by enhancing their reputation, allowing them to express their convictions, entertaining them, or satisfying their sense of duty. As with post hoc attempts to make rational choice theory compatible with voting, here the criteria of rationality are so all-encompassing that rational choice theory becomes an unfalsifiable tautology.

In Chapter 6 Green and Shapiro take up rational choice models of legislative behavior. Rational choice theory shows that any parliamentary majority in favor of a set of legislative policies is unstable, in that a different majority can be found that will support a different policy combination. This should lead to aimless parliamentary "cycling" between different legislative equilibria; since this does not often occur, it could mean that manipulated or brokered legislative outcomes are masquerading as the unique will of the parliamentary majority. The unsettling consequences for democratic theory are apparent. But, Green and Shapiro ask, how well are rational choice models of parliamentary behavior borne out in practice? Such writers as Tullock accept that cycling is infrequent, but account for this anomaly by imputing parliamentary stability to logrolling, coalition building, and a host of other rational-choice-friendly post hoc possibilities that sidestep the question of verisimilitude by relying on ambiguities in their depiction of legislative "equilibrium" and "stability." Moreover, when rational choice work that compares the degree of instability produced by different legislative rules—since the theory suggests rules should be decisive—does not produce the hypothesized results, the theory is altered tautologically, such that "*when the assumptions of the model hold*, the prediction holds" (*Pathologies*, 144, emphasis original).

Finally, Chapter 7 considers "spatial theories" of electoral competition—in other words, theories that model candidates' issue positions by comparing them to graduated voter preferences that can be mapped as points on a line segment. Spatial electoral theories start with the postulate that candidates will converge toward the position of the "median voter," portraying themselves as *nearly* indistinguishable moderates so as to capture all the votes to the left or the right of the political center-point. Green and Shapiro complain that, despite the many analytic complications that have been added to this simple picture, spatial voting hypotheses have not been tested against posited stratagems that are not readily captured by such models, such as the manipulation of candidates' personal images; and that when, all too infrequently, spatial theories are tested, they do not seem to explain many American election campaigns. On the other hand, spatial models that seek verisimilitude tend to predict all possible outcomes, including the *divergence* of candidates' positions; and they leave unanswered the question of the *magnitude* of the various forces driving candidates away from equilibrium. Moreover, as with rational choice models of parliamentary behavior, spatial behavior models are often tautologized, Green and Shapiro contend, by their use of unmeasurables such as "risk aversion, discounting of future outcomes, beliefs about the likely behavior of others, [and] utilities derived from outcomes other than electoral victory" (*Pathologies*, 175-76). With such vaguely defined forces at work, "it is unlikely that spatial models . . . can be estimated statistically" (ibid., 176).

A few remarks might bring some perspective to the debate over whether such practices are indeed blameworthy by highlighting parallels between them and the practices, and methodology, of economics—where rational choice theory originated (but see Murphy below).

Rational Choice Theory in Political Science and Economics

An appropriate starting point is the objection, made below by Ferejohn and Debra Satz, Morris Fiorina, and Kenneth Shepsle, that Green and Shapiro's list of pathologies seems to require that rational choice theory be subjected to "state-of-the-art statistical analysis" (Fiorina, 90) in order to qualify as empirically substantiated. Observers of the debate may find this argument surprising: if anything, one might have expected the *critics* of rational choice theory to champion humanistic approaches to social science against rational choice reductionism. Yet it turns out that rational choice theory is itself seen by some of its most prominent proponents as more humanistic (that is, as suffering fewer of the distorting effects of scientism) than are the critics' standards of proof.

In reply, Green and Shapiro point out that *Pathologies* does not "advocate the exclusive use of quantitative methods in political science" (below, 245). To equate science with statistics would, Green and Shapiro suggest, be as wrongheaded as the rational choice pathologies they identify: in both cases, scholarship would be driven by researchers' precommitment to particular methods rather than by their determination to understand political phenomena. All they ask, Green and Shapiro write, is that scientific attitudes toward data selection, measurement, and reasoning prevail, "whether the mode of inquiry be ethnographic or statistical" (ibid.; cf. *Pathologies*, 172). Is it possible that their critics have, nonetheless, correctly detected a hyperpositivist tendency that, despite Green and Shapiro's intentions, is somehow implied (if not entailed) by their argument?

Here recourse to the recent history of economics may be useful. Until the middle of this century, the mainstream methodological view, derived from both classical and Austrian economists (see Hausman 1992b, 123, and Caldwell 1982, 103-4), emphasized "the self-evident nature of the basic postulates of economic theory" (Caldwell 1982, 99). And basic economic assumptions were not only seen as obviously true; they were unfalsifiable in principle, since they were held to apply only *ceteris paribus*—that is, in the absence of countervailing factors, which John Stuart Mill called "disturbing causes." Since such disturbances are frequently or always present, economic theory was thought unable to predict exactly what will happen in a given instance. On the other hand, economic theory *was* held to be realistic in the sense that its assumptions do hold good when no disturbances are present. Two independent claims are at work here: first, that economic assumptions identify efficacious initial conditions that are universally present in human affairs—the self-evidence postulate; second, that the predictions following from these assumptions are inexact, because other conditions may counteract them in a given instance—the *ceteris paribus* postulate.

In the 1940s and 1950s economists began to abandon the classical/Austrian orthodoxy. Terence Hutchison's *The Significance and Basic Postulates of Economic Theory* (1938) pioneered the new, positivist approach that would eventually lead to Milton Friedman's enormously influential "The Methodology of Positive Economics" (1953). Hutchison argued that basic economic assumptions (such as instrumental rationality), being untestable in principle, are devoid of scientific merit. "The price of unconditional necessity and certainty of propositions of pure logic and mathematics (and of propositions of pure theory) is," he wrote, "complete lack of empirical content" (Hutchison 1938, 27). For

> the *ceteris paribus* assumption makes out of an empirical proposition that is
> concerned with facts, and therefore conceivably can be false, a necessary ana-

lytical-tautological proposition. . . . The *ceteris paribus* assumption sweeps all the unknowns together under one portmanteau assumption for a logical "solution." (Ibid., 1938, 42)

Norman Schofield points out below that the prepositivistic method criticized by Hutchison is still practiced by microeconomists—who continue to derive postulates about economic interactions from rational choice assumptions (the very ones that have, in turn, been borrowed by some political scientists). But while microeconomists may be accused of relying on the *ceteris paribus* self-evidence of their models as a substitute for extensive empirical research, macroeconomists, who study economy-wide aggregate phenomena, adhere more closely to the instrumentalist version of positivism that is widely accepted as the "official" economic methodology. According to instrumentalism as formulated by Milton Friedman, a theory should be judged by its predictive accuracy, not the realism of its assumptions. Thus, macroeconomists tend to assess the validity of generalizations that have relatively weak theoretical foundations by seeing how well they account for statistical data, or they simply make predictions based on statistical regularities that have no theoretical foundation at all.[3]

All four of Green and Shapiro's "pathologies" are (they contend) objectionable for reasons that are strikingly similar to both Hutchison's positivism and Friedman's instrumentalism. That is, they are "pathological" inasmuch as they inhibit the testing of rational choice theory by definite predictions. When Green and Shapiro allow only those post hoc, falsification-avoiding expansions of rational choice theory that can survive subsequent attempts at predictive falsification; when they demand that the theory predict magnitudes and specify observables in ways that can be tested; when they disavow ad hoc shrinkages of the domain of application because this averts falsification by inaccurate predictions; and when they condemn searches for confirming rather than falsifying evidence, they are attempting to secure predictions that can serve as tests of the theory's validity. Given the association in economics between Friedmanite predictivism (see Caldwell 1992) and (macroeconomic) statistical testing, it is understandable that Shepsle should characterize Green and Shapiro as "political statisticians . . . contemptuous of anything short of . . . systematic, comprehensive, and sophisticated data analysis" (below, 219).

Strictly speaking, however, Green and Shapiro's methodological posture is agnostic. They compare rational choice claims against a range of methodological criteria—Hempelian, Popperian, Friedmanite, and Lakatosian—that mirror the variety of methodologies to which rational choice theorists appeal. Green and Shapiro's enumerations of methodological "pathologies," then, merely hold rational choice theory to its own advertised standards. What these standards share, however, is a commitment to judging theories by their predictive accuracy. An unintended consequence of Green and Shapiro's immanent methodological critique is to expose a tension between this predictive criterion for the success of rational choice theory and the implicitly prepositivist defenses of the theory adumbrated by its most astute advocates below.

For example, several contributors to this volume contend that, instead of being vilified, post hoc theorizing should be applauded by those interested in the empirical merits of rational choice theory—since post hoc amendments are designed to incorporate empirical findings into the theory. Only if one's aim is to test a theory against its predictions will one object to post hoc theory expansions (or ad hoc shrinkages)—since such amendments make the theory's predictions unfalsifiable. And, like the prepositivist economists, Fiorina (below, 88) emphasizes "the importance of *ceteris paribus*."

Yet most of the defenders of rational choice do not repudiate the aspiration to discover social-science laws testable by their predictions; indeed, several explicitly endorse this aspiration. If one accepts that laws, or lawlike regularities, can be falsified by incorrect predictions, how can one oppose predictivism?

One way is to endorse one of the central tenets of the prepositivist economic approach: the postulate of the *self-evident applicability* of the laws in question. Thus Fiorina, Shepsle, Ferejohn and Satz, and Dennis Chong express something like a conviction that rational choice assumptions are obviously true—like the basic postulates of microeconomics, in the old view. Chong, for instance, writes that "there is an essential degree of rationality in most behavior" (below, 39), and Fiorina interprets Mancur Olson's *The Logic of Collective Action* as arguing that (*ceteris paribus*) there is a *universal* tendency for people to behave in ways that will frustrate large-scale collective action in the absence of selective incentives. These sentiments echo those of Mill; of the Austrian economists Friedrich von Wieser (see Hutchison 1994, 213) and Ludwig von Mises (1981); and of the great expositor of the prepositivist orthodoxy, Lionel Robbins—all of whom held that "the propositions of economic theory . . . are obviously deductions from a series of postulates" that "are so much the stuff of our everyday experience that they have only to be stated to be recognized as obvious" (Robbins 1935, 78-79).

The Future of Political Science?

Ironically, the parallels between rational choice theory and prepositivist economics are even clearer when one notices the *official* hegemony of instrumentalism across *both* levels of economics. Just as Green and Shapiro show (e.g., *Pathologies*, 30-31) that rational choice theorists invoke a variety of predictivist doctrines in support of practices that are, according to those very doctrines, pathological, even microeconomists profess allegiance to Friedmanite instrumentalist predictivism—despite their failure to investigate the accuracy of the predictions generated by their assumptions (not to mention the accuracy of the assumptions themselves). Although microeconomic assumptions are quite similar to rational choice theory in their abstraction from reality (and their content), microeconomists accept in principle that their predictions must, to be worthwhile, be tested—some day, and preferably by someone else.

Why did instrumentalism supplant the prepositivist economic orthodoxy? Less than a decade after Hutchison's first assaults on the classical/Austrian view, Richard Lester conducted a survey showing that businesspeople do not necessarily try to maximize expected returns (see Hausman 1992b, 159)—contradicting an "obvious" microeconomic assumption. In response, Fritz Machlup took up the task of defending microeconomics on predictivist grounds. Like Friedman, Machlup suggested that economists should learn from up-to-date positivism (logical empiricism) that good theories need not use realistic assumptions. Realist forms of positivism should be discarded, he argued, and theories should be measured against the success of their predictions. The only apparent alternative would have been to accept that Lester's results *falsified a theory* that, however flawed in its *assumptions*, did generate "fairly good results in many applications" (Machlup 1956, 488; cf. Ordeshook below, 184). But Machlup's and later Friedman's instrumentalism left open the possibility that economics would be falsified by inaccurate *predictions*. (How likely is it that an unrealistic theory will make accurate predictions?) So instrumentalism came to be interpreted as licensing economic theorists to bracket not only the realism of their assumptions but that of their predictions, too.

Most of the contributors to this volume, in contrast, argue that rational choice assumptions are realistic, but may not be predictive because of disturbing causes. In short, rational choice assumptions are both self-evidently true and unfalsifiable. Like prepositivist economics, this view is vulnerable to Lester-like evidence against the assumptions' realism—such as that amassed below by Robert P. Abelson and Robert E. Lane. It is far from inconceivable, then, that an instrumentalist version of rational choice theory (e.g., Downs 1957, 21) will supplant the realist view in political science, as it has in economics. On that day, we can probably expect that the political science "stars" will be those who produce formal models of extremely limited empirical relevance, and that researchers concerned with empirical data will be thought "dunces" who aren't bright enough to do the really important work: theorizing (Mayer 1993, 70). As Thomas Mayer writes, "the typical academic economist . . . feels less like a scientist when gathering data, or thinking about data, than when doing the mathematics of a paper" (ibid.). Even though it should encourage hypothesis testing rather than formal speculation, economists have treated instrumentalism as "a carte blanche for making whatever assumptions provide a tractable model. Formalists have found this highly convenient, since it seems to imply that their 'if-then' reasoning can by itself solve empirical science problems" (ibid., 51-52).

It has become almost routine for prominent economists to bemoan the distance between economic theory and reality. As long ago as 1971, Nobel laureate Wassily Leontief condemned "the ephemeral substantive content of the arguments behind the formidable front of algebraic signs" generated by the "unbridled enthusiasm for mathematical formulation" (quoted, Mayer 1993, 2). In the previous year, Frank Hahn had referred to the "scandalous . . . spectacle of so many people refining the analyses of economic states which they give no reason to suppose will ever, or have ever, come about" (quoted, ibid.). More recently, Arjo Klamer wrote that "most members of the profession . . . will confess, usually at unguarded moments, that their highly sophisticated research produces ultimately meaningless results," and he asked how long "irony and cynicism [can] sustain the economics profession" (quoted, ibid., 3). And Franklin Fisher has deplored, as producing the "games that economists play," the "strong tendency for even the best practitioners to concentrate on analytically interesting questions rather than on the ones that really matter for the study of real-life industries" (quoted, ibid., 63). The same problem afflicts public choice theory. The originator of the bureaucratic budget-maximization hypothesis, William Niskanen, now writes (1993, 151) that "much of the [public choice] literature is a collection of intellectual games. Our specialty has developed clear models of first and second derivatives but cannot answer such simple questions as 'Why do people vote?'" While macroeconomists use instrumentalism to justify predictions bereft of theoretical underpinnings, microeconomists—and public choice theorists—use a degenerate form of instrumentalism to sanction implausible theories with scant predictive power.

Uniting Theory and Data

Instrumentalism bridges a gap that confronts virtually all science: the distance between facts and our understanding of them; precise laws and inaccurate predictions. There are at least two important reasons for this fissure.

The first problem is that outside the laboratory (and even within it), the world is usually too complex to allow the complete isolation of the variables in which one is interested. Only a unified and true theory of everything, encompassing all the more limited theories human beings can understand, would apply with precision at all times and in all places. Thus, even if the hypothesized independent variable is present in a given case, other possible causes of the dependent variable are likely to be present as well, ruining predictions about the magnitude produced by the hypothesized cause. Moreover, "disturbing causes" may offset the action of the independent variable, diminishing the dependent variable or making it disappear. While a true theory may predict that X will cause Y to occur, not-Y may yet occur in the presence of X because of the overpowering effect of other variables. Self-interested voters might tend to vote their pocketbooks, but their nationalistic education might obviate this tendency. The question is which tendency will, in a given instance, predominate, and the answer may very well have to wait until after the fact.

The problem of complexity encourages prudent scholars to attach *ceteris paribus* clauses to their theories. But this can obliterate their predictive power, making them suspect in the eyes of positivists such as Hutchison and Friedman. Yet in theory, if not in practice, the instrumentalist alternative, like Green and Shapiro's critique of rational choice theory, sacrifices theoretical realism to the pursuit of predictions. This is why Green and Shapiro are taken to task for (allegedly) privileging the statistical over the plausible. As Ferejohn and Satz write, an understanding (*Verstehen*) of human behavior in terms of human intentions is "necessary for any explanatory . . . rather than merely predictive or descriptive" science (below, 74).

The second problem is the unobservability of some real causes, such as gravity. In the physical sciences this problem can be solved by instrumentalism: one can ignore the verisimilitude of one's assumptions about unobservables in favor of worrying exclusively about the predictions they generate. But in the social sciences, theories that provide *Verstehen* must include assumptions about unobservable mental states, and these are not consistent enough across all people at all times to produce accurate behavioral predictions unless they are defined so broadly that the "predictions" are empty tautologies.[4] Similar actions—such as the votes cast by several different electors, or the budget-maximizing actions of several different bureaucrats—cannot simply be treated as equivalent for predictive purposes, for they may have different motivations. Even when disturbing causes *are* held constant, we want to know whether the agents in a given real-world instance actually have the particular attitudes that constitute the initial conditions of a nontautological social-science theory.

That is what Lester asked about microeconomic theory. His answer was, Not always. The response of Machlup and Friedman was to render the question nugatory by severing any direct link between observed behavior and plausible independent variables. This accomplished, theoretical and empirical research became dissociated from each other: microeconomic model-building now takes place without regard to the verisimilitude of the posited initial conditions, and realistic theoretical assumptions no longer check macroeconomic predictions.

The middle chapters of *Pathologies* show why this process has not yet been completed in political science. True, one category of rational choice research consists of formal mathematical derivations of equilibrium solutions to largely imaginary problems, based on admittedly unrealistic initial-condition assumptions. But in a second category is rational choice research into observed behavior. Since rational choice assumptions are no more universally applicable than are those of any other nontautological model, research of this type sometimes fails to make accurate predictions. In response, researchers who, were they in economics, would tend to disregard the theoretical implications, instead either (1) expand the theory toward tautology, so it can predict more (or all) outcomes; or (2) resort to ad hocery, admitting that nontautological rational choice theory tends to apply unpredictably, not universally. Green and Shapiro deride the first stratagem as post hoc theory development and the second as arbitrary domain restriction.

A more radical, yet constructive critique of rational choice theory could be imagined, however, based on the belief that social science should offer realistic (in the sense of *verstehende*) explanations of human actions. Since unrealistic modelling implies a repudiation of this proposition, rational choice theorists who want to avoid the cynical irrelevance that characterizes modern economics should be congratulated, not chastised, for modifying their theory, whether (2) explicitly (by means of arbitrary domain restriction) or (1) implicitly (by further tautologizing the definition of rationality, subsuming behavior previously studied by social psychologists, "ethnographers," and the like).

Such modifications, however, fly in the face of the assumption that nontautological rational choice theory is universally applicable. Tautologizing rational choice or restricting its applicability means renouncing a priori assumptions about what causes will be at work in any given instance. Precisely because we cannot know in advance whether people will be instrumentally rational, we cannot predict their behavior. Post hoc or ad hoc rational choice theory allows Weber's categories of intrinsically valuable, traditional, and emotional action; Green and Shapiro's "habit, blunder, and the like" (*Pathologies*, 27); Abelson's and Michael Taylor's "expressive" action; and so forth, (1) to be incorporated into rational choice theory, or else (2) to set its limits.

Yet Green and Shapiro oppose this approach because, committed (at least for purposes of argument) to one or another form of predictive testing, they must condemn post hoc and tautologizing alterations that immunize a theory from falsification by inaccurate predictions. Their alternative (and that of Taylor and Stanley Kelley below), which would narrow the predicted applicability of rational choice theory by spelling out a list of theoretically justified (hence predictable) domain restrictions, will inevitably encounter the very indeterminacies they criticize in "universalistic," a priori rational choice theory. For while such lists increase the relevance of the theory's initial conditions in the remaining domains and reduce the need to appeal to the *ceteris paribus* clause, we can assume that some degree of unobservability and complexity will always remain, continuing to debar accurate point predictions (or retrodictions) or even comparative statics. Although rational choice theory's accuracy will have improved, it will still be "falsified" in real-world applications; both its assumptions and its conclusions will remain unrealistic (as with all valid but incomplete theories), and if economics continues to show the way, this may well lead, in reaction, to instrumentalism.

What is needed is a form of scientific method that uses theory to explain facts; restrains theory with facts; yet allows for an imperfect fit between the two. Such an approach would both encourage domain restrictions *and* accept that untheorized inexactitude or inapplicability does not falsify theories. It would thereby sanction rational choice research that uses ad hoc criteria of applicability—or tautological formulations of "rationality." By allowing the domain of rational choice to shrink when its predictions prove false, the needed approach would recognize that any theory that could completely specify its conditions of inapplicability with no trace of ad hocery would be part of a perfectly comprehensive Laplacean determinism, of a sort to which human beings cannot aspire (see Murphy below). With such godlike knowledge, no empirical research would ever be necessary (cf. Chong below, 45–46; Ferejohn and Satz below, 82). By allowing its domain to expand to the point at which many "irrational" behaviors are redefined, on the other hand, the needed method would recognize that nothing rides on whether a given behavior is described as "rational"—so long as it is clear what one means by the term.

Such a method requires treating theories as ideal types[5] (cf. Lane below, 124) which are derivable from any source (but which, in the social sciences, provide *Verstehen*); which are devised to explain imagined patterns of behavior; *but which are not falsified by inaccurate predictions of actual behavior,* because variations in initial conditions, and disturbing causes, may always interfere. Like the positivism Daniel Diermeier discusses below (62–63), the ideal-type view denies that the purpose of prediction is to falsify *theories,* rather than to falsify the hypothesis that a certain theory applies to a certain case. The purpose of empirical research, therefore, is to confirm or falsify the possibility that a *particular* event is an instance of the operation of a certain "law"—that is, research may demonstrate that the posited cause is present and has not been undone by countervailing forces (cf. Shepsle below, 220). Ideal-type formal models have no scientific value until empirical research begins to assess the extent of their applicability and the magnitude of their effect in particular cases. (One may, of course, define a "particular case" as broadly as one wants.) The main goal of social science is the determination of how far, in given cases, the initial conditions of theoretically derived hypotheses hold good and are not "disturbed."

In this view, only empirical research can falsify or verify the hypothesis that a certain ideal type explains a certain phenomenon in the real world. *All* logically coherent theories are true in the sense that if their initial conditions hold, all else being equal, then the posited consequences will always follow (cf. Chong below, 49). But if the purpose of theory building is to develop ideal types whose hypotheses are relatively *accurate*, the question is whether the initial conditions *do* hold and whether all else *is* equal. In social science, morever, these constraints must not be merely fortuitous, as under instrumentalism; the accuracy of one's hypotheses must flow from the accuracy of one's assumptions. The ideal-type approach does sanction a certain amount of theoretical fantasizing, since any number of logically coherent assumptions (even when subject to the *verstehen* requirement) *might* prove applicable in the real world, and it is vital to think through the consequences of one's assumptions (i.e., the consequences if one's ideal-type initial conditions are present, are capable of producing the posited effects, and are not counteracted). But the ideal-type approach also builds into theorizing a bias toward interaction with empirical research—for any theory, that is, which is intended to be scientifically relevant.

It is a peculiarity of *verstehende* theories that unless counteracted, their initial conditions automatically produce the effects posited by sound deduction. If one is self-interested or instrumentally rational then, *ceteris paribus*, certain behavioral effects follow as a matter of course. There is no question as to whether the unobservable force (the mental state) is capable of producing the consequent behavior, as there might be a question about whether gravity can pull two bodies toward each other; no empirical investigation is needed to determine the efficacy of mental states in producing behavior if they are present and are not defeated, say, by ignorance about appropriate means. Thus, any internally coherent *verstehende* ideal type, no matter how fanciful, may be said to be applicable (to *all* of reality) if it relies heavily enough on the *ceteris paribus* clause and on the mere assumption that its initial conditions are "obviously" present. But only some *verstehende* ideal types will turn out to apply (to a specific *part* of reality) without heavy reliance on these assumptions. Empirical research is required if we are to distinguish whether, in a given instance, a valid theory is of the first or the second type.

The advantage of the ideal-type approach is that, by placing the inexact fit of theory and reality at center stage, it redirects scientific research away from attempting to use empirical data to verify or falsify laws, instead using it to show how close or how far competing "laws" come to explaining actual behavior in a given case. This obviates the dilemma social scientists must face when their theories are, inevitably, unable to predict behavior: either come up with endless excuses about the inaptness of the test, or beat a quasi-instrumentalist retreat from the empirical fray into ivory-tower theorizing. The ideal-type approach circumvents the dilemma by recognizing from the outset that scientific laws cannot be held to all-or-nothing standards in the real world. No humanly devised theory can predict the frequency or magnitude with which ideal-typical behavior, or an approximation of it, will appear in reality. A theory cannot be falsified by a single bad prediction, or even a string of them, once we recognize that each falsification concerns only the application of the theory to a particular case, and shows merely that the theory is less than universally applicable to the real world.

Since no negative result can be considered a definitive "test" of anything but a theory's applicability in the specific instance examined, the assumption that a theory that has always produced relatively accurate predictions in the past will continue to do so in the future is unwarranted; until we achieve perfect knowledge, conditions may unexpectedly change. The most accurate explanations will tend to be retrodictions (unless we unexpectedly achieve omniscience); the best social science will be historical. However, once one has discovered a theory whose initial conditions (which may include path-dependent historical circumstances) obtain and are not counteracted in the given cases, one may make the theory the basis not only of scientific retrodiction, but of practical predictions of future likelihoods. Upon these, one bases the design of one's legislation or one's bridges (cf. Ordeshook below). But the difference between "engineering" and science always should always be kept in mind.

The ideal-type approach has many similarities to the prepositivist economic orthodoxy. Chief among these are that they both emphasize what Daniel M. Hausman (1992b) calls the "inexact nature" of social science; and that in both, "empirical studies are used to suggest plausible subsidiary postulates, and to check on the applicability of the theoretical framework to given situations" (Caldwell 1982, 103). There is one key difference, however. The old view, especially in its Austrian version, vitiated its commitment to check the empirical applicability of a framework by assuming, a priori, that economic assumptions were not just ideal types, but laws that were (largely if not perfectly), in fact, reflected in the real world. The tenet of self-evidence militates against doing empirical research to determine the extent of a theory's accuracy in a given instance. This tenet, in other words, is the source of the universalistic apriorism Green and Shapiro attack.

Yet by holding rational choice theory to its predictivist methodological canons, Green and Shapiro leave instrumentalism as the only viable alternative to universalism. No "partial universalism" can undo the gap between data and predictions—unless it is a "universalism" so partial that it institutionalizes the gap, refusing to assume that theories bear any resemblance to reality beyond that which is proven, case by case. In this way the ideal-type approach incorporates Green and Shapiro's antiuniversalism, without their predictivism—and the antipositivist sentiments of many of Green and Shapiro's critics, without their apriorism.

One of the more important implications of this synthesis is to legitimize not only inexact predictions and ad hoc/post hoc theory alteration, but searches for confirming evidence. If the task of empirical research is to see whether, and to what extent, a theory explains a particular slice of reality rather than to see whether reality falsifies a theory, positive evidence will be even more valuable than the negative kind.

The problem with many searches for confirming evidence is that they aim to prove the universal applicability of the assumptions underlying the theory. Accordingly, they illegitimately extrapolate from favorable cases and ignore unfavorable ones. The reviewer of Lewin's book in the journal *Public Choice*, for example, attempts to brush aside its troubling findings as "very selective," inasmuch as Lewin "fails to mention any experiments in public choice and rational choice theory" or to discuss the many cases in which self-interest does play a political role (Cain 1993, 379). As a response to the overly broad question with which Lewin opens the book—"Is it self-interest or public interest that predominates in public life?"—the reviewer asks legitimate questions. But, implicitly taking an even broader approach, the reviewer must ignore Lewin's evidence *against* self-interested voters, politicians, and bureaucrats.[6] The reviewer's preoccupation with (unidentified) confirming evidence could only be relevant to the disconfirming evidence Lewin presents if one views the purpose of public choice theory as the establishment of universally predictive laws, rather than the explanation of particular events.

Rational Choice Theory As an Ideal Type

Olson's *The Logic of Collective Action*, by contrast, is a model of ideal-type research.

Olson's argument is directed against "group theory" in political science, which held that individuals join groups (and, by implication, that they vote) on the basis of their collective self-interest. Olson points out that in groups with large memberships, such as labor unions and business lobbies, the contribution of each member to the achievement of collective goals is negligible, so the potential members' interests would better be served by free riding on others' contributions than by making pointless sacrifices for the collective benefit. Therefore, the observed existence of large groups requires some other explanation than collective self-interest. Olson finds this explanation in selective incentives that benefit group members, such as various services offered to the members of business lobbies; in the case of unions, "compulsory membership and picket lines are . . . of the essence" (Olson 1965, 71). Without such "incentives," the self-interest assumption of group theorists would generate a point prediction of zero collective action in large groups, and would therefore be falsified in virtually every case. ·

As Fiorina notes below, however, zero is not *Olson's* point prediction, even in the absence of selective incentives (cf. *Pathologies*, 82). Unlike group theorists—and public choice theorists—Olson notes that groups may consist of "altruistic individuals"; unlike rational choice theorists, he concedes that groups may contain "irrational individuals" (Olson 1965, 2; cf. ibid., 108). In such cases, selective incentives may not be needed to get people to join large groups.

By interpreting Olson's caveats as invocations of the *ceteris paribus* clause alone, Fiorina suggests that Olson posits an always-present *tendency* for large groups to require selective incentives, albeit a tendency that may be offset by "a host of other factors" (below, 88; cf. Chong below, 39). The a priori conviction that certain initial conditions always apply (while allowing that countervailing forces may offset them) entails the self-evidence of a theoretical assumption, and therefore violates the ideal-type method. An alternative would be to interpret Olson as saying that there may be different kinds of people, and that his theory does not apply to all of them: when considering altruistic and irrational people, in short, the initial conditions do *not* obtain. Undoubtedly Fiorina is right to point out that people often fail to behave selfishly or rationally *despite* satisfying the antecedent condition of having selfish or rational dispositions. In such cases, conflicting factors (such as ignorance or mixed motives) may need to be invoked by means of the *ceteris paribus* clause. But surely there can be no reason to assume, a priori, that people are always self-interested or rational, even *ceteris paribus*.

Olson qualifies his admission that the rationality and self-interest assumptions may not apply in some cases by suggesting that this is "usually of no practical importance" (1965, 2). Just how important it can be, however, becomes clear in the closing pages of his book, where Olson turns to discuss "noneconomic lobbies" and "groups that are characterized by a low degree of rationality" (ibid., 160, 161). In these cases, he proposes, "it would perhaps be better to turn to psychology or social psychology than to economics for a relevant theory" (ibid., 161).

Thus, by insisting that the presence of instrumental rationality and self-interest must be proven in each instance, Olson is drawn to agree—both with most of its defenders in this volume, and with such fierce critics as Lane—not only that rational choice theory can be compatible with other explanations, but that it can *facilitate* them. As Susanne Lohmann (below, 131) argues, "without a theory of how much people should contribute to a public good if they are rational and self-interested, there is no way of assessing whether empirical contribution patterns reveal altruism, systematic misassessments of the probability that a given contribution will be decisive, or total incomprehension on the part of the individuals involved." Were its practitioners less determined to protect rational choice theory *in general* from "falsification" by any single instance (or less prone to proceed as if such instances do not exist), they might more freely recognize that their theory lends great credibility to alternative approaches, such as social psychology, public opinion theory, and intellectual and cultural history, in the many *particular* cases in which its predictions are inaccurate (cf. *Pathologies*, 67; Weber 1949, 102).

Chong's paper exemplifies the other way to use rational choice theory as an ideal type: by expanding its boundaries to include "so-called extrarational incentives" (below, 40). Instead of restricting its domain of applicability, he deals with recalcitrant data by incorporating them into a broader version of it. The danger here is the temptation to ignore social-psychology constructs that cannot easily be interpreted as "rational."[7] If due caution is exercised, however, Chong's tautologizing approach would seem to be an acceptable remedy for the unrealistic assumptions and empirical irrelevance of rational choice theorizing discussed by Green and Shapiro.

Rational choice theorists should do more than tolerate alternative forms of explanation. Properly understood, their greatest contribution may be to demonstrate how *infrequently* political behavior exemplifies instrumental rationality—let alone the instrumentally rational pursuit of self-interest. But this is a matter for research, not speculation.

NOTES

1. I disregard the claim, made early in Buchanan and Tullock's *The Calculus of Consent*, that public choice theory assumes only instrumental rationality and

is agnostic about the types of ends (e.g., selfish or altruistic) that individuals pursue (Buchanan and Tullock 1962, 17).

As in most instances where this claim prefaces an exercise in economic theory, Buchanan and Tullock do, in fact, go on to assume self-interested ends, and accordingly they abandon their "praxiological" or thin-rational agnosticism (ibid., 29) in favor of thick-rational, *Homo economicus* assumptions. There seem to be three reasons for this retreat.

First, as do most economists, Tullock and Buchanan need to supplement the sparse requirements of instrumental rationality with the assumption that individuals are selfish "to a degree sufficient to make prediction and explanation possible"; otherwise, we would not be able to say whether prices reflected instances of "individual buyers deliberately pay[ing] to sellers higher prices than is necessary to secure the product or service purchased, [or of] . . . sellers deliberately accept[ing] lower prices than buyers are willing to pay" (Buchanan and Tullock 1962, 18). The praxiological/"thin"/rational-choice approach, Buchanan and Tullock argue, "cannot develop hypotheses about the results of political choice in any conceptually observable or measurable dimension. To take this additional step," they must therefore "move to . . . a more narrowly conceived submodel" in which not only rationality but selfishness is assumed (ibid., 29).

Second, Buchanan and Tullock juxtapose their "essentially economic approach to collective activity" against what they take to be the orthodox political science "assumption that the representative individual seeks not to maximize his own utility, but to find the 'public interest' or 'common good.'" The terms of this juxtaposition require Buchanan and Tullock to portray political actors as people who do *not* equate their own utility with the public interest or common good, and who *are* therefore "profit-seeker[s]" (ibid., 20).

Finally, Buchanan and Tullock seem to assume that, even granting that the same motivations drive people's economic and their political behavior, it follows that political agents must be motivated by self-interest. But this interpretation of the symmetry assumption overlooks the possibility that people could be consistently *selfless* in both the economy and the polity (which the young Marx envisioned), or that they could display a consistent *mixture* of selfish and selfless motives in both spheres.

My public choice/rational choice division also departs from Lohmann's (32) equation of rational choice theory with behavior that is both rational and self-interested; and from Dennis Mueller's (1989) treatment of literature on both thick-rational (e.g., rent-seeking) and thin-rational (e.g., legislative cycling) phenomena as falling under the rubric of public choice theory. This treatment contradicts Mueller's thick-rational equation of public choice with "the application of economics to political science" (rather than vice versa); i.e., the application to political science of the view "that all men pursue their private interests" (Mueller 1989, 1).

2. Page references to *Pathologies* in this introduction and in Green and Shapiro's reply are identified as such. Unidentified parenthetical page references in the introduction and the reply refer to other chapters in this volume, while unidentified parenthetical page references elsewhere in this volume refer to *Pathologies*.

3. This is a simplification; formal rational choice theory has, in fact, been applied not only to microeconomics but macroeconomics since the advent of the New Classical effort to provide microtheoretical, rational-expectations foundations for macroeconomics.

4. The latter problem can be illustrated by referring to the most aprioristic of the prepositivist economists, Ludwig von Mises, who criticized Weber's use of ideal types precisely because they are not universally applicable laws. Von Mises's tautological version of rational choice theory, "praxeology," appears to be what Buchanan and Tullock have in mind when they retreat from "praxiology," or rational choice theory as instrumental rationality in the "thinnest" sense, to the more definitely selfish assumptions of the *Homo economicus* ideal type (see n1 above).

Von Mises (1981, 81) defines as "the fundamental law of action" (on which economics is to be grounded) the apodictic certainty that people will act to achieve whatever it is that they "subjectively conside[r] mo[st] important," and he criticizes Weber (1978, 24-25) for failing to see that value-rational, affective, and traditional behavior are, by (von Mises's) definition, instrumentally rational. The difficulty is that such a thin definition of instrumental rationality generates a tautology that says little about human behavior (except that, as von Mises defines the term, it is always and everywhere "rational"). Without using distinctions among rational actions as von Mises defines them—distinctions of the sort provided by Weber's "thicker" ideal types—how, for example, are we to distinguish prices that reflect "individual buyers deliberately pay[ing] to sellers higher prices than is necessary to secure the product or service purchased" from prices that reflect sellers who "deliberately accept lower prices than buyers are willing to pay" (Buchanan and Tullock 1962, 18)?

Weber advises that in such cases—i.e., in all cases in which actual behavior is the topic of inquiry—we rely on empirical investigation (or on extrapolation from other investigations) into whether a given price was the outcome of instrumental bargaining or else exemplified, say, action taken for its intrinsic worth or for emotional or traditional reasons. Weber uses as an example "the generalization called Gresham's Law" (Weber 1978, 10), which is but "a rationally evident anticipation of human action under given conditions and under the ideal-typical assumption of purely rational action. Only experience," he writes, "can teach us how far action really does take place in accordance with it. This experience does in fact demonstrate that the proposition has a very far-reaching validity" (von Mises's translation of Weber 1978, 10, in von Mises 1981, 86).

In reply, von Mises denies that Gresham's Law applies only "under the ideal-typical assumption of purely rational action," but then he admits that Gresham's Law does not always produce an accurate prediction of people's behavior. While continuing to affirm that even behavior that is not predicted by the Law is "rational" in his sense of the word, von Mises allows several circumstances in which "the assumptions of the law do not apply," adding however that "experience teaches that for the mass of creditor-debtor relationships these assumptions do apply" (von Mises 1981, 87). As the reader may readily affirm, this is precisely Weber's position, in almost exactly the same words.

Von Mises and Weber agree that (1) *ceteris paribus* and (2) whenever its initial conditions apply, Gresham's Law accurately predicts that bad money drives out good. The question, then, is how to determine when these two conditions are satisfied—which cannot be done a priori. The apparent difference between their positions stems from Weber's effort to emphasize the importance of empirical investigation, which leads him to call the ideal type in question "so-called 'Gresham's law'" (von Mises's translation, 1981, 86). Von Mises's response is, in effect, that it is a *real* law. But this response obscures the fact that von Mises, too, in retrodicting actual behavior, must treat the regularity in question as an ideal type of purely contingent, a posteriori *applicability* to a given case.

It is evident from the chapter in which his critique of Weber appears ("Sociology and History," ch. 2 of von Mises 1981) that von Mises needlessly exaggerates the aprioristic implications of his view because in his mind, he is still fighting the *Methodenstreit* against the German Historical school of economics.

5. There are several differences between the methodology set forth here and Weber's view of ideal types (see Weber 1949, ch. 2, and Weber 1978, pt. 1, ch. 1). I have retained from Weber the idea of theoretical constructs with no necessary empirical referent; but, *inter alia*, the notions that these constructs may be wholly false or wholly true, and that they can be used to characterize natural as well as social science, may go beyond Weber's account.

6. The reviewer's only comment about this evidence is that it does not adequately "operationalize and test" the self-interest axiom in the areas it covers, by which he seems to mean that "self-interest" should be tautologized to include altruism, and that survey results probing mental states should be ignored in favor of overt behavior.

7. Chong (below, 42–43, 47) prefers this dangerous approach because of his fear that many non-rational choice theories are so "sociological" that they lack microfoundations. But see Schumpeter 1950 (cf. Prisching 1995) and Converse 1964 for methodologically individualistic accounts of the origin of irrational beliefs. I believe Chong may have an unnecessarily restrictive view of what constitute adequate microfoundations, leading him to reject ad hoc invocations of noninstrumental, nonselfish motivation.

Robert P. Abelson

THE SECRET EXISTENCE OF
EXPRESSIVE BEHAVIOR

The rational choice assumption that any chosen behavior can be understood as opti-mizing material self-interest is not borne out by psychological research. Expressive motives, for example, are prominent in the symbols of politics, in social relationships, and in the arts of persuasion. Moreover, instrumentality is a mindset that is learned (perhaps overlearned), and can be situationally manipulated; because it is valued in our society, it provides a privileged vocabulary for justifying behaviors that may have been performed for other reasons, and encourages the illusory belief in the universali-ty of rational choice.

Every autumn, John Doe traveled a long distance for something he claimed was important, and this aroused the curiosity of a rational choice theorist.

"What do you do there?" he asked.

"I dote," John replied. "I dote on Sally, my granddaughter."

"You go all that way to *dote*? How do you benefit from it?"

"Benefit?" asked John, puzzled. "I dunno, I just dote on her. Little Sally, she's really something. She'll do great things some day—make money, be famous, maybe even be president."

The theorist considered this. "Well, do you think your doting makes any difference?" he asked.

"Difference? How do you mean? I guess Sally likes to be doted on. When she's a teenager, she might not. Those teenagers. . . ."

Robert P. Abelson, Professor Emeritus of Psychology and Political Science, Yale Univer-sity, New Haven, CT 06520, is the author of *Statistics as Principled Argument* (Erlbaum, 1995) and coauthor of *Candidates, Issues, and Strategies* (MIT, 1963), *Theories of Cognitive Consistency* (Rand McNally 1968), and *Scripts, Plans, and Goals* (Erlbaum, 1977).

"No, no. I mean, does your doting make it any more probable that she'll do great things than if you don't dote?"

"More probable? Never thought about it. She'll do great things anyway. I like her best of all my grandchildren."

John's questioner became exasperated. "You spend a lot of money and effort to go and dote, without expecting your doting to make a difference?"

"Should I?"

"Oh, yes," said the rational choice theorist. "It's a law of human nature. Your actions are anomalous."

Troubled, the theorist pondered the matter for many years. In the meantime, John Doe died without knowing his granddaughter's achievements. The theorist, further perplexed, wondered whether Doe had considered the possibility that he would die before the benefits of his doting could be enjoyed.

The rational choice theorist never solved the riddle, but he posed the issues in a famous paper entitled "The Doter's Paradox."

Reinventing Psychology

As a social psychologist who has written previously on the general subject of human rationality (Abelson 1976; Abelson and Levi 1985), and as the only psychologist in this symposium issue, I confess that I come to the present arena with a certain sense of aggravation. Almost every participant in this controversy is arguing about psychology, but with the exception of Robert Lane and Michael Taylor, virtually no one has taken notice, much less advantage, of what psychologists know about the issues.

Rational choice theorists have tried to reinvent psychology without a genuine commitment to the empirical study of behavior. With flair, they have theoretically analyzed hypothetical beings, and have occasionally come up with something of mathematical consequence. If people were found to confirm propositions developed by such theorizing, rational choice would become a dazzling *tour de force*. Conversely, the almost complete absence of descriptive success, as laid out so thoroughly by Green and Shapiro, is a major disappointment.

To a psychologist, it is frankly no surprise that rational choice models receive such poor empirical support. As applied to ordinary citizens, such models are at best manifestly incomplete; at worst they are seriously misleading.[1] There is a double problem: the axiomatic requirements of rational choice are too demanding; but even were this not so, the presupposition that behavior is necessarily instrumental to material goal attainment is too restrictive.

With regard to the former problem, there has already been a strong challenge to rational choice theory by a cluster of psychologists whose most central figures are Amos Tversky and Daniel Kahneman, supported by a group of revisionist economists including Richard Thaler and George Loewenstein. They have shown that contextual variables such as the manner in which preferences are elicited, the wording or "framing"[2] of options, the point of initial reference, the prominence of norms of fairness, and many others, lead in the laboratory to systematic deviations from rational choice predictions, and that related anomalies can be found in aggregate field data. Expositions of these challenges appear in various sources (Kahneman, Knetsch, and Thaler 1991; Kahneman, Slovic, and Tversky 1982; Kahneman and Tversky 1984; Loewenstein and Elster 1992; Neale and Bazerman 1991; Nisbett and Ross 1980; Quattrone and Tversky 1984; Thaler 1991; Tversky 1994).

I will concentrate on the second problem: the unrealistic, excessive reliance on instrumental motives. I will discuss a number of empirical findings bearing on a meaningful and important class of noninstrumental motives, and the implications of these findings for rational choice theory.

Instrumental vs. Expressive Motives

The grammar of rational choice employs only the instrumental case, in which everything people do is a deliberate means to a self-interested, material end. This stance produces the absurdism of the parable of the doter, and of portions of the rational choice literature. Regarding behavior as payoff-driven may often enough produce useful insights, but insistence on universality is counterproductive. As Green and Shapiro observe, "The hypotheses that flow from rational choice theory would be more insightful were there a clearer distinction between rational action and other modes of behavior" (203).

Whatever other differentiations one might want to make, there is a very useful distinction between instrumental behavior and *expressive* behavior. When I use the term "instrumental," I refer to deliberate, rational planning and choice in self-interested pursuit of the prospect of future material benefit. By contrast, I intend "expressive" to refer to spontaneous enjoyment or value-expressive action, performed for its own sake, with no apparent rational consideration of material consequences for the actor.[3] Consider, for example, the incredible ferocity of demonstrations at clinics offering abortions, the fervor of the opposition to fox hunting in England, the hullabaloo over whether the Confederate flag should be flown over the statehouse of Georgia, or the famous uproar caused by two sprinters who gave the Black Power salute during the Olympic awards ceremony in 1968. It is a tortuous exercise to try to articulate a rational, self-interested instrumentality in examples such as these, and this lends strong intuitive credence to the potential power of noninstrumental, value-expressive motives.

By way of empirical support, David Sears and his colleagues (Kinder and Sears 1985; Sears and Funk 1990, 1991), referring to group-based, value-expressive attitudes and acts as *symbolic politics*, have assembled a good deal of evidence that political attitudes about many issues, including health care, abortion, welfare, and school busing[4] depend surprisingly more on symbolic factors than on self-interest, whether individual or collective.

Psychologists have studied a number of basic properties of the contrast between instrumental and expressive motives. A simple device is to classify objects such as consumer products according to whether they are strictly instrumental or directly pleasurable. One correlate of this difference in function is the appropriateness of different marketing appeals. Take a coffee pot, on the one hand, and bottled perfume on the other. Consider the two appeals, "Very durable and convenient to use," and "Expresses the real you." Intuitively, the former is applicable to the coffee pot and the latter to the bottle of perfume, while the reverse connections are proverbial lead balloons. Indeed, research on the persuasiveness of the two types of appeal for the two types of product supports this clear intuition (Shavitt 1989).

The instrumental orientation can be conceived in part as a mindset that can be explicitly switched on or off. Different types of individuals (and organizations) have different mixes of settings. Some individuals (rational choice theorists in particular) virtually always have their settings on, while others have them almost exclusively off.

In one study of such individual differences (Prentice 1987), students were asked to name their six favorite possessions. Those whose choices were mainly instrumental (bookcases, calculator, meal tickets . . .) or mainly expressive (guitar, family heirloom, cat . . .) were subsequently exposed to short, persuasive communications about unfamiliar issues. The arguments used were either instrumental ("The secession of Staten Island from New York City will have favorable financial consequences for the New York area"), or value expressive ("The secession of Staten Island from New York City is morally correct"). The relative favoritism for instrumental or expressive possessions proved to be a reasonably good predictor of which type of argument was more effective.

The mindset of instrumentality is also predictably sensitive to contextual variation. Gerald Salancik (1974) elicited from students in a large undergraduate class several behavioral indicators of being intrinsically interested in the course (such as reading outside materials on which they would not be tested). He also obtained records of grades (at that point in the course)—to gauge self-interestedness. Later, he induced a transient instrumental orientation by asking the students to finish a number of incomplete sentences such as, "Generally, I raise my hand in a classroom *in order to . . .*" whereas other students were given stems of the form, "Generally, I raise my hand in a classroom *because . . .*" [emphasis added]. He then obtained an overall course satisfaction rating. In the "*in order to*" condition, grades were by far the best predictor of course satisfaction, whereas in the "*because*" condition, satisfaction depended instead on the extent to which the student enjoyed the subject matter.

The possibility that instrumental orientation can be switched on or off limits the applicability of predictions based on self-interest. A study by Donald Kinder and Lynn Sanders (1994) on whites' opposition to affirmative action in college admission policy is a case in point. Self-interest (having college-entry children vulnerable to harm) was related to expressed opposition to affirmative action only under special circumstances. If respondents were simply asked whether they were for or against colleges reserving openings for black students, their responses had no relationship to their self-interest. Even when the introduction to the question invoked the opposing arguments of minorities' historical disadvantage versus the "unfair advantage" given them by affirmative action, there was still no relationship of attitude with self-interest. Only when the affirmative action argument was framed as "reverse discrimination" was there a (slight) correlation between opposition to it and self-interest. The authors of this study summarize the matter thus: "Interests can be activated; more often they are not" (Kinder and Sanders 1994, 400).

One might suppose that a self-interested mind set, once activated in a given domain, would remain permanently operative in that domain. The same supposition could be made about a self-expressive mind set, however, and the conditions for "fixing" one or the other deserve exploration.

In one interesting experimental paradigm, an instrumental orientation does survive sharp situational alterations, albeit with a somewhat surprising side effect. In a series of experiments, Mark R. Lepper, D. Greene, and Richard E. Nisbett (1973) studied what would happen in the long run if participation in an activity that had always been sheer fun were one day externally rewarded. Using nursery-school children as subjects, the experimenters introduced promises of systematic rewards into ongoing free play sessions, and studied subsequent behavior. It turned out that children who were given the promised rewards for engaging in a particular activity—playing with magic markers—later spontaneously avoided this activity when the reward was no longer offered.[5] By contrast, children not rewarded for using the markers continued to play with them in the later session.

That type of experimental procedure is called the "overjustification paradigm": two reasons exist for engaging in the designated activity, when only one is needed. The intrinsic (expressive) reason in this particular study, *it's fun*, comes to be dominated by the extrinsic (instrumental) reason, *it's in order to get the reward*. Play is turned into work, so to speak. When the work no longer pays off, the activity loses its former appeal. From a self-interested point of view, it is irrational to work for a zero wage. What goes beyond rationality is that a perfectly enjoyable activity has lost its intrinsic appeal, tarnished by its association with reward.[6] This might be considered a case of the *overpersistence* of an instrumental orientation.

In other psychological domains, instrumental and expressive orientations may remain persistently in competition. Consider a thoughtful son sending flowers to his mother upon her return from the hospital, whereupon she mails him a check to cover the cost. The participants are treating the relationship in clashing ways: in the terms used in psychology, the mother is following the rules of an "exchange" relationship, while the son is behaving on a "communal" basis (Clark and Pataki 1995, 292–95). Exchange relationships are based on the give-to-get principle. If we provide rewards to people, the account goes, we expect that they will provide rewards to us (including social rewards such as affection and praise). For the relationship to survive, a rough equality of net benefits must accrue to each party.

The exchange view is intuitively rather persuasive. Reciprocity of gift giving, dinner invitations, picking up the tab, and so on, clearly are widespread social norms among friends. Even when a stranger does a favor for someone, the recipient feels social pressure to respond.

By contrast, in communal relationships the partners do not expect or desire to keep track of relative rewards, as in the initial stages of close relationships, or in relationships between people with manifestly unequal resources, such as parents and young children. The importance of the question of who owes whom how much in a social relationship varies sharply with the mindsets of the people involved—which are, in turn, systematically affected by specifiable contextual variables, and can be reliably manipulated in the laboratory (Clark and Mills 1979).

Competition between instrumental and expressive motives also turns up in studies of altruism, attraction to social groups, intergroup conflict, and many other areas of psychology that are relevant to politics. In none of these areas is the instrumental pursuit of self-interest a law of human nature. It is an option that is partly a matter of voluntary personal style and partly under the (usually implicit) control of situational factors.

The Learning of Rational Choice

It is sometimes argued by rational choice theorists that if people are not making optimal decisions, it is because they have not been properly trained.[7] The level of sophistication in rational decision making is indeed quite low among untrained people—even for college students and professors, such as those who participated in a study by Richard P. Larrick, James N. Morgan, and Richard E. Nisbett (1990). These researchers gave their subjects brief instruction in the subtle applicability of basic cost/benefit principles to everyday contexts. After this training, the subjects were more likely to disregard sunk costs, pay attention to opportunity costs, and so on.

However, learning a few distinct principles does not automatically convert dunderheads into complete rational thinkers. Realizing that goal probably requires persistent training covering many domains of application. There is one group of people—economists—who receive such training as a matter of course. Larrick et al. found that economics majors and faculty members were more instrumentally rational than their academic counterparts to begin with, and learned the most from their experimental training.

The question of negative side effects of rationality training has been raised by Robert H. Frank, Thomas Gilovich, and Dennis T. Regan (1993). They have assembled evidence showing that economics professors are more likely to refrain from donations in support of public goods; that economics students less frequently invoke conceptions of fairness, and behave more often with aggressive self-interest in experimental games, even *to their own detriment*; and that these tendencies increase as students move through college.

The Tyranny of Instrumentalism

If instrumental and expressive orientations are both major alternatives in good standing, why does instrumental reasoning command so exalted a status that rational choice theorists can unabashedly pretend that expressive action doesn't exist? Two considerations stand out. The most obvious is the greater ease of formally modelling the behavioral consequences of instrumental thinking. Second, along with the ease of formal manipulation, instrumental constructions enjoy general public endorsement because they are more easily communicated, perhaps more readily learned in childhood,[8] and more serviceable as handy public accounts of many behaviors—political and otherwise—that may not actually have been instrumentally motivated (at least not as theorists model them). This is especially true in our culture, which applauds cleverly calculated action in the service of goal attainment. This is, after all, the story line of pragmatism, the profit motive, and the ideology of individualism.

Ordinary people as well as prominent decision makers want others to believe in their good intentions and rationality, especially when they have behaved frivolously or irrationally.[9] It is relatively easy to come up with reasons that are simultaneously deceptive to others and to oneself. Indeed, a strong case has been made that people typically have no awareness of the true reasons for their behavior (Nisbett and Wilson 1977). When asked to provide reasons for their attitudes or behavior, people typically give externalized propositions rather than expressions of inner feelings (Wilson, Dunn, Kraft, and Lisle 1989). It is much more common to hear people say, "I like the candidate because he will cut government spending" than "I like the candidate because my friends like him."

Not only are people disposed to provide reasons that justify a previous behavior, they also hesitate to make choices if they can't come up with a reason, or if they don't know which of two reasons will prove apt. Eldar Shafir, Itamar Simonson, and Amos Tversky (1993) have provided several sets of data suggesting the psychological importance of reasons—and showing that axioms of rational choice are violated by the psychological use of reasons.[10]

Two features of the instrumental orientation seem to be popular in the construction of reasons, either before or after choice. *Material self-interest*, usually financial, tends to be a privileged justification. This is highlighted in an experimental demonstration by Christopher Hsee (in press) of what he called *elastic justification*. Hsee gave subjects a choice between two proofreading tasks with different rates of pay per unit of text. One task was to proofread an address directory—pretty boring work. The other was proofreading personal ads, a job with an appeal that people might be reluctant to admit. When the unit pay rate was fixed at 24 cents for the directory and 17 cents for the personal ads, subjects overwhelmingly preferred the stodgy but financially superior alternative. However, when the pay rate for the personals was made elastic by the instruction "pay rate to be determined later; ranges from 4 cents to 30 cents," there was a sizeable degree of erosion in the popularity of proofreading the directory in favor of working on the personals.

Hsee had predicted this result. It cannot be explained by some peculiar attraction of the elastic wage itself, since there was no decline in the popularity of working on the directory when the alternative task was to proofread picture-frame ads for an elastic wage. Hsee's interpretation is that in the elastic wage condition for proofreading personals, subjects imagine that they will get lucky and actually earn a *higher* wage for doing the titillating task, thereby instrumentally justifying an otherwise frivolous, self-indulgent choice.[11]

Note that this construal of the choice situation is instrumentally irrational in its overconfident assessment of the likely value of the elastic wage. In fact, an intransitive triad of choices occurs; when, in a separate condition, subjects were given a choice between proofreading personal ads at a fixed 17-cent wage and proofreading the same ads at an elastic 4-cent-to-30-cent wage, they strongly preferred the fixed rate. This is an empirically well-established type of preference, which Tversky and Kahneman ([1974](1982) call "risk aversion in the domain of gains."

A rational choice theorist might argue that the subjects' defections from proofreading the directory to proofreading the personal ads for an elastic wage are indeed rational, and merely indicate a real preference for the more interesting material. But then it would be puzzling why this "real" preference was not manifest when it was offered at a fixed wage of 17 cents in competition with the dull task at 24 cents. If the theorist responds by maintaining that the elastic wage condition led the subject to *discover* his real preference, one question is why such a discovery process is necessary for a pleasure motive but not for a financial motive; a second question is why the elastic wage manipulation is particularly suitable for such discovery. There are unanswered questions here, but research of this kind is capable of making sense out of the otherwise mystifying on-again, off-again character of the financial incentive.

Other effects arising from the socially privileged status of self-interest justifications (as opposed to justifications apparently lacking in self-interest) are suggested in a penetrating paper entitled "The Power of the Myth of Self-Interest." Its authors, Dale T. Miller and Rebecca K. Ratner (1995), adduce evidence that laypeople experience discomfort when they take actions seemingly incongruent with their self-interest. Further, they tend to regard the behavior of others as intelligible when self-interested, and odd when effortful but not self-interested. In Miller and Ratner's data, respondents considered it rather strange for a heterosexual to organize a demonstration for gay rights, or a man to lead a pro-choice rally. Similarly, people grossly overestimate the empirical relationships between social category membership and the opinions and behaviors seemingly consistent with the self-interests of that category. For example, the actual gender difference in endorsement of abortion rights is practically nil, but both male and female subjects believe that the difference is substantial.

I conclude as I started, challenging the working hypothesis (if not absolute belief) of rational choice theorists that all behavior is self-interested and reflective, with actors calculating and optimizing the instrumental potentiality of possible actions. From the perspective of research findings in psychology, my claim is that the instrumental pursuit of self-interest is a sometime state of mind. Its structure must be learned, and opportunities for its application recognized and acted upon. These contingencies depend on the person and the situation, and the instrumental orientation typically faces competition from expressive and other non-instrumental tendencies.

I have conjectured that the blind spot of rational choice theorists for expressive motives is due to their penchant for formalisms—which are easier to apply in the instrumental case—as well as a general cultural overemphasis on the self-interested pursuit of material gain. In correcting for the near-sighted view that human behavior is unremitting, selfish instrumentalism, the first step is to acknowledge that this position has boundaries. The second step is to identify those boundaries empirically and theoretically, perhaps aided by a decline in the self-isolation of rational choice theorists from the relevant insights of psychologists.

NOTES

1. An example of gross theoretical overreach, in my opinion, is the claim by Gary S. Becker, Michael Grossman, and Kevin M. Murphy (1992) that drug addiction is rational behavior. Their evidence is a handful of findings that the consumption of addictive substances is consistent with consumer models that include price elasticity. Many other aspects of addiction are left unexamined in their desultory empirical coverage, and as Green and Shapiro point out (59–65), evidence that costs (and/or benefits) affect a behavior at the margins does not demonstrate the rationality of engaging in the behavior itself.

2. Kinder and Sanders (1994), noting the influence that the particular framing of policy options has on the recruitment of political support, refer to the "war of [the] frames" (376).

3. The instrumental and expressive categories are not defined by the logic of necessary and sufficient features; rather, they are specified by "family resemblance" (Rosch and Mervis 1973). The several features listed for instrumental and for expressive behavior characterize the prototypic members of each of these two categories. A potentially mischievous confusion arises from the possibility that people can take actions—such as choosing a vacation spot, or signing up for piano lessons—that are instrumental to goals of entertainment or self-expression. Such mixed cases, falling between the two prototypes, are not really of independent interest. They have often been used by rational choice theorists to form a garbage category that explains, post hoc, the failure of pure material self-interest to account for some phenomenon. This strategy is nonfalsifiable and it forestalls

the recognition that not all behavior is instrumental. To convey the most distinctive features of expressive action, I set aside the mixed case of planning to enjoy oneself, and focus on spontaneous expressive behaviors consistent with the injunction in the athletic shoe commercial: "Just do it!"

4. The claim that opposition to school busing has no relation to self-interest has created a chain of controversy. It has been discovered in at least one racial hot-spot that while busing attitudes are unrelated to self-interest, the *behavior of protesting* against busing does correlate with self-interest (Green and Cowden, 1992). But that correlation may be inflated by a tangential process: racists without at-risk children may feel excluded from protests advertised as emanating from angry parents. This point is due to Miller and Ratner 1995.

5. If the reward comes as a surprise, intrinsic interest is maintained. To spoil the fun, the extrinsic motive must be psychologically present during the play period. Incidentally, the reward was a "Good Player Award," a shiny paper medallion mounted on a rectangle of construction paper. The utility of this thing is unclear, but it has high incentive power for kids.

6. The evidentiary support for the phenomenon has survived a flurry of criticism from reinforcement theorists, who were understandably perturbed by its negative implications for token economies. The large early literature on this is reviewed capably in Deci and Ryan 1985.

7. A largely discredited version of this argument holds that people will naturally learn by experience to be rational. This sounds more plausible than it turns out to be. Among many of the real-world difficulties (see Abelson and Levi 1985, 293–94; Einhorn and Hogarth 1978) is that corrective feedback from the outcomes of decisions is often biased, seriously delayed, or absent altogether.

8. Lepper, Greene, and Nisbett (1973) posed to their sample of three-year-old children questions such as: "Suppose that before you can eat foofers you have to eat greebles. Which do you think you would like better, foofers or greebles?" Virtually every child knew that foofers were yummy and greebles yucky, and that the former was a reward for enduring the latter. It is clear that concepts of reward and punishment, benefits and costs, and so forth, are learned early and are deeply embedded in public knowledge systems.

9. The motivation to cover one's apparently foolish behavior with reasonable justifications has been extensively studied under the rubric of "insufficient justification" within dissonance theory (Festinger 1957). In commenting on the tendency to invoke reasonable dispositions as justifications for our actions, a prominent dissonance theorist (Aronson 1968) wrote, "We are not rational animals so much as rationalizing animals." In related vein, a well-known game theorist (name withheld) once seriously joked, "Rationality is sloth-moderated greed constrained by formless fears, rationalized."

36

10. Politicians, of course, are extremely sensitive to the need for reasons that will be publicly acceptable as justifications of their voting records.
11. A comparable effect, consistent with this interpretation, obtained when the address–directory wage was made elastic.

Dennis Chong

RATIONAL CHOICE THEORY'S
MYSTERIOUS RIVALS

Although rational choice theory has enjoyed only modest predictive success, it provides a powerful explanatory mechanism for social processes involving strategic interaction among individuals and it stimulates interesting empirical inquiries. Rather than present competing theories to compare against rational choice, Don Green and Ian Shapiro have merely alluded to alternative explanatory variables such as culture, institutions, and social norms, without showing either how these factors can be incorporated into a more powerful theory, or how they are inconsistent with rational choice theory. It is likely that any eventual theory of the origin and maintenance of social institutions, norms, and values will have to reserve a central place for rational action.

Donald Green and Ian Shapiro's *Pathologies of Rational Choice Theory* raises serious questions about whether the growing popularity of rational choice theory in political science is based on scientific criteria. Few of the criticisms raised in *Pathologies* have not been aired previously (e.g., Rosenberg 1992; Blaug 1980; Cook and Levi 1990; Monroe 1991), but Green and Shapiro have, more than other critics, accompanied their arguments with an extensive review of empirical rational choice literature.

The book starts with the premise that the value of any theory has to be

Dennis Chong, Department of Political Science, Northwestern University, Evanston, IL 60208, telephone (708) 491–2642, the author of *Collective Action and the Civil Rights Movement* (Chicago, 1991), thanks Chris Achen, Patti Conley, Daniel Diermeier, Tim Feddersen, Jeffrey Friedman, Marissa Martino Golden, Jim Johnson, Jack Knight, Anna Marshall, Richard McAdams, Ben Page, Barry Preisler, and Michael Wallerstein for their valuable comments.

measured against its empirical power. After examining research on voter turnout, collective action, and spatial models of legislative behavior and party competition—substantive areas in which rational choice theory has claimed its greatest successes—Green and Shapiro conclude that the theory has contributed surprisingly little to our understanding of politics. The testable propositions of rational choice theory, they claim, have been falsified or subjected to inconclusive tests, or else are so banal as to be obviously true. An even more serious problem, in their view, is that research employing rational choice reasoning typically suffers from a variety of methodological flaws or "pathologies" that inhibit scientific progress. Among the prime defects of rational choice analysis are that its hypotheses are vague, inconsistent, or untestable; that evidence is gathered and interpreted in a biased fashion; that competing theories are not considered when assessing the evidence; and that post hoc amendments to the theory are introduced to explain away disconfirming evidence. These methodological problems, Green and Shapiro argue, stem from rational choice theorists' attempt to develop a universal theory of politics. Although they do not oppose the scientific study of politics, Green and Shapiro contend that general laws of human behavior are unlikely to emerge from it. Instrumental rationality, they are convinced, cannot account for all social phenomena; some events are better explained by culture, norms, and psychology.

Before I take up these arguments, I first want to outline a few modest virtues of the rational choice approach, illustrated by examples drawn from the areas of political participation and collective action. Then I will return to some of the central criticisms presented by Green and Shapiro.

Probably the greatest virtue of their book is that it will be instrumental—as in this symposium—in sparking or renewing debate on the nature of theory and model building, the prospect of a general theory of political action, the criteria for evaluating scientific theories, the relationship between explanation and prediction, the difference between conceptual and empirical progress, and the connections between theories, models, and data. But despite raising important issues, Green and Shapiro add disappointingly little substance to these debates and their argument is marred, ironically, by some pathologies of their own. In particular, *they* tend to view evidence selectively, sometimes offer no evidence for their claims, often take both sides of an issue, and, most important, provide no constructive solutions to the problems they identify because they do not develop rival explanatory hypotheses.

Moreover, by concentrating single-mindedly on the degree to which rational choice explanations have (or have not) been verified, they overlook how the theory supplies a powerful causal mechanism that is a prerequisite

to interesting empirical inquiry. Alternative hypotheses often identify social regularities without clearly specifying their causal mechanisms—in
other words, they fail as explanations. Because Green and Shapiro mistakenly feel that they bear no burden to weigh rational choice theory against
alternative explanations, they do no better than to muster half-hearted al-
lusions to vague alternative cultural, psychological, moral, and institutional
hypotheses. Since I take Green and Shapiro to task for not presenting a
constructive discussion comparing rational choice to competing explanations, I close by examining just how we might understand the relationship
between economic and sociological theories of action.

Theories and Research Agendas

Rational choice theory builds on the assumption that people choose,
within the limits of their knowledge, the best available means to achieve
their goals. They are presumed to be instrumentally rational, meaning that
they take actions not for their own sake, but only insofar as they secure desired, typically private ends.

This theory, it seems to me, has considerable intuitive plausibility and, at
the very least, is a compelling point of departure for social analysis. Individual actions are seldom perfectly rational, but there is an essential degree
of rationality in most behavior. Analysts therefore do well to see how far
this idealized explanatory model comports with actual behavior (Popper
1961, 141).

Like any good theory, rational choice theory raises interesting issues for
study and charts a program and methodology of research. By tracing social
institutions, collective action, and social change to the actions of individuals, the theory follows the principle known as methodological individualism. People's actions are, in turn, explained in terms of their preferences,
beliefs, opportunities, and choices. It is instructive to compare the premises
of the rational choice model with the assumptions underlying so-called sociological approaches, which give priority to values (Barry 1978; Elster
1989a). In their ideal form, sociological explanations ground the motivation for behavior in people's attachment to social norms rather than in
their assessment of opportunity costs. Rational choice or economic explanations, on the other hand, focus on the intentions of the agent, who
chooses among alternative courses of action depending on the rewards
promised by each one. Rational behavior is motivated by the relative at-
tractiveness of different alternatives rather than by internal regulation provided by values or dispositions.

Rational choice theory thus reframes many conventional research questions by asking how rational individuals would behave in different environments of choice. This approach was essential in pointing out the difficulty of motivating self-interested actors to take collective action on behalf of public goods. Instead of assuming, as in earlier group theories, that individuals will naturally take action that is in their collective interest, rational choice theory implied that, paradoxically, individuals will refrain from contributing even if they stand to benefit from the collective good. Since people can potentially receive the benefits of such goods without paying for them, they will not readily contribute to their provision.

The logic of collective action (Olson 1971), which has proved applicable to a remarkably broad range of social and economic situations, proceeds from the assumption that cooperation must be explained in terms of the individual's cost-benefit calculus rather than the group's, since the group is not itself rational, but can only consist of rational individuals. In the classic examples of collective action problems, such as preserving the environment, maintaining a common natural resource, participating in national defense, and engaging in social protests, group members gain when all individuals do their share, but the marginal benefit of a single contribution is outweighed by its cost. What is best for the group, therefore, is not necessarily best for the individual. Studies of collective action using laboratory experiments, game theory, and historical cases have tried to identify the conditions under which rational actors are likely to cooperate even though they have a strong incentive to be free riders. Collective action problems are typically solved by changing the incentive structure facing individuals, or by inducing cooperative behavior through repeated social interaction. In the political realm, it also appears that social norms, principled commitments, and expressive or symbolic benefits are often needed to motivate participation in collective action. Whether these so-called extrarational incentives stretch the rational choice model or break it is the source of much controversy in the field (Benn 1979; Frank 1988; Hirschman 1982; Margolis 1982; Scitovsky 1976).

Likewise, the related puzzle of why people bother to vote had not always troubled students of elections before the advent of rational choice theory. Traditional sociologists and political scientists traced group variation in voter turnout to differences in the extent to which group economic and noneconomic interests were made salient in electoral campaigns. Farmers, for example, were thought to turn out more than average because they were especially vulnerable to government economic policy. In general, those who paid close attention to politics, such as lawyers, professors, and business people, voted more frequently because they saw more clearly than others the costs and benefits of alternative policies. From this perspective, the motivation to vote may also stem from an interest in furthering moral and religious convictions through government action, or from social pressure to abide by group norms. Although the discussion in this literature was conducted at the group level, the implication was that voting was instrumental in that individuals acted according to their broadly defined group interests (Lipset et al. 1954).

The rational choice account of voting, however, reveals that the policy benefits one can expect from voting will almost always be insufficient to repay the cost of gathering information and going to the polls. This implies that people require other inducements to vote, such as civic duty, social pressure, the value of exercising voice, and the like. Thus far, we have no powerful theory—rational choice or any other kind—about how these factors motivate individual action. Since the problem of voter turnout has not been solved by any rival theory, it is not, strictly speaking, an "anomaly" for rational choice theory, but simply an unsolved problem for all relevant theories. Only when a theory cannot account for a problem that another theory has already solved does it have an anomaly on its hands. An unsolved problem is less damaging to a theory than an anomaly because a theory's status depends largely on how it handles problems that a competing theory has already solved (Laudan 1977, 17). The fact that rational choice theory has fallen short in explaining voter turnout, therefore, is no reason to abandon the theory. Until there is a rival theory that solves the paradox of voting, it will not be the problem that ate rational choice.

Causal Mechanisms

Some of the discoveries of rational choice theory may appear merely to restate earlier observations or to be obvious. But even when deductions from a particular model reproduce what was already known, rational choice theory is valuable for specifying a causal mechanism behind the phenomenon in question (Elster 1989b; Little 1991). Exploration of this underlying mechanism sheds light on the range of circumstances in which the regularity will hold, and on when it is likely to be contradicted. In the study of social movements, it has frequently been observed that collective action piggybacks on existing community organizations (McAdam 1988). People who were affiliated with churches and fraternal organizations, for instance, were more likely to be active in the civil rights movement (McAdam 1982; Morris 1984). This is the kind of empirical regularity that is commonplace in social science research. As it stands, we do not know specifically what it is about organizational membership that facilitates contributions to public goods. One possible mechanism is that cooperative conventions established out of self-interest within enduring community networks and organizations provide the foundation for large-scale cooperation. Contingent cooperation in large-scale ventures is facilitated when collective action comprises a federated network of community groups and organizations (Hardin 1982). Monitoring is feasible in these smaller groups, and cooperation or defection can be rewarded or punished in the context of everyday interaction with friends and associates. A person who refuses to contribute to a community-wide effort may suffer damage to his reputation and lose companionship and future opportunities for beneficial exchanges with those in his immediate reference groups (Chong 1991). Rational choice theory therefore leads the researcher to examine whether social institutions and patterns of social exchange within communities create favorable conditions for cooperative behavior.

By exploring the mechanism of rational calculation in the context of repeated social interaction, we can derive further hypotheses about circumstances that would, theoretically, foster cooperation by lengthening individual time horizons. Therefore, the addition of a lower-level mechanism to explain a social regularity is not simply philosophically satisfying in the sense of offering microfoundations (Stinchcombe 1991); rather, exploration of the implications of this individual-level mechanism yields further deductions about the relationship between structural conditions and aggregate outcomes. For example, black migration to cities and burgeoning black college attendance between the 1930s and 1950s would be expected to promote collective action by creating structural conditions that permitted regular social exchange and community building among blacks (McAdam 1982). In contrast, organizations whose members pay dues, but enjoy few opportunities for direct social exchange, are predicted to be less conducive to producing public goods.

Alternative social science theories, such as structural explanations, are frequently imprecise about causal mechanisms. Such explanations would often be strengthened if they more explicitly considered the role of individual choice. The causal impact of structural change on revolutionary collective action, for instance, depends crucially on how people experience their social arrangements and how their beliefs about their condition and opportunities change as a result of changes in state capacity or social and economic relations. These beliefs constrain how well people are able to develop effective organizations and overcome collective action problems in order to wage conflict against existing authorities (Skocpol 1979; Taylor 1989).

Similarly, functionalist explanations of social institutions that identify how they contribute to the maintenance of society gloss over the mechanisms by which individuals create and defend such arrangements. According to Kingsley Davis and Wilbert Moore's (1945) functionalist account of social stratification, for example, a status system guarantees that adequate incentives are available to attract the most able individuals to the most important social positions. In the interest of society, individuals with the necessary aptitudes must be given an incentive (such as higher income and status) to undergo the education and training that is required for such occupations. The standard critique of functionalist explanations holds, however, that we cannot account for a system of social stratification by pointing to how it serves the general interests of society. One must still ask how and why individuals support such a social arrangement. Furthermore, the functionalist argument assumes that high social status actually does correspond to the more important roles and positions in society when, in fact, this is only partly true. Gang leaders and mob bosses receive more than their share of praise within their own circles. Moreover, individuals must have a personal interest in acquiring status and in granting esteem to others, if functionalist explanations are to be valid. "Social needs can affect individual behavior only as far as they are translated into individual motivations—either by appeal to the various individuals' self-interests in a narrower sense, or by appeal to their personal loyalties—that is, to their personal concern for the interests of some other individuals, or for the interests of some organizations or social groups" (Harsanyi 1966, 358). This is why, within every social group (street gangs and criminal organizations included), status is granted only to individuals whose actions further the interests of those bestowing the status.

Likewise, as I will elaborate later, social-psychological theories of the sort favored by Green and Shapiro—such as reference group theory—which attempt to explain conformity in small groups based on patterns of identification and social contact, underspecify the causal relationships between membership and beliefs. Again, one must incorporate strategies, choices, and interests in explaining how individuals are prone to identify themselves and the ideas and values to which they are likely to conform.

Why Is Rational Choice Popular?

By taking an unusually limited view of what constitutes scientific progress, Green and Shapiro fail to acknowledge the contributions made by rational choice theory in developing a conceptual framework, raising novel research questions about the microfoundations of social processes, and addressing these questions by exploring new causal mechanisms. Their evaluation also gives no weight to the theoretical research in rational choice that uses abstract, game-theoretic models to work out the logical consequences of rational behavior under various assumptions about actors' desires, beliefs, and circumstances.

Many of Green and Shapiro's criticisms have the quality of half-truths: for all the confirming instances they supply, there is also much evidence to the contrary. For example, Green and Shapiro claim that the popularity of rational choice theory is not due to successful deductions from it, but because it tends to roam freely in areas that are data poor, such as the study of legislative behavior as opposed to public opinion (195). Their evidence for this claim, however, is not systematic: they provide no breakdown, for example, of the frequency of rational choice studies in different realms, nor do they contemplate alternative explanations for the distribution of rational choice research. There is, after all, no shortage of aggregate- and individual-level electoral data on the factors that are correlated with voting turnout, and yet rational choice theorists (regrettably perhaps) seem quite determined to wrestle with that issue. There are also numerous qualitative and quantitative studies of interest groups, community action, social movements, and other forms of political participation to which rational choice theorists have devoted attention.

An alternative hypothesis is that rational choice theory has been less prevalent in the data-rich field of public opinion because rational choice practitioners are more interested in behavior than in opinions and attitudes. The shift toward rational choice in political science and away from explanations relying largely on attitudes and values was accompanied by a shift in emphasis toward behavior and action rather than expressions of intentions, and toward strategy and politics—typified, perhaps, by decision making in legislatures—rather than social-psychological dynamics that are divorced from political calculation.

Method-Driven Research and Post Hoc Theorizing

Green and Shapiro contend that rational choice is method driven rather than problem driven and that, as a result, rational choice theorists look only for evidence that is consistent with their theory—sometimes to the point of fitting the data to the theory—and do not approach problems open-mindedly, using whatever theoretical knowledge is available (42–44). While this accusation can probably be levied with justification against some studies in every tradition, including rational choice, counterexamples are, once again, easy to locate. If rational choice theorists only seek confirming instances for their theory, it must be perverse that they return repeatedly to what many consider to be hard, even hopeless, cases or puzzles for the theory, including not only the particular problem of explaining participation in elections but the general issue of explaining uncoerced contributions to public goods.

It is unclear at best, moreover, how Green and Shapiro reconcile their accusation about method-driven research—which suggests that disconfirming evidence is ignored—with their jibes at the tendency of rational choice theorists to alter their assumptions about actors' information sets, risk levels, desires and goals, and decision-making capacities when rational choice predictions fall short (29–30). Modifications of rational choice theory are derided by Green and Shapiro for being post hoc explanations, yet such modifications are meant to improve the theory in the light of disconfirming evidence.

Similarly, Green and Shapiro criticize the lack of realism of rational choice theory even while they discourage efforts to make it more realistic. While rejecting the realism of rational choice explanations of voting and collective action, Green and Shapiro (36–37) cite the existence of multiple rational choice models of such phenomena as evidence of the unfalsifiability of the theory—rather than as competing attempts to improve its explanatory power. In any research program, different analysts will naturally rework the basic assumptions of the model when the implications of the model do not accord with the evidence. Green and Shapiro would prefer that rational choice theorists stop tinkering with their models, concede that instrumental rationality cannot be applied in every realm due to "the recalcitrant complexity of the political world" (185), and thus give up their aspiration to develop a general theory of social action. Social science is law governed, according to Green and Shapiro, but not governed by the same laws everywhere.

Ad hoc revisions are rightly avoided when they create conceptual tangles within a theory that reduce its problem-solving capacity. For instance, when Anthony Downs (1957, 270) tried to save his economic model of voting by arguing that people go to the polls in order to do their share in preserving a democratic system, he violated his main assumption that one chooses among alternative actions based solely on the relative advantage of each action to oneself alone. Green and Shapiro, however, appear to distrust ad hoc modifications merely because they seem too easy to construct. Leaving aside whether they are easy or difficult to devise—I think the latter is more accurate—ad hoc modifications are not always bad practice. Indeed, we cannot trace the development of such theories as Newtonian mechanics and evolutionary theory in the natural and biological sciences without taking ad hoc modifications into account. By definition, an ad hoc modification increases the empirical power of a theory and therefore is a progressive development. Avoiding ad hoc modifications by restricting the domain of a theory shrinks that theory's empirical reach. While an ad hoc modification should generate additional tests of the theory, it is debatable whether those additional tests need to be identified immediately, as opposed to being developed later (Laudan 1977, 115–17).

I should add that not all of those who are sympathetic to rational choice research share the view that instrumental rationality can explain all social action. Researchers understandably attempt to employ whatever theory they think has the most explanatory potential. In recent years, this has led to the widespread application of rational choice across many domains, even when individual practitioners within each realm are not convinced that rational choice is universally applicable.

Instead of trying to impose arbitrary rules about the limits of rational choice theory, perhaps we should make our assessments based on the research it enables. Discussion of the limits of the theory among those who are more sympathetic to the rational choice enterprise than Green and Shapiro has produced some general boundary conditions. For example, John Harsanyi has pointed out that acts of altruism or morality are more likely to occur when the costs of doing so are small. Likewise, sociological factors can lead to the development of personal friendships and commit ments and motivate actions on behalf of people other than oneself (Harsanyi 1969; Sen 1977). These and other limitations of the theory will have to be uncovered in the course of research, not by a priori declaration.

Furthermore, we will still want to establish generalizations about when these exceptions will occur—that is, when alternative mechanisms need to be invoked—and thereby move systematically to a more encompassing theory. In typical fashion, Green and Shapiro's prescriptions on this issue cut both ways. On the one hand, they discourage efforts to develop a general theory of politics, but, on the other hand, they criticize what they call "arbitrary" restrictions on the domain of rational choice theory in the sense that they are not derived from the theory itself (44–46).[1] However, we cannot get beyond arbitrary boundary conditions for a theory without moving in the direction of a more elaborate and general theory.[2]

Alternatives to Rational Choice Theory

In order to justify scrapping rational choice theory, we need a viable replacement, so it is reasonable to ask critics to propose alternatives to contrast against rational choice explanations. The first hint that Green and Shapiro will refuse the invitation is their caveat that rational choice theories are sometimes formulated in ways that are tautological, capable of explaining any possible outcome or empirical fact. When this is the case, they argue, they aren't obliged to provide an alternative. "Whatever its particular content, if an empirical theory is formulated in this porous fashion, its defender may not legitimately fault the skeptic for failing to propose an alternative" (184). It escapes me, however, how someone else's presumably tautological theory prevents one from formulating a sounder theory that explains the facts to which the first theory was directed and, in addition, has the virtue of being falsifiable.

A theory cannot be rejected because of disconfirming facts; it can only be supplanted by a superior theory. But Green and Shapiro feel absolved of the responsibility for proposing alternative theories not only because rational choice theory is supposedly tautological, but because they claim that it was never shown in the first place to possess greater explanatory power than existing theories (182–83). But even if this were true, it is akin to saying that because rational choice didn't play by the rules, its opponents aren't required to, either. I should note that Green and Shapiro do not substantiate the claim that rational choice did not, on scientifically meritorious grounds, supplant alternative theories. They do not trace citation patterns, examine the reasons behind the success and failure of competing theories in various subfields, or document the extent to which inconsistent evidence undermined older theories.

In fairness, Green and Shapiro do make a half-hearted attempt to identify some alternatives to rational choice hypotheses. "Rational choice theorists who have advocated partial universalism," they write, "have left unexplored the extent to which a phenomenon is explained by individual maximization as opposed to habit, blunder, and the like" (27). Toward the end of the book, they claim that "in the course of examining different rational choice literatures we have mentioned a variety of alternative hypotheses for particular political phenomena: normative, cultural, psychological, and institutional. The criticism that we offer no alternative theory must be interpreted, therefore, to mean that we offer no theory of comparable generality or range" (184). However, the speculative factors they name are not explanatory theories. They are variables that might have causal impact via some unspecified mechanism. Green and Shapiro provide no substitute psychological theory of individual agency nor any discussion of what gives institutions and norms their causal power over social action (e.g., do they influence behavior by altering individual incentives, changing preferences, providing information, coordinating beliefs, or what?).

The two chapters in the book devoted to voter turnout and collective action problems offer no alternative theories to compare against rational choice. Green and Shapiro occasionally allude to the influence of social-psychological and moral factors (e.g., group loyalties, emotions, political identities, ideology, obligation, altruism) that they believe fall outside the rational choice approach. They venture, for example, that demonstrations and riots may not be instrumental acts, but simply reflect frustration and anger (184–85); therefore, such phenomena may not be explainable by a rational choice theory. However, besides identifying variables like these, Green and Shapiro make no effort to spell out a competing theory that explains when such mass actions are likely to occur.

Are There Free Riders?

Green and Shapiro's predilection for nonstrategic, noninstrumental motivations is evident when they question the frequency of free riding. We would do well to consider whether the alternative explanation they sketch is more accurate or fruitful than a rational choice analysis. Green and Shapiro wonder if, in many alleged cases of free riding, people are really trying to get something for nothing. "As an empirical matter," they contend, "it is far from an established fact that people are holding back resources for causes they value in the hopes that others will pay" (83). They argue that many instances of failed collective action may simply be the product of indifference, apathy, ambivalence, distaste, or lack of interest rather than shirking, since we do not know how much people value specific public goods nor whether they agree that political action is the best route to obtaining them (80).

We may examine this issue by considering the 1994–95 impasse between the owners and players in major league baseball over such issues as salary caps and free agency (van Dyck 1994). What would rational choice theory, or its possible competitors, have predicted about whether the owners could break the players' union? Non-rational choice theorists might explain cooperation or defection among the players to be a function of their values and group norms—such as their strength of commitment to free agency or to their union, their willingness to join group ventures, or their desire to help fellow group members. The problem with these explanatory variables is that they are in very close proximity to the phenomenon that we wish to explain, since they invoke an underlying disposition or commitment to act in a particular way that is exemplified by the behavior in question. Moreover, such explanations are seldom clear about how and when these values will motivate action. Therefore, even if there is a close correspondence between people's values and their behavior, the regularities so identified do not amount to a flexible, fertile theory that generates interesting deductions.

Rational choice theory cannot generally offer a precise prediction of what level of defection will take place or when it will occur. Most rational choice models do not have much practical predictive value in those re spects. Theories rarely explain facts exactly because theories are based on idealized, isolated systems that do not usually pertain in the actual world. We also cannot readily assess the initial conditions of real situations with sufficient accuracy to match against the premises of our models. Crucial data about individual beliefs and preferences that are needed for predictions are often ascertainable only after the event has already occurred (Scriven 1988). Consequently, rational choice models are predictive only in the ideal sense that if their assumptions are found to apply in a given situation, then certain outcomes should logically follow.

The low *predictive* strength of a theory, however, does not undermine its *explanatory* power (Little 1993). Although rational choice theory probably could not have told us the absolute level of free riding among baseball players, it could produce some insight into which categories of player would have been most likely to defect in the absence of a settlement. Players near the end of their careers, players in deep financial straits, players unlikely otherwise to make it to the big leagues, international players—in general, players who need the money most and who have weak relationships to other players—are the likeliest strikebreakers, since the benefits they receive would likely outweigh future reprisals. On the basis of rational choice theory, we can also predict, with some accuracy, the kinds of preventive actions the union is likely to take to prevent defections, such as frequent meetings to shore up solidarity, real or implied warnings against those who might defect, threats of subsequent retaliation on the playing field, and concerted efforts to define the issue in terms of individual rights rather than money. The union is inclined to take these measures—monitoring, offering selective incentives, indoctrination—if it believes that players are in varying degree tempted to return to work—that is, to free ride. However, this temptation may be kept in check by awareness of the repercussions, and possibly by normative beliefs reinforced by the union. While the use of such countermeasures is a standard derivation from the logic of collective action, it is not suggested by explanations that trace choices to underlying values, habits, or dispositions. Also, none of the tests of the theory involve asking the players for the reasons behind their choices; instead, the predictions (or retrodictions) are based on a model that assumes that the ballplayers face a collective action problem in which the temptation to defect varies according to personal circumstances.

Survey Evidence

Green and Shapiro, on the other hand, rely heavily on self-proclaimed motives to challenge the prevalence of free riding. Moreover, they sift through the evidence of such motives in a highly selective manner. For example, they cite survey data on professed "apathy, ambivalence, or antipathy toward politics" (81) as evidence against free ridership. In considering the opinions of those who opposed the Three Mile Island power plant, but contributed no money to the oppostion, Green and Shapiro find that some had never heard of the opposition organization, some believed that nuclear power was not a serious threat, and some opposed joining any group. They conclude that many of these people cannot be accused of free riding (ibid). Similarly, they cite interviews with members of the Confederation of British Industry showing that selective incentives were not the only reason mentioned for membership; respondents also mentioned the collective benefits of counteracting labor organizations (84–85). But Green and Shapiro fail to discuss how to protect our research against people's tendency to present reasons that make their actions morally defensible. In explaining their failure to participate in collective action, would we expect free riders to come right out and admit their free ridership, or is it not more plausible that they would make excuses that protect their self-image? (In his candid autobiography, the civil rights leader James Farmer [1985] confesses that he tried to manufacture a credible excuse to dodge participation in the freedom rides through the South because he feared the campaign was too dangerous.)

I have difficulty squaring Green and Shapiro's naive use of survey data to oppose the free-rider hypothesis with their refusal to accept survey results showing that people think their individual participation has a pivotal impact on the provision of a collective good. Such evidence has been used by some defenders of rational choice theory to show that people may cooperate because they overvalue the benefits of their own contributions to an organization or social movement. Green and Shapiro doubt if these individuals would say the same thing if they were questioned more closely— if they were asked, say, whether the organization or its policy goals would change if they were to drop out (86). Apparently, the kind of "blunder" Green and Shapiro feel is a powerful explanatory factor in other contexts is implausible in this circumstance. Of course, it may be the case that the respondents *would* think differently if the survey questions were better framed, but that they think and act as they do because they do *not* frame the matter so sharply. Similarly, when rational choice researchers contrast survey results showing mass support for a public good, such as a clean environment or gun control, against the low level of material contributions to these causes, Green and Shapiro call it a "peculiar line of defense" (82) for those committed to analyzing behavior rather than expressions of preference.

Green and Shapiro's reliance on survey data to discredit the logic of collective action also contradicts Green's claim elsewhere, drawing on his own research on opposition to court-ordered busing schemes, that people are not rational when they answer survey questions even though they may be rational when they act. Green and coauthor Jonathan Cowden (1992) reach this conclusion after discovering a significant statistical relationship between objective measures of self-interest and *participation* in antibusing protests, but little relationship between self-interest and *opinions* about school busing.

This kind of analysis might appear to be exactly what Green and Shapiro have in mind when they recommend invoking different theories and laws to explain different events. But parsimony would seem to recommend a better solution than to treat individuals in dichotomous terms, operating according to one model in surveys and another when they act. Opposition to busing may be a product of group conformity. If one's friends and neighbors oppose busing, if the politicians one admires oppose busing, if one thinks busing is unsound, one will receive net benefits by indicating in a survey that one is opposed. Protesting, however, is more costly than is a mere expression of opinion. Those who become involved in protests are typically going to need additional benefits to offset the higher costs. Naturally, then, parents who live in predominantly white neighborhoods and parents without the resources to enroll their children in private schools are more likely to act, because they feel they stand to gain more by preventing busing from occurring in their district. Nevertheless, they still might have to employ measures to deter shirking by those who are tempted to free ride. This reasoning can reconcile observations about people's opinions and their actions without introducing two separate causal mechanisms.

I should add that social factors—such as the desire to get along with one's friends—that affect expressions of opinion are also likely to undercut the relationship between narrow self-interest and protest activity. People who do not have children, or who can transfer their children to private school, will sometimes be drafted by their neighbors to engage in protest for the same reason that they will be inclined to agree with the predominant community view on the issue.

I do not mean to attack or defend surveys in principle, but to point out that they should not be used selectively. Both Green and Shapiro's readings of the survey results and the alternative interpretations I have proposed are speculative, because expressions of motivation are raw data that result from an unclear process. We have to develop some consistent rules about how such evidence is to be evaluated. People's professed reasons cannot be the sole criterion for understanding their behavior; if it were, the social sciences would be largely directed toward interviewing people to find out how they explain their own actions.

Extrarational Strategic Behavior

Green and Shapiro contend that the motivation to participate in collective action may not be "palpable incentives or disincentives" but rather "such norms as 'doing one's share,' 'every little bit counts,' or 'cheaters never prosper'" (73). In short, some amount of participation appears to be noninstrumental, since individuals value participation for ideological or moral reasons. Participation is, to this extent, explained by underlying commitments and values rather than the cost-benefit calculus.

How and when do these norms work? Are they themselves products of self- or collective interest? Rational choice analysts have explored these issues because they, too, have sensed that people often relish involvement in certain forms of collective action. When participants in collective action are motivated by extrarational considerations, however, they tend not to pursue them independently of other motivations. Even in the modern civil rights movement, which was infused with moral and religious conviction, there is evidence both of free ridership and of social mechanisms (including monitoring and social pressure) that were instituted to minimize it. Thus, the expressive or moral benefits of participation are not doing all of the work.

Moreover, even if we factor in the kinds of extrarational incentives that Green and Shapiro seem to think are crucial, we are still typically left with problems of coordination or "assurance." Extrarational motivations, such as zeal and moral outrage, are not sufficient to explain how collective action in favor of civil rights originated. Acts of altruism and compliance with norms tend not to occur unconditionally, but to depend on feelings of social obligation that are contingent upon the choices of others. These additional considerations are better represented by coordination games that present different strategic considerations to participants than the prisoner's dilemma game on which Green and Shapiro focus. In assurance games, for instance, people tend to shirk so long as few people are active, but they weigh in when the movement grows beyond a certain point. Therefore, while collective action may struggle to get off the ground, people may rush to join after a critical mass is achieved (Chong 1991).

The point is that rational choice analysis of strategic behavior is likely to be important in any examination of collective action, whether we make simple or complex assumptions about motives. Social norms, expressive and symbolic actions, and even habitual behavior tend to have strategic components that are amenable to rational choice analysis, even if instrumental rationality does not appear to be the whole story. The joint venture (204) that Green and Shapiro recommend among contending theoretical approaches in the social sciences would have been better served had they spent more effort discussing how separate traditions might complement each other. In that spirit, I will spend the remainder of this essay sketching how such a venture might proceed in the study of social norms and values, which in Green and Shapiro's view are motives for behavior that lie outside the boundaries of rational choice.

Social Values and Self-Interest

Green and Shapiro venture that rational choice theory will diminish in popularity as more empirical testing is conducted (196). A more likely scenario is that rational choice analysis will increasingly expand into such noneconomic domains as social norms, cultural values, ideology, and group identification, which Green and Shapiro place outside the scope of the theory. Green and Shapiro apparently think variables can be neatly compartmentalized into those that are compatible with rational choice theory and those that are not. But whether social norms and values belong in a separate cultural or symbolic realm, or are themselves amenable to rational choice reasoning, can be settled only by further research.

This may eventually result in a proliferation of distinct theories for different areas of social inquiry—the "middle-range" theories recommended by Green and Shapiro (188). But parsimony demands that we first investigate whether any of the recalcitrant social phenomena can be explained by rational choice. For example, it would be sensible to study whether the formation of group norms and values can be explained by more or less explicit calculations of interest.

According to reference-group theory, people tend to pattern their values and behavior after those who have social backgrounds similar to themselves, since they are likely to share interests and perspectives. It is an elementary principle of political socialization that beliefs and values are likely to stem from one's social origins. In Tibetan Buddhism, when the Panchen Lama dies, he is reincarnated somewhere. Whoever is the reincarnation of the Lama can be discovered through a series of divine signs, so senior lamas use oracles and examine the surfaces of holy lakes for clues to his identity and location. Using these leads, they turn up a number of children who might prove to be the reincarnated Lama. One of these children is eventually chosen, based on his ability to recognize a variety of objects that belonged to the deceased Lama. In theory, the new Lama could be located anywhere, but political and religious leaders are acutely aware that the geographical location of the new Lama broadly hints at his future political inclinations. Therefore, when the Panchen Lama died in 1989, the whereabouts of the reincarnated Lama were the subject of much political controversy, since the new Lama would be an influential voice on the question of Tibet's future relationship with China. The betting was that if the Panchen Lama turned out to be a boy in China with parents who supported the Beijing government, he would probably favor maintaining existing ties to China when he grew up; but if he were plucked from a family of anti-Communist Tibetan exiles in India, he would be inclined to support the movement for political independence. Knowing what was at stake, religious and political authorities fought over where the search should be concentrated (Kristof 1990). All of which might lead us to ask, Whatever happened to the idea of the one true Panchen Lama?

An important contribution of the postwar Columbia school's research on opinion formation and political choice was to show how a person's attitudes and actions are shaped and reinforced by her so-called reference groups (Berelson, Lazarsfeld, and McPhee 1954). These groups include not only closely related individuals, such as family, friends, classmates, and coworkers, but also more abstract categories of associates, such as professionals and members of social classes, who have a hand in molding attitudes and opinions. Social interaction, discussion, and the circulation of ideas within these groups lead to shared opinions on matters of common interest such as religion, culture, politics, and morality. People develop common evaluations and norms as the influence and conformity processes within their social groups tend toward social equilibrium. While conformity to group norms and values may be a response to overt inducements—threats of ostracism or retaliation, for example—people are often simply trying to develop a coherent understanding of events and situations with the assistance of their immediate social circle. There are individual and collective incentives for group members to coordinate their actions around conventions, including social norms, morals, and even empirical beliefs.

One of the prime manifestations of this phenomenon in politics is the convergence of public opinion during election campaigns, as people try to make sense of the issues and candidates. Green and Shapiro (183) contend that rational choice arguments about how people employ shortcuts to gather information, such as relying on the endorsements of interest groups or politicians, have not been placed in competition with old-time social-psychological theories, for which they show great fondness (68, 70), such as the reference group theory I have just described. They claim that rational choice theory sometimes does nothing more than restate implications of reference-group theory using rational choice terminology.

Without a clearer specification of the causal mechanism behind social learning, however, the implications of reference-group theory are not obvious. The theory requires further elaboration of individual motivation—such as the pursuit of individual or group interests—to explain the kinds of values around which people will coordinate and the circumstances under which they will change their values. As the theory stands, it suggests implausibly that any pattern of conformity may manifest itself and that group values will survive intact indefinitely across generations. A model of social conformity needs a starting point in the form of people with sufficient motivation to assess the consequences of political alternatives and form opinions on the basis of these evaluations (Luce 1959). Such people provide the energy behind the diffusion process.

The more motivated individuals who are the driving force behind social conformity processes are characterized by higher levels of interest in politics. They may make their decisions on the basis of either personal benefits to be derived from election outcomes or, more likely, their perception of benefits for the groups with which they identify. It is also fair to assume that their social position gives them personal incentives to remain informed about political affairs. Bernard Berelson, Paul Lazarsfeld, and William McPhee (1954) identified such individuals as opinion leaders. We can suppose that such individuals gather information during the campaign in order to establish which candidate serves their interests.

Therefore, a promising model of social norms and values that gives a more central role to rational choice would assume that class or group homogeneity is a product of group interests. Awareness of such interests is developed through a process of opinion leadership, in which more motivated and independent individuals influence less interested voters. If group interests are preeminent, then social mobility out of one's social class will lead gradually to the formation of new political preferences, despite continuing discussions with members of one's former group. By introducing the concepts of individual and group interests, we give the opinion formation process a starting point lacking from a model in which individuals are passive; at the same time, the elaborated model yields insights into the kinds of political values that will be attractive to members of different groups, and the circumstances in which values are likely to change.

In contrast, the pure sociological model predicts that values imprint themselves and become impervious to change once they are internalized. But this deduction cannot be sustained in the face of the evidence. Studies indicate that values change when the social support for them is undercut, as when white Northern students in the 1930s traveled to the South for their college education and subsequently developed more intolerant racial attitudes (Sims and Patrick 1936). The female subjects of the famous Bennington College study held steadfastly to their liberal college political beliefs only when, following graduation, they were able to maintain a social network that was similar in ideological composition to their reference groups in the Bennington community (Newcomb et al. 1967). By the same token, the new Panchen Lama will presumably adjust his values in the direction of his new associates' views to the extent that he can be weaned from his social origins.

One appealing feature of this rational choice model is that it can handle the observations that people are often guided by values and dispositions that are not acquired through conscious calculation, and that they may not respond promptly to changes in opportunity costs. Indeed, many acts of conformity seem to involve complete ignorance of the consequences and potential benefits of alternative choices. Does this mean that people are sometimes motivated by social values that are inconsistent with self-interest? Not if we refuse to regard the pursuit of self-interest in overly calculating terms. As Harsanyi (1969) noted, "people regard their existing customs as superior to alternative patterns of behavior because they have little reliable information about what it really would be like to live with any of these alternatives" (527). Cultural inertia, then, is not always inconsistent with rational decision making. No individual has the resources to evaluate thoroughly all the choices he must make, so by conforming to the status quo he takes advantage of community leaders or the cumulative wisdom of the community; in effect, he operates on the assumption that existing practices have already survived a trial-and-error test (Dollard and Miller 1941). Still, we have to wonder why people develop such strong emotional attachments to the patterns of behavior they develop through socialization. It may be, as Donald Campbell (1975) has speculated, that blind conformity is adaptive early in life because it improves the rate of information transmission from parents to their offspring. In the formative stages of life, it may simply be better to follow one's elders unquestioningly than to stop and assess the conventional wisdom.

In addition, even if people do not deliberately calculate that adopting certain norms and values will serve their interest, they are likely to see that they have an interest in conforming to group norms, because conformity can be valuable in itself. The specific opinions with which one agrees may not be as important as the display of one's willingness to belong. Unconventional opinions, by the same token, are telltale signs that one is a potential troublemaker whose behavior cannot be reliably predicted. Thus, a major reason people attach significance to opinions may be that they provide clues to deeper behavioral dispositions.

These examples may well strike Green and Shapiro as further instances of how rational choice theory often renders a social phenomenon "intelligible" by making it the unintended consequence of rational individual action without showing that such a process actually *did* occur. It may be the case that the observed outcome could have been derived from quite different initial conditions or from non-rational choice premises. My purpose in this last section, however, has been merely to show that it is not obvious that social norms and values lie entirely outside of rational choice theory and thus require separate theoretical treatment. The first step in making this argument is to explain how certain processes of value formation and change can be traced to the operation of individual interests and more-or-less conscious strategic calculation. The theoretical explanation of value formation and change developed here assumes that people seek both material and social goals given limited information and restricted group memberships. The next step is to derive further testable implications of the model, such as how values will change when an individual experiences upward social mobility. In this painstaking fashion, we gradually improve the explanatory power of our models. Although I doubt that Green and Shapiro would disagree with this process, it is regrettable that they never provide any similar discussion of how rational choice theory might be strengthened, or how it matches up against competing theories.

NOTES

1. Curiously, Green and Shapiro do not think that a specified relationship between two variables (e.g., X is related to Y when Z is present, but not otherwise) constitutes an arbitrary domain restriction (45). In practice, such specifications are almost always entirely arbitrary in the sense that we have no theoretical reason why the relationship holds under some circumstances, but not others.
2. I owe this point to Jim Johnson.

Daniel Diermeier

RATIONAL CHOICE AND THE ROLE
OF THEORY IN POLITICAL SCIENCE

In their survey of empirical research based on rational choice theory, Don Green and Ian Shapiro point to a list of methodological deficiencies or "pathologies." The main problem with Green and Shapiro's list lies in the standards they use to evaluate the achievements of rational choice theory. These standards are derived from a view of empirical research that is deeply questionable and, in the stated form, inconsistent with both standard insights in contemporary philosophy of science and the established practice in the most successful empirical sciences.

If rational choice—like political science—claims to be an empirical science, then eventually its accomplishments have to be judged empirically. In this sense, a critical assessment of the empirical success of rational choice theory is an important enterprise. In *Pathologies of Rational Choice Theory*, Don Green and Ian Shapiro conclude that a number of methodological deficiencies or "pathologies" plague empirical applications of rational choice models—"fundamental and recurrent methodological failings rooted in the universalist aspirations that motivate so much rational choice theorizing" (33). Green and Shapiro argue that these mistakes "stem from a method-driven rather than a problem-driven approach to research, in which practitioners are more eager to vindicate one or another universalist model than to understand and explain actual political outcomes" (33).

Green and Shapiro's argument can be summarized in three propositions:

Daniel Diermeier, Graduate School of Business, Stanford University, Stanford, CA 94305-5015, wishes to thank David Austen-Smith, David Baron, Jon Bendor, Randy Calvert, Dennis Chong, Gary Cox, Ulrich Druwe, Jeffrey Friedman, Jim Johnson, Keith Krehbiel, and Keith Poole for valuable comments on this paper, an earlier version of which was presented at the 1993 Annual Meeting of the Political Science Association.

P1. There is a list of methodological characteristics that are undesirable in an empirical science and are thus to be avoided.

P2. Empirical applications of rational choice theory are more likely to commit (a subset of) these mistakes than other types of empirical analysis in political science.

P3. These pathologies are not due to an historical coincidence (such as deficiencies in training or interest), but are rooted in fundamental characteristics of rational choice theory, especially its universalist aspirations and the lack of (empirical) specificity in the rational actor assumption.

Note that P1 and P2 are logically independent. While P2 is a meta-empirical claim asserting a certain empirical regularity in scientific behavior, P1 is a methodological claim identifying certain kinds of scientific behavior as undesirable. Since Green and Shapiro's verdict concerning rational choice theory depends on both claims, invalidating either one is sufficient to reject their main argument. P3, of course, is only relevant if P2 and especially P1 are defensible. If P3 holds, however, its impact is considerably more powerful than the conjunction of P1 and P2, since it suggests that the identified failings can only be corrected by fundamentally altering or even abandoning the rational choice enterprise.

In the following section, I will criticize these statements in turn. The main emphasis will be placed on P1, since the issue of methodological standards is presumably the most important one for the practicing political scientist.

Methodological Pathologies?

To claim that rational choice theory exhibits "pathologies" presupposes certain criteria of methodological "health." Such standards could be delineated either by providing explicit standards or—using Wittgenstein's technique of "family resemblance"—by providing paradigmatic cases of good theorizing. If it turns out, as I wish to show, that Green and Shapiro's methodological criteria are inappropriate for an empirical science, then their attempt to demonstrate that rational choice theory fails to satisfy them is irrelevant for the evaluation of rational choice applications.

In order to criticize these criteria most effectively, I will rely heavily on examples from Newtonian physics. The reason is not that I assume that rational choice theory is as successful as physics. This, of course, would be an absurd claim. Rather, Newtonian physics is undoubtedly one of the paradigmatic cases of a successful empirical theory. Yet Newtonian physics exemplifies the very features that Green and Shapiro identify as characteristic pathologies of rational choice theorizing. Moreover, these features are not small deficiencies in an otherwise grand theory. Modern philosophy of science has identified these features as characteristic of theories that success-fully account for empirical phenomena.

Unfortunately, Green and Shapiro provide neither a list of such criteria, nor do they point to paradigmatic cases of good theorizing. Thus, their list of pathologies has to be used to reconstruct their methodological stan-dards. In Chapter 3, Green and Shapiro identify methodological patholo-gies grouped into the following categories:

1. Post-Hoc Theory Development
2. Formulating Tests
   a. Slippery Predictions
   b. Vaguely Operationalized Predictions
3. Selecting and Interpreting Evidence
   a. Search for Confirming Evidence
   b. Projecting Evidence from Theory
   c. Arbitrary Domain Restrictions

First I will argue that in their original formulation, Green and Shapiro's standards are not sound. Then I will reconstruct the intuition underlying these standards in the language of modern philosophy of science, to demonstrate that the so-called pathologies are perfectly normal character-istics of successful theories in the empirical sciences, and that relying on Green and Shapiro's implicit criteria would hinder scientific progress in political science.

Post Hoc Theory Development

According to Green and Shapiro, rational choice theory places great em-phasis on the development of post hoc accounts of known facts (34). This is not a pathology. It is a standard feature of normal research, i.e., research guided by a paradigm (Kuhn 1962). What Green and Shapiro call "post hoc theory development" Thomas Kuhn would call "puzzle-solving." Cre-ating a model that shows how a hitherto inexplicable phenomenon can be shown to be rational is analogous to normal scientific behavior in theoreti-cal physics.[1] Indeed, puzzle solving is what drives cumulative research in a discipline guided by a paradigm.

Given Green and Shapiro's stated preference for a problem-driven rather than a methodology-driven approach to the study of politics (33), puzzle-solving—the explanation of a known but so far unexplained fact by means of a theory—should not cause any methodological concern. What Green and Shapiro may have in mind, however, is the tendency to stop with puz-zle-solving, failing to generate hypotheses that may be used to test the newly proposed solutions to the empirical puzzles. They charge that

62

post hoc theories are not only tested inadequately, the manner in which they are developed tends to be in tension with empirical testing. To the extent that theorists exploit the ambiguity in the meaning of rationality to transform successive disconfirming instances into data consistent with a newly recast theory, one must question whether the succession of theories is susceptible to empirical evaluation in any meaningful sense.

> Given the lack of specificity about what it means to be a rational actor, it is not obvious what sorts of behaviors, in principle, could fail to be explained by some variant of rational choice theory. (36, 34)

Of course, this challenge to rational choice theories only makes sense if individual theoretical statements, such as the rational actor assumption, *can* be tested in a meaningful sense. Since the 1930s, an abundance of work in the philosophy of science has challenged such a claim as naive. Here I will consider only two examples: Hempel's covering-law approach[2] (Hempel 1965) and the so-called Duhem-Quine Hypothesis (Lakatos 1970; Quine 1953; Quine and Ullian 1978).

The covering-law approach states that in order to explain a particular empirical fact we have to demonstrate how this fact (E) can be logically deduced from a set of general statements ($L1$-Lr) and a set of initial conditions ($C1$-Ck). Hempel restricted this scheme to explanations of singular sentences by empirical generalities or "laws." Theoretical explanations, according to Hempel, do not directly explain singular phenomena; rather, they systematize a variety of empirical generalizations. But for the sake of argument, let us assume that the core assumptions of rational choice theories are among $L1, \ldots Lr$.[3]

According to the covering-law approach, these assumptions are *never* directly testable. Rather, what is tested is always the *conjunction* of $L1, \ldots Lr$ and $C1, \ldots Ck$.[4] So if our model predicts E, but not-E occurs, then from a logical point of view, *any* of the antecedent conditions can be given up. A particular claim can only be tested if all the other statements that make up the antecedents are assumed to be true. If a rational choice theorist wants to test a particular game-theoretic model, he has to assume, among other things, that actors maximize a particular utility function, know the game form, know that the game form is common knowledge, never use a weakly dominated strategy, and so forth. If he wants to test the maximization hypothesis itself, he has to assume that the game form suggested matches the actual decision situation, that it is common knowledge, and so on.[5] So if rational choice theorists are more willing to drop an initial condition or modify a particular model than to reject the rational actor premise, there is nothing logically wrong with it. One can criticize the refusal to give up the rational actor assumption only on pragmatic grounds, by arguing, for instance, that it somehow hinders the progress of science.

This insight has found a pronounced expression in the Duhem-Quine

Hypothesis, which can be formulated in the following two statements (Stegmüller 1986): (1) A theory is accepted or rejected as a whole, not through the acceptance or rejection of particular components of the theory. (2) A rejection of a theory based on a critical experiment is impossible.

The rationale behind this thesis is that empirical evidence may "falsify" only a conjunction of statements, not an isolated statement. Hence theories can always be adapted to deal with troubling observations without having to abandon any given core assumption, such as the rational actor assumption.

The fundamental question, of course, is: which particular parts of a theory should be modified in the absence of any ironclad logical imperative? Quine suggests following rules of simplicity and conservatism. Central parts, such as the rational actor assumption, should be modified only as a last resort, and only if the subsequent theory is considerably simpler than its predecessor. Rational choice theorists follow exactly these rules when, for instance, they refuse to give up the assumption that politicians are primarily office-motivated—the better fully to explore the logical and empirical consequences of this premise. Similar behavior has been repeatedly documented as prevalent in the most successful of the natural sciences (Kuhn 1962; Sneed 1979; Stegmüller 1986).

To be sure, nobody is obliged to subscribe to Hempel's or Quine's approach to testing. For their complaint to be relevant, however, Green and Shapiro must demonstrate how testing of a particular proposition, such as the rational actor assumption, can be a meaningful enterprise—a formidable task, given sixty years of philosophy of science that point in precisely the opposite direction.

Formulating Tests

Green and Shapiro condemn the use of unobservables in rational choice theories. "Arguably the most important source of slipperiness in model building," they write, "is the multiplication of unobservable terms, which causes the complexity of the theory to outstrip the capacity of the data to render an informative test" (39). Most of what was argued in the previous section also applies here. In this section, however, I want to focus on the independent issue of the role of unobservables in empirical theories.

A general form of Green and Shapiro's argument concerning problems with unobservables goes as follows: By definition, unobservables cannot be measured. Thus theories that contain unobservables cannot be tested empirically. Since rational choice theories contain unobservables, they cannot be tested empirically. Therefore they are unscientific.

This challenge to rational choice theory is, however, only relevant if (a) the existence of unobservables can be avoided, and (b) unobservables diminish the empirical content of a theory—neither of which is true.

The problem of unobservables has been well recognized in the philosophy of science literature, under the heading of "theoretical terms," terms that do not express measurable phenomena alone (Carnap 1979; Hempel 1965; Ramsey 1960; Sneed 1979). Early analyses of such empirical theories as Newtonian physics recognized the prevalence of theoretical terms, such as "mass." Building on these insights, Joseph D. Sneed's important analysis rejects the traditional distinction between observables and unobservables. Sneed introduces the notion of a "T-theoretic term," where T is the theory in question. An entity is T-theoretic if its measurement presupposes the validity of theory T (Balzer 1982).

Consider, for instance, rational choice uses of roll-call data that use a "revealed preferences" argument. Now, revealed preferences themselves presuppose (rational) choices in a particular choice situation. The concept of (revealed) preferences is thus T-theoretic; it presupposes the validity of rational choice theory. It is a trivial consequence of the existence of T-theoretical terms that T cannot be tested in the usual way, since testing T requires measurement, but measurement presupposes the validity of T.

At this stage one may be tempted to argue that the presence of T-theoretical terms would be a fatal blow to any empirical theory. This, however, would be a rather serious misconception. All empirical theories that have been analyzed by philosophers of science contain T-theoretical terms (Balzer 1982; Balzer, Moulines, and Sneed 1987; Dreier 1993; Stegmüller 1986). Among these theories are Archimedian statics, classical particle mechanics, classical electrodynamics, Dalton's theory, special relativity theory, thermodynamics, genetics, general equilibrium theory, theory of accounting, macroeconomics, and psychological behavioralism.

Green and Shapiro claim that it is not the mere presence of unobservables that causes problems in testing rational choice theories, but the high ratio of unobservables to observables. This is baffling. Even one unobservable would lead to the supposed testability problem. Moreover, rational choice theories do not seem to excel in the proliferation of theoretical terms. Preferences and beliefs (in imperfect information models) seem to be the main ones.[6] But even if the ratio of theoretical to nontheoretical terms were indeed high, then rational choice theory would be in good company. Newtonian classical particle mechanics (CPM) contains three fundamental terms: distance, force, and mass. Two out of three (force and mass) are CPM-theoretic (Balzer 1982; Sneed 1979; Stegmüller 1986).

While there is no logical reason that theories *must* contain theoretical terms, successful empirical theories do. Sneed contends that this, in part, stems from the fact that T-theoretical terms are crucial in considerably simplifying a theory.[7] Further, they allow scientists to increase the content of a theory and to develop new prognoses. A T-theoretical term is typically introduced into a theory with constraints that restrict the set of empirical facts consistent with it. Requiring that an entity be "conservative" is a typical example of such a constraint. In Newtonian mechanics this refers, for example, to the requirement that objects have the same mass even if they appear in different mechanical systems. In rational choice theory, preferences are assumed to be constant across choice situations. Comparative statics analysis can then be used to vary observable parameters, such as institutional features, and predict changes in observable behavior. Thus, theoretical terms are not only unavoidable; they fulfill a critical role in the development of successful theories. Indeed, it may be precisely the explicit use of theoretical terms that accounts for the success of rational choice theory in political science, since it allows the systematization and logical connection of hitherto unrelated empirical regularities.

But what about the empirical content of a theory containing theoretical terms? Sneed has suggested a formal solution building on the work of Frank P. Ramsey (1960). While the details of this procedure, the so-called "Ramsey-Sneed" elimination, are mathematically quite demanding, the basic idea is rather simple. It requires one to represent a given theory formally as a set-theoretic entity, a "predicate," and then to replace the existing theoretical terms by variables and quantify over these (now free) variables using existential quantifiers (Sneed 1979; Stegmüller 1986). Intuitively this means that the Ramsey-Sneed statement of a theory only claims the existence of some entities connecting the observable phenomena. The result is a statement that expresses the empirical content of the whole theory, but only contains empirical entities that can be measured without referring to theory T. The main practical implication of the Ramsey-Sneed elimination is the formal demonstration that one can use theoretical terms without having to fear that this leaves the theory devoid of empirical content. In the case of rational choice theory, this means that whether preferences are directly observable or not is logically independent from the question of whether rational choice theory has empirical content.

Since theoretical terms are not only unavoidable, but fulfill a variety of useful purposes, such as allowing comparative statics analysis, prohibiting theories that contain theoretical terms would thus not only eliminate all the empirical science since Archimedes, but also restrict political science to theoretically trivial generalizations of particular data sets.

Selecting and Interpreting Evidence

With respect to the selection and interpretation of evidence by rational choice theorists, I will focus on the issue of arbitrary domain restriction. Green and Shapiro write:

> Arbitrary domain restriction occurs when an empirically testable set of limiting conditions is lacking, but retreat is sounded anyway. There is in other words a critical difference between specifying the relevant domain in advance by reference to limiting conditions and specifying as the relevant domain: "wherever the theory seems to work." (45)

To illustrate their argument, Green and Shapiro give the example of the theory of gravity. They ask the reader to consider what would happen if red apples did not confirm the predictions of Newtonian physics. They conclude that one would not be impressed by a theory that is supposed to work for other falling bodies, but does not work for red apples. But ironically, this is precisely what repeatedly happened to Newtonian physics. Perhaps the most important case was Newton's theory of light, which was originally a sub-theory of general particle mechanics. After a series of failures, the domain of Newtonian mechanics had to be restricted to "nonlight particles." Another example is the orbit of Mercury. Newton's theory never worked for this planet. So its application was "arbitrarily" restricted and Mercury's orbit was left as a puzzle, indeed an anomaly, until Einstein's theory of general relativity could account for it (Kuhn 1962). Of course, it would have been foolish to give up Newton's theory, which worked so well in most areas, just because of one anomaly. Once again, a supposedly pathological characteristic of rational choice theory turns out to be a standard and fruitful feature of successful empirical science.

The confusion presumably stems from the belief that theories in some sense determine their domain. If this were true, a post hoc restriction of the domain would be inappropriate. Recent studies in the philosophy of science have indicated that this "auto-determination" intuition is highly problematic (Kuhn 1962; Sneed 1979). Sneed has suggested that theories should be interpreted as ordered pairs consisting of a *core*, C, which expresses the mathematical content of a theory, and a set of *intended applications*, I. The empirical claim of a theory then consists in the statement that C can successfully be applied to I.[8] Theories can be modified by changing either the mathematical core or the intended applications. Progress will consist in either strengthening C or extending I. Regress consists of relaxing C or restricting I. All these variants are common procedures in empirical sciences.[9]

In this context it is worthwhile to consider Green and Shapiro's response to the suggestion that rational choice theory is either a family of theories, a methodology, or a paradigm (192). Green and Shapiro state that such perspectives are inconsistent with the claim that rational choice offers a unifying theoretical approach to the study of politics. Using Sneed's concept of a theory, however, it can be demonstrated that a family-of-theories approach is consistent with (potentially) universal applicability. The key idea is the distinction between fundamental and specific laws. Fundamental laws apply to all intended applications, specific laws only to subsets. Again Newtonian mechanics perfectly exemplifies this distinction: its fundamental law is Newton's Second Law, linking force, mass, and acceleration.[10] Special laws include the law of gravitation, whose intended application, or domain, is the set of large bodies, such as planets; and Hooke's Law, which applies to phenomena such as springs. Specific laws link the fundamental law to measurable phenomena. The fundamental law systematizes a variety of previously unrelated and more specific laws.

Thus, in rational choice theories of candidate competition, some researchers assume policy-motivated candidates, while others follow Downs's suggestion and assume pure office-seeking motivation (see Calvert 1985). The former assumption may be more appropriate in cases where disciplined parties compete for office, the latter where the competition is among political entrepreneurs. Both assumptions are, of course, untestable, yet they allow us to link the rational actor assumption to empirical realities. In the particular case of candidate competition under uncertainty over voters' ideal points, these assumptions, in conjunction with the rational actor assumption, lead to different empirical implications: convergence in the Downs model, nonconvergence in the Calvert-Wittman model. So, in conjunction with a particular assumption concerning motivations, the rationality assumption generates precise and testable implications.

Throughout their book Green and Shapiro hint at the possibility that the rational actor assumption may be tautological (e.g., 36). Although they never provide a rigorous argument that this is indeed the case, suppose for the sake of the argument that it were. Would this matter? First of all, it is important to distinguish between the content of a *statement* and the content of a *theory*. While a particular statement, such as the fundamental law of a theory, may be tautological, the conjunction of fundamental law, specific law, constraints, and so on, typically will not. It is precisely the assumption of particular motivations in particular applications that would guarantee the empirical content of rational choice models *even if the fundamental assumption of rational action were indeed tautological*. The empirical content of rational choice theory then derives from the fact that those particular motivations are constant across different institutional settings, allowing one to compare, for instance, voting under plurality rule to voting under runoff majority rule.

Once again, Newtonian physics offers an example of how this works. The second Newtonian Law strictly speaking *is* tautological.[11] Classical particle mechanics, of course, is not. The reason is that additional (general and specific) laws allow us to apply the theory in its intended domain.

What, then, is the role of Newton's Second Law? It fulfills precisely the same role as the rational actor assumption in rational choice theory. It links and systematizes isolated empirical regularities.

In their final chapter, responding to critics who might accuse them of advocating a naive falsificationism, Green and Shapiro claim that this criticism can, in turn, only be made from a Lakatosian standpoint (181). The previous discussion has demonstrated that this conclusion does not follow by any means. Moreover, according to both Kuhn's concept of paradigms and Sneed's structuralist reconstruction of empirical theories, the so-called pathologies of rational choice theory are perfectly acceptable and indeed consistent with characteristic behavior in the most successful natural science. The challenge for Green and Shapiro, then, is to demonstrate that their criticism of rational choice theory is consistent with *any* reasonable position advocated by students of empirical science. By a "reasonable" position I mean one that does not declare typical scientific behavior, such as that exemplified in Newtonian physics, to be unscientific or bad science.

My challenge to Green and Shapiro's claims should not be taken to imply that rational choice political science is as successful as physics, or even that, in its present state, it is empirically more successful than the collection of mutually inconsistent middle-level approaches that had dominated political science before the advent of rational choice theory. Rather, criticizing Green and Shapiro from the standpoint of philosophy of science reveals that their central objections to rational choice lack any sound theoretical justification.

Meta-Empirical Fallacies

Let us now focus on P2. Just as much as P1, P2 must hold true if Green and Shapiro's argument is to be judged as valid. The following critique, then, is independent of the previous criticisms, but sufficient to reject Green and Shapiro's argument.

P2 is an empirical claim. Of course, it is not an empirical claim about political behavior, but about political science. So we are talking about science from a metascientific perspective. Since, presumably, there are no shared empirical criteria for a meta-empirical analysis, let me use the very criteria Green and Shapiro suggest for empirical work and apply them to their own meta-empirical claim.

Green and Shapiro neither provide an explicit sampling procedure, use control groups, formulate an explicit null hypothesis, appropriately operationalize rejection criteria, or avoid slippery predictions and the search for confirming evidence.[12] They rely on a collection of case studies, rather than, for instance, taking a random sample from the *American Political Sci-*

ence Review or the *American Journal of Political Science* during the last 10 years and comparing rational choice papers with other contributions. Doing so would have enabled them to (1) formulate an appropriate null hypothesis—for instance: that there is no difference between rational choice-based papers and other papers in political science, in terms of their conformity to a specific set of scientific standards; (2) make a strong case for it; and (3) reject it, if necessary, on the basis of the sample data. In the absence of such a careful examination, Green and Shapiro commit the very fallacies of which they accuse rational choice theorists: they are unclear about alternatives, vague about operationalization, and relentless in their pursuit of confirming evidence.

Should they respond that it is somewhat inappropriate to criticize their metascientific analysis using criteria that are intended only for an empirically successful theory of politics, would they not—post hoc—be engaging in arbitrary domain restriction?

Green and Shapiro's argument thus faces the following dilemma. Either P1 is sound and we indeed are faced with methodological pathologies, but P2 lacks justification, since it relies on the very fallacies condemned by P1; or P1 has to be given up, in which case P2 may very well be accepted. But then the criticism of rational choice theory, as compared to other forms of political science research, is irrelevant, since it is based on inadequate criteria. Indeed, since many of the P1 "pathologies" turn out to characterize the most successful sciences, one must consider whether P2 amounts to an endorsement of rational choice theory.

*   *   *

The previous discussion has demonstrated that the main deficiency of Green and Shapiro's critique lies in the standards they use to evaluate rational choice theory. These standards are derived from a view of empirical research that is deeply questionable, and is, in the stated form, inconsistent both with standard insights in contemporary philosophy of science and with the established practice in the most successful empirical sciences. This does not mean, of course, that there are no methodological problems in the application of rational choice theories to measurable phenomena. It only suggests that Green and Shapiro's treatment fails to address this question. Indeed, it confuses rather than clarifies the relevant issues.

Among those issues are the relationship between (typically) deterministic game-theoretic equilibrium predictions and stochastic empirical analysis, the ad hoc use of equilibrium refinements, the role of learning and evolution in rational choice models, the lack of explicit measurement theories in many areas, and, finally, the operationalization of the very specific characteristics of extensive game forms. The debate over rational choice would do well to shift from imaginary battles to the rational discussion of these genuine methodological problems.

NOTES

1. A nice example is the quantified Hall effect, which was treated as an aberration or "dirt effect" until it was demonstrated to be consistent with the laws of quantum physics. This example of "post hoc theorizing" was worth a Nobel Prize for its discoverer, von Klitzing.
2. Green and Shapiro mention this approach in Chapter 2.
3. This holds once rational choice theory is completely "axiomatized." In this case the mentioned empirical generalizations are merely theorems that follow from the axioms of the theory. But then, of course, it is sufficient to include only the axioms of the theory among the list of premises. Note that Hempel's argument relies on the so-called "statement view" of theories, i.e., the view (borrowed from metamathematics) that theories are sets of sentences (or propositions) that are closed under logical implications. Newer developments have questioned this interpretation of theories (Sneed 1979; Stegmüller 1986). The details of this debate, however, are irrelevant for our purpose, since Hempel's insight is preserved in these new approaches.
4. If we subscribe to a falsificationist theory of testing, this follows directly by *modus tollens*.
5. This is especially important for the literature on experimental games.
6. At this stage this claim can only be a conjecture. To my knowledge, there is only one explicit reconstruction of a rational theory, namely Downsian electoral competition (Dreier 1993).
7. This is not just a matter of taste. As will become clear later, the empirical content of a theory "purged" of theoretical terms, the Ramsey-Sneed statement, is an enormously complicated entity.
8. This is an overly simplified version of Sneed's sophisticated argument. His argument, however, extensively uses set- and model-theoretic arguments. For details see Sneed 1979.
9. For an extensive list of examples see Sneed 1979, Balzer 1982, and Balzer, Moulines and Sneed 1987.
10. Recall that both mass and force are theoretical entities.
11. For a formal proof see Gaehde 1982.
12. In their last chapter, Green and Shapiro mention the important contributions by, for example, Gary Cox and Mathew McCubbins (1993), Roderick Kiewiet and McCubbins (1991), and Keith Krehbiel (1991). Here, their methodological discussion focuses on measurement problems that are prevalent in this area of political science and have nothing to do with the previously identified methodological pathologies. Further, such important work as Snyder 1990, 1991 and Poole and Rosenthal 1991 is still omitted.

John Ferejohn and Debra Satz

UNIFICATION, UNIVERSALISM, AND RATIONAL CHOICE THEORY

Green and Shapiro's critique of rational choice theory underestimates the value of unification and the necessity of universalism in science. The central place of intentionality in social life makes both unification and universalism feasible norms in social science. However, "universalism" in social science may be partial, in that the independence hypothesis—that the causal mechanism governing action is context independent—may hold only locally in certain classes of choice domains.

In *Pathologies of Rational Choice Theory,* Donald Green and Ian Shapiro argue that rational choice theory has not made a substantial contribution to our knowledge of politics. While this shortcoming might be due to the theory's simply being false, Green and Shapiro locate much of the responsibility for this explanatory inadequacy in a "syndrome of fundamental and recurrent methodological failings rooted in [its] universalist aspirations" (33). Its "pathologies" serve simultaneously to protect rational choice theory from disconfirming evidence and to prevent it from developing testable hypotheses about the political world. The resulting insulation of theory from data threatens to make rational choice theory at best an intellectual diversion, and at worst an ideological exercise.

In making their argument, Green and Shapiro consider several areas that have received attention from rational choice theorists. They argue that the accumulated empirical contributions in these areas have not added up to

John Ferejohn, the Carolyn S.G. Munro Professor of Political Science and a Senior Fellow of the Hoover Institution at Stanford University, Stanford, CA 94305, and Debra Satz, Department of Philosophy, Stanford University, Stanford, CA 94305, thank Bruce Bueno de Mesquita and the editor of this journal for comments on an earlier version of this paper.

very much—and that where rational choice theorists have made empirical contributions, these have tended to be trivial (11). While we agree with some of Green and Shapiro's assessments of particular studies, we think that their characterization of the rational choice enterprise is inaccurate and that their recommendations for its improvement are misguided.

We object to two parts of Green and Shapiro's argument. First, their conception of what constitutes a contribution to knowledge is too narrow: it excludes much good social science. Specifically, it is a mistake to identify the empirical contribution of a theory only with its explanatory successes. Theories play other important roles in guiding empirical social science research. The very notion of explanatory success depends on a prior (theoretical) characterization of what exactly needs to be explained. Consider, for example, the way that rational choice theories made the act of voting problematic in ways it had not been in earlier theories. This shift meant that it was now voting rather than nonvoting that a successful theory needed to explain. Rational choice models of legislatures also made the apparent stability of majoritarian processes appear puzzling and, as a result, shifted attention away from explaining change and toward explaining stability. In both cases, rational choice theory shifted the explanatory agenda and guided subsequent theoretical and empirical work.

Theories also place constraints on what counts as an acceptable explanation of a phenomenon. When Anthony Downs proposed that electoral behavior and candidate strategic choice be embedded within a unified model that recognized their interdependence, he greatly increased the demands that proposed explanations of either voter or candidate behavior would have to satisfy. Acceptable explanations of either phenomenon would henceforward need to account for interactions between candidates and voters.

More generally, by unifying apparently diverse phenomena, theories can change the way we look at the empirical world and alter the way social scientists do their work. We are not claiming that theoretical unification is always good or even feasible. Unification needs practical rather than epistemic justification, just as do other scientific norms, such as parsimony or tractability. Unification is desirable where possible not because we know, a priori, that the world really is unified. If the apparently diverse phenomena really are unrelated, if the world really is complicated rather than simple, norms of unity and parsimony could misdirect scientific work (Dupre, 1992). There are, however, powerful practical reasons to accept such norms as part of a regulative strategy for research. Much scientific progress has consisted of the development of theories with an ever wider range of application and, hence, explanatory potential (Kitchen, 1981). It is sensible to begin with the hypothesis that the political world can be understood in terms of a limited number of general principles, while keeping open the possibility of rejecting that idea later on.

Our second objection is that Green and Shapiro present a one-sided and misleading account of the role "universalism" plays in scientific explanation. The authors argue that the commitment to universalism—to the development of general laws that apply over wide domains of activity— leads rational choice theorists to engage in various slippery practices when applying their theories to empirical situations. The aspiration to vindicate general laws, say the authors, leads to post hoc theorizing, the proliferation of theoretical entities, and the selective use of evidence (in particular, arbitrary domain restriction); these "pathologies" save the universalist theory from empirical refutation, but only by depriving the theory of empirical content. The result, according to Green and Shapiro, is a political theory with precious little to say about politics.

We think these conclusions are unwarranted for two reasons. The first reason, which we note here but leave to others in this symposium to address, is that the various pathologies attributed to rational choice theorists might actually be instrumental or even necessary to the development of what Lakatos calls a progressive scientific research program. That is, the driving force behind many of the practices that Green and Shapiro point to might not be the desire to "save" the theory but, instead, an effort to deepen the conception of what "rational behavior" requires both in general and in specific situations. Moreover, this development might be a good thing. Rational choice theorists have increasingly adopted models of interaction which make fewer and fewer arbitrary assumptions about strategic play. The past thirty years have witnessed changes in the strategic representations of choice situations and in the conception of rationality itself. For example, there has been a transition away from neoclassical models which posit fixed prices, through cooperative game-theoretic structures in which coalitions can freely make binding agreements to coordinate play, and on to noncooperative models of political phenomena in which costless commitments are not possible. Partly as a result of this shift toward finer-grained strategic representations, the concept of rationality has been extended in various ways to apply to the formation of beliefs and expectations as well as to the pattern of choice among actions.

This evolution has greatly challenged received ideas as to what rational play would look like in numerous empirical domains and has generated new theoretical expectations as to what should occur in various circumstances. Often, this internal evolution has led in the direction of producing less determinate predictions about strategic play. Thus, some patterns of behavior that, when examined from earlier viewpoints, were thought to be irrational, appear "rationalizable" from a more recent perspective. These developments were not generated by an attempt to insulate rational choice theory from refutation but were the result of a genuine effort to follow out the consequences of the paradigm itself.

The second reason that we object to Green and Shapiro's characterization of the role of universalism, on which we shall focus, is that we believe that some version of universalism—including what Green and Shapiro call "partial" or "segmented" universalism—is necessary for any explanatory enterprise. Accounts of empirical phenomena are *explanatory* (rather than merely predictive or descriptive) insofar as they show how those phenomena can be seen as instances of causal laws or *mechanisms*. Explanations, as distinguished from descriptions, identify causal mechanisms that are held to apply across all relevantly similar contexts. Causal mechanisms are universalistic in that they can be represented independently of situations in which they are supposed to obtain.[1]

In order to count as being situation–independent, causal mechanisms need to satisfy several properties. They must not contain terms which refer to individual objects, dates or temporal periods; or, if they do, these must be derivable from more general statements that do not. They must be universal in their application and not be simple finite conjunctions of confirming instances (i.e., descriptions). Without formal properties of this sort, scientists would be unable to appeal to underlying mechanisms as explanations.[2]

More controversially, we argue that a particular form of universalism has a special place in social-scientific explanation. Social-science explanations must, we claim, be compatible with intentional descriptions of human agents. That is to say, it is a necessary constraint on a social science explanation that the agents whose actions are required to make it work be capable of forming the intentions appropriate to those actions. A successful social-science explanation presupposes that the behavior in question be describable as being intentionally brought about by human agents seeking goals and holding beliefs.[3] In this sense, intentional explanations are privileged in the social sciences. This privileging is "weak," however, in that it does not exclude the possibility that a good social-scientific explanation can proceed without explicit reference to intentions. Social-scientific explanation need only be compatible with intentional explanation, even if a nonintentional explanation is preferred for explanatory purposes.[4]

Obviously, this "weak compatibilism" is inappropriate in explaning human behavior that is the result of external physical processes—for example, the effects on behavior of exploding a bomb. Such explanations, in any case, are not *social*-science explanations—they are physical ones. Physical explanations appeal to causes that do not respect the fragile boundaries of our bodies.[5]

Unification and Theory Assessment

The standards Green and Shapiro use to assess contributions to knowledge are both arbitrary and too narrow to constitute useful criteria for evaluating theories. First, Green and Shapiro put forward aprioristic and unsound criteria for judging theories. They are, for example, critical of theories that rely on a proliferation of theoretical or unobservable entities, and of theories that do not generate unique predictions. Second, they fail to recognize the contribution of studies that identify new problems, or that unify apparently diverse empirical phenomena.

We shall not say very much about the use of unobservables in empirically useful theories, as it is explored in detail elsewhere in this symposium. But the notion that a good theory must yield unique predictions is, we think, an ad hoc requirement. While it might have been better, from the standpoint of testability, if the theory of natural selection predicted a unique evolutionary path, the theory is no less valid for failing to produce such strong results. Similarly, in many circumstances the rationality of actors may not be a severe constraint on the kinds of actions they can take. In such cases, rationality alone does not powerfully (uniquely) explain their actions, even if it is true that all the actors are rational.[6] This does not mean that such explanations are false or unilluminating, but only that other constraints or conditions must be appealed to if a more *complete* account of the action is desired.[7] The extent to which explanations require additional contextual information of this sort is an empirical, not an a priori matter.

Moreover, a theory can be empirically illuminating by identifying what needs explanation. One contribution of the rational choice literature on voter turnout—perhaps the main contribution—is that it shifted attention to explaining why some people vote, as opposed to why some people do not. Where many earlier studies portrayed nonvoting as a species of social deviance—a symptom of personal or social disintegration—the Downsian view shifted the explanatory burden to explaining why normal, well-adjusted people would vote. Whatever Green and Shapiro think of the various attempts to provide positive accounts of voting within a rational choice framework—appeals to strategic factors, norms, or systematic misperceptions—the point is that any plausible theory of voting is now required to bear this explanatory burden.

An additional contribution of that literature is that it promised to unify diverse empirical phenomena within a single theoretical framework. For it raised the possibility—since explored more deeply by John Ledyard (1984) and by Thomas Palfrey and Howard Rosenthal (1985)—of explaining voter turnout in terms of factors endogenous to the electoral process. In such studies, the benefits and costs of the voting decision, and the probability that a single vote will be decisive, are both determined (endogenously) within the larger context of competition among candidates and parties.

The hypothesis that one's decision to vote depends significantly on these variables is an empirical claim that is not entailed by a commitment to any version of rational choice theory. This claim is, strictly speaking, stronger than either the assertion that voters are rational (as in Riker and Ordeshook 1968) or that they calculate in some other way (as in Ferejohn and Fiorina 1974). Thus, the truth or falsity of rational choice theory is not directly at stake in these studies. What is at issue is whether it is more promising to attempt a unified study of electoral phenomena that includes voters and candidates in the same strategic framework, or whether we should retain a more compartmentalized approach. If, indeed, it turns out that there are empirically important strategic interconnections among voters, candidates, contributors, etc., then the Downsian unification will have been a good strategy for discovering this.

We can see several other examples of the value of theoretical unification as a research tactic among studies Green and Shapiro cite. David Mayhew's classic, *Congress: The Electoral Connection*, is exemplary in showing how apparently diverse aspects of congressional behavior can be understood as arising from the interaction of "single–minded" reelection seekers. In much the same way, Keith Krehbiel's *Information and Legislative Organization* and Gary Cox and Mat McCubbins's *Legislative Leviathan* each show how a wide range of congressional actions can be understood as the result of more basic causal processes. The main contribution of each of these studies is in showing how diverse empirical phenomena can be understood as instances of underlying general causal mechanisms. Even if none of these studies had provided an improved statistical account of any specific behavioral phenomenon, they would remain outstanding additions to our understanding of congressional behavior and organization. By showing that apparently diverse empirical phenomena are instances of an underlying single causal mechanism, these studies suggest ways to examine that mechanism directly in a wider range of institutional settings. This is a particularly important contribution in fields in which experiments are difficult to conduct and where, therefore, we are limited in our ability to test or compare theories.[8]

Why Universalism Is Indispensible to Explanation

Green and Shapiro propose, in place of the universalistic view that people make choices in the same way in all circumstances, a more modest position that permits explanatory accounts to vary situationally. While some of our own writing (Satz and Ferejohn 1994) is cited in support of this view, we think Green and Shapiro have overstated the case for rejecting the universalist commitment in rational choice theory. There are two reasons for this conclusion. First, contextual dependence is not incompatible with universalism. Individuals could use different intentional calculi in different contexts while still conforming to general (though possibly relatively complex) laws.

Second, we do not believe it is possible to abandon universalist aspirations: *some form of universalism* is unavoidable if one seeks explanations rather than mere descriptions. The examples of good research cited by Green and Shapiro suggest that they should endorse this idea as well.

Consider two salutory studies, authored by John Aldrich and Morris Fiorina (Aldrich 1980; Fiorina 1994), which Green and Shapiro present as instances of desirable "mid–level" explanation (190). Both studies are lauded for not depending on (or presenting) theorems but, rather, for constructing solid empirical generalizations that tell us something new about the phenomena in question. But why do Green and Shapiro find such empirical *generalizations* to be explanatory? The explanatory punch of the Aldrich and Fiorina papers comes, in reality, from the fact that they do rely on general theorems that have been derived from universalistic premises (even though these authors do not explicitly defend these premises). Both Aldrich and Fiorina rely on rational choice theory to generate the hypotheses they examine.

Nonuniversalistic accounts framed in terms of local and concrete observations lack explanatory punch for roughly similar reasons for which Green and Shapiro criticize the use of "arbitrary domain restrictions." A completely nonuniversalistic account will have a completely ad hoc range of application. Given their description of these studies, Green and Shapiro offer no reason to think that Aldrich's and Fiorina's explanations would generalize to any domain beyond their actual cases. Why aren't generalizations of this sort mere descriptions? We believe, on the contrary, that the Aldrich and Fiorina accounts have explanatory appeal precisely because they rest on rational choice theories and, to that extent, present us with a deeper understanding of the phenomena they examine.

Perhaps what Green and Shapiro really object to in rational choice theory is the assertion that individuals act to maximize utility across all circumstances, and that it is the utility maximization hypothesis that explains most human behavior. But, depending on how this idea is fleshed out, we do not think that someone committed to rational choice theory must hold it.

Following Green and Shapiro, we distinguish between universalism and partial universalism. Partial universalism recognizes that the explanatory power of rational choice theory could be domain specific. One kind of partial universalism—one that we argued for in an earlier work (1994)—is the idea that rational choice theories might provide more powerful statistical explanations in settings where structural forces act to constrain preferences, beliefs, or choices. Thus, even though agents are assumed to maximize their utility in every circumstance, utility maximization does not provide an equally powerful explanation in every setting. In this version of partial universalism, the assumption of utility maximization is retained, but its explanatory power depends on the operation of contextual forces shaping preferences and beliefs, or setting up penalties for departures from rational action. We might attribute the relatively weak explanations of behavior when stakes are very low—such as in the case of the voting decision—to this phenomenon.

We may distinguish a second form of partial universalism, in which agents act as utility maximizers in some settings but not in others. The classical formulation of instrumental rationality evolved to help understand economic production and exchange, and, for all we know, might not be as useful in explaining other kinds of decisions, such as the choice of a marriage partner. In some settings agents may make choices for moral reasons, such as honoring their commitments, and the behavior generated by such choices need not be consistent with maximizing behavior. In other settings, where they don't have reason to care greatly about the consequences of their acts, individuals may choose whimsically or act so as to minimize regret.

Thus, according to the second form of partial universalism, it seems possible that the way people make choices may depend on features of choice situations. But this stance still retains some powerful universalistic commitments. Explanatory accounts still draw their strength from showing how observed phenomena are instances of more general causal processes—for example, we could still explain agents' choices of a marriage partner in terms of their intentions.

Intentionalism, Charity, and Rational Choice Theory

Both of these forms of partial universalism are consistent with the idea that the central explanatory project for social science—the explanation of human action—entails a commitment to intentional explanation, a commitment that carries with it, at minimum, a further commitment to partial universalism. We cannot give a complete defense of this claim here but shall, instead, sketch an argument that we present in more detail in another paper (Ferejohn and Satz, 1994).

We claim, first, that in everyday life, human agents must and do make use of intentionalist interpretation in order to make attributions about mental states. Second, we claim that this form of intentionalism must satisfy a pragmatic test—it must allow its holders to make good predictions as to how others will behave in a wide variety of settings—so that it is "generative," and cannot consist of mere tautologies. In order to satisfy these requirements, we claim that this "folk intentionalism" must be describable in universalistic terms. Finally, we claim that successful intentional scientific accounts must "track" folk intentionalism, and therefore inherit its universalistic features.

We agree with Donald Davidson that understanding others would be impossible if, in everyday life, people did not try to explain behavior in terms of intentions. When we see someone gesturing wildly at us as we drive down the street, most of us would not be inclined to view the behavior as a mere physical phenomenon like a bolt of lightning, but would try to see it as reflecting some intention—for example, a desire to warn us of some impending danger, to gain our assistance in an emergency, or perhaps to convey some pithy epithet. The disposition to see a substantial amount of human behavior as intentional is sometimes called a charity principle. A principle of this sort must be widely shared for language and culture to be possible.

While there are good reasons to think that people generally are disposed to charitable interpretation, it is not at all clear that what the content of this disposition is. Clearly, a completely stated charity principle would necessarily contain a lot of social and psychological theory and would evolve as these theories change. This content must, we think, be pretty widely shared within the community if the charity principle is to be a useful pragmatic guide for interpretation.

A charity principle does not, in any case, tell anyone how to interpret any particular behavior; it is, instead, a disposition to seek intentional accounts of whole patterns of activity. It is a tendency to attribute coherence or meaning of a certain kind to disparate phenomena rather than being content with literal descriptions. Nor does a charity principle commit its holder to the view that all actions are consciously brought about by agents. Intentionality can be given a relatively wide construction, permitting, for example, such subconscious intentions as the Freudian account of "slips of the tongue."

On its face, intentionalism—the view that much human behavior can be described as intentional and can therefore be seen as action—is weaker than rationality. Individual action could easily be intentional without satisfying any of the standard principles of rationality. For example, an individual's preference may not be independent of her choice situation. More puzzling is the experimental evidence of "preference reversal" (Lichtenstein and Slovic 1971; Grether and Plott 1979). In these experiments, an individual is given two "structurally identical" choice situations which differ only in how the alternative choices are described. The differing descriptions lead many individuals systematically to make different choices. The actions in question seem to be intentional—the experimenters structure the situations to provide assurance that the individuals have reasons to make the choices they do, are conscious of making comparisons, understand the instructions, and so on—but it is hard, at first glance, to see how they could be interpreted as rational. However, if we define the descriptions of a choice (or a subject's perception of it) as part of what he has a preference for, then preference reversal phenomena can be trivially rationalized.

Our point here is not that the standard rationality axioms and intentionality really are identical—they are not. Rather, our point is that to distinguish between them requires an additional hypothesis: that preferences are independent of choice situations. Classical rationality requires that if an individual chooses x over y in situation A, where x and y are interpreted as completely specified courses of action, she cannot rationally choose y over x in another situation (in which both are available). Where choices are based on preferences but preferences can depend on the situation, choices would be classically understood as intentional but not rational.

The orthodox distinction is overly rigid in implicitly characterizing behavior not satisfying the independence principle as irrational. Much behavior in this category might conform with weaker "rationality" principles. In the spirit of marking out the disputed boundaries of rational behavior, we can identify a variety of weaker forms of rationality that do not satisfy the independence hypothesis but which are not, on the other hand, completely ad hoc. The most commonly known of these are regret principles, according to which actors construct situation–specific preferences from more basic preferences.[9] Sen's well–known example of polite choice—wanting as much cake as possible but also not wanting to take the largest piece remaining on the plate—is another interesting example.

Richer examples arise when people make choices among objects based on the object's intrinsic characteristics.[10] In these cases, intra–individual aggregation processes—structurally similar to those arising in social choice theory—generate individual choice. Such choices will not generally satisfy the requirement of situation independence, even if they can be seen as intentional.

Both the principle of charity and that of intentionality are weaker than classical rationality conceptions. But although they are closely related, charity principles must satisfy a test of usefulness that intentionality by itself does not require. A charity principle must, above all, permit its users to distinguish action from behavior and attribute meanings and intentions to others in a wide range of novel situations (generativity), and to form expectations and predictions about their behavior (nontriviality). To be useful in sustaining social interaction (or social explanation), charity principles cannot be completely ad hoc. Rather, for a charity principle to do any work, an observer must be able to get some independent idea of the preferences and beliefs the subject would be likely to hold in a given situation. Regret principles—whether or not they are descriptively accurate—meet this formal test, and we suspect that many other nonrational choice theories would as well.

Thus, in our view, real charity principles—principles that people could actually employ to attribute intentions to others—occupy a middle ground between mere intentionality and classical rationality. It may be the case that people, in many settings, employ a charity principle that satisfies the independence hypothesis, or perhaps even the stronger hypotheses of expected utility theory. And, even if they do not, they may be brought to recognize the normative attraction of such a principle when presented with the bizarre consequences of their own decisions. If this is the case, we would expect classical rationality theories to perform well in these domains. But charity principles that fail to satisfy strict independence may still exhibit sufficient regularity to be explanatorily useful. If this is true in some domains of action, other forms of intentional explanation may be available.

Green and Shapiro are wrong to give up on the possibility of general explanatory accounts of human action in favor of seeking low-level generalizations. The fact that central features of human existence—language use and acquisition, culture, etc.—rest on intentionality and charity, implies that universalistic explanation is possible in social science. Of course we cannot know, in advance, the level of generality explanatory accounts may achieve. That is part of the reason that social scientists disagree so intensely about the nature of choice and rationality.

* * *

Rational choice theory is best understood as what Green and Shapiro call a family of theories or, better, a field of endeavor, rather more like physics or biology than like Newtonian mechanics or Darwinian selection. Such a description permits us to understand the range of intense disagreements among rational choice theorists about what motivates human agents. By characterizing rational choice theory as a field of endeavor, we can see why its boundaries—what counts as rational choice—are disputed and cannot be usefully fixed by an historically arbitrary definition. In particular, it becomes clear how theories that do not satisfy one or more of the standard (maximizing) conceptions of rationality (such as regret theories and various theories of nonbinary choice) can be part of the same explanatory enterprise.

In our view, the requirement that social explanations be compatible with intentional explanation constrains what counts as good social science. Because society is composed of human beings, social science explanations have to be compatible with psychological processes. This means both that it is physically possible for people to act as the social explanation requires, and to hold or form the relevant beliefs and desires. There is no escape from the need to attribute some form of rationality to human agents: none of Green and Shapiro's preferred explanatory styles obviate this necessity.

The question of what *form* such attribution should take is an empirical one. We cannot completely describe what counts as rational action a priori without exploring the nature of choice in a given domain. When confronted with new choice situations, we are often required to reassess what rationality requires, and it has often turned out that a much larger range of behavior can be seen as rational than had been previously thought. Green and Shapiro complain about this descriptive voraciousness but we think it does not need apology. It would be an expression of enormous hubris to think we could specify, in advance of empirical observation, the nature of the things people value, the kinds of beliefs and expectations they might form, or what technical opportunities confront them.

Moreover, if we recognize that preferences and beliefs may exhibit some degree of context dependence, their formal properties will depend on actual choice situations. Consider, for example, the standard normative argument against holding cyclical preferences: the money pump. A person holding cyclical preferences would be unable to resist the temptation to accept an indefinite sequence of wealth–reducing exchanges, leading either to a very bad situation or to the disappearance of the individual as an actor. But the power of the money pump argument presupposes, for example, that some feature of the choice environment could turn such an unfortunately endowed individual into a money pump. The existence of such a feature is, surely, an empirical rather than an a priori matter. Thus, the attraction of the classical rationality norm (which entails acyclic preferences), as distinguished from some weaker form of intentionality, might depend on features of a specific choice environment.

Our main argument is that social science research inherits a commitment to universalism from its explanatory aspirations. The feasibility of universalistic accounts, on the other hand, arises from the centrality of intentional explanation. This "universalism" may only be partial, in the sense that the independence hypothesis—the hypothesis that the causal mechanism is sufficiently independent from its contexts of realization that it may be separately described—that stands behind any form of universalism may take on different forms in different domains. Without some form of independence, however, explanation becomes inseparable from description and social science becomes impossible. The examples of good research that Green and Shapiro offer exhibit nontrivial independence hypotheses that permit their accounts to be explanatory.

The aspiration to unity and the quest for universalistic explanations have spurred progress in every science. By ruling out universalism on philosophical grounds, Green and Shapiro surrender the explanatory aspirations of social science. Such a surrender is both premature and self-defeating. And, insofar as intentionality is itself a ground for universalism, it is also unwarranted.

NOTES

1. Jon Elster (1990) distinguishes causal mechanisms, which do not have fully specified domains of application, from more completely characterized causal laws. For the purposes of the present argument we do not need to maintain this distinction, so we use both mechanisms and laws as instances of universals. Causal mechanisms, while possibly weaker than causal laws, seem characterizable in ways that are sufficiently situation independent to count as universals.

2. This list is paraphrased from Nozick 1993, 5.

3. This constraint does not require that the behavior in question was *actually* brought about intentionally, and certainly not that it was done consciously; it requires only that it *could* be described as having been done in that way. So we could admit that some actions have subconscious causes.

4. We argue elsewhere that this form of compatibilism does not commit us to any strong form of methodological individualism. Individuals, preferences, and beliefs may all be socially formed or constructed. All we require is that somehow preferences, beliefs, and actions come into line in an appropriate manner (Satz and Ferejohn 1994).

5. It would be another story if what we were interested in explaining was *why* the bomb was exploded.

6. Recent work on noncooperative games suggests that in many strategic settings, rationality accounts may exhibit this kind of indeterminacy.

7. Ferejohn 1991 argues that cultural elements might interact with rational choice theory to produce more determinate predictions in some settings.

8. We are not thereby committed to the view that complete causal explana-

tions of all phenomena are possible. For one skeptical treatment of completeness, see Dupre 1992.

9. A recent example of a regret-based choice theory is found in Loomes and Sugden 1982. See also Bell 1982.

10. For a recent description of attribute–based choice see Hurley 1989.

Morris P. Fiorina

RATIONAL CHOICE,
EMPIRICAL CONTRIBUTIONS,
AND THE SCIENTIFIC ENTERPRISE

Don Green and Ian Shapiro's Pathologies of Rational Choice Theory, *despite the impressive amount of work that has gone into it, is undercut by a number of serious misunderstandings of the use of the rational choice approach by students of American politics. Furthermore, Green and Shapiro adopt an extremely pinched notion of an empirical contribution and an outmoded and idealized view of the scientific method. If their standards were adopted, it would be difficult to allow that anyone in political science has made an empirical contribution, or that political science is a scientific enterprise.*

In *Pathologies of Rational Choice Theory*, Don Green and Ian Shapiro (hereafter, GS) have provided political science with a useful critical review of the far-flung rational choice (hereafter, RC) literature. Many of the critical observations they make about specific studies are on the mark. Nevertheless, I completely disagree with their bottom line. I have been working in the political science vineyards for 25 years, the bulk of that work has been empirical, and I am RC down to my DNA. But if GS are correct, I must be deluded: with perhaps one exception (190), what I have done that is RC makes no empirical contribution, and any empirical contributions I have made are not RC. Obviously, I disagree.

Morris P. Fiorina, Department of Government, Harvard University, Cambridge, MA 02138, telephone (617) 495–9270, telefax (617) 496–5149, the author of, *inter alia, Congress—Keystone of the Washington Establishment* (Yale, 1989), *Retrospective Voting in American National Elections* (Yale, 1981), and, most recently, *Divided Government* (Macmillan, 1992), wishes to thank the usual suspects for their comments and suggestions.

Contrary to the central assertion of the GS critique, the RC research program has made major empirical contributions. How could it have prospered otherwise? Are we to believe that RC scholars have snookered everyone else in the discipline except for a few clear thinkers like GS? I have been the target of too many clear-thinking critics to believe anything like that. The negative verdict reached by GS reflects an excessively restrictive notion of what constitutes an empirical contribution, as well as an unrealistic view of scientific research. Careful statistical tests of precisely formulated hypotheses are one kind of empirical contribution, but not the only kind. Moreover, however accurate GS's observations about the abstract scientific failings of RC theory, a moment's reflection suggests that such failings are common to all political science research—indeed, to all of scientific research.

Before turning to these two general points—the nature of empirical contributions, and a realistic view of scientific research—I will offer some clarifications and corrections of GS's characterization of the RC enterprise.

The Rational Choice Enterprise

"Critics tend to ignore or heap scorn on the RC approach without understanding it fully. They dismiss its assumptions or scientific aspirations, or they get it wrong in elementary ways. Not surprisingly, practioners generally ignore them" (ix). Although self-characterization probably was not what GS had in mind, these sentences pretty well sum up my reaction to *Pathologies*. I am genuinely impressed by how much effort GS have put into their critique of several extensive literatures, but I believe that their failure to achieve a clear understanding of what RC people are doing prevents them from making a truly positive contribution. GS are not alone, however; despite its growing usage, RC continues to be widely misunderstood. For purposes of weighing the charges in *Pathologies*, four misunderstandings are most important.

1. An 800-lb. Gorilla or a Thousand Blooming Flowers?

A generation ago, RC scholars were a small minority facing a skeptical, if not hostile, discipline. Consistent with the stylized findings of social-psychological research, such an unfriendly environment fostered in-group solidarity. But times have changed—anyone who was on the job market in those days can only marvel at the general acceptance of RC today. With that acceptance has come diversity within the RC community. RC today is not a monolithic movement—if it ever was.[1] I suspect the only thing that all RC people would agree upon is that their explanations presume that individuals behave purposively. Beyond that, every manner of disagreement—theoretical, substantive, methodological—can be found. [2] RC is an approach, a general perspective within which many different models can be located. It is not surprising that GS can paint portraits of RC scholars contradicting each other over matters of logic, data, and interpretation. That is only a natural reflection of the diversity of scholars who operate under the general rubric. The situation becomes even more complicated when scholars from other traditions take rational choice formulations and adapt them for their own uses. Such scholars understandably are unconcerned about maintaining the metatheoretical purity of rational choice formulations. GS, however, use them as examples of RC scholars being untrue to their theoretical principles.[3]

2. Universalism?

Certainly, one can cite rational choice scholars who write ambitiously—if not grandiosely—about constructing unified theories of political behavior. But have we forgotten so soon representatives of other traditions who harbored similar grand ambitions? Talcott Parsons, David Truman, and David Easton were not exactly modest in this regard. Not every scholar who found a structural-functionalist, a groups, or a systems perspective useful shared the universalist ambitions of these theorists; similarly, not every RC scholar shares the universalist ambitions of a few RC theorists.

From this standpoint, the GS attack on "domain restriction" is ill considered, inasmuch as domain restriction is one of the ways in which RC folk explicitly recognize the limits of their explanations. No one would defend what GS call "arbitrary" domain restriction—declaring a model not applicable simply because it does not fit the data. But most domain restrictions are "principled," in that the theory specifies why they should not fit the data.

Thus, if one were to construct a legislative model based on David Mayhew's (1974) assumption of "single-minded seekers of reelection," it would not be an arbitrary restriction to say that the model does not apply to amateur legislatures or city councils where the evidence indicates that members routinely quit for non-electoral reasons. That would be a perfectly justified recognition that other models should be utilized where reelection is not highly valued.

A more general example comes from the study of mass participation.

GS characterize as "peace with honor" Aldrich's conclusion that voting turnout is beyond the domain of RC models. Much as I envy this Wolfin-geresque phrase, it is not sufficient to dispose of Aldrich's argument. In fact, GS should praise Aldrich for rejecting the "universalism" that they find so objectionable. Like Aldrich, I teach my students that RC models are most useful where stakes are high and numbers low, in recognition that it is not rational to go to the trouble to maximize if the consequences are trivial and/or your actions make no difference (Fiorina 1990).[4] Thus, in work on mass behavior I utilize minimalist notions of rationality (1981, 83), whereas in work on elites I assume a higher order of rationality (1989, chs. 5, 11).

3. The Importance of Ceteris Paribus

Mancur Olson's (1965) theory of collective action is widely misinterpret-ed. It does not predict that there will not be groups organized to achieve collective goods; nor does it predict that no individual would join such a group in the absence of selective incentives. Rather, Olson's theory pre-dicts that—ceteris paribus—it will be more difficult to organize groups for broad, general purposes than for narrow, special purposes, and that—ceteris paribus—individuals will be more likely to join small groups organized for narrow purposes than large groups organized for general purposes. In other words, contrary to GS's reading (81), Olson's theory makes no ab-solute or "point" prediction of zero participation. It predicts relative differ-ences and comparative statics (e.g., as individual responsibility decreases, individual incentives to join decline), but the absolute levels of organiza-tion, suitably measured, are determined by a host of other factors. These factors are lumped together in the ceteris paribus condition.

Critics of RC accounts often assume that a monocausal explanation is being offered because they fail to realize that RC propositions typically are stated with a ceteris paribus condition. Such an assumption is always made whenever there is an attempt to apply a model empirically. Only if all the other factors mentioned by GS ("normative, cultural, psychological, and institutional") were fully incorporated could any RC model generate an absolute or "point" prediction. Since we can never know all of the relevant variables, let alone measure all of them accurately, the empirical predictions of all models in political science—not just RC models—are about relative differences and comparative statics predictions.

Thus, I would not be at all concerned if legislative outcomes were not exactly located on the legislative median, even if there were every reason to believe we had identified it accurately. Numerous factors other than median-voter logic surely operate in real legislatures. But if the median were to shift significantly to the right, while outcomes shifted to the left, that would trouble me.

4. Explanatory Parts, Not Wholes

The fourth misunderstanding is associated with the third. When being trained in RC, students are taught to focus—to restrict their attention to one or two aspects of a situation or process (a "stylized fact" or two), and to explain it on the basis of one or two considerations. That is simply the nature of the enterprise: tractability requires simplification. As a consequence of this tradeoff, an RC model, even in principle, is ordinarily only part of an explanation. RC scholars work out "logics," "principles," and problems, and seek to apply them to situations.[5] But that is not to assert that only one logic or principle is operative in a situation. Only an empirical test that gets 100 percent of the variance can show that.

When NASA put astronauts on the moon (and brought them back), its scientists and engineers did not rely on a single overarching model. They relied on literally hundreds of models and theories to construct the equipment, train the personnel, design the organization, and make the round trip. No single model would have accounted for more than a few aspects of the total enterprise. Analogously, there will never be a single RC model of a real presidential campaign, of the U.S. Congress, or of the federal regulatory process. What we are engaged in is the construction of scores of models that focus on different aspects of political institutions and processes. One or two models might help to explain a specific feature of an institution or process (e.g., Krehbiel 1991 on specialization and restrictive rules), but the explanation of broader institutional patterns normally will require several models used in combination (e.g., Cox and McCubbins 1993 on congressional parties).

Empirical Testing and Empirical Contributions

> What has this literature contributed to our understanding of politics? . . . A large proportion of the theoretical conjectures of rational choice theorists have not been tested empirically (6).

During a recent college vacation, my son, an English major, expressed an interest in viewing some classic films that had not been part of his educational experience. His mother, an English major 25 years ago, happily accompanied him to the video store. After watching *Casablanca*, my wife dabbed the tears from her eyes and asked (rhetorically, I think), "Weren't the love scenes beautiful?" Our son gave her a puzzled look: "What love scenes?" he inquired.

I thought immediately of Green and Shapiro. Unless the researcher grapples with the data, and arises panting and covered with the residue of rejected alternative models, GS ask: "What empirical contribution?" Here lies much of the disagreement I have with them. The notion of empirical research that "contributes to our understanding of politics" is far more general than the notion of testing a specific theoretical proposition. This is why the GS critique of several large RC literatures misses the mark.

Consider a work by one of my teachers, Richard Fenno's *Congressmen in Committees* (1973). In this book Fenno moves from his earlier structural-functional approach to an RC framework. Members of Congress have goals, they gravitate (self-select) to committees where those goals can be met, they adopt strategic premises (previously called "norms") that facilitate the achievment of their goals, they structure committee processes to attain their goals, and they reach equilibrium when their goals are met through committee membership. Fenno's book is highly empirical, but it is not based on random samples of committees or members, contains no multivariate equations or even significance tests, and doesn't explicitly consider and reject alternative explanations. Moreover, the theoretical account is built on the same data that it is used to explain. By the standards used in *Pathologies*, it is pretty clear that Fenno's study makes no empirical contribution.

I certainly hope that GS will be disturbed by this claim. Perhaps they would concede that not all empirical contributions need be of the highly statistical sort. Perhaps qualitative, nonrandom, even selective evidence can be of some value. Or perhaps they would say that Fenno's real empirical contribution lies less in his work than in the work of those who emulated him, taking his framework and applying it to new committees and members. All of those "perhapses" are just the point. An empirical contribution can be many things, only one of which is state-of-the art statistical analysis.

For example, it boggles the mind that anyone would deny the empirical contributions that resulted from the work of Mancur Olson. The working out of the prisoner's dilemma/collective action logic has as strong a claim as any to being the most important political science contribution of the twentieth century. GS will gnash their teeth when Olson wins a Nobel Prize.[6]

Olson provided a simple explanation for an empirical finding familiar to political scientists: the full spectrum of economic interests is not equally represented by interest groups.[7] But more generally, his work suggested that the question was not only why people did not associate in interest groups, but also why they did. This led scholars to think harder about the importance of leadership or entrepreneurship in the formation of groups (Frolich, Oppenheimer and Young 1971; Moe 1980; Walker 1991) and the nature of the benefits from group membership (Moe 1980). Jane Mansbridge (1986, ch. 10) insightfully applied Olson's ideas to explain why forces supporting the ERA used strategies that seemed to hinder adoption of the proposed amendment.

Moving farther afield, Lawrence Dodd (1977) used a collective- action logic to construct an imaginative account of the periodic decline and resurgence of Congress. Olson (1982) used his work to offer a provocative explanation of cross-national and cross-temporal variation in economic growth. And Elinor Ostrom (1990) relies on collective action logics in her sweeping comparative account of how different societies have dealt with common resource problems. Now, GS can discount any and all such work. They can suggest that the very use of such adverbs and adjectives as "insightfully," "imaginative," "provocative," and "sweeping" is a recognition that no real empirical contribution has been made. But I daresay that if they do, their sympathizers will begin abandoning ship.

Every empirically based modification, generalization, or even rejection of Olson is an empirical contribution stimulated by his work. Every extension of his ideas to new arenas is an empirical contribution. Every incorporation of his ideas in larger explanatory accounts is an empirical contribution. Even seeming counter-examples that lead people to see matters in a new light are empirical contributions. For example, Robert Bates (1995) notes that the international coffee cartel showed a stability that seemed to defy the implications of collective action theory. According to Bates, the explanation for this (theoretically) puzzling situation is that a major consumer—the United States—helped the cartel enforce its pricing as a byproduct of U.S. anti-communist foreign policy.

Empirical contributions made by theories lie on a continuum from the specific to the general. On one extreme are precise theories that generate counterintuitive or previously unthought-of propositions that are carefully tested and confirmed. One thinks of teams of experimental physicists lowering sensitive instruments into deep mines in search of traces of theoretically predicted but never-observed particles. On the other extreme are "theories" that serve as organizational rubrics for various hypotheses that appear to have some vague connection with each other. One thinks of structural functionalism and systems theory. Although RC theories fall far short of the standards common in experimental physics, in terms of empirical contributions they are a significant improvement on the so-called theories that have held sway in the past.

The Nature of Scientific Research

The GS concept of scientific method seems to run something like this:

1. Formulate a specific hypothesis.
2. Think of all possible alternative hypotheses.
3. Gather all the data necessary to test the various hypotheses.
4. Do all the appropriate tests using state-of-the-art statistical methods.
5. Draw the appropriate conclusions based on universally accepted canons of statistical and scientific inference.

Every student learns something like this in high school chemistry and physics, but like many other textbook portraits it has little resemblance to reality. Political scientists don't operate that way in practice; nor do natural scientists, as I learned in a decade at Caltech. GS remind me of Captain Renault (Claude Rains) in *Casablanca*: Post hoc theory development, slippery predictions, and selective interpretation of evidence? *Here? In political science? GS are shocked! Shocked!*

One could go further than this, and suggest that the textbook model of scientific method adopted by GS might not even be a useful ideal, however difficult to meet in practice. If I were to test competing rational choice and symbolic politics explanations of voting behavior and conclude that the evidence supported the former, would partisans of symbolic politics really be convinced? No more than I would be if they did the test and concluded the opposite. All of us have perspectives and commitments that inevitably show through in our work. It is these very perspectives and commitments that motivate us to search diligently for confirming evidence, to dissect contrary evidence, and to critically examine studies not consistent with our perspectives and commitments.

What keeps these human imperfections from leading to manipulation of results, suppression of evidence, selective interpretation, and the general corruption of the scientific enterprise? Very simply, the collective nature of the scientific enterprise provides the safeguards. Scholar 1 makes an argument and offers some evidence, Scholar 2 offers an alternative argument, Scholar 3 offers conflicting evidence, and others rush to join the fray. The debate proceeds according to accepted rules of logic, inference, and evidence. Any kind of dishonesty, or even an unintentional but egregious error, is a cardinal sin that threatens one's reputation, if not career—a fact reflected in the vituperation that often emerges in academic controversies.

The community of interested scholars monitors the debate and evaluates the arguments, the evidence, and importantly, the debaters themselves. The community treats each individual debater as a data point. Each may be characterized by measurement error, but over time, as theory, data, and (dare I say it?) even judgment accumulate, the research community forms a collective determination.[8]

Certainly, I applaud GS's call for quantitatively more, and qualitatively more careful, empirical work. But who in the legislative subfield has put together a wider array of data on the congressional parties than RC scholars Cox and McCubbins, and who in the legislative subfield is a more painstaking empirical worker than RC scholar Keith Krehbiel? I applaud GS's concern for greater methodological self-consciousness and higher standards of evidence. But where do you find more concern for such matters than in the ongoing RC debate over whether congressional committees are preference outliers?[9] I agree that scholars should avoid sweeping policy recommendations on the basis of simple formal models, but the lawyers' eager grasp of such models suggests that they have been making sweeping policy recommendations on the basis of much less.[10] GS are inexplicably blind to the contribution that the rational choice research program has made toward achieving the goals they hold dear.

As for our colleagues (and even some friends) who are anti-RC down to their DNA, I can only remind them that political science is a big tent, with room inside for all. If your comparative advantage lies with those "normative, cultural, psychological, and institutional" alternatives that GS believe provide such promising alternatives to rational choice, develop them in detail, just as we whose comparative advantage lies in the realm of RC have developed our models. The theory of comparative advantage predicts that more progress will occur this way than if, say, RC folk try to do political psychology, and GS try to do RC. So long as we communicate in good faith, the friendly competition will make us all better scholars, and will make political science more worthy of its name.

NOTES

1. Failure to appreciate that fact leads GS (5) to quote me inaccurately. My "quip" that "contemplating the empirical achievements of rational choice theory 'is a bit like dwelling on the rushing accomplishments of Joe Namath'" actually reads: "Tullock chooses to concentrate on the empirical *public choice* literature [my emphasis]. This is a bit like dwelling on. . . ." (Fiorina 1979, 48). Virginia school public choice is a variety of RC, but not a synonym for it. My remark expressed Rochester-Caltech school skepticism about the (then) questionable empirical contributions of the Virginia school.

2. For example, even in a relatively narrow subfield—legislative studies—one

can find a wide range of sometimes intense disagreements (Shepsle and Weingast 1995).

3. Thus, Carol Uhlaner, a student of that well-known RC scholar, Sid Verba, becomes an RC theorist in GS's treatment (52). Uhlaner attempts to incorporate group mobilization into the analysis of turnout. Groups are an obviously important influence on turnout to anyone with sociological training, although one not addressed by mainstream RC theorists. GS discount Uhlaner's effort, but recent work by Rosenstone and Hansen (1993) indicates that she was clearly on the right track.

4. More precisely, giving little or no thought to what you are doing *is* maximizing behavior when little or nothing is at stake and/or your actions make little or no difference. It is not that rational choice models cannot explain such behavior, just that they do not say anything very interesting about it. People vote when the benefits exceed the costs, just as people buy a tomato when they prefer the tomato to anything else they could do with the money. In neither case is the proposition very interesting, even if obviously true. If your primary interest lies in *why* people view the act of voting as beneficial or why they like tomatoes, other models will be more useful.

5. For elaboration, see Fiorina 1995.

6. In all candor, so will I. How did our elders in the discipline collectively permit an economist to abscond with an idea whose lineage in Hobbes and Hume should have made it a familiar part of our intellectual capital?

7. "The flaw in the pluralist heaven is that the heavenly chorus sings with a strong upper-class accent" (Schattschneider 1960, 34–35).

8. Is it at all inconsistent for an RC scholar to put such an emphasis on community? Nope. Noncooperative game theory models demonstrate that coooperative behavior generally can be an individually rational (Nash) equilibrium in repeated games.

9. For citations see Londregan and Snyder 1995.

10. Consult the *Journal of Law, Economics, and Organization*, published by GS's colleagues at the Yale Law School.

Stanley Kelley, Jr.

THE PROMISE AND LIMITATIONS
OF RATIONAL CHOICE THEORY

Pathologies of Rational Choice Theory *is a valuable survey and critique of re-search in the rational choice tradition, but one that slights that tradition's past and potential contributions to the study of politics. The authors rightly note limitations of rational choice theory but understate what it has to offer political scientists, for they fail to focus clearly on its essentials; adopt too narrow a basis for evaluating scholarship; and wrongly identify rational choice theory with the shortcomings of some scholarship that makes use of it.*

Although it will aggravate some and inspire partisan glee in others, political scientists concerned about either their discipline's future or their own can learn a great deal about rational choice theory from Donald Green and Ian Shapiro's *Pathologies of Rational Choice Theory*. Laying out a large body of ideas for scrutiny, as they have in their book, is akin to charting a large body of water: It is a valuable professional service that can increase our knowledge of the direction and character of prevailing currents and alert us to reefs and shoals. The body of ideas that Green and Shapiro choose to chart is substantial, influential, and almost certain, at some time, to lie athwart the path of a young political scientist. Many, including many of those who call themselves rational choice theorists, will find the outlook Green and Shapiro bring to their task to be congenial. The other

---

Stanley Kelley, Jr., Department of Politics, Princeton University, Princeton, N.J. 08544, telephone (609) 258-4763, telefax (609) 258-4772, the author of *Interpreting Elections* (Princeton, 1983), thanks Douglas Arnold, Larry Bartels, Fred Greenstein, Jeffrey Herbst, Jonathan Krasno, Alan Ryan, Glenn Shafer, and William Wohlforth for their comments on this article.

shore they would have us seek is one well populated with generalizations about politics that are interesting, important, widely applicable, and well supported by evidence. If they have any irrational phobias about methods, none are on display in this book.

It would be remarkable if an enterprise like Green and Shapiro's left no room for disagreement, however, and of course no such miracle has occurred. That enterprise, welcome though it is, is problematic on its face. They are attempting to evaluate an ongoing intellectual movement by examining its accumulated fruits at a particular time, fruits embodied in particular pieces of scholarship by particular scholars. How seriously should we take averages and totals when making such an evaluation? Much poor work might mean that a set of bad ideas is leading many scholars astray; it could also mean merely that good scholarship, of whatever variety, is always scarce. What do the worst and the best work in a genre tell us about the genre's potential? The worst, nothing; the best, something, certainly, but quite probably not enough to bring optimists and pessimists together on the matter. Moreover, scholars agreed about much else can disagree about the scales in which rational choice theory ought to be weighed and about what to put on each side. It will be unsurprising, then, that I strike a different balance in assessing rational choice theory than Green and Shapiro do, even though I share their major intellectual goals and sympathize with many of their particular criticisms.

My summary view is that they sell rational choice theory short, although less short than their title's hyperbole would suggest. Having reached that judgment, I am happy to recommend their book to young scholars who find rational choice theory attractive, but I am much less comfortable about recommending it to scholars whose training and temperament incline them to side against rational choice theory. The former can surely profit from Green and Shapiro's criticisms of work like theirs. The latter may simply have their inclinations strengthened and thus overlook, to their detriment and the discipline's, ideas and resources from which their intellectual projects could profit.

What Is It?

As a thing is, let it be judged. Is "rational choice theory" an internally consistent set of highly credible and unambiguous propositions designed to explain the phenomena of politics and society? Of course not. Neither Green and Shapiro nor (as they acknowledge) most rational choice theorists regard rational choice theory as *a* theory in this sense. What is it, then? I have been referring to it as a "body of ideas," and that term is surely accurate, if vague. The body of ideas labeled "rational choice" includes (sometimes conflicting) theories about particular phenomena and, associated with them, conjectures, puzzles, models, some tests of theories, interpretations of events and patterns of behavior, and much discussion of all of the above (and more). Following Green and Shapiro, we may speak of a "family of theories," provided we recognize that not all the members of the family are full-fledged theories. What justifies lumping these things together—fully fledged and fledgling—and putting the label "rational choice" on them?

The lumping and labeling are justified when (and insofar as) a certain way of thinking about social and political phenomena figures in these various sorts of intellectual enterprises. To try this way of thinking on for size, proceed (roughly) as follows: (1) Identify the agents (classes of individuals, kinds of groups) associated with a phenomenon or situation (broadly or narrowly defined) that you seek to understand. (2) Identify the goal or goals of these agents as they relate to the phenomenon or situation. (3) Delineate the features of the agents' environment that may aid or impede them in achieving their goals. (4) Determine the kind and quality of information that the agents possess about this environment. (5) Identify the courses of action the agents might take to achieve their goals within the bounds that their environment, and their knowledge of it, impose. (6) Identify, from among these possible courses of action, the ones that realize the various agents' goals most efficiently.

You now have a list of intellectual tasks. Complete the tasks successfully, and you know the possible routes that the agents may take to reach their goals and, among these, which routes are optimal for each. You know, in short, what the "choice" of rational choice theory refers to, and what "rational" agents should choose to do. You still lack a theory that can be tested by observation or experiment, however, although you now have the ingredients for one.

Such a theory (although not necessarily a good one) emerges when you take a seventh step, that is, when you *predict* that the rational choice for any agent will be its actual choice, or *explain* any agent's actual choice by showing it to have been its optimal choice.[1] Your theory will normally be what Carl G. Hempel (1965, 335–76) calls "deductive-nomological" *in form*—that is, you will have presented your prediction or explanation as the *expected* result of certain conditions, in a way that may be rendered thus:

In circumstances $c_1, c_2, c_3, \ldots c_n$, a rational agent will do x.
M is a rational agent.
Therefore, M will do x.

Being a sensible social scientist, however, you will want immediately to qualify your prediction, *M* will do *x*, by telling all and sundry that you mean it to be interpreted as a statement of tendency only, not as a proposition expected to hold without exception. Why? Because you know that the intellectual road that you took to arrive at your theory is highly unlikely to have led you to an invariant law of behavior. You will therefore want to be understood as predicting that *M* will do *x unless other factors intervene*, thus preparing your line of retreat while hoping that other factors intervene weakly or rarely enough to make *x*'s chances of occurring appreciably better than random.[2]

Now, let us suppose that *x* is an event or action of some significance. If you find that in fact *x* occurs with some considerable regularity, you will deserve praise because your theory—until supplanted by some more general or better-performing one—is in the running as at least a partial account of *x*. You will merit still more praise if the fact or frequency of *x*'s occurrence was previously unknown. Why the make-believe about invariant laws? Why present a theory as if it leads to an invariant law when in fact it does not? Because (for many at least) the forms of reasoning appropriate to invariant laws are more thinker-friendly than those appropriate to chance-statements, it being easier to deduce one such law from another than it is to derive one chance-statement from another. If one makes clear what one is doing, the argument goes, one can for now play the game of "as if," and make the necessary corrections later (Gibson 1960, 146–47).

The theory that you now have in place is in its essentials a "rational choice" theory, but its superficial resemblance to the more elegant theories of that genre may be slight. Indeed, your theory could look a lot like a case study leading up to an explanation of one person's decision, while a more elegant theory, seeking wider applicability and perhaps abstracting from many such cases, might concern itself with a class of decisions in a broadly defined kind of situation. The more elegant theory might also greatly simplify its description of such a situation—reducing the cast of agents to a minimum, attributing but one goal to each such agent, sketching the agents' environment in a few strokes only—in a search for parsimony. Mathematics may play no part in your theory but figure prominently in the presentation of the more elegant one. Theorists who use mathematics sacrifice a part their potential audience in doing so, but gain in their ability both to reason about complex relationships and to convey that reasoning with clarity and precision. Abstraction, simplification, and mathematics—though commonly associated with rational choice theory—are not essential to it (and are in no way the target of Green and Shapiro's criticisms of it). Evaluating rational choice theory as such (as opposed to evaluating particular pieces of scholarship in that mold) requires us only to decide how much and how well the seven-step procedure outlined above promises to increase our understanding of social and political phenomena.

Evaluating the Rational Choice Approach

What is wrong with the rational choice approach as just construed? One major count in Green and Shapiro's indictment can be put very simply: The adepts of the school have thus far produced few generalizations about politics that are nonobvious, testable, tested, and well supported by the evidence. Let us ignore the issue posed by the "few" in this charge—I have not done the relevant counting, and one person's mountain is another's molehill—but consider the merits of its remaining elements as a basis for measuring the promise of a theory or an approach.

In this regard one point to make, certainly, is that we should be careful about dismissing or discounting a theory because some of its predictions are "obvious." As a case in point, Green and Shapiro—praising Morris Fiorina for research on state legislatures in the rational choice tradition (190)—temper their praise by noting that his hypothesis was "not obviously counterintuitive." Why the discount? Evidently, because others have entertained hypotheses rather like Fiorina's. Although scholarship as well as journalism normally finds man-bites-dog more interesting than dog-bites-man, an hypothesis correctly deduced from some more general proposition is a different and better thing than an isolated guess to the same effect, even if everyone knows the guess to be a good one. It is hard to imagine a theory that would explain much human behavior that would not also predict many things we already know to be true; what we would gain from such a theory would be order and connectedness in our view of the world, as well as (probably) some, but not endless, surprises. We should care about the surprises, but we should value the order and connectedness, too.

A second point: The tried and true findings (surprising or unsurprising) that a theory yields are but one legitimate ingredient in an adequate assessment of its promise and of the value of the work that it inspires. To base evaluation only on "results" narrowly defined is to ignore byproducts and timing: A student may learn a good deal in studying for an examination that he or she fails, and failure now is not necessarily failure later. Timing figures in another way as well. If, as Larry Bartels has noted, the notion of a Caucus-race nicely describes competition for presidential nominations since 1968 (1988, 274–93), it describes competition among approaches in political science at least as well.[3] The discipline offers an array of these—old and new and varying in clarity, coherence, and suggested ranges of applicability—and asks its young initiates to guess which will take them fastest and farthest in the direction they want to go. In making such guesses—that is, in deciding on a strategy for studying something one wants to study—a thoughtful assessment of the pros and cons of these various approaches is likely to be more helpful than the current reading on the scoreboard.

For that reason let us put ourselves in the place of a young political scientist about to embark on a study of something unexplained and important. Let us imagine that he or she is problem-oriented and not method-oriented (to adopt Green and Shapiro's distinction), and that his or her ambition is to *explain* the phenomenon selected for study—not merely to collect information about it, to illustrate some logical properties of the situation in which it occurs, or to show what a particular *type* of explanation of it might look like. What might rational choice theory have to offer our young scholar? What kinds of considerations might enter into his or her assessment of it?

One such consideration might be the ability, in principle, of rational choice theory to yield explanations; another, its potential range of application. Whatever may be the count to date of rational choice hypotheses that have survived rigorous testing, it is clear that the approach *can* produce falsifiable explanations and predictions. The same cannot be said of all competing approaches. It is clear also that rational choice theory can make some contribution to the understanding of a relatively wide range of political phenomena. We know that human beings are often calculating animals, and it is easy to believe that knowledge about efficient ways to reach goals might suggest causes of important kinds of goal-seeking behavior. Some other approaches have an inherently narrower range of potential usefulness—those, for instance, that amount mostly to an injunction to study some particular thing (either as an independent or a dependent variable or both) on the grounds that it has been neglected. Even if the thing in question is important and the neglect real, such approaches are likely to contribute less than rational choice theorizing to the connectedness of thinking about politics. Why should one care about connectedness? Because good theory helps in organizing knowledge of the world, as well as in discovering it.

Since neither the rational choice approach nor any existing alternative to it is a key that will open all doors equally well, our young scholar, in considering its pluses and minuses, should also take into account the nature of the phenomenon that he or she proposes to study. Among the most important of the many things in which a student of politics may be interested are power (people's abilities to do things and the distribution and sources of such abilities), political culture (the beliefs and values that relate to political institutions and practices), and the factors that influence the making of consequential choices. Knowledge about the most efficient strategies to achieve various goals is likely to contribute more to the study of the last of these subjects than it is to the study of the other two, though all are of obvious importance for understanding government.

Moreover, the contribution of such knowledge to understanding political choices will vary across situations. The optimal way to achieve a goal may sometimes be impossible to identify, or possible to identify only by calculations so heroic as to be utterly implausible for any real agents. In such situations the rational choice approach is not promising. It may also be unpromising when a population of agents in which we are interested is quite capable of calculating the best way to achieve a goal, but cares too little about the goal to bother doing so—or is typically called upon to make calculations in circumstances unconducive to making them well—although in such cases, identifying the rational routes to goals may still inspire efforts to change actual behavior, or may offer a basis for evaluating it.

When will the rational choice approach help to predict, or explain, behavior? When will actual choices be likely to coincide with what are the most efficient choices from the agents' points of view? A list of conditions that favor such a coincidence would surely include these five: Uncomplicated goals for agents, widely available knowledge about ways and means to achieve these goals, choices that continually repeat themselves, agents who care a great deal about their goals, and situations that reward (appreciably) choices of efficient means and punish (severely) choices of inefficient ones. It is no accident that microeconomic theorists and many students of Congress find the rational choice approach a congenial way to think about the phenomena they study, since the five conditions just noted hold, at least roughly, for many of the things in which they are interested.[4]

Our young scholar might end a survey of the possible contributions of a rational choice approach with an inventory of his or her talents, and by asking this question: If my best efforts to follow the seven-step, rational choice procedure fail to produce a testable explanation that in fact tests out, where will I stand?

What should we say in reply? I believe we should tell our scholar that such an "unsuccessful" project may nonetheless make a valuable contribution to knowledge, if the phenomenon under study is important, poorly explained or unexplained, and reasonably susceptible to the kind of analysis that the rational choice approach involves. At the very least, that sort of analysis is likely to yield an interesting description of the phenomenon, and, better yet, it may produce a partial explanation of it. Green and Shapiro correctly describe as banal the assertion that "cost reduces turnout to some degree," but good measurements of that degree—for the turnout of voters, or any other political activity of importance—are valuable and not at all commonplace. Further, a "failed" application of the rational choice approach may, if the reasons for expecting actual and rational behavior to coincide were good enough, yield a puzzle that stimulates new thought; or it may pave the way for later success. In applications of the rational choice approach, success may easily owe a great deal to failure, for the latter may have shown the insignificance of variables once thought to be important, or the significance of variables whose significance was unappreciated.

Our canvass of the considerations a young scholar might bring to an assessment of rational choice theory (which can end here) should have established these points: Many considerations may validly figure in assessing an approach—more, undoubtedly, than I have noted here. No good reason exists for believing that all young scholars either will or should find that such an assessment will lead them to identical conclusions about the contributions that the rational choice approach (or any other) may make to their particular scholarly projects. Good reasons do exist, however, for believing that the rational choice approach may contribute to the study of some important kinds of phenomena.

Pathologies

In what I have said so far I may seem to have forgotten Green and Shapiro's characterization of rational choice scholarship as infected by various sorts of pathologies. I have not. Among the more important of the maladies they identify are these: Elaborate theorizing with little attention to operationalization and testing, or to the realities of what is being theorized about; marshaling evidence for hypotheses selectively and testing them in a biased fashion; "explaining" non-facts; "saving" hypotheses by recasting (but not retesting) theories to take account of disconfirming data; failing to consider possible alternative explanations of data that appear to confirm rational choice hypotheses; and bending and stretching the notion of rationality to make hypotheses essentially unfalsifiable. Let us ask two questions: How pathological are these "pathologies"? What is their connection to rational choice theory?

To the first question, a few words in reply should suffice. Little is to be said on behalf of most of the practices that Green and Shapiro condemn, and some of them, if deliberate and intended to deceive, are shameful (for instance, the biasing of tests or the selective use of information to make plausible what is not). If no cheating is involved, however, at least one of the "pathologies"—the "saving" of hypotheses—merits a brief defense. Scholars who nurse a poorly performing theory beyond the point when others would have turned off its life-support system may be wasting their time, but they are otherwise doing nothing wrong. Sickly ideas, like sickly people, may conceivably respond to treatment, and then survive and prosper. Infinitesimals are a case in point. They were once scoffed at as a possible foundation for the calculus, until Abraham Robinson convinced mathematicians that they could indeed serve as such, and do so in a most helpful way.[5]

The second question is the crucial one for those who would make a fair-minded assessment of rational choice theory. Does the rational choice approach have any *necessary* connection to the pathologies Green and Shapiro attribute to it? Here we should note two things, both of which lead us to a negative answer. First, these pathologies infect the work of scholars identified with many different schools of thought. No one has as yet cross-tabulated any reasonable index of the incidence of pathological blemishes with membership in such schools, but, until someone does, it seems reasonable to believe that no set of scholars has any corner on them. Second, theories don't engage in poor scholarly practices, scholars do. Perhaps an approach *could* involve a fallacy or contradiction so beguiling that it could be said to encourage degenerate scholarship, but rational choice theory seems to involve nothing of the sort, and Green and Shapiro fail to identify any such direct link between the theory and the pathologies. To the extent that the work of rational choice theorists displays the pathologies, the fault lies with the theorists and not the theory.

That rational choice theorists are neither uniquely nor universally guilty of the bad practices of which they stand accused by Green and Shapiro is, of course, no reason to ignore the authors' rightful criticisms of particular practices. A young scholar attracted to the rational choice school would, in my opinion, be especially well advised to heed their criticism of theory that is advanced with too little knowledge of the phenomena of the real world to which it is intended to relate. This sin is not the worst of those to which Green and Shapiro call attention, but it may be the easiest to fall into. A good mentor may say (correctly) that theories need not—should not—reflect all the complexities of the real world, that they are "maps" of the real world whose usefulness depends in part on their simplifications of it. True, but it is equally true that it is a map of New Jersey, not one of Middle Earth, that can be helpful to the driver who wants to get from Princeton to Secaucus.

Years ago Jacob Viner, noting the irrelevance of the classical theory of international trade to a greatly changed world, suggested a way for economists to go about their constructing of theoretical models (1955, 100–130).[6] Start, he said, by listing all variables suspected of significance and by indicating their probable relationships. Turn next to empirical research to determine the least significant of these. Setting these aside, proceed (cautiously) toward models that permit rigorous deductions about the variables and relationships for whose importance there is empirical evidence. In Viner's view (ibid., 129) such a procedure would help to insure theorists' consideration of important variables that might otherwise be omitted "because of oversight, traditional practice, difficulty of manipulation, or unsuitability for specific types of analytical manipulation to which the researcher has an irrational attachment." The procedure would also be likely, he argued, to increase awareness of the possible effects of variables omitted from a theory, and thus greater caution in interpreting it, better understanding of findings associated with it, and "some measure of guidance as to the further information and the new and improved techniques of analysis that would be most helpful." Viner's suggestion, given to economists two years before the publication of Anthony Downs's *An Economic Theory of Democracy*, is good advice (it seems to me) for Downs's progeny in political science. The young scholar attracted to rational choice theory should proceed with caution and humility in a field that has produced little good empirical research, and—whatever the field—he or she should emulate older theorists in whom great talent for theory is joined with great knowledge of the phenomena they seek to explain. I shall attempt no exhaustive list of such theorists, but Gary Cox, Morris Fiorina, and David Mayhew are names that come readily to mind.

The Importance of Not Winning

At the end of their book Green and Shapiro tell us that social science would gain if it were seen by social scientists "less as a prizefight between competing theoretical perspectives, only one of which may prevail, and more as a joint venture in which explanations condition and augment one another" (204). I agree, the more readily because the specialties and approaches long associated with political science have in fact jointly contributed to significant intellectual ventures.

Consider the ways of thinking that the authors of *The Federalist* brought to the task of justifying the government they proposed. That task required (among other things) a persuasive account of the way in which the new government would work in practice; to provide it, Madison, Hamilton and Jay looked in part to the probable goals of various agents (presidents, armies, state governments, etc.), assumed that these agents (when they

could) would adopt means appropriate to their goals, reviewed the probable circumstances in which agents would be placed, and so made predictions, many of which still strike us as remarkably astute. But of course this
implicit rational choice approach, noted as such by Green and Shapiro, was
not the only one employed, as anyone who has read *The Federalist* knows.
Its authors brought a variety of complementary perspectives to their eluci-
dation of the Consititution. Would *The Federalist* be improved by rewriting
it as an exclusively rational choice analysis of the Constitution? By excis-
ing that kind of analysis from it? Sustaining an affirmative answer to either
of these questions is something that only the most intellectually parochial
among us would attempt.

Contributing to the proper design and functioning of political societies
is a goal that activates many contemporary political scientists, as it did our
founders; and now, as at the founding, it is clear that many ways of thinking can contribute to realizing that goal. Conceivably, rational choice theorists might someday banish other approaches from political science, or
their critics might someday succeed in exiling rational choice theorists
from the discipline. Either sort of "victory" would be profoundly impover-
ishing. Fortunately, neither seems imminent or likely.

NOTES

1. Predicting that an agent's actual choice will be one from an identifiable set
   of those satifactory to it, or explaining an agent's actual choice by showing
   it to have been one of an identifiable set of satisfactory choices, would also
   give one either a rational choice theory, or something very like a rational
   choice theory.
2. Brian Barry finds the intellectual source of the rational choice approach (or,
   as he calls it, the "economic approach") in the philosophy of Jeremy Bentham. Compare his account of Benthamite analysis with the seven-step procedure outlined above (1970, 9–10):

   > What then, are the salient characteristics of the Benthamite analy-
   > sis? Its most important assumptions are: that men tend to act rational-
   > ly in the pursuit of their ends; that most men in all societies want
   > power, status and economic goods; and that internalised restraints on
   > the pursuit of these are less significant than sanctions which make use
   > of them (public disapproval, legal punishments, etc.). Its characteristic
   > method is to work out how men rationally pursuing power, status,
   > and economic goods would behave in a certain set-up, and then to
   > suggest that men in the real world behave sufficiently similarly to
   > make the conclusions applicable.

3. Bartels's reference is to a passage in Lewis Carroll's *Alice's Adventures in Wonderland* in which the Dodo organizes a demonstration caucus-race for Alice (Bartels 1988, 273):

> First it marked out a race-course, in a sort of circle, ("the exact shape doesn't matter," it said,) and then all the party were placed along the course, here and there. There was no "One, two, three, and away!" but they began running when they liked, and left off when they liked, so that it was not easy to know when the race was over. However, when they had been running half-an-hour or so, and were quite dry again, the Dodo suddenly called out, "The race is over!" and they all crowded round it, panting, and asking, "But who has won?"

4. For further discussion of the circumstances in which rational choice theories may have greater or lesser explanatory power see Gibson (1960, 156–78), Barry (1970, 40–46), and the sources cited by Green and Shapiro (193).
5. I owe this example to Richard Jeffrey.
6. This essay of Viner's is not well known, even among economists, but he himself thought it one of his best.

Robert E. Lane

WHAT RATIONAL CHOICE EXPLAINS

Rational choice theories have been falsified by experimental tests of economic behavior and have not been supported by analyses of behavior in the market. Politics is an even less fertile field of application for rational choice theories because politics deals with ends as well as means, thus preventing ends-means rationality; voters have partisan loyalties often "fixed" in adolescence; political benefits have no common unit of measurement; "rational ignorance" inhibits rational choices; and there is no market-like feedback to facilitate learning. Research comparing public and private efficiency does not support rational choice. Ironically, while law and business schools are now employing better microeconomic theories, political scientists are taking up rational choice theory, regardless of the disconfirming evidence.

It was a brilliant, simplifying question: Could one account for economic behavior by observing the relations of supply and demand to prices while assigning market participants only two qualities, *rationality,* meaning stable, transitive preferences, and *greed,* meaning the attempt to maximize the achievement of these preferences? If one could do so, then by adding a few assumptions about market circumstances, budget constraints, competition, and information, one could specify the conditions for market equilibrium. Kenneth Arrow (1987, 204) reports that for the marginalists (chiefly Jevons, Walras, and Menger), the "rationality hypothesis was the maximiza-

Robert E. Lane, a former president of the American Political Science Association and the Eugene Meyer Professor Emeritus of Political Science, Yale University, P.O. Box 208301, New Haven, CT 06511, telephone (203) 432-3266, telefax (203) 432–6196, is the author of *The Market Experience* (Cambridge, 1991).

tion of [consumer] utility under a budget constraint." When it was seen that demand was a function of *all* prices, it was then "possible to formulate the general equilibrium of the economy." The payoff to economic theory of the rationality and maximization hypotheses was substantial.

If the rational choice hypothesis worked such wonders in understanding the market, the idea should certainly be applied to politics. After all, buyers and voters are the same people with the same endowments. To Green and Shapiro's triumvirate of Arrow (1951), Anthony Downs (1957), and Mancur Olson (1965) may be added the names of James Buchanan and Gordon Tullock, as pioneers in importing game theory and other (e.g., Hotelling 1929; Black 1958) forms of rational choice economics into political science.

Unfortunately, the brave and conscientious efforts of rational choice theorists to examine only environmental variables severely limits attention to the characteristics of the decision makers involved. In *Pathologies of Rational Choice Theory* Donald Green and Ian Shapiro have revealed that this approach has not been shown to work in politics. Before them, studies by Herbert Simon (e.g., 1967, 1979, 1982, 1987), Amos Tversky (1969), Tversky and Daniel Kahneman et al. (e.g., 1982, 1987), Arrow (1987, 1989), Hillel Einhorn and Robin Hogarth (1981, 1985, 1987), Richard Herrnstein (1990, 1993), Richard Thaler (1980, 1987), Stephen Lea et al. (1987), and research presented at a 1984 Princeton conference, a 1985 Chicago conference, by the Russell Sage program in behavioral economics, and so forth have provided persuasive evidence that rational choice theory does not work very well in market economics, either.

After briefly reviewing this evidence, I will seek to explain why the political domain is even less hospitable to rational choice analysis than is the market, and, in general, why almost any theory of human behavior that ignores the qualities of the actors is likely to fail. An example of the uses of rational choice in explaining governmental inefficiency is then followed by some speculations on the future of rational choice analysis.

I. RATIONAL CHOICE IN THE MARKET

Thaler (1987, 96–98), a war-weary veteran of the battles between behavioralists and rationalists (psychologists and economists), summarizes the arguments and cites some evidence in a passage I take the liberty of further summarizing here. First I quote Thaler's statement of the rationalists' arguments and then I allude to his description of the rebutting evidence:

"1. *If the stakes are large enough, people will get it right.*" But studies of preference reversals show that these were more frequent with larger stakes (Thaler 1987, 96, citing Grether and Plott 1979).

"*2. In the real world people will learn to get it right.*" But "accurate learning takes place only when the individual receives timely and organized feedback," which is rare, and in any event repetitive decision making leads to overconfidence, impairing rationality (Einhorn and Hogarth 1987). In general, there is substantial evidence that "experience does not necessarily lead to learning" (Thaler, 96).

"*3. In the aggregate, errors will cancel out.*" This remark should be used with caution since the errors that have been discovered by the psychologists studying decision making are systematic. (Thaler, 96).

"*4. In markets, arbitrage and competition eliminate the effects of irrational markets.*" Experiments by Russell and Thaler (1985) with rational and quasirational agents revealed the conditions necessary for rationality: "We find," said Thaler, "that these conditions are quite restrictive and are unlikely to occur in any but the most efficient of financial markets." Moreover, "in goods markets, a mistake by one individual will generally not create an arbitrage or profit opportunity for someone else. . . . Mistakes can persist" (Thaler, 97).

"*5. Where is the [alternative] theory?*" Originally psychological research offered only a collection of anomalies, but now Tversky and Kahneman (e.g., 1987) and Einhorn and Hogarth (e.g., 1987) have "developed descriptive theories that can account for the observed behavior. These explicitly descriptive theories cannot be derived from normative axioms. Nevertheless, they are theories, and they seem to do a good job of predicting behavior" (Thaler, 97).

"*6. Economic theory has done very well so far, and if it is not broken. . . .*" Thaler (98) argues that microeconomic theory has not met satisfactory tests of success, and suggests that the only satisfactory test would be one which, if the evidence did not support the rational choice predictions, would be accepted as disconfirmatory. With some implied doubt, he hopes such an agreement would put an end to the interminable debate. As we shall see, Thaler's doubt seems justified.

In a more extensive review, Lea et al. (1987, 529) find that the theories of riskless choice in demand theory, of choice under risk, of intertemporal choices, of consumer behavior, of gambling behavior, and of savings all fail to predict behavior. Overall, "rationality in itself was an inadequate theory of behavior."

Again in summary fashion, let us look at two kinds of further evidence that rational choice theory fails to explain economic behavior: direct experimental tests of its underlying hypotheses, and field tests of how it works in the market.

Experimental Tests

Universal comparisons versus dyadic comparisons. Rational choice theory holds that choices among relevant goods involve comparing all goods against each other to make correct choices dictated by preference schedules. But in a set of experiments using reinforcement theory, Herrnstein (1990) shows that, in fact, people tend to compare goods by pairs ("matching theory"), rejecting the less favored alternative in any pair before making the next comparison. This *meliorative* dyadic comparison process may produce suboptimal choices; but that is, indeed, what happens in market choices. Herrnstein points out that a theory that explains what happens is superior to a theory that must regard actual behavior as an aberration from expectations.

The logic of collective action. In *The Market Experience*, I have compared psychological research on social loafing with Olson's (1965) theory of the logic of collective action (Lane 1991, 47–49). Social loafing research initially has exactly the outcomes predicted by the logic of collective action: when individuals undertake collective tasks they work less hard than when they do the same tasks individually, i.e., they are free riders. But social loafing research then goes on to show that under certain relatively simple conditions free riding tends to disappear or to be greatly reduced. These conditions are that the individuals involved know how their own contributions to collective efforts compare with the contributions of others, or that they know of the differences between their effort when working alone and when working with others. When the subjects of a collective grading experiment were told that someone might contact them to ask how they arrived at their judgments, their free riding declined, although it did not disappear. Thus, rather simple remedial measures easily available to most groups, such as letting members of a group know what others are doing or simply letting them know that their contributions are monitored, may greatly reduce free riding.

Invariance and reversible preferences. Rational choice theory presupposes that preferences are stable (invariant) and transitive, but in a variety of experiments Tverksy and Kahneman (1974, 1987) have shown, for example, that the requirement of invariance is violated when people are confronted with identical probabilistic outcomes presented in one case as preventing loss of life and in another case as achieving gains in protecting lives. They strongly prefer the first option to the second, although the options are identical in their consequences. In experiments presenting risk of monetary loss and possibility of monetary gain, the same violation of invariance is evident. In another experiment with financial losses and gains, "the majority choice is risk averse in [one formulation] and risk seeking in [another] although the the two problems are essentially identical" in the two formulations (1987, 75). In still other experiments "certainties" are chosen over essentially equivalent "probabilities." These framing effects violate "not only expected utility theory but practically all other normatively based models of choice" (1987, 75).

Risk assessment. Other studies of risk assessment reveal further deviations from the rational choice model. Einhorn and Hogarth (1987) summarize their analysis as follows: "The real world of risk involves ambiguous probabilities, dependencies between probabilities and utilities, context and framing effects . . . regret . . . 'illusions of control' . . . and superstitions. . . . Given the richness of the phenomena before us, our biggest risk would be to ignore them." In another set of experiments, Alice Isen (1983) has shown that mood also influences risk assessments: in gambling experiments, people in a good mood will wager more tokens but fewer dollars than do controls. The theory is that people in a good mood will take special precautions to preserve that good mood. It has long been known (e.g., Posner 1973) that people do not use all the information in their possession in assessing risks, discarding crucial information in order to simplify their decisions.

Without reviewing the large literature on positivity, especially in politics (e.g., Lau et al. 1979), one may observe the irony that people in bad moods are more accurate in assessing the probable outcomes of an event. Thus, if rationality serves to maximize one's utility (happiness), one will be happier if one is unhappy while planning how to be happy.

Effects of stress and cognitive overload. Rational choice is unrelenting in its requirements for stable and transitive preferences and utility-maximizing behavior, but much research shows that under conditions of stress, people are, in fact, less rational. O. R. Holsti (1979) found that in international affairs, stress impaired the rationality of decisions, while Irving Janis and Leon Mann (1977) analyze the way in which stress blocks the processes of rational thought. Cognitive overload has been examined in detail; it is the basis for Simon's theory of bounded rationality and has long been the subject of studies by other cognitive psychologists (e.g., Miller 1967). Harold Schroder and Peter Suedfeld (1971) show how cognitive complexity increases with the complexity of a situation up to a point of overload and then descends rather sharply towards more simplistic forms of thinking. But rational choice theory does not distinguish between normal situations and those that are stressful or overly taxing.

Money: illusion and symbol. In addition to the so-called money illusion (reliance on money denominations instead of the purchasing power of money) that is frequently deplored by economists (Lane 1991, 96–114), money is loaded with symbolic freight: when money is at stake, stress and the attendant irrationality increases; people vary in how hard—or easy—they find the task of controlling money; they treat it with distrust and suspicion; they are overly—or insufficiently—retentive; they treat it as saturated with evil or as a good in itself; they use it to punish themselves as well as to benefit themselves. All of this makes a hash of the view that money is a neutral medium in the service of the rational choice of goods. Most economic and political rational choice theories, unfortunately, depend on such a view.

Moral behavior. Does rational choice theory allow for altruism? As Green and Shapiro (18) point out, the political science arm of rational choice is divided on this issue. Some economists have made prodigious efforts to reconcile rationality with altruism (Collard 1978; Margolis 1982; Frank 1988), not by describing how altruistic motives and behavior play a part in market behavior, but by showing how altruism is compatible with rationality—e.g., by demonstrating that a *reputation* for altruism is good for business—or even with self-interest: e.g., by arguing that it is in one's own best interest to satisfy one's conscience. This amounts to redefining *rationality* so as to make rational choice theory unfalsifiable.

Similarly, Kahneman, Jack Knetsch, and Thaler (1987, 104–106, 108–109) have explored how concepts of fairness violate the normal maximizing principles of rationality. For example, people will refuse a clear monetary benefit to themselves if they think that for some reason the offer is "unfair." People also tend to think that although it is fair for a vendor to increase his profits because of invention or efficiency increases, increased profits due to lower supply costs should be shared with one's customers. Like altruistic behavior (when considered as an empirical phenomenon, rather than being defined out of existence), people's commitment to fairness is evidence that rational choice assumptions are false.

Rationality assumptions are not necessary for equilibrium theory. The rationality assumption is, as Arrow (1987, 202, 203) points out, not necessary for market explication. It would be possible, he continues, to envisage the "creation of an economic theory based on other hypotheses than rationality." (Arrow suggests such an alternative hypothesis is habit, which George Katona [1975, 219] contends is the most frequent basis for buying.) "The use of rationality in . . . [Keynes's and Milton Friedman's] arguments," Arrow suggests, "is ritualistic, not essential." For "rationality hypotheses are partial and frequently, if not always, supplemented by assumptions of a different character," ad hoc hypotheses that do the work of explication.

Why then do rational choice economists, and now political scientists, cling to the rationality assumption? I think rationality is inserted to *justify*, not explain, the market. As Richard Zeckhauser (1987, 264) says in a rather wistful footnote: "Maybe we can even learn to divorce the rationality debate from our views on how well the market performs."

Market Tests

Armed with the idea that people tend, with various degrees of ends-means rationality, to maximize their satisfactions, whatever they are, and that money buys a lot of satisfaction (if not happiness), rational choice economics claims that in many markets it predicts behavior fairly well. Certainly it will predict the behavior of firms better than that of individuals; regarding the latter, let me merely advert to some rational choice failures. Given its record regarding risk assessment, we should not be surprised that rational choice theory fails accurately to interpret insurance markets. In buying earthquake insurance, for example, people are more influenced by the experience or cautions of their friends than by the actual risks they confront (Kunreuther et al., cited in Hogarth and Reder 1987, 18). Labor markets are unpredictable by rational choice theory because there are two alternative sources of utility to be maximized: income (the price effect) and leisure (the substitution effect). Financial and commodities markets, which come as close to perfect auctions as may be found, are theoretically unpredictable because prediction relies on the claim that people's tastes are homogeneous and universal, which raises the question of why they would engage in trade (Arrow 1987, 205). As Zeckhauser (1987, 260) puts it, not only is Las Vegas "an affront to the rational decision model . . . [but] the vast volumes that are often traded on commodities and futures exchanges are no less of an affront," especially since the model calls for perfect, or at least equal, access to information. In part this failure stems from the reluctance of rational choice theorists to embrace "process benefits," the pleasure of gambling (or work) as an activity in itself without regard to outcomes. Nor is savings behavior explained by rational choice. Saving, Arrow points out (1987, 206), "is not proportional to income. From which it would follow that distributional considerations matter. (In general, as data improved, it has become increasingly difficult to find any simple rationality based model that will explain savings, wealth, and bequest data.)"

Moreover, while participation in elections has seemed paradoxical to rational choice theorists, economists, at least, and by inference rational choice theorists, have thought such participation to be a simple function of budgetary constraints. In his *General Theory* (1936, 96) Keynes wrote that "the propensity to consume is a fairly stable function so that, as a rule, the amount of aggregate consumption mainly depends on the amount of aggregate income." But empirical research again found variability where economists like Keynes assumed a constant relationship. Katona (1975, 70) comments: "Three decades after World War II . . . evidence of the instability of the consumption function in the United States is overwhelming." Apparently, the budgetary constraints on which rational choice theory relies are insufficient to explain participation even in the consumer market.

In short, it is far from clear that, as Thaler suggested a rationalist would argue, "economic theory has done very well so far." Arrow (1989) contends that "the impossibility of carrying out . . . [rationality] calculations is manifest from everyday observation and confirmed by the inability of economists using our theory and our computing power to make good forecasts—even good contingency forecasts."

II. RATIONAL CHOICE IN POLITICAL SCIENCE

But perhaps the political arena is *more* congenial than the market to the assumptions and procedures of rational choice theory. In what follows, except for a brief excursion into bureaucratic behavior, I will confine my rebuttal of this view to mass phenomena, elections, public opinion, and parties, disregarding legislative and committee behavior.

Both Karl Mannheim and Harold Lasswell spoke of politics as the domain of the irrational. They did not mean that people were more unreasonable in politics than in other domains, but rather that, because politics deals with the ends or purposes of society, the ordinary processes of ends-means rationality could not be applied. Popper (1983, 380–83) made the same point: a planned society encountered the problems of reconciling different concepts of life, for which the processes of reason but not rationality were appropriate. Similarly, Weber distinguishes between *Wirtrationalität*, the rationality of fitting means to ends, and *Zweckrationalität*, the "rationality" of deciding among ends. In elaboration of this point we might recall Burke's and Oakeshott's belief that tradition and experience are far better guides to political choices than rationality. Schumpeter (1950, 122–23) contrasts the irrationality of politics with economic life, the source of "the rational attitude," going so far as to suggest that "all logic is derived from the pattern of economic decision." The idea that the political is, in any event, *less* rational than the economic is borne out by a closer comparison of the two realms.

What to Maximize?

The benefits of market activity are thought to be measured by homogeneous, fungible units: measurable, infinitely divisible, easily stored and traded money, which Schumpeter called "the most saleable of all commodities." In contrast, the benefits from political activity are often symbolic and nonmaterial, hard to measure, idiosyncratic among individuals and heterogeneous among groups. These benefits often stem from identification with a group (party, race, nation) or an ideological label such as "conservative" or "liberal" (Kinder and Sears 1985). Because these identifications are often acquired early—there is some evidence that adolescence is a period in which political learning acquires a kind of "fix" that persists, with only gradual change, throughout adulthood (Sears 1983)—responses to current political stimuli are sluggish and erratic. These symbolic identifications are themselves highly valued, leading people to exercise their reason to defend their identifications rather than to calculate the probable benefits of switching loyalties. It is certainly not irrational to defend one's prejudices, but that defensive policy will confound efforts to find examples of rational choices designed to benefit the individual by choosing parties which and candidates who offer economic gain. Self-interest is recondite under these circumstances.

This is just the kind of situation, however, in which partisans of rational choice theory as well as "economists revel in showing how apparently anomalous behavior is in fact consistent with the maintained hypothesis" (Hogarth and Reder 1987, 6). This tendency leads to "thin" versions of rational choice theory (Green and Shapiro, 17–18) that permit *any* coherent set of values to be the subject of maximization. Such theories run into the same problem of unresearchable tautology as that which characterizes the concept of utility in economics. As Joan Robinson (1964, 46) wrote, "Utility is a metaphysical construct of impregnable circularity; utility is the quality in commodities that makes individuals want to buy them, and the fact that individuals want to buy the commodities shows that they have utility." That is, unless the analyst specifies what people are seeking to maximize, all choices are "rational" choices. But "thick" versions of rational choice theory that specify the content of utility will have trouble predicting political choices from political stimuli when these choices are guided by the symbolic identifications mentioned above and thus are largely independent of the stimuli presented by candidates and parties. On the surface, it seems reasonable to suppose that people seek different kinds of goods by different kinds of strategies: love in one way, social esteem in another, ideological confirmation in a third, material welfare in yet a fourth.

Collective vs. Individual Action

While one may buy things to benefit only oneself, one can only rarely vote for a candidate, party, or policy without (if one is successful) conferring whatever benefits one anticipates receiving upon others, as well as oneself. But it is also true that one is not likely to receive the anticipated benefits unless others also vote in the same way, making the voter we have in mind a beneficiary of *their* votes. There are two difficulties for rational choice theory here: each person gets a "free ride" only if others also benefit; and the implied interdependence of utilities is a violation of neoclassical rules as well as an infringement on the methodological individualism of rational choice theory.

Political Ignorance

Learning is taught. Partly due to television (Ward et al. 1977), parents take pains to teach their children market skills at an early age; they generally delay political teaching until much later—if they do it consciously at all (Easton and Dennis 1969). People who believe that *they*, and not others or society, control what happens to them tend to learn from experience much more readily than those who believe their fates are controlled by outside forces. The market doctrine of self-reliance encourages the belief that each is the source of his or her own destiny, but democracy offers only a diluted version of this direct sense of individual responsibility for one's fate. Since rationality is often identified with learning, the conditions that favor learning also favor rationality. Hence we may expect that learning in particular and rationality in general will be lacking in political behavior. This expectation is supported by a study conducted by Amos Tversky and Daniel Kahneman.

Tversky and Kahneman (1987, 90) offer a short list of the reasons why people fail to learn in markets. Their central assumption is that learning occurs when systematic "feedback" provides information about errors that can be "adapted" for future use. But in markets, trial and error does not lead to learning under the following conditions:

> (i) outcomes are commonly delayed and not easily attributable to a particular action; (ii) variability in the environment degrades the reliability of the feedback, especially where outcomes of low probability are involved; (iii) there is often no information about what the outcome would have been if another decision had been taken; and (iv) most important decisions are unique and therefore provide little opportunity for learning. (Ibid.)

The most notable thing about these barriers to learning in the market is how very much more prevalent most of them are in politics. Compared to market outcomes, political outcomes are more delayed. They are almost never strictly attributable to an individual's own acts. The political environment offers few of the regularities of the market: instead of the same set of products available at roughly the same "prices" at the same places, there is a shifting set of candidates and policies from election to election, and varying degrees of distracting external conflict. While information about counterfactuals is limited in both domains, unique decisions are more common in politics because, except for the presence of the same parties, all elections are "unique," given the variation in their historical settings.

Schumpeter (1950, 258, 262) points out that

> In the ordinary run of often repeated decisions [in the market] the individual is subject to the salutary and rationalizing influence of favorable and unfavorable experience. He is also under the influence of relatively simple and unproblematic motives and interests which are but occasionally interfered with by excitement.

In political life, by contrast, the citizen is dealing with things unfamiliar to his own experience and uncorrected by trial and error. As a consequence,

> the typical citizen drops down to a lower level of mental performance as soon as he enters the political field. He argues and analyzes in a way which he would readily recognize as infantile within the sphere of his real interests. He becomes primitive again. His thinking becomes associative and affective.

How does rational choice theory fare where people's thinking has become "associative and affective"?

Zeckhauser (1987, 258) has produced a table that specifies the conditions under which rationalist and behavioralist approaches to human action are appropriate. A modified version of his table highlights the implausibility of rationalistic understandings of politics.

Rationalist	*Behavioralist*
Steady state	Adaptive
Recurring situation	Unique situation
Continuous allocation	Discrete allocation
States of the world identified	States of the world need to be identified
Alternatives clear	Alternatives need to be identified
Price taking	Negotiations or strategic pricing
Goods	Time, health, faith, love
Subject to arbitrage	No poaching

Even when stated in this telegraphic fashion, we can identify many market-politics differences.

Although some (e.g., Thaler 1987) doubt that market circumstances offer a stable environment (steady state), it seems clear to me, for the reasons given above, that market circumstances tend to be "steadier" than political circumstances (although to a Russian in 1995 this might not be apparent). A possible exception is the business cycle, but this affects political choices almost as much as it affects market choices (Hibbs 1987, 141–210). The question of "continuous" versus "discrete" allocation reminds us again of the lumpiness of political goods as contrasted to market goods, discussed above in reference to the uniqueness of political choices. The need to identify relevant states of the world, and that of discovering various "alternatives" to any particular proposal, are surely more characteristic of politics than of markets—if only because markets offer choices continually while politics offers choices only intermittently and in confusing, partisan contexts.

The political analogy to the economy's "price-taking" behavior is "party taking" or party identification. In the case of price taking, individuals choose among current offerings, but choices determined by party identification are influenced by historical shifts that may have occurred a generation or more earlier. Regarding Zeckhauser's next item, the nature of the goods to be "bought," we might interpret two of the conditions favoring behaviorism as distinctly political: the "faith" embodied in symbolic identification and the form of "love" known as charisma. Finally, the "arbitrage" versus "no poaching" comparison raises two different issues. When arbitrage occurs, rationalist approaches may be appropriate because arbitrage tends to present to choosers a common price or policy that bridges their differences. In this sense, both markets and politics are subject to arbitrage.

"Poaching" generally refers to the appropriation of someone else's assets—for example, hiring an employee who has been trained by another firm. By extension, it means no-holds-barred competition. In consumer markets people do not think of themselves as members of the firms they patronize, whereas in elections voters do think of themselves as members of the parties they support. Voters are partisan in a way that even the devoted brand loyalist is not; they are socialized early into their parties; their membership is (still) often part of their identities; when their party is defeated *they* suffer defeat. Does this kind of partisan competition encourage rationality? I doubt it. Just as one would be unlikely to characterize the partisanship of supporters of sports teams as products of rational choice, one would be unlikely to say that competing party identifiers were rational in their partisanship. Thus, political competition is less hospitable to rational choice theory than is market competition.

There are other reasons for believing that politics is an arena much more favorable to behavioral theory than to rational choice theory.

The Irrationality of Mass Political Participation

The more important the choice, the more rational the deliberation. In the consumer market, at least two measures of "importance" are available: the expensiveness and durability of a good. George Stigler (1961, 529) makes the point that the more expensive an item, the more prospective purchasers deliberate and weigh alternatives. Katona (1965) contrasts the habitual nature of everyday purchases with the careful planning involved in the purchase of durable goods. In elections these two measures are at odds: the price of voting is negligible but the duration of the choice is substantial. One might think that a low-cost investment in a durable good would be ideal for encouraging participation, but there is a third consideration: the probability that a person's act will make a difference. It is this consideration that leads Downs (1975) and his followers to suggest that voters are "rationally ignorant." But what kind of rationality is this? In the market, ignorance about the goods one buys is considered irrational and, as Stigler points out, one invests time and attention proportionate to the durability, as well as the expensiveness, of the goods one buys.

The decision to participate in an election is supported by an irrational belief in the effectiveness of one's own actions. This belief has been called "the illusion of control" (Langer 1983), an illusion reinforced by the need to believe that one is in control of one's own fate. It is an illusion reflected, for example, in the belief that such symbolic acts as cheering for a team or *selecting* (as contrasted to being given) a lottery ticket influence the outcome. We now face a paradox: an irrational motivation is required to counteract people's "rational ignorance" so that they can choose a durable good more rationally.

Presumably, it is not just winning an election that people care about; they also care about the policies that might flow from their team's winning, and the benefits they hope to receive from these policies. But this is a chain of contingencies beyond the calculation of most people, even when they are experts in politics. Such remote and uncertain chains of contingency generally fail to elicit rational responses; indeed, sometimes it seems that only prophetic powers will serve in the place of ordinary instrumental rationality.

People are more rational when their self-interest is clearly engaged. One implication of the attenuated chain of contingencies is that people cannot easily see where their self-interest lies. Perhaps for this reason, or perhaps because symbolic identifications with party, race, and nation determine opinions and voting patterns, people do not seem to be motivated much by self-interest in politics. David Sears and Carolyn Funk (1991) review the abundant evidence that those with higher stakes in a policy outcome generally behave no differently from those whose self-interest would be unaffected by that outcome. Thus, the attitudes and behavior regarding school bond issues of those with children in school were little or no different from those without them; with respect to busing, those with affected children were little different from those whose children would be unaffected; those whose jobs might be affected by affirmative action were minimally different from those whose jobs would not be affected; the attitudes of the unemployed toward government support of full employment were only trivially different from jobholders. Similarly, recipients of public services, such as welfare, had attitudes toward such services that were no different from those who did not, but who were similar in other respects; and compared to matched others, the attitudes of the elderly were no different toward age-related benefits, nor were those of crime victims different on crime issues.

In contrast, self-interested attitudes and voting emerged with respect to taxation among the general public, and toward policies affecting the security of their jobs among public employees. Sears and Funk (47) conclude that "personal self-interest generally has not been of major importance in explaining the general public's social and political attitudes," with those two exceptions. Material self-interest certainly can influence voting decisions, but in mass politics this influence is generally weak.

Since rational choice theories usually put the maximization of self-interest at center stage, they tend to contradict the insight that, in voting, it is "rational" to be irrational. In the market, by contrast, material self-interest is at least a plausible first-order explanation of behavior.

The Relation between Persons and their Environments

Although much of the criticism of rational choice theory has rightly focused on the rationality assumption, I would like to draw attention to something else, namely the implicit assumption that in the social sciences (including economics), human properties can be homogenized and then waved away with the *ceteris paribus* caveat, while attention focuses on variation in such environmental factors as price and budget constraints, party competition, or the costs of voting. For predicting, say, traffic flows, variation in preferences may be unimportant (as long as circumstances remain constant—the stable-state assumption that has been questioned in economics), but for predicting, say, responses to fashion (Earl 1983, O'Shaughnessy 1992), variation in tastes may be crucial. One cannot safely assume that market or political behavior, however aggregated, has the properties of traffic analysis rather than fashion. It is for reasons of this kind that all behavior is the *joint* function of persons and their environments. Alfred Marshall (1938, 16) contended that "the economist studies mental states rather through their manifestations than in themselves," but this explanation does not excuse rational choice theories that, far from ignoring mental states, make them central to the analysis while simply *assuming* their content. In my opinion *any* fixed assumptions of this sort are misleading, because behavioral manifestations are governed in part by the character and development of the mental states in question.

A little history of psychological explanation is in order. In 1968 Walter Mischel, reviewing a variety of psychological studies, found that the situations in which people find themselves explain at least as much of the variance in their behavioral responses as do their personal traits. This is close to what economic rational choice theorists claim: if we assume the personal traits of stable preference ordering and utility maximization, then situational variations in price and budgetary constraints can explain most of the variance in consumer and other behavior. But when psychologists then attempted to create an environmentalistic psychology (e.g., Magnusson 1981), they found that it was no better. For situations were recalcitrant to proper theorizing about behavior when treated in isolation from personal traits. It did not take them long to understand that "much of the interesting variance is in the interaction between person and situation" (Bem & Funder 1978, 485). Lest this seem to be foreign turf to economists, it must be pointed out that psychologists are interested in explaining the incidence, prevalence, and rates of change of a variety of kinds of aggregate behavior, including matters of interest to economists, workplace behavior, and consumer behavior. One is not surprised, therefore, that when Gary Becker (1976) covers some of the same territory, he has to introduce ad hoc psychological variables to attempt to do the job (Simon 1987, 29–31) — and even then his "explanations" omit important environmental (that is, historical) variables (Berk and Berk 1983).

Explaining Government Inefficiency

While electoral turnout, ideological "distortion" of vote maximizing behavior among political parties, "irrational" commitments to unpopular positions by presidents and legislators, and other similar matters in the public domain are notoriously difficult for rational choice theory to explain, I want to turn to an area in which rational choice seems to do better. Rational choice theory predicts that government enterprises will be less efficient than private enterprise. The reasons flow from the premises of methodological individualism: each person is assumed to be motivated primarily by self-interest rather than by role norms or devotion to the public interest (when these norms and ideals conflict with perceived self-interest). This assumption applies to legislators commissioning an enterprise, bureaucrats running it, and citizens appraising it. That is, in their "ordering by preference among all possible outcomes of choice," the various political actors place their own welfare at the top of the ordering, regardless of countervailing normative claims.

Two substantial and careful studies comparing the relative efficiencies of public and private enterprise (Wolf 1988 and Borcherding et al. 1982) come to the same conclusion: with only a few exceptions, public enterprises (such as hospitals, banks, transportation, utilities, etc.) are less efficient than comparable private enterprises. But does rational choice explain this outcome?

I wish to draw attention to two questions in these accounts of governmental inefficiency: What does rational choice theory add to ordinary market theory or even to common sense? And how much of the explanation of governmental inefficiency is compatible with rational choice theory? Charles Wolf (1988, 17) sets forth the following condition for efficiency: "Efficient use of resources at any point in time requires that prices of outputs be equal to marginal costs." He points out that market enterprises (except for monopolies and firms with increasing returns to scale) must, as a requirement for staying in business, meet this condition, whereas public enterprises, which may be subsidized by taxes, need not. True enough, but this is a proposition from general market economics that does not depend on theories of rational choice. Wolf goes on to say that private firms have incentives to innovate and to adopt new cost-saving technologies, incentives public firms lack. Furthermore, unlike private firms, where investment decisions are governed by the relation between costs and income, in public enterprises the chief investor is a legislature with interests other than profitability. The theory that individuals maximize their (material) self-interest does not explain this difference between public and private managers; conversely, no theory of rational choice is needed to show that wherever managers profit from innovation, they are more likely to innovate than managers who reap no such benefit. This is why, as Thaler said, "maybe we can even learn to divorce the rationality debate from our views on how well the market performs."

Wolf advances other reasons for the superior efficiency of private enterprises. In private enterprises, unlike public ones, there are incentives for keeping employment costs to a minimum. While public managers (like managers of firms with market [monopolistic] power) may find it to their advantage to pay higher-than-market wages and overhire in order to advance their claims for larger budgets (a rational choice hypothesis), public managers may also do so because they identify with the welfare of their employees (a hypothesis inconsistent with rational choice theory). Wolf also holds that market accountability is more stringent than accountability to central accounting bureaus, but that is, at least in part, because he has already excluded from consideration noncompetitive pockets of market power.

Rational choice theory holds that managers of public enterprises are motivated by personal self-interest instead of by the announced goals of their enterprises. Wolf disagrees: in public enterprises, he says, "internalities or organizational goals become elements in the utility functions that agency personnel seek to maximize" (67). On balance, it seems to me that where rational choice theorists agree with Wolf their theory adds nothing to ordinary market economics (Simon's [1987] claim), and where they disagree, Wolf understands the variety of motives of public managers better than rational choice theorists do.

At least one political economist (Dowding 1991, 175) who has attempted rational choice explanations agrees: "Pluralists, elitists, statists can all use the rational choice method . . . but the method will itself not generate the thesis which will prove the most empirically robust."

It was once said that there were three perfect organizations: Standard Oil of New Jersey, the Prussian army, and the Society of Jesus. How, without tautology, can we explain the efficiency of the Prussian army and the Jesuits with theories devised to explain the efficiency of business firms?

III. THE FUTURE OF RATIONAL CHOICE

Thaler (1987, 99), no friend of rational choice, asks all parties to agree that two propositions are false: "(1) Rational models are useless. (2) All behavior is rational." Although Herbert Simon ([1986] 1992, 33) points to the usefulness of rational choice models, he suggests that to define the "conditions of perfect utility maximization rationality in a world of certainty or in a world in which the probability distributions of all relevant variables can be provided by the decision makers . . . might be compared with a theory of ideal gases or of frictionless bodies sliding down inclined planes in a vacuum," a theory that is worth having even though "the real world of human decisions is not a world of ideal gases, frictionless planes, or vacuums" (34). Rational choice models should cease to be confused with descriptive models accounting for economic or political behavior. They are aids to thought. Put differently, rational choice is to decision theory what Weber's ideal types are to sociology. What is now needed is a set of *testable* propositions (and a sensitivity to evidence) that, when tested, will mark out the area where rational choice is a reliable guide to economic and political behavior.

Many applications of rational choice have proved useful both as heuristics *and* as explanations of reality. For instance, I am told that game theory has been helpful in understanding bargaining and negotiations of all kinds, but especially in international relations — although without scrutiny of the "confirming" evidence by some team as able as Green and Shapiro, one must avoid the too- willing suspension of disbelief that prevailed in other areas for the past three decades.

Does rational choice have a future, not just as a heuristic, but as an interpretation of reality? In spite of its failure to predict or explain the phenomena it addresses, most commentators believe it will persist undaunted. Herrnstein (1993, 138) believed that because of its centrality to the methods of economic analysis, rational choice is "impregnable. . . . No criticism of the hypothesis will ever be successful." Tversky and Kahneman (1987, 89) observe that "the assumption of rationality is protected by a formidable set of defenses in the form of bolstering assumptions that restrict the significance of any observed violation of the model. In particular, it is commonly assumed that substantial violations of the standard model are (i) restricted to insignificant choice problems, (ii) quickly eliminated by learning, or (iii) irrelevant to economics because of the corrective function of market forces." Mary Zey (1992, 27), a sociologist, comments that "rational choice theory survives counterevidence by placing no limits on implausibility or inconsistency of its inferred utilities and by appealing to the undeniable fact that organisms may calculate incorrectly, be ignorant, forget, or have limited time horizons." The consequence, she says, is that rational choice inhibits "our understanding of human behavior . . . [and] the advancement of theories that explain the real world."

It is at this point that interesting questions of scholarly self-policing arise. How has rational choice theory managed to survive peer review? Wassily Leontief (1982, 207) argues that peer review can be perverse as well as constructive. He writes that in economics departments, the disciplinary codes enforcing orthodoxy "remind one of those methods employed by the Marines to maintain discipline on Parris Island." In politics, only true believers are thought competent to referee rational choice manuscripts: having learned a skill, rational choice theorists are inclined to believe in the efficacy of that skill, and believing in its efficacy, they endorse work employing that skill. Even though such critics as Simon, Arrow,

Tversky and Kahneman, and now Green and Shapiro seem to have the better case, if the impregnability hypothesis is correct, these critics may also prove to be relatively ineffectual.

Three analogies (they are no more than that) may help. For many years dialectical materialist theories of history survived, at least in European universities, in spite of an "ad hocery" in defining materialism (Kamenka 1985) that was essentially no different from the "ad hocery" in rational choice research. History killed Marxist historicism, but there is much that is questionable in the very concept of the murder of a theory by the march of events. Note that in violation of principles set forth by Lakatos (1970), no alternative theory of history has emerged to take the place of the Marxian materialist dialectic.

Freudian theories of the mind, or rather (because Freud, like rational choice theorists, had no theory of mind) Freudian theories of the psyche, were said to survive not only because their doctrine was impregnable (criticism was merely "resistance"), but also because Freudianism took root in nonacademic establishments designed to advance the doctrine rather than subject it to critical review. The National Institute of Mental Health gravely wounded psychoanalysis by refusing to fund "cures" that could not be substantiated or shown to be better than less expensive procedures. But perhaps the mortal blow, at least to theories of schizophrenia and depression, came from the alternative paradigm presented by physiological and pharmaceutical research and therapy. Like Jung, Freud survives today at the margins of literary studies but not (much) in medical schools. Yet peer review seems not to have contributed very much to the demise of this self-reinforcing theory.

At one time "learning theory," based on the theories and research of Pavlov, Watson, Hull, and, in the form of operant conditioning, Skinner, dominated academic psychology in American universities. Unlike the other two in this list of dead or dying theories, learning theory was based on research, even though most of the evidence came from the behavior of rats, pigeons, and other nonhumans. Again like rational choice theory, learning theory had no concept of mind (except as a receptacle for the history of previous reinforcement); Skinner (1972) said, in fact, that the notion of "mind" was invented to enhance the idea of human dignity. Learning theory lost its dominance when research into cognition and affect developed superior capacities to explain the things learning theory explained—and much more. It was a genuine case of an academic discipline curing itself without outside muscle or historical *coup de grace*.

The latter two of these three examples reveal the power of Lakatos's (1970) and Kuhn's (1962) insight that an alternative theory is needed to displace a no-longer-credible one. Green and Shapiro—wisely, I think—do not offer an alternative to rational choice theory. But there is one, or rather, several.

As a consequence of the invalidation of rational choice in economics, there are now two versions of microeconomics competing with each other. In addition to the formal version incorporating rational choice and taught in economics departments, there is an informal behavioral or cognitive version, increasingly adopted by law schools for their programs in law and economics (Ellickson 1989) and taught in marketing courses and industrial organization and behavior courses in business schools. (Is this because there are real-world consequences for business students trained to believe invalid theories — as there are for theories of macroeconomics, quite independent of microeconomics, in governmental policy?) Departments of sociology and of psychology (every third issue of the *Annual Review of Psychology* has a review essay on consumer behavior) are groping toward an alternative microeconomics, as well. This second microeconomics relies on psychology, sociology, and a growing body of decision theories free of rational choice assumptions but often employing theories of subjective expected utility open to modification by empirical research (Simon [1986] 1992). The new cluster of theories has multiple foci: industrial organization and behavior, the psychology and sociology of work, labor policy, and consumer behavior and marketing. Some marketing texts (e.g., Engel et al. 1978; Mullen and Johnson 1990) hardly mention the formal version of microeconomics, relying instead on theories derived from the major social and cognitive psychologists. Simon's work, the basis of much non-rational choice decision theory (reviewed in Simon 1986), stems from such early works as Cyert and March 1963, while theories of industrial organization flow from the transactional theory of Ronald Coase ([1937] 1988) and Oliver Williamson (1975), and from such sociological work as is now assembled in Smelser and Swedberg 1994. The research published in the *Journal of Economic Behavior and Organization*, the *Journal of Consumer Research*, and the *American Sociological Review* has none of the elegance of rational choice theory, but it has something else: empirical validity that is subject to revision by disconfirming evidence.

It would be one more irony if political science were to adopt rational choice just as it is being displaced in business schools and other places where empirical validity is still important. Were this to occur, political science would mimic the hermetic irrelevance of the contemporary study of literature, in which Jung and Freud are treated as serious guides to the human mind.

Susanne Lohmann

THE POVERTY OF
GREEN AND SHAPIRO

Donald Green and Ian Shapiro argue that rational choice scholarship in political science is excessively theory-driven: too few of its theoretical insights have been subjected to serious empirical scrutiny and survived. But rational choice theorizing has the potential to identify and correct logical inconsistencies and slippages. It is thus valuable even if the resulting theories are not tested empirically. When Green and Shapiro's argument concerning collective dilemmas and free riding is formalized, it turns out to be deeply flawed and in many respects outright false. Their mistake is common enough: they misclassify a variety of collective dilemmas as prisoner's dilemmas. Because they misunderstand the theory of rational choice, Green and Shapiro allege that it is refuted by empirical findings that, in fact, support it.

In recent decades, rational choice theory has become the rising star of political science. Even though rational choice scholars constitute a minority of political scientists, they publish a disproportionate number of articles in the *American Political Science Review*; they are sought after by leading political science departments; and, after achieving intellectual dominance in some subdisciplines of the field of American politics, they are beginning to make inroads into international relations and comparative politics. Given the importance of rational choice scholarship in political science, it is

---

Susanne Lohmann, Department of Political Science, University of California at Los Angeles, Los Angeles, CA 90095, telephone (310) 825–1277, telefax (310) 825–0778, thanks Richard Anderson, Jonathan Bendor, Rupen Cetinyan, James DeNardo, Jeffrey Frieden, Jeffrey Friedman, Miriam Golden, Jack Hirshleifer, Howard Rosenthal, Adam Simon, and George Tsebelis for insightful comments.

clearly valuable to have a public discussion of its strengths, limitations, and philosophical underpinnings.

The strength of rational choice theory is its potential to provide explicit and rigorous models of political processes and institutions that allow us to derive empirically testable hypotheses and to understand precisely how political outcomes vary as a function of environmental factors. Perhaps the most serious intellectual threat to the rational choice approach comes from empirical findings that challenge the rationality assumption.

For example, rational choice models of imperfect or incomplete information are based on the assumption that players employ backwards induction and Bayesian inference, effortlessly computing equilibria over which a rational choice theorist might slave for months. Assumptions of this kind are inconsistent with a large body of experimental evidence suggesting that people (i) often fail to do backwards induction, and (ii) do not generally employ the Bayesian logic when processing new information. Instead, people use heuristic rules of thumb, and their inferences are subject to cognitive biases (Kahneman, Slovic, and Tversky 1982; for a critical assessment of the literature on judgment under uncertainty, see Cosmides and Tooby 1992).

Similarly, the description of the standard game-theoretic model assumes that players not only know each others' equilibrium strategies and beliefs, but that they also know that all players know each others' equilibrium strategies and beliefs, and that they know that all players know that all players know each others' equilibrium strategies and beliefs, ad infinitum. Trivially, this "common knowledge" assumption implies that players are in agreement about the game that is being played. (It does not exclude the possibility of incomplete or imperfect information.) However, in many real-world situations people appear to hold different beliefs about the game that is being played. James DeNardo (1995) provides an empirical critique of the game-theoretic underpinnings of nuclear deterrence theory along these lines. He shows that people's beliefs about nuclear strategy, nuclear deterrence, and the arms race are highly heterogeneous. Perhaps surprisingly, this result holds not only for the beliefs held by laypeople, but also for those of security experts who "know" the relevant game theory.

Leading game theorists are responding to the intellectual challenges implicit in empirical findings of this kind.[1] Reinhard Selten, who won the Nobel Prize in Economics for his seminal contributions to game theory, has all but turned his back on the rationality assumption; instead he is devising laboratory experiments that explore how people actually reason. Other economists are developing models in which players learn about each others' strategies and beliefs in the course of many iterations; under some conditions, such play converges to the equilibrium prescribed by game theory. Evolutionary game theory explains systematic deviations from rationality with reference to structural constraints in the evolutionary environment. Mathematical theories of cultural evolution examine the relative fitness of social norms (see Selten 1989 and Hirshleifer 1985 for surveys and references).

In-Principle vs. In-Practice Critiques of Rational Choice Theory

Against this background, Donald Green and Ian Shapiro's *Pathologies of Rational Choice Theory* is a disappointment. Theirs is primarily a critique of rational choice theory as it is allegedly practiced, rather than an assessment of its substantive strengths and limitations: they claim misbehavior on the part of rational choice theorists instead of subjecting the approach itself to serious scrutiny. Indeed, the book might have been more appropriately titled *Pathologies of Rational Choice Theorists*.

In particular, Green and Shapiro argue that rational choice scholarship is excessively theory-driven. The complaint that rational choice scholars allocate too little of their time and efforts toward empirical work is not new, though. Wassily Leontief, also a Nobel laureate in economics, compiled some relevant data: of all articles published in the *American Economic Review* from 1972 to 1976, 50.1 percent consisted of formal theory without any data, and another 21.2 percent contained analysis without formal theory *or* data. The corresponding figures for 1977-1981 are 54.0 percent and 11.6 percent, respectively (Leontief 1982). In political science, numerous surveys of rational choice scholarship call for more empirical work (see, for example, Krehbiel 1988).

It never occurred to me that one could fill a whole book developing this complaint in excruciating detail (Leontief made his point in a two-page letter to the editor). In Green and Shapiro's defense, however, their argument is rather complex and goes well beyond the standard complaint. Their central hypotheses are these:

1. More often than not, rational choice scholars fail to formulate empirically testable hypotheses.
2. When they formulate empirically testable hypotheses, these are rarely subjected to serious empirical scrutiny.
3. When rational choice hypotheses are tested, the tests are often so poorly devised as to be irrelevant to evaluating the models.
4. When such tests are properly conducted, the empirical findings tend to undermine rational choice theory or to lend support for propositions that are banal.

130

5. These flaws do not merely arise due to sloppiness, but are a necessary
consequence of the scholars' universalist ambitions.

Green and Shapiro present a considerable amount of anecdotal evidence, but this evidence does not always sustain their hypotheses. They suggest both that rational choice scholars put too little time and effort into empirical work, and that the implications of rational choice theory are contradicted by a large body of evidence. Yet much of the evidence Green and Shapiro cite was gathered by rational choice scholars.

Because they misunderstand the theory of rational choice, Green and Shapiro repeatedly discuss empirical findings that support the theory as if these findings refuted it. The structure of Green and Shapiro's argument is as follows: rational choice theory implies A, which is inconsistent with empirical finding B. In many of the examples provided in *Pathologies*, however, rational choice theory actually implies B', which is something very close, or even identical, to B.

Ex post, B' may appear banal—but since B' is inconsistent with Green and Shapiro's intuition A, they can hardly argue that this result was obvious *ex ante*. The implications of rational choice theory often replace firmly held, yet logically self-contradictory, intuitions. Here it is useful to maintain some historical perspective: many theoretical implications of rational choice scholarship were strikingly powerful and counterintuitive when first expressed, including Arrow's (1951) paradox and Olson's (1965) free rider problem.

Green and Shapiro's universalist claim about the universalist ambitions of rational choice scholars is partially contradicted by their own literature review (Ch. 2). Some early rational choice scholars indulged in a cultist universalism that denies the legitimacy of alternative modes of inquiry, and some still do so today. But the field has matured as it has entered the mainstream, and successive generations of scholars have embraced "partial universalism" or "segmented universalism" in ever greater numbers (these oxymorons are due to Green and Shapiro, 26–27). Today many rational choice theorists believe that rational choice can explain part, but not all, of what goes on in any given political domain, and that rational choice explanations tend to be more successful in some domains of political life than in others (see, for example, Tsebelis 1990, ch. 2; Satz and Ferejohn 1994).

Since Ockham, scientists have valued parsimony in explanation ("entities should not be multiplied needlessly"). Political scientists have long attempted to explain political behavior in terms of incentives faced by political actors; rational choice is one way of doing so parsimoniously. Based on the assumption that political actors respond in a coherent way to incentives, one can identify a sparse set of assumptions that logically implies a particular action. One does not thereby assert that political behavior is driven by instrumental motivations alone. Moreover, the rational choice approach is bound to be more useful when applied in domains with high-powered incentives, where a "rational" response has high payoffs, than in domains with low-powered incentives, where learning effects or selection pressures are weak.

There are good reasons to reject the notion that the rationality paradigm is universally applicable and powerful. Even then, inquiries into the nature of bounded or limited rationality must necessarily rely on rational choice theory to provide a benchmark against which anomalies can be identified and systematic deviations mapped out. For example, without a theory of how much people should contribute to a public good if they are rational and self-interested, there is no way of assessing whether empirical contribution patterns reveal altruism, systematic misassessments of the probability that a given contribution will be decisive, or total incomprehension on the part of the individuals involved.

Underlying Green and Shapiro's literature review is the attitude that rational choice theorizing is irrelevant unless its theoretical claims are tested empirically:

> We contend that much of the fanfare with which the rational choice approach has been heralded in political science must be seen as premature once the question is asked: What has this literature contributed to our understanding of politics? We do not dispute that theoretical models of immense and increasing sophistication have been produced by practioners of rational choice theory, but in our view the case has yet to be made that these models have advanced our understanding of how politics works in the real world. (6)

To examine the validity of Green and Shapiro's skeptical attitude toward theorizing, I will formalize their argument about collective dilemmas and free-riding. I will demonstrate the potential of rational choice theorizing to provide an organizing framework for our thinking about political processes and institutions, to explicitly spell out which assumptions drive the results, and to avoid logical inconsistencies and slippages. In the same way, the historical emphasis of rational choice scholarship on theory-building can be interpreted as a response to the loose reasoning that pervaded mainstream political science in the past and, judging by Green and Shapiro's performance, still constitutes a problem. To the extent that Green and Shapiro prefer to avoid logical inconsistencies in their reasoning, they may appreciate the value of the formal models I develop even though I do not subject my theoretical findings to empirical testing.

Social Dilemmas and Free Riding

Sometimes people who act rationally to further their individual interests produce an outcome that is suboptimal in the aggregate. Green and Shapiro illustrate such collective dilemmas with the Chinese barge parable:

> A gang of Chinese laborers manually [tugs] barges up the Yangtze River. Although the laborers are paid according to the number of barges that reach their destination, this incentive system is insufficient to entice the laborers to pull. No single laborer's efforts have more than a trivial effect on the progress of the barge, and the success of the team effort is a collective good to which each laborer is entitled regardless of effort. Left to pursue their own interests, therefore, the workers fail to pull the barge and therefore receive no pay. The barge moves only after the laborers themselves consent to the hiring of a taskmaster to whip them. (73)

Each laborer would be better off if the cooperative outcome could be achieved; that is, if some or all laborers exerted effort, the barge moved, and the laborers got paid. But, according to Green and Shapiro, rational choice theory predicts the noncooperative outcome in which no laborer exerts effort, the barge does not move, and the laborers do not get paid. Most political scientists would agree with Green and Shapiro's conclusion: for self-interested individuals, cooperative behavior is not individually rational unless it is enforced by institutions that monitor and sanction uncooperative behavior or provide selective incentives for cooperation. Yet, in the real world, people often resolve collective dilemmas without resorting to institutional solutions. Such observations are consistent with the possibility that people are not purely self-interested; their cooperation may be due to their concern for the welfare of others, adherence to social norms, or other noninstrumental motivations.

As Green and Shapiro correctly note, there is nothing in the logic of rational choice theory that would exclude such motivations. Indeed, the Chinese barge dilemma could be solved easily if the laborers had, say, a "taste for exercise" (88).[2] But theoretical "solutions" of this kind are clearly cop-outs. I fully agree with Green and Shapiro that such "slippery predictions and post hoc embellishments" (85) are worthless to the extent that their primary purpose is to save the rational choice paradigm. Like Green and Shapiro (97), I believe that rational choice theory should be conceived narrowly as a theory about the behavior of instrumentally rational and self-interested individuals, so as to keep rational choice explanations analytically distinct from other explanations. My formal argument is based on this narrow definition.

Green and Shapiro's description of the barge parable is ambiguous and incomplete. Formalizing it requires an explicit statement of assumptions. (This is one reason why formal models are valuable.) For example, Green and Shapiro assert that "the laborers seek wages while avoiding physical exertion" (73). This assumption does not restrict the functional form of the laborers' utility function, other than requiring that the laborers' utility increases with their pay and decreases with their effort. Again, Green and Shapiro say that any one laborer's efforts have a "trivial" effect on the progress of the barge, leaving unclear whether the barge would not move at all if only one laborer pulled, or whether it would simply move too little or too slowly. If the efforts of one laborer are insufficient, there remains some ambiguity as to whether the barge would move only if all laborers actively pulled it, or whether some laborers can move the barge even if others fail to pull. The parable is also worded as if each laborer faces a binary choice: pull the barge or don't pull the barge. This leaves out the possibility of pulling hard, pulling desultorily, or pulling at some other point on a continuum of effort. Finally, it would appear that individual efforts must be unobservable; otherwise, the laborers could distribute the pay they receive when the barge reaches its destination according to their levels of exertion.

Given these ambiguities, I offer two formal models of the barge parable in the hope that the reader will be convinced that at least one of them is a fair depiction of the setting Green and Shapiro have in mind. Both models assume unobservable efforts. The first model stipulates that the laborers face a binary choice of pulling the barge or not pulling the barge, and that no laborer alone can get the barge to move. In one variant of this model, I assume that the barge moves if and only if all laborers pull; in a second variant, it is sufficient for a strict subset of laborers to exert effort. The second model allows for a continuum of effort, and it stipulates that an increase in effort on the part of any laborer leads to an increase in the speed by which the barge moves toward its destination. It turns out that the implications of the second model are sensitive to the functional form of the laborers' utility functions.

A First Model of the Barge Parable

The first model builds on an extensive literature dealing with voluntary contribution threshold games (Lipnowski and Maital 1983; Van de Kragt, Orbell and Dawes 1983; Bliss and Nalebuff 1984; Palfrey and Rosenthal 1983, 1984, 1985, 1988, 1991a, 1991b; Rapoport 1985). If the barge arrives at its destination, each laborer receives a payment of 1. The barge moves if and only if all laborers exert effort. Here, the choice is binary: labor or abstain. To labor means to incur a cost C, which is strictly less than 1. The laborers' decisions are made simultaneously.

The game has two pure strategy equilibria. The first equilibrium corresponds to the one identified by Green and Shapiro: no laborer exerts effort, the barge does not move, and the laborers forego their pay. Suppose each laborer believes that no other laborer will exert effort. Since the barge will move only if all laborers exert effort, each laborer is better off abstaining, and receiving a payoff of 0, than working and obtaining a negative payoff $(0 - C)$. Since all laborers go through identical calculations, they all abstain. Thus, their beliefs that no laborer will exert effort are fulfilled in equilibrium.

A second pure-strategy equilibrium implements the cooperative outcome: each laborer exerts effort, the barge moves, and the laborers receive a positive payoff $(1 - C)$. Suppose each laborer believes all other laborers will exert effort. Since the barge will move only if all laborers work, each laborer's effort is decisive in determining whether the barge will move. Each laborer is better off working and receiving the positive payoff $(1 - C)$ than abstaining and obtaining a zero payoff. Since all laborers go through identical calculations, they all exert effort. Thus, their beliefs that each laborer will exert effort are fulfilled in equilibrium.

In the symmetric mixed strategy equilibrium (formally characterized in Appendix I), the probability p that each laborer exerts effort lies strictly between zero and one. For this to be the case, each laborer must be indifferent between exerting effort and abstaining, which can only mean that the expected payoffs of the two courses of action are equal. Equivalently, the expected probability that the laborer's effort is decisive in getting the barge to move, multiplied by the benefits he receives if the barge moves, must be equal to the cost of effort. This indifference condition implicitly defines the equilibrium probability p as a function of the parameters of the problem: the number of laborers involved and the cost of effort. (Recall that the benefits are normalized to 1.)

Given the random nature of the laborers' strategies, the probability that a sufficient number of laborers will exert effort to ensure positive payoffs lies strictly between zero and one. The model thus predicts that the cooperative outcome will be achieved sometimes but not always, depending on the random realization of the laborers' effort strategies.

Clearly, then, the zero-effort outcome is just one of multiple equilibria. The argument that rational self-interest on the part of the laborers necessarily leads to the noncooperative outcome is thus false. Green and Shapiro err in contending that "when a social dilemma exists, conventional rational choice models—which make no allowance for strategic error and stipulate no special utility from 'doing the right thing'—predict that no player will adopt a cooperative strategy" (77). (Green and Shapiro recognize the potential for multiple equilibria but erroneously assume that this possibility arises only in infinitely repeated games [78].)

The interesting question, then, is not whether the laborers can achieve the cooperative outcome at all, but whether they can achieve the equilibrium they unanimously prefer (see also Taylor 1987). The answer to this question lies outside game theory. It is a weakness of game theory that it has nothing to say about the individuals' beliefs even though these beliefs in effect determine which one of multiple equilibria is "selected." But it is the application of game theory to the problem at hand that demonstrates that incentives alone are insufficient to explain cooperation.

In real-life situations, players may coordinate on a particular equilibrium by using information and shared understandings that are not part of the formal description of the game; such an equilibrium is referred to as a "focal point" (Schelling 1960). The cooperative equilibrium is focal; after all, the laborers agree unanimously that they are better off with that outcome. If the laborers are able to coordinate with each other to the point where they can jointly hire a taskmaster (as Green and Shapiro seem to assume), it is not obvious why they cannot, by the same token, coordinate to achieve the cooperative equilibrium without resorting to a taskmaster.

This argument is strengthened by the fact that the taskmaster solution is a costly one. It is reasonable to assume that the taskmaster must be paid for her efforts, and that the whippings dealt by the taskmaster are costly. (It is possible, however, that the mere threat of being whipped induces the laborers to exert effort, so that they experience no pain in equilibrium).

The case for the institutional solution cannot be based on theoretical considerations, as Green and Shapiro erroneously assume. But it can be based on empirical findings suggesting that the cooperative equilibrium may be fragile. In experimental settings, individuals faced with strategic uncertainty in the presence of multiple Pareto-ranked equilibria often fail to coordinate on the cooperative equilibrium (Van Huyck, Battalio, and Beil 1990).

The model developed so far can be modified by assuming that the barge moves only if at least k out of n laborers exert effort, where k lies strictly between 1 and n. In this case, there exists one zero-effort equilibrium, as above.

In addition, there are multiple pure-strategy equilibria in which exactly k laborers exert effort, while nobody else does, and the public good is provided with certainty. (The number of such equilibria is equal to the number of combinations of n objects taken k at a time.) Suppose everybody believes that exactly k clearly identified laborers will exert effort, while the remaining $(n - k)$ laborers abstain. The former set of laborers will be referred to as the k group, the latter as the $(n - k)$ group. Since the barge will move only if at least k laborers exert effort, a member of the k group knows that his effort is decisive in determining whether the barge will move. Each member of the k group is better off working and receiving the positive payoff $(1 - C)$ than abstaining and obtaining a zero payoff. Since exactly k laborers are expected to exert effort, the members of the $(n - k)$ group know that their effort makes no difference. Each of them is better off abstaining from work and receiving a payoff equal to 1 than working and obtaining the payoff $(1 - C)$. Thus, the laborers' beliefs that all members of the k group will exert effort, while all members of the $(n - k)$ group abstain, are fulfilled in equilibrium.

Finally, in the symmetric mixed-strategy equilibrium (formally characterized in Appendix I), the probability p that each laborer exerts effort, and the probability that sufficient labor will be forthcoming to ensure positive payoffs, both lie strictly between 0 and 1.

In terms of aggregate welfare, the pure-strategy equilibria that implement the cooperative outcome dominate both the zero-effort and the mixed-strategy equilibria. While the cooperative equilibria lead to the same level of aggregate welfare, however, they differ in their distributional implications. In the modified version of the model, each laborer prefers the set of equilibria where k other laborers exert effort while he abstains. Given this distributional conflict, coordination is more difficult. (Game theory does not predict whether or how the coordination problem will be overcome.)

In this situation, the symmetric mixed-strategy equilibrium has the appealing focal property that the laborers' expected payoffs are identical, even if each laborer's expected payoff is lower than the average payoff in any of the cooperative equilibria. The notion that the laborers randomly choose to exert effort or abstain may, of course, be ruled out either on a priori or empirical grounds. But clearly, the case for an institutional (taskmaster) solution requires demonstrating the infeasibility of equilibria that implement the cooperative outcome without resorting to an institution. This is true *a fortiori* if the institution under consideration is costly.

The theory developed so far can be reasonably criticized on the grounds that its predictions are weak. Given the multiplicity of equilibria, the model is compatible with the following empirical findings: (i) the socially optimal number of individuals contribute to the public good, and the public good is provided; (ii) no individual contributes to the public good, and the public good is not provided; (iii) too few individuals contribute to the public good, and the public good is not provided; (iv) too many individuals contribute to the public good, and the public good is provided.

This does not mean that the theory is immune to falsification. The theory does place some restrictions on the data that would allow for its statistical assessment in repeated laboratory trials (see, for example, Palfrey and Rosenthal 1991a, 1991b). Such testing requires some auxiliary hypothesis, such as the hypothesis that the individuals coordinate on the same equilibrium in each trial. In the k-out-of-n game, if the individuals coordinate on one of the pure-strategy equilibria, the model predicts that either 0 or exactly k contributions will be made in each period; in other words, either the public good is never provided, or its provision is certain. Any other outcome would require us to reject the model. If the individuals coordinate on the symmetric mixed strategy equilibrium, any number of contributions can be observed in equilibrium, but in repeated trials standard statistical tests can assess whether the observed frequencies of contribution and public good provision deviate significantly from the equilibrium probabilities implied by the model. (Clearly, the experiment must be designed carefully to avoid the confounding effects of cooperation-furthering repeated play.)

Nevertheless, in the presence of multiple equilibria, the criticism that rational choice theory places too few restrictions on observed data is well taken. But this is not Green and Shapiro's criticism. They believe that rational choice theory is problematic because it predicts the noncooperative outcome as the *unique* equilibrium. In fact, the weakness of game theory is that it allows for too many cooperative equilibria.

Claims about the empirical failings of rational choice theory are invalid to the extent that they build on Green and Shapiro's flawed theoretical argument. *Pathologies* cites a great deal of empirical evidence that people can and often do overcome collective dilemmas. Green and Shapiro interpret this evidence as inconsistent with the alleged point prediction of rational choice, namely that voluntary and costly contributions to a public good will be zero:

> Even a very low rate of collective action may nonetheless involve an anomalously large number of participants since the point prediction stemming from Olson's account anticipates a participation rate of zero. Mitchell (1979), however, finds that among the millions of members of environmental organizations, about 100,000 join for reasons that cannot be linked in any plausible way to selective incentives. Comparable if not larger numbers describe individual financial contributions to national election campaigns (Sorauf 1988, 44-47) or protesters who travel long distances to demonstrate in Washington (Walsh and Warland 1983). (81-82)

If the collective dilemma under consideration can be classified as a prisoner's dilemma game, then the unique prediction of rational choice theory is indeed zero turnout, zero contributions, or zero effort. In many cases, however, collective dilemmas are more appropriately classified as variants of a public goods game; the Chinese barge parable is one example. In this case, empirical findings suggesting that people do in fact cooperate are *qualitatively* consistent with rational choice theory. It is entirely possible, of course, that the *quantitative* predictions of the theory (such as its point prediction about the amount of collective action) are way off. But Green and Shapiro's account does not provide sufficient information to allow us to assess this possibility. In their view, such information would be redundant, since they believe that *any* positive amount of collective action constitutes a falsification of rational choice theory. In fact, a rejection of rational choice theory would have to be based on a comparison of its quantitative predictions and the observed patterns of collective action.

Green and Shapiro's mistake is common enough: they erroneously try to fit the standard collective dilemmas of political science into the one-shot or finite prisoner's dilemma mold, in which the noncooperative outcome is indeed the unique equilibrium. (Green and Shapiro allow for the possibility that collective action problems could arise in games other than the prisoner's dilemma [75n4], but their discussion of social dilemmas and free riding in Ch. 5 partakes exclusively of the prisoner's dilemma paradigm.) Green and Shapiro could argue that many rational choice theorists also make this mistake. Their literature review shows that many rational choice scholars share the view that rational choice theory predicts no voluntary contributions to public goods. But this only demonstrates that rational choice scholars can be wrong about their theory. What rational choice theory implies is a matter of logic, not of what claims well-known political scientists at high-status research departments have made in leading political science journals.

A Second Model of the Barge Parable

One rather artificial feature of the model developed so far is that each laborer faces the binary choice of exerting either zero or all-out effort. In practice, such choices are more continuous in nature. When the model is modified accordingly, the results correspond to those of the standard public goods game in public economics (see Samuelson 1954 and Hirshleifer 1983; see also Mueller 1989 for a survey). (The formal model and its solution are documented in Appendix II.)

Suppose each laborer can choose any hourly level of effort. The speed at which the barge moves is determined by the laborers' joint efforts: the number of hours it takes for the barge to arrive at its destination is a decreasing function of each laborer's level of effort per hour. Once the barge arrives at its destination, the laborers jointly receive a payment, which is shared equally. Each laborer's utility increases with his hourly rate of pay and decreases with the effort he exerts per hour. I assume that the marginal disutility of effort increases with effort.

For any one laborer, the individually rational level of effort maximizes his utility function subject to the constraint relating his efforts to the speed of the barge (which in turn affects his hourly rate of pay). The collectively optimal level of effort for each laborer maxmizes the sum of the laborers' utility functions subject to that same constraint. Both the individually rational and the collectively optimal levels of effort are strictly positive. But effort is undersupplied in equilibrium relative to the collective optimum. The reason is that the laborers don't take into account the positive externalities of their efforts on each others' utility levels. The individually rational and collectively optimal levels of effort are equal only if there is no free rider problem, which is the case if the number of laborers is equal to one. Green and Shapiro's zero-effort prediction, on the other hand, is obtained for the special (and empirically rather unrealistic) case in which that number is infinite.

Green and Shapiro's zero-effort prediction can also be obtained as a corner solution of my model if utility is linear in both pay and effort, and the relative weight placed on the effort term is sufficiently high. However, it is clear from Green and Shapiro's description of the problem that they regard the zero-effort outcome as the unique equilibrium that does not hinge on the *specific* functional form of the laborers' utility function.

The model allows us to conduct comparative statics on the number of laborers involved. The equilibrium level of effort decreases as that number increases. The model is thus consistent with the notion that smaller groups overcome the free rider problem to a greater extent than do larger groups—without resorting to group socialization effects and the like. This result is usefully contrasted with the comparative statics that are implicit in Green and Shapiro's assertion that the point-prediction implied by Olson's theory of collective action is zero effort (81); rather implausibly, they view this prediction as valid regardless of the number of laborers involved. A more careful reading of Olson would have yielded a comparative statics statement that is inconsistent with Green and Shapiro's interpretation of his theory: "the larger the group, the farther it will fall short of providing an optimal amount of a collective good" (Olson [1965] 1971, 35). Olson did not formalize his intuition, but he must have had in mind a public goods game similar to the one I develop above.

The implication that the severity of the free-rider problem increases with the number of individuals involved is consistent with standard laboratory experiments (see, for example, Darley and Latané 1968). Green and Shapiro mistakenly interpret such empirical findings as a rejection of rational choice:

> Another anomaly is that even though a social dilemma game features a dominant strategy, and thus any one person's actions should not be affected by the choices made by others, players are indeed sensitive to the behavior of others and to the condition of the collective good. (90–91)

Once again, their false conclusion follows from their erroneous belief that defection is necessarily a dominant strategy on the part of rational, self-interested individuals in collective dilemmas.

Cheap Talk and Cooperation

Similarly, Green and Shapiro list other empirical results as inconsistent with rational choice theory:

> From the standpoint of game theory, nonthreatening communication between players who are unable to make binding agreements should have no influence on cooperative behavior in social dilemma situations. . . . What in fact happens, however, is that experiments in which subjects are permitted to communicate generate much higher levels of cooperation than treatments in which communication is not permitted (Linder 1981). Dawes, McTavish and Shaklee (1977), for example, found that about 70 percent of the participants in eight-person, one-shot dilemmas defected when no communication was permitted, as opposed to 28 percent when communication was permitted. . . . Lest one think that what is going on reflects merely the process of becoming acquainted with others, growing to like them, and donating to newly acquired friends, Dawes et al. (1977) show that group conversation unrelated to the allocation problem at hand produces no increase in cooperation. That individuals who are allowed to communicate cooperate with others in their group, despite the incentive to defect, represents [an] anomaly. (89–90)

Well, not necessarily. Rational choice theory implies that pre-play communication cannot affect the outcome of a prisoner's dilemma game, in which each player's dominant strategy is to defect. However, there are many social dilemma situations in which communication can further cooperation.

Thomas Palfrey and Howard Rosenthal (1991a) have developed a formal game of costless communication prior to the costly contribution toward the provision of a public good. Consider the following numerical example.

A public good is provided if two out of three individuals contribute, in which case each individual gets a payoff equal to 1. Each individual has a cost of contribution that is randomly drawn from a uniform distribution defined over the interval [0,1.5]. She is privately informed about her cost. In the first period, each individual can costlessly send one of two messages, "C" (standing for "I will contribute") or "NC" (standing for "I won't contribute"). Individuals are not committed by their promises; that is, an individual who sends the message "C" may subsequently choose not to contribute, and vice versa. In the second period, each individual can choose to make a costly contribution to the public good, or she may refrain from doing so.

Clearly, individuals "babble" in some of the equilibria of this game; that is, each individual sends one of the two messages—"C" or "NC"—independently of her actual cost, and all other individuals rationally ignore this uninformative message. Thus, Green and Shapiro's intuition that nonthreatening, nonbinding communication has no impact on individuals' incentives to cooperate is valid in some cases.

But there are also informative equilibria. In them, an individual sends the message "C" if her cost lies below a cutoff point; otherwise, she sends the message "NC." The individuals' contribution strategies then depend on how many individuals previously announced "C." Each individual makes a costly contribution if her cost lies below a cutoff point whose value depends on how many individuals previously promised to contribute.

One such informative equilibrium (formally characterized in Appendix III) allows information about the distribution of costs to be transmitted by "cheap talk" (Farrell 1988; see also Crawford and Sobel 1982). In this equilibrium, the probability that the public good is provided is higher in the presence of cheap talk than if there is no possibility of communication.

Cheap talk, then, allows individuals to influence each others' contribution strategies and thereby affect the probability that the public good is provided. In the equilibrium under consideration, each individual makes the following tradeoff: by announcing that she will contribute, she increases the probability that the public good will be provided, but she also increases the probability she will be a member of the coalition that contributes. Individuals whom Nature assigned a low cost of contribution consequently have strict preferences to announce "C," while high-cost individuals strictly prefer to announce "NC." Costless communication thus has real effects on the probability that the public good is provided, even though individuals are not committed to keep their promises (and in many cases have incentives to deviate from their prior announcements).

At first glance, it seems reasonable to speak of people as "lying" or "reneging on their promises." But it is worthwhile noting that this terminology does not necessarily make sense in signaling games. Suppose we interpret the individuals' "C" and "NC" messages as standing for "my cost lies below the critical cutoff point" and "my cost lies above the critical cutoff point," respectively. Then the same equilibrium is played out in "real terms"—but now the individuals' messages are "sincere."

The public goods game analyzed above is not a pure prisoner's dilemma game. On the one hand, the individuals' behavior is subject to a conflict of interest—each of the three individuals would like to free ride on the contributions of the other two. But the individuals also have a common interest, namely to ensure that a coalition of two contributors is formed. Indeed, behind their veil of ignorance (that is, before they are privately informed about their individual-specific cost parameters), the three individuals would unanimously agree that the two who could do so at lowest cost should contribute to the public good. Since costs are unobservable, this prescription cannot be implemented in a straightforward way. However, communication allows for (imperfect) coordination, with the potential of decreasing the probability that too few or too many individuals contribute, increasing the probability that the two lowest-cost individuals contribute, and increasing the probability that the public good is provided.

In short, nonbinding, nonthreatening communication has the potential to affect individuals' contribution strategies in social dilemmas that are not prisoner's dilemmas, contrary to Green and Shapiro's claim that one factor

> that should *not* resolve a true social dilemma, according to rational choice accounts, [is] interpersonal communication. . . . Absent binding commitments, communication may be regarded with suspicion, since promises are presumably intended to deceive others into cooperating while one defects. (78)

Empirical findings that communication affects cooperation do not necessarily constitute a rejection of rational choice theory. To assess the empirical performance of rational choice theory, one would first have to examine whether the situation under consideration is a prisoner's dilemma. If it is, then Green and Shapiro are correct in identifying an anomaly. If it is not, then rational choice theory is qualitatively consistent with the data. To assess the empirical performance of rational choice theory more precisely, one would once again have to compare the quantitative predictions of the theory and the observed patterns of communication and contribution. Palfrey and Rosenthal (1991a) do so experimentally for the communication and contribution game described above, with mixed results.

In Green and Shapiro's defense, it could be argued that they were not aware of the Palfrey and Rosenthal (1991a) article (which is not cited in their bibliography). The failure to conduct a comprehensive literature review is not the most serious flaw of their work. More importantly, their misassessment of the potential of cheap talk stems from their unfortunate tendency to see prisoner's dilemmas behind every bush.

"The Paradox That Ate Rational Choice Theory"[3]

Green and Shapiro introduce their chapter on the problem of voter turnout with the following statement:

> Rational choice theorists have characterized voter turnout as a collective action problem in which individuals are asked to sacrifice time and transportation costs on behalf of a public good, the election of a particular candidate or party. Although rational citizens may care a great deal about which person or group wins the election, an analysis of the instrumental value of voting suggests that they will nevertheless balk at the prospect of contributing to a collective cause since it is readily apparent that any one vote has an infinitesimal probability of altering the election outcome. Why take the time to vote when the election outcome will be unaffected by one's ballot? Unless rational citizens find the act of voting gratifying—because, say, they enjoy democratic participation or seek the status rewards of being seen at the polls—they will abstain and foist the costs of voting onto others. (47)

Green and Shapiro thus claim that rational choice predicts zero turnout. This is indeed the prediction of some early, and rather primitive, rational choice models of voting (see, for example, Riker and Ordeshook 1968). The decision-theoretic logic of these models is based on an exogenously given probability of being decisive that is taken to be very small. This logic becomes questionable once it is recognized that the probability of being decisive depends endogenously on the number of voters turning out. Green and Shapiro correctly summarize the game-theoretic critique of the early rational choice voting literature:

> The probability of casting a decisive ballot, which appears as an independent variable, is in turn a consequence of the decision to vote. If many people vote, one's chances of being decisive are trivial; if this reasoning leads others not to vote, then one's own vote will prove decisive (Meehl 1977). (57)

It follows that for some nonempty set of strictly positive costs of voting over two distinct alternatives, zero turnout is not an equilibrium: each individual would want to deviate from the equilibrium prescription of abstention.

John Ledyard (1984) shows that for some nonempty set of strictly posi-

144

tive costs of voting over two distinct alternatives, equilibrium turnout will be strictly positive. Even though this insight might be considered a banal result, it was an important theoretical breakthrough given the flawed—but widely accepted—logic of earlier rational choice models suggesting that rational and self-interested individuals will always abstain from voting if participation is costly.[4]

Ledyard's positive turnout result shifts the terms of the debate. The question is no longer: Is rational choice theory logically consistent with the observation of positive turnout? We now know that rational choice theory is qualitatively consistent with the observation that people turn out in elections. But Ledyard's work left several questions unanswered. Is rational choice theory logically consistent with the observation of large turnout? Even if it is, is the rational choice "explanation" of large turnout empirically relevant? Does it have testable implications that can guide empirical work? How well does the rational choice approach do when compared to competing approaches?

The second breakthrough in the game theory of electoral participation came with Palfrey and Rosenthal 1985. Here the authors proved that for a nonempty set of strictly positive costs of voting, there exists an equilibrium for which participation rates approximate one hundred percent—even if voters are purely self-interested and the electorate is "very large." (This high turnout equilibrium coexists with a low turnout equilibrium.) Their result relies on the assumption that voters are completely informed about each others' preferences and costs of voting. Under incomplete information, the unique equilibrium involves vanishingly low (albeit strictly positive) turnout numbers.

Thus, the question of whether rational choice theory is logically consistent with the observation of high turnout can be answered in the affirmative: the high turnout equilibrium is one of multiple equilibria in the complete information case. It exceeds the compass of this article to summarize the intuition underlying Palfrey and Rosenthal's complex model in any detail. For the skeptical reader, I offer one example that builds on the threshold model developed earlier so as to demonstrate that a rational choice model can, as a matter of principle, be logically consistent with high participation rates even if the electorate is very large (see also Palfrey and Rosenthal 1993). Because of its simplicity, the example I give is highly artificial. It is advanced to prove a theoretical point and not meant to be of empirical relevance. The reader who would like to understand how the high turnout equilibrium obtains in a more realistic model is referred to Palfrey and Rosenthal 1985.

Suppose there are 50 million voters who get a payoff equal to 1 if candidate A wins and 0 otherwise, and 50 million voters who receive a payoff equal to 1 if candidate *B* wins and 0 otherwise. Let the cost of voting (*C*) lie strictly between 0 and .5. The voters' decisions are made simultaneously. The candidate who gets a simple majority of the vote wins. In the event of a tie, the election winner is determined by the toss of a fair coin.

First, it is useful to check whether zero turnout is an equilibrium. Suppose the equilibrium prescription is for all voters to abstain. Then the election winner is determined by a toss of the coin, and the expected payoff to each voter is .5. A voter who deviates from the equilibrium prescription and votes for his preferred candidate would receive the payoff (*1* − *C*), which is greater than .5. Given that all other voters are expected to abstain, each voter is better off deviating. It follows that zero turnout is not an equilibrium.

Next, let us check whether universal turnout is an equilibrium. Suppose each voter's equilibrium strategy is to turn out and vote for his preferred candidate. Correspondingly, each voter believes that all other voters will turn out. Then the election ends with a tie: each candidate gets 50 million votes. The winner is determined by a toss of the coin, so the expected payoff to each voter is (.5 − *C*). A voter who deviates from his equilibrium strategy and abstains would break the tie. As a consequence, his preferred candidate would lose. The payoff of deviating is 0, which is smaller than (.5 − *C*). Thus, the voter has no incentive to deviate from his equilibrium strategy. Moreover, the voters' belief that everybody will turn out is consistent with their equilibrium turnout behavior. It follows that universal turnout is an equilibrium. (This equilibrium coexists with a mixed strategy equilibrium in which some voters may abstain.) The universal turnout result hinges on the assumption that each candidate has the same number of supporters. More generally, turnout approximates 100 percent if the two sides are not too unequal (Palfrey and Rosenthal 1993).

In the end, the winner is determined by a random toss of the coin, and each voter's expected payoff is (.5 − *C*). The voters would be better off if they could credibly commit to abstain, in which case the winner would also be determined by a random toss of the coin, but each voter's expected payoff would be .5. In a one-shot game, the cooperative outcome of universal abstention is unachievable: due to the competitive nature of the game, the voters are trapped into playing an equilibrium with costly participation (Palfrey and Rosenthal 1983).

This example demonstrates that rational choice theory is, in principle, consistent with the implication of high turnout. Moreover, it illustrates the illogic of equating voter turnout with cooperation and voter abstention with lack of cooperation, as Green and Shapiro do when they misclassify the problem of voter turnout as a prisoner's dilemma (75).

Nevertheless, there is still some question about whether the rational choice explanation of voter turnout is empirically relevant. Palfrey and Rosenthal showed that under incomplete information, voter turnout is vanishingly low if the electorate is large. Clearly, incomplete information about voter preferences or voting costs is a closer approximation to reality than is the complete information assumption. Palfrey and Rosenthal conclude that

> in very large electorates the only voters are citizens with net positive benefits from the act of voting, citizens whose sense of duty outweighs any cost in voting. We have come full circle and are once again beset by the paradox of not voting. (64)

Palfrey and Rosenthal thus establish the empirical irrelevance of rational choice theory (defined narrowly as a theory that does not allow for noninstrumental motivations) as an explanation of high voter turnout. This does not imply that their formal model is worthless. It identifies precisely which assumption drives the low-turnout result. From a theoretical perspective, we only now fully understand the precise nature of the paradox of voter turnout. The rational choice literature on this paradox is an excellent example of intraparadigm critique and debate leading to intellectual progress.

Does the rational choice analysis of electoral turnout generate empirically testable hypotheses that can usefully guide empirical work? One variant of the Palfrey and Rosenthal model assumes that voters are incompletely informed about each others' costs of voting. These costs range from some negative value to some positive value; that is, some voters have negative costs of voting, while others have positive costs of voting. Since negative costs of voting are formally equivalent to positive costs of not voting, one interpretation of the Palfrey and Rosenthal model holds that voter turnout is partly motivated by citizen duty. Given my narrow definition of rational choice theory, I would not classify such a model as a pure rational choice model; it is a hybrid in which some individuals have noninstrumental motivations, but all individuals respond rationally to incentives. (However, positive costs of not voting may also arise when abstentions are sanctioned by the state or by interested groups. In this case, the Palfrey and Rosenthal model would fulfill the definition of a pure rational choice model, suggesting that its classification as a hybrid model is rather tenuous.)

In general, the comparative statics derived from rational choice models of electoral turnout do well when tested empirically; that is, changes in electoral turnout vary systematically with changes in key parameters (the costs of voting, the polarization of the candidates' policy positions, the size of the electorate, the closeness of the election, and the like), as predicted by the theory. Grofman 1994 concludes that rational choice models can usefully guide empirical work if we restrict attention to their comparative statics "at the margin" instead of their point predictions.

Together with Stephen Hansen, Palfrey and Rosenthal (1987) tested their hybrid model using electoral turnout numbers in budget referenda for Oregon school districts, with good results. The equilibrium conditions from the voting game were used to estimate the distribution of net voting costs across individuals, making use of turnout data from a cross-section of constituencies that varied in size. Hansen, Palfrey, and Rosenthal's estimate of the average cost-benefit ratio of voting allows for some "back-of-the envelope" calculations suggesting that the average cost of voting corresponded to an after-tax wage of about $5.00 per hour (30). They found that many voters appeared to vote for instrumental reasons. Their most interesting conclusion, however, was that the size of the electorate had no independent explanatory power for turnout, once one controls for the free-rider problem of participation, as prescribed by the theory. In other words, the fundamental rational choice calculus of voting does not appear to differ across electorates of different size: "Any sociological distinctions between large groups and small groups," the authors conclude, "appear to be largely captured by our model of the free rider problem" (31). This finding undermines one tenet of "partial universalism," namely that the explanatory power of the rational choice approach is greater when the theory is applied to small-group settings than to mass phenomena. It is worthwhile noting that strong empirical findings of this kind are possible only because the theory places strong restrictions on the data.

Earlier, I agreed with Green and Shapiro that a rational choice explanation that invokes noninstrumental motivations is worthless to the extent that its primary goal is to save the rational choice paradigm. This is not the goal of Palfrey and Rosenthal's hybrid model; after all, their theoretical analysis ultimately rejects rational choice theory (narrowly defined) as an explanation of voter turnout. Instead, their model generates a set of empirically testable predictions. From an empirical perspective, its status as a hybrid rational choice model is irrelevant. The important question is how well the hybrid model does relative to its competitors. It obviously does better than a pure rational choice model that is inconsistent with observations of high turnout (at least under plausible conditions, such as incomplete information). But the hybrid model also does better than non-rational choice models that rely exclusively on noninstrumental motivations, on sociodemographic characteristics of the electorate, or on economic conditions. Such models do not explain why electoral turnout varies systematically with voters' participation incentives.

With some qualifications, I agree with Green and Shapiro's recommendations for empirical rational choice scholarship:

The coherence and explanatory power of [rational choice] models could be enhanced if the commitment to universalism were discarded in favor of what we have termed partial universalism, or the view that rational maximizing is but one of several factors at work in the turnout decision and that the influence of strategic considerations is likely to vary across people and decision contexts. Although a synthesis of different theoretical perspectives entails a sacrifice in terms of theoretical parsimony, it offers a number of advantages. First, the coherence of rational choice theory would be improved by placing such phenomena as adherence to norms of civic duty or expression of partisan enthusiasm into a separate explanatory category from that of the more manifestly instrumental motives, such as the desire to reap the expected benefits of casting the decisive vote or the aversion to wasting time waiting in line. Sharpening the theoretical boundaries in this way helps reduce the conceptual strain that occurs when seemingly habitual, expressive, or rule-directed behaviors are forced into an interpretive scheme that recognizes only utility maximization. Second, a more synoptic view of the causal process that governs the decision to vote could enable rational choice scholars to move beyond interminable post hoc theorizing about why so many people vote to more nuanced and informative research. . . . Freeing rational choice theorizing from the requirement that each facet of the explanation be consistent with utility maximization and the convention that a single (read parsimonious) decision calculus applies to all citizens provides researchers with greater latitude to anticipate [novel facts]. (69–70)

At first glance, scholars who follow Green and Shapiro's recommendations are vulnerable to their question, "What observation would in principle be inconsistent with a theoretical framework that allows for post hoc insertion of idiosyncratic tastes, beliefs, and probability assessments as explanatory devices?" (69). However, the Hansen, Palfrey and Rosenthal analysis demonstrates that rational choice theory can place meaningful and testable restrictions on the data even if voters are partly motivated by citizen duty. Similarly, Palfrey and Rosenthal (1991b) rely on rational choice theory to map out systematic deviations of observed behavior from the predictions of the theory. In doing so, they successfully discriminate between the hypotheses that individuals are altruistic and that they systematically misassess the probability that their contribution to a collectively valued enterprise is decisive.

I strongly disagree with Green and Shapiro when they belittle the theoretical contribution of rational choice scholarship to the paradox of voter turnout as "ethereal speculation about why rational citizens vote" (71). Even though they review the relevant decision- and game-theoretic literature, they fail to appreciate the subtleties of the argument sketched above. For example, after reviewing Ledyard's positive turnout result, Green and Shapiro comment:

Over the years, many scholars (e.g., Schram [1991]) have announced with great satisfaction that their models of rational behavior predict "positive turnout." This seems to be an especially popular claim to make in abstracts to articles (e.g., Feddersen 1992; Morton 1991). Of course, the domain of positive numbers (integers, really) encompasses quite a wide range of potentially observable outcomes. Notably, authors seem reluctant to commit to any such very positive number as 104,000,000, roughly the number of voters nationwide who cast ballots in the 1992 national election. Perhaps this is because it is not clear from the models themselves whether voters will outnumber, say, exit pollsters. (57n16)

The reason rational choice scholars continue to emphasize the positive turnout implication of their models is that many political scientists still erroneously assume that rational choice theory *necessarily* predicts zero turnout. Amazingly, Green and Shapiro belong to this group, even though they should know better:

Many forms of collective action, including voter turnout, share the general characteristics of a Prisoner's Dilemma game. . . . In the language of game theory, it is said that defection represents a "dominant strategy." (75)

In other words, Green and Shapiro do not appear fully to understand the implications of the game-theoretic models of voter turnout they summarize. Ledyard's positive turnout result is clearly inconsistent with their (false) claim that the problem of voter turnout has the characteristics of a prisoner's dilemma, in which zero turnout would be the unique equilibrium.

While one may question Green and Shapiro's understanding of rational choice theory, one can hardly object to their desire to see how well the theory describes political reality. Political science would have been well served had Green and Shapiro directed their efforts toward the empirical testing they call for, rather than toward a literature review attempting to demonstrate the pathologies of rational choice theorists.

APPENDIX I

A public good is provided if n out of n individuals contribute. Their contribution decisions are made simultaneously. If the public good is provided, each individual receives a benefit whose value is normalized to 1. For each individual, the cost of contribution is equal to C, where $C < 1$.

The symmetric mixed strategy equilibrium of this game requires each individual to contribute with probability p, where p solves the indifference condition

$$b(n - 1; n - 1, p) = C, \qquad (1)$$

and $b(a_1; a_2, a_3)$ is the binomial probability that a_2 Bernoulli trials lead to a_1 successes when the probability of a success is given by a_3. The probability that the public good is provided is given by $b(n; n, p)$, where $0 < b(n; n, p) < 1$.

For example, in the case of $n = 7$ and $C = .3$, the individual probability of contribution is given by .818, the probability that the public good is provided by .245.

The model is now modified as follows. The public good is provided if k out of n individuals contribute to the public good. In this case, the symmetric mixed-strategy equilibrium requires each laborer to contribute with probability p, where p solves

$$b(k - 1; n - 1, p) = C. \qquad (2)$$

The public good is then provided with probability

$$\sum_{v=k}^{n} b(v; n, p), \text{ where } 0 < \sum_{v=k}^{n} b(v; n, p) < 1.$$

For example, in the case of $n=7$, $k=5$, and $C=.3$, there are multiple solutions. In one of these, the individual probability of contribution is given by .746, the probability that the public good is provided by .748.

APPENDIX II

There are n laborers indexed $i = 1, \ldots, n$. Each laborer can choose his hourly level of effort e_i from the real line; that is $e_i \in [0, \infty)$. (The assumption that effort can take on any value between zero and infinity is made for simplicity only. The model is easily modified to allow for a finite-valued ceiling for effort. Such a modification would complicate my argument without leading to any qualitatively interesting insights.)

The speed at which the barge moves is determined by the laborers' joint efforts: the number of hours H it takes for the barge to arrive at its destination is a decreasing function of each laborer's level of effort per hour. For concreteness, I assume a specific functional form for this relationship:

$$H = 1/(e_1 + e_2 + \ldots + e_n). \qquad (3)$$

This functional form has the appealing property that the barge never arrives at its destination if all laborers choose to exert zero effort ($H = \infty$);

whereas it arrives instantaneously if one or more laborers choose to exert infinite effort ($H = 0$).

Once the barge arrives at its destination, the laborers jointly receive a payment that is normalized to 1. They share this payment equally; that is, each laborer gets $1/n$. His pay per hour of effort is thus $1/n$ divided by H, that is, $1/nH$.

Each laborer's utility increases with his hourly rate of pay and decreases with the effort he exerts per hour:

$$U_i = 1/nH - 1/2\ e_i^2. \tag{4}$$

The quadratic term reflects the assumption that the marginal disutility of effort increases with effort. This assumption is made to avoid corner solutions—all laborers choosing zero or infinite effort—that would result if utility were linear in both hourly pay and effort. Without loss of generality, the effort variable is premultiplied by one-half to simplify the first-order condition.

Substituting the constraint (3) into the utility function (4) yields

$$U_i = (e_1 + e_2 + \ldots + e_n)/n - 1/2\ e_i^2. \tag{5}$$

The first-order condition for laborer i's maximization problem is given by

$$\partial U_i / \partial e_i = 1/n - e_i = 0. \tag{6}$$

The individually rational level of effort is thus given by

$$e_i^* = 1/n. \tag{7}$$

The collectively optimal level of effort solves the first-order condition

$$\partial \sum_{i=1}^{n} U_i / \partial e_i = 1 - e_i = 0, \tag{8}$$

resulting in

$$e_i^{**} = 1. \tag{9}$$

The individually rational level of effort e_i^* is thus positive; but a comparison of the individually rational and collectively optimal levels of effort, e_i^* and e_i^{**}, shows that effort is undersupplied in equilibrium: $e_i^* < e_i^{**}$. These two levels of effort are identical only if $n = 1$, that is, if there is no free-rider problem. Green and Shapiro's zero-effort prediction, $e_i^* = 0$, is obtained for $n = \infty$.

The model allows us to conduct comparative statics on n:

$$\partial e_i^*/\partial n < 0. \tag{10}$$

The equilibrium level of effort thus decreases as the number of laborers increases.

APPENDIX III

A public good is provided if two out of three individuals contribute, in which case each individual gets a payoff that is normalized to one. Each individual i has a cost of contribution c_i that is randomly drawn from a uniform distribution defined over the interval [0,1.5], where $i = 1,2,3$. Each individual is privately informed about her cost. In the first period, each individual can costlessly send one of two messages, "C" (standing for "I will contribute") or "NC" (standing for "I won't contribute"). Individuals are not committed by their promises; that is, an individual who sends the message "C" may subsequently choose not to contribute, and vice versa. In the second period, each individual can choose to make a costly contribution to the public good, or she may abstain from doing so.

One informative equilibrium of this game has the following structure. In the communication stage of the game, individual i sends the message "C" if her cost c_i lies below the cutpoint $\hat{c}$, $0 < \hat{c} < 1$; otherwise she sends the message "NC." In the contribution stage of the game, the individuals' strategies depend on how many individuals previously announced "C." Individual i makes a costly contribution if her cost c_i lies below the cutpoint $\tilde{c}_j$, where j is the number of individuals who sent the message "C" in the communication stage.

The equilibrium cutpoints $\hat{c}$, $\tilde{c}_0$, $\tilde{c}_1$, $\tilde{c}_2$ and $\tilde{c}_3$ solve

$$\hat{c} = \tilde{c}_2, \tag{11}$$

$$b(1; \ 2, \ \tilde{c}_2/1.5) \ (1 \ - \ \tilde{c}_2) \ + \ b(2; \ 2, \ \tilde{c}_2/1.5) \\ [b(2; 2, \tilde{c}_3/\tilde{c}_2) - 1] = 0, \tag{12}$$

$$\tilde{c}_3 = b(1; 2, \tilde{c}_3 / \tilde{c}_2), \tag{13}$$

$$\tilde{c}_0 = \tilde{c}_1 = 0. \tag{14}$$

Equations (11)–(13) imply that

$$\hat{c} = \tilde{c}_2 = .724. \tag{15}$$

$$\tilde{c}_3 = .462. \tag{16}$$

Given the individuals' communication and contribution strategies, the public good is provided with probability

$$b(2; 3, \tilde{c}_2 /1.5) + b(3; 3, \tilde{c}_2 /1.5) \, b(2; 3, \tilde{c}_3 /\tilde{c}_2) = .411. \tag{17}$$

It is useful to compare the equilibrium outcome that obtains if there is no possibility of communication. In this case, one of multiple equilibria requires individual i to contribute if her cost c_i lies below the cutpoint c^* and abstain otherwise, where c^* solves

$$c^* = b(1; 2, c^*/1.5), \tag{18}$$

or, equivalently,

$$c^* = .375. \tag{19}$$

The public good is then provided with probability

$$b(2; 3, c^*/1.5) + b(3; 3, c^*/1.5) = .016. \tag{20}$$

NOTES

1. In this essay I use the expressions "game theory" and "rational choice theory" interchangeably.
2. It is worthwhile noting that another frequently cited explanation of why people are able to overcome collective dilemmas is inconsistent with the rational choice paradigm: the notion that individuals contribute to a collective enterprise because they overestimate the probability that their contribution is decisive. Opp (1989) provides evidence suggesting that political activists and non-activists have heterogeneous beliefs about this probability: activists are more likely to believe that political engagement can make a difference. From the perspective of rational choice theory, this finding appears to constitute an anomaly. However, I have developed a rational choice model of collective action that implies heterogeneous beliefs about the probability that an individual action will be decisive, consistent with Opp's evidence (Lohmann 1993).
3. Fiorina 1990, 334.
4. Ledyard's insight was obscured by some unfortunate modelling choices. In

passing, Ledyard established the positive turnout result for elections with two distinct alternatives. But he then argued that the policy positions of competing candidates would converge to the median voter's position, in which case voter turnout would drop to zero, given the lack of distinct alternatives.

James Bernard Murphy

RATIONAL CHOICE THEORY
AS SOCIAL PHYSICS

Donald Green and Ian Shapiro discover a curious gulf between the prestige of rational choice approaches and the dearth of solid empirical findings. But we can understand neither the prestige of rational choice theory nor its pathologies unless we see it as a variant of the equilibrium analysis found in physics, economics, and biology. Only such a global perspective on rational choice theory will reveal its core assumptions and the likely shape of its future in political science. In this light, the growing dominance of rational choice theory in political science is all but inevitable and its pathologies are all but inescapable.

In their recent book, *Pathologies of Rational Choice Theory*, Donald Green and Ian Shapiro carefully document various rhetorical strategies employed by rational choice theorists to immunize—if I may reverse the medical metaphor—their hypotheses from hazardous contact with empirical pathogens (i.e., data). These strategies range from the "high theorists'" sublime disdain for the empirical to their colleagues' desperate attempts to modify, or to restrict the domain of, hypotheses in danger of disconfirmation. The empirical world is such a "buzzing, blooming confusion" that even carefully designed experiments rarely produce unambiguous results; in many cases we cannot trust what we think we see right in front of us. It is not surprising, then, that all theoretical enterprises build in some degree of protection from what are aptly called the brute facts. If these self-immunizing strategies are indeed pathologies and if, as we shall see, they are

James Bernard Murphy, Department of Government, Silsby Hall, Dartmouth College, Hanover, NH 03755, thanks James Shoch for his helpful comments and suggestions.

pervasive in microeconomics, evolutionary biology, and even physics, then one might justifiably wonder where to look for healthy science. Is the advancement of knowledge promoted best by researchers who limit their claims to what is empirically warranted, or by researchers who dogmatically push a theoretical program ahead, damning the torpedoes? Green and Shapiro seem to prefer the former; we may often be stuck with the latter.

Given the gap between the enormous prestige of rational choice approaches and the rather meager empirical success of these approaches, Green and Shapiro (195) are right to insist that "the widespread influence of rational choice models in political science calls for an explanation." Indeed, some defenders of rational choice argue that the empirical success of rational choice approaches *must* be substantial; otherwise, the high standing of these approaches within the discipline would be inexplicable (195)! When challenged to furnish evidence of these empirical breakthroughs, however, rational choice theorists in political science will often refer to alleged successes in economics or biology (180). "It may be," Green and Shapiro write, "that we are witnessing a curious phenomenon in which rational choice theories are fortified in every discipline by reference to their alleged successes elsewhere, when a more global view of things would reveal the emperor to be, if not entirely naked, somewhat scantily clad" (180). The disciplinary focus of their book prevents them from exploring this "global view." This is unfortunate: such a view is necessary if we are even to attempt to understand the inevitable rise of rational choice theory in political science, the ubiquity of its vices, its underlying assumptions, and its future course.

Political Economics or Political Physics?

Green and Shapiro reiterate conventional accounts of rational choice as the use of microeconomic analysis in the explanation of political behavior. Voters are consumers; politicians are entrepreneurs; *homo oeconomicus* is everywhere—in the voting booth and the legislature as well as the shopping mall (1, 194). There is no doubt that the proximate cause of most rational choice models was microeconomics and that the founders of rational choice approaches in political science were economists. By borrowing the methods of economics, political scientists also borrowed the prestige of economics. But the ultimate source of rational choice approaches to political science is physics. Microeconomics simply lifted equilibrium analysis, utility maximization, and the accompanying systems of differential equations and matrix algebra directly from the classical mechanics of pre-entropic energy physics. By borrowing the methods of physics, economists also borrowed its prestige. Some rational choice theorists understand that their theories of political behavior are metaphorical: by microeconomic analogy, voters are metaphorical consumers, policies are metaphorical commodities, and so on. What is rarely grasped is that these economic theories are themselves metaphors: *homo oeconomicus* is a particle, the commodity-space is a force field, utility is energy, disutility is work, force and marginal utility are vectors, energy and utility are scalars, the component force along an axis in equilibrium is the price of a commodity in equilibrium, and so forth (for details see Mirowski 1989). In short, rational choice theory only seems to be based on an analogy between economic man and political man, between voting and consuming; ultimately, rational choice theory is based on an analogy between the issue-space of political deliberation and the vector-space of classical mechanics, between the trajectory of agenda-setting and the trajectory of particles.

We cannot begin to understand the prestige, the assumptions, and the pathologies of rational choice theory until we see it as a version of social physics. Rational choice theory is one variant of a much larger research program of equilibrium analysis that applied nineteenth-century energy mechanics first to engineering, then to microeconomics, then to biology, then to operations research, and now to political science. Indeed, virtually every discipline that aspires to the mantle of science does so by adopting the paradigm of classical mechanics. As we shall see, rational choice theory, neoclassical economics, and evolutionary biology all borrowed not just the mathematical formalisms of physics, but an entire theoretical apparatus, an entire set of assumptions, aspirations to predictive determinism—and characteristic pathologies. At the theoretical core of this research program is the *extremal* principle that the objects of inquiry behave in such a way as to maximize or minimize the values of certain variables. The calculus of maxima and minima that makes possible the description of physical equilibria was developed, for just that purpose, by Leibniz and Newton. Thus, it cannot be said, as it often is, that rational choice theory finds its origins in the work of Hobbes, Grotius, or even Bentham.[1]

Not only does the hierarchy of all sciences rest on the degree of their similarity to physics, but developments in physics continue to call the shots in other disciplines—consider the recent spread of chaos and catastrophe theory from mathematical physics to biology to economics.[2] In fact, one of the newest theoretical statements of a version of rational choice theory (Satz and Ferejohn 1994) signals a transition from the analysis of individual particles in classical mechanics (methodological individualism) to the analysis of gases in statistical thermodynamics (structuralism). If you think that this analogy with physics is far-fetched, consider this statement: "Rational choice theory can be applied wherever there is patterned behavior:

for example, it can be applied to the behavior of gas particles when heated, and to the behavior of the temperature of a room when someone enters" (ibid., 75n). When Green and Shapiro (ix, 10) applaud the scientific aspirations of rational choice theory, this must, I suggest, imply the aspiration to imitate physics.

What does it mean to imitate physics? Certainly not the slavish pseudophysics of the nineteenth-century energetics movement, in which the language of energy, force-fields, electricity, and magnetism were used to describe economic and political phenomena. Rather, like neoclassical economics, there must be a translation of the concepts of mechanics into a familiar disciplinary lingo expressing a new interpretation of physical laws and principles, so that, for example, the conservation of energy becomes the conservation of utility plus expenditure. What counts is not a theoretical approach that explicitly apes physics, but one that embodies a set of differential equations and variational principles describing a system in equilibrium.

Why imitate physics? Because ever since the seventeenth century, physics has been the exemplar of scientific inquiry. If you want to convince a community of inquirers that you have a viable research program, what could be more rhetorically effective than imitating physics? But I do not wish to suggest that the imitation of physics is necessarily an explicit strategy to maximize some agenda; the role of physics as a regulative ideal in scientific explanation is largely a tacit one. By proposing the move from an individualist to a structuralist model of rational choice theorizing, Debra Satz and John Ferejohn may not have deliberately intended to replicate the transition from classical to statistical mechanics, but their comment about the behavior of gases nicely reveals the tacit program.

What strikes Green and Shapiro as an overweening aspiration for a universal theory of politics seems more understandable if the enterprise is really social physics. Seeing rational choice theory as social physics helps account for the paradox that the prestige of equilibrium models in political science does not depend upon empirical success in political science (nor even in economics). Rational choice theory borrows its prestige from the theoretical, empirical, and technological success of classical mechanics. When rational choice theorists appeal to explanatory success in evolutionary biology or in microeconomics to defend equilibrium analysis, what they are really appealing to is not biological theory or economic theory per se, but rather the deployment of physics by those disciplines.

Moreover, seeing rational choice theory as social physics helps differentiate the core theoretical assumptions of the model—the ones that are derived from physics—from the peripheral assumptions that come and go. Green and Shapiro focus on the latter, namely, assumptions about rationality, choice, and individual agency; but the core assumptions of equilibrium analysis require no reference to these. Unless we understand these core assumptions, we will never make sense of the paradox that some versions of rational choice theory jettison all assumptions about rationality, choice, and individual agency. Nor will we understand why attacks on rational actor assumptions about human psychology, about agency, about rationality have, over the course of a century, led to nothing more than a dialogue of the deaf. A focus on the core assumptions of equilibrium analysis reveals that a social physics need not make any assumptions about human nature, human psychology, and rationality.[3] Human beings, for the purposes of social physics, are particles moving through a commodity or issue space along a path defined by the constrained maximization of utility. The "rationality" of rational choice actors has about as much content as the rationality of the mass-point in a force field; after all, classical mechanics in physics used to be called "rational" mechanics. Both the actor and the mass-point are only metaphorically rational in the sense that their behavior maximizes some function and moves, in conjunction with other forces and within constraints, toward some kind of predictable equilibrium.

Why should physics take note of the pseudo-scientific findings of psychology or the speculation of philosophers? Sophisticated economists warn against giving utility any psychological interpretation; and Satz and Ferejohn (1994) argue that rational choice explanations do not rest on any psychological or philosophical view of rationality. Indeed, they argue further that rational choice theories are likely to be strongest where actors are so constrained that they do not make choices. Equilibrium analysis in political science could well move to a statistical or population mechanics, perhaps leaving the study of individual choice to another science. If rational choice theory really is social physics then one would expect it gradually to lose interest in rational choice.

A Theology of Equilibrium Analysis

The rhetorical strategies of many rational choice theorists reveal a deeply held faith in their research program: a faith that social and political behavior must, at bottom, be tractable to the mechanics of equilibrium analysis. Green and Shapiro call this global faith into question by asking what empirical findings can be adduced to support it. Now in the case of certain logical and mathematical truths, belief in their truth is perfectly rational even when direct evidence seems to contradict them. If you show me two balls in each hand and then combine them to yield three balls, I will doubt my eyes before I abandon my faith in arithmetic. The question is: in the absence of either logical necessity or compelling empirical evidence, what accounts for the prestige of equilibrium analysis and the seemingly unshakable faith of many proponents?

Two core assumptions of classical mechanics help account for its status as a paradigm of knowledge and its diffusion into evolutionary biology, operations research, engineering, economics, and political science. These assumptions underpin all equilibrium analysis. First, classical mechanics demonstrates the optimality of nature. The trajectories of particles always minimize some quantity; nature is perfectly efficient in this Leibnizian best of all possible worlds. Second, classical mechanics makes prediction possible by abstracting causal relationships from the path-dependence of history; hence the Laplacian dream of perfect knowledge of the future based on present conditions alone. In equilibrium mathematics, all motion is optimally efficient—indeed, without extremal principles, equilibrium analysis could not yield point predictions. And through differentiation, the historical path of a particle has no bearing on its force or, in equilibrium, its position.[4] Thus, the mathematics of equilibrium analysis is not some neutral formalism that can be deployed to describe any set of theoretical assumptions about causal relations. The calculus of extremal principles was designed to describe the behavior of mass-points and forces in a vector space; it can be used to describe the behavior of voters and consumers only insofar as their behavior is analogous to the mechanics of particles.[5] A rigorous evaluation of rational choice theory would require a detailed examination of the analogies and disanalogies between political behavior in an issue space and particle behavior in an energy field.

The metaphysical assumptions behind classical energy physics were theological in origin. The calculus of variational principles derived from Leibniz's conviction that the world is the optimal solution to a problem in constrained maximization. Laplace's influential vision of perfect predictive determinism derived from his understanding of divine omniscience. Although the seventeenth century prided itself on its rejection of Aristotelian teleology, early modern physics was profoundly teleological in structure. Just as Aristotle had insisted that nature makes nothing in vain, so modern physicists insisted that nature economizes in its expenditure of motion and energy.

The conceptual apparatus and first formalization of these principles in the calculus of maxima and minima have their origins in Leibniz's theodicy. There has always been a tension between the Christian faith in God's benevolence and the empirical reality of evil and suffering. Leibniz saw a solution to this quandary in the calculus of constrained optimization (see Elster 1975, 34, 110). Not all the aspects of the best imaginable world are compossible: the maximum of order is constrained by the maximum of diversity, for example. God's challenge is to maximize the net goodness of the world by jointly optimizing order and diversity. Anticipating the logic of microeconomic analysis, Leibniz even describes God as an entrepreneur who allocated resources in such a way as to create the maximal goodness with the minimal expense (Elster 1975, 34, 181).[6]

Leibniz's metaphysics, physics, and calculus were developed by his friend, Maupertuis, into the principle of least action, according to which all motion in nature follows the path of least action. That is, motion seeks to minimize the product of time and distance (Maupertuis [1744] 1964, 55, 68). It is widely agreed that the principle of least action has been one of the most fruitful generalizations in the history of physics—in part because it has admitted of a variety of theoretical interpretations. It can be found today in the Lagrangian formulation of quantum mechanics. Physicists differed, of course, about whether nature was "really" optimally efficient, or if this teleology was merely a fiction required by the mathematics of equilibrium analysis.

Ironically, the teleology of classical mechanics made even more intuitive sense in its application to the analysis of economic and political phenomena: if particles seek maximal efficiency, why not assume that people do, too? If physical systems achieve a balance of forces in a stable equilibrium, why not assume that markets or legislatures can? All explanation presupposes some kind of order in the world; the order of least action—of stable equilibria defined by the calculus of extremal principles—is an optimal order in many senses of the word optimal.

In Leibniz we also find the origin of the other fundamental dimension of equilibrium analysis: the emancipation of prediction and explanation from historical time. Indeed, the differential calculus was developed precisely to enable physicists to measure velocity and acceleration at a given instant—that is, with no reference to the past trajectory of the body in question. In a revealing passage, Leibniz extends his analysis from the physical to the social:

> In effect, time contributes nothing to this estimate. Looking at a body of a given mass and a given velocity, cannot one estimate its force without knowing in what time frame and by what path it had perhaps acquired the velocity it has? It seems to me that one can judge here by the present state alone without knowing the past . . . [otherwise] it would be as if one said that a man is richer because he had spent more time earning the money. (Cited in Elster 1975, 164; my translation.)

Leibniz's foray into social physics is, as we shall see, unfortunate; it turns out that consumer behavior cannot be predicted on the basis of current income alone. Old money really is different from new money. But Leibniz's commitment to the ideal of explanation as a system of equations of state, abstracted from historical time and path, continues to be the ideal of all equilibrium analysis.

The most famous description of the regulative ideal governing all explanation in physics, natural or social, is that of Laplace:

> An intelligence knowing all the forces acting in nature at a given instant, as well as the momentary positions of all things in the universe, would be able to comprehend in one single formula the motions of the largest bodies as well as of the lightest atoms in the world, provided that its intellect were sufficiently powerful to subject all data to analysis; to it nothing would be uncertain, the future as well as the past would be present to its eyes. (Laplace 1820, cited in Nagel 1979, 281n)

In short, classical mechanics promised human beings an approximation of divine omniscience. Only God, being outside of time, was thought to be able simultaneously to grasp past, present, and future. No need, then, to study the origins, development, growth or historical path of an entity: just describe its initial state, the structure of the field in which it moves, and its conditions of equilibrium, and proceed to predict or retrodict.

Within physics, however, the Laplacian ideal had to be severely restricted due to the discovery of entropy, hysteresis (casual relations dependent upon history), and indeterminacy. There are many examples of hysteresis in human affairs as well (see Elster 1976). James Duesenberry, for example, has demonstrated the hysteresis of consumer behavior. One cannot predict current spending and saving behavior on the basis of current income alone, since people strive to maintain the standard of living to which they have become accustomed (Duesenberry 1952, 85). Paul Samuelson said that to introduce hysteresis into equilibrium analysis "takes the subject out of the realm of science into the realm of genuine history" (cited in Mirowski 1989, 390). Samuelson's comment suggests why equilibrium analysis continues to inspire such faith, hope, and love: the alternative is to reduce social science to mere history!

That real physics can admit the existence of hysteresis while its imitators cannot is just one of the ironies of the social dynamic of physics envy.

Pathologies of Equilibrium Analysis

In every field of application, beginning with physics, the Leibnizian and Laplacian ideals of optimal order and perfect predictive determinacy, as embodied in a set of differential equations joined to some variational principle, developed pathologies similar to those described by Green and Shapiro. Philip Mirowski points out that in nineteenth-century physics we find: "assertions that it did not matter what the actual process underlying a theory was; the demotion of intuitive plausibility as a criterion of theory choice; increasing denial of direct sensory access to the workings of phenomena; that formalization and quantification came to be embraced for their own sake; and that technical utility became more admissible as a positive criterion for theory choice" (Mirowski 1989, 27). Many of these pathologies grew out of the difficulties of framing a conservation principle to serve as a fixed benchmark against which physical transformations could be measured. In the nineteenth century, the teleology of least action was applied to energy. God so designed nature that energy could never be created or destroyed, but only transformed and communicated. This assumption seemed to be at odds with the experimental findings of energy dissipation. Eventually, the laws of thermodynamics (and a new statistical mechanics) reconciled experimental findings with the teleological principle of conservation of energy: energy was conserved, but not necessarily in a usable form—despite the fact that energy had previously been defined as the capacity to do work. Here we see the usual pattern in equilibrium analysis: when a hypothesis or theorem is confronted with intractable contrary evidence, falsification is avoided by skillful modification (ibid., 11–98). However, physicists saved the principle of the conservation of energy by developing a whole new theoretical context within which it could be preserved. This was no mere exercise in curve-fitting.

Social physics continues to be dominated by the pre-entropic energy physics of the middle of the nineteenth century, before statistical mechanics, before hysteresis, before indeterminacy—in short, before classical mechanics abandoned its universal aspirations and became limited to particular domains of inquiry, and before physics evolved in radically new directions. In social physics, by contrast, we see a case of arrested development—it is still, for the most part, 1870. Perhaps this is what Norbert Wiener meant when he said of economists that they imitated the trappings of physics but never understood the intellectual attitudes behind the trappings (Mirowski 1989, 357).

It is not quite accurate to say that neoclassical economics borrowed or adapted classical energy physics; neoclassical economic theory just *is* that borrowing and that adaptation. The three simultaneous discoverers of neoclassical theory, Jevons, Walras, and Menger, all discovered it in the energy physics of their engineering textbooks of the 1870s. Utility was now located neither in the commodity nor in the consumer, but in the energy that linked consumer to commodity in the commodity space. (It is thus misleading to describe theirs as theories of subjective utility). In partial equilibrium analysis, consumers conveniently maximize this utility function until they come to rest at the point where it meets the budget constraint. In general equilibrium analysis, a hypothetical auctioneer jointly optimizes all preferences against all constraints, through mathematical mysteries independent of temporal or path-dependent processes. Of course, there were concerns that utility could not be directly measured, and debates over whether it should be understood ordinally or cardinally. Paul Samuelson sought to escape from these disputes through his theory of revealed preference. Observed choices, however, can hardly ground a preference ordering which is then used to explain those choices. If choices change over time, is it evidence of inconsistency or of changed preferences?

Satz and Ferejohn (1994) concede the weakness of rational choice theory to predict the choices of consumers or voters, admitting that equilibrium analysis may work best where individual action is severely constrained, as in the case of the behavior of firms or parties. Yet when economists have examined actual price-setting behavior to test the hypothesis that firms maximize dollar returns, they have discovered that firms not only do not know their schedule of optimal prices, but that they tend to set prices based on unit costs plus a customary markup—in many cases, truly suboptimal behavior. Milton Friedman defends neoclassical analysis against such findings by insisting that firms *must* behave as if they were maximizing returns; otherwise, they would be driven out of business by "natural selection" (Friedman 1953b). In the presence of such logical truths, what force do mere facts have? Alexander Rosenberg shows that Friedman's claim is either false or vacuous:

> Is the hypothesis that returns are maximized over the short run, the long run, the fiscal year, or the quarter? If we make the hypothesis specific enough to test, it is plainly false. Leave it vague and the hypothesis is hard to test. (Rosenberg 1994, 391)

Friedman's attempt to deploy natural selection in defense of his faltering microeconomic theorem buttresses Green and Shapiro's contention that rational choice theories tend to be fortified by reference to their alleged successes in other disciplines.

Although economics was the first to claim scientific status by imitating physics, evolutionary biology also borrowed the prestige of physics by adopting equilibrium analysis. In the 1930s, R. A. Fisher showed that the equation governing the change of gene frequencies at a single locus with two alleles under natural selection could be expressed as an extremum principle: The Fundamental Theorem of Natural Selection. George F. Oster and Edward O. Wilson (1984, 272) cite the comment that "physics-envy is the curse of biology" and then add: "This has been nowhere more true than in evolutionary theory." The "adaptationist program" of "optimization models" that has dominated Anglo-American evolutionary theory for the past 50 years is nothing more than the constrained optimization mechanics of nineteenth-century physics partially modified by linear programming research (Oster and Wilson, 1984). One begins with the Leibnizian assumption that God created nature optimally: natural selection carefully designs every trait of an organism to optimize fitness, constrained only by the optimal fitness of every other trait. Since not all optimal traits are compossible in one organism, even suboptimality is explained by the law of optimality, just as evil is explained by the constraints on God's quest for maximum goodness. The research design closely parallels linear programming analysis in engineering and operations research. Having identified a problem facing an organism, such as its need to forage for food or to defend itself from predators, a behavioral or morphological trait is then designated as the solution. In the words of Oster and Wilson (1984, 273), the biologist "plays God" by creating an optimal design for the trait and then comparing it to nature.

Here we see that the teleological assumption of optimal design removes history from evolutionary theory: just as the adaptiveness of organisms to their niche was once thought to reflect the wisdom of God, now it is said to reflect the wisdom of natural selection. The adaptationist program in evolutionary theory, as a variant of equilibrium analysis, predicts (or rather retrodicts) future states from present knowledge of the organism and its environmental constraints. Organisms are not understood as the product of a unique path of historical inheritance, but as solutions to current problems. Thus, even natural history can only aspire to scientific legitimacy by denying that time plays an important role in the explanation of evolution. "The crucial difference between engineering and evolutionary theory is that the former seeks to design a machine or an operation in the most efficient form, while the latter seeks to infer 'nature's design' already created by natural selection" (Oster and Wilson 1984, 272). Optimization theory achieves this result by using the mathematics of equilibrium analysis: a state space, a set of strategies, one or more optimization criteria (or fitness functions), and a set of constraints (ibid. 1984).

The optimal design is then compared to nature. "If the two correspond, then nature can be regarded as reasonably well understood. If they fail to correspond to any degree (a frequent result), the biologist revises the model and tries again" (Oster and Wilson 1984, 273). At first blush this may seem like sound scientific procedure, but let us consider. If the two correspond, then nature is understood: does this mean that nature is merely correctly predicted, or that it is actually explained? It cannot mean the latter, for the correspondence might be due, not to adaptation to the current constraint, but to fortuitous pre-adaptation to an entirely different constraint. Feathers might be predicted as an ideal solution to the aerodynamics of flight, but we know that they evolved for warmth (Rosenberg 1985, 243). Only knowledge of the specific historical path of a species can distinguish current adaptation from fortuitous pre-adaptation. On the other hand, when the optimal model does not correspond to nature, Oster and Wilson concede that an exercise in curve-fitting is customary, ensuring that whatever empirically observed trait we choose will be guaranteed to be the optimal solution to some set of equations and constraints.

In one amusing example of ingenious ad hoc hypothesis-modification, a biologist named Orians calculated the optimal size of food items for a bird that must search for and catch prey and return with it to the nest. To explain the failure of the model accurately to predict the actual size of food items, Orians hypothesized that the birds spend less time searching for optimal prey than they should because of the competing demand to visit the nest often enough to discourage predators. The optimality of the foraging behavior is constrained by the optimality of the defensive behavior: we return to Leibnizian theodicy. "By allowing the theorist to postulate various combinations of 'problems' to which manifest traits are optimal solutions, the adaptationist program makes of adaptation a metaphysical postulate, not only incapable of refutation but necessarily confirmed by every observation" (Lewontin 1984, 244). John Maynard Smith defends optimization models despite the force of this critique. While conceding that ad hoc modifications of models is common even in his own work, he insists that this procedure is legitimate so long as one admits that the first version has been disconfirmed. "What is not justified is to modify the model and at the same time to claim that the model is confirmed by observation" (Smith 1984, 297). But given the bias in all fields against publishing negative results, how are we to check the temptation to prepublication curve-fitting designed to modify one's model to the point where one can claim in print that it has been confirmed?

Like the most resourceful rational choice theorists, Smith has another fallback position: if equilibrium analysis does not yield accurate point predictions, then at least claim an accurate marginal prediction. Unfortunately, however, optimization theorists, whether in economics, biology, or political science, often "move seamlessly between point predictions and marginal predictions" (Green and Shapiro 1994, 41) without admitting that they are conveniently lowering the threshold of empirical confirmation. For example, Smith (1984, 297) suggests that Orians can rescue his original model, which failed as a point prediction, if it "fits more closely in species less exposed to predation," that is, if the vector of marginal adaptiveness has the right direction.

It never occurs to Smith or other optimization theorists to consider the rival hypothesis that perhaps the behavioral or morphological trait in question may not be adaptive at all, let alone optimally so. This would require that one confront the conviction that this is the best of all possible worlds and the presupposition that the point of science is to demonstrate that the world is optimally ordered, rather than asking whether it is.

Green and Shapiro (195) point out that equilibrium analysis flourishes in the most data-poor environments; in data-rich environments, it becomes all too obvious either that the description of initial conditions is false and misleading or that historical factors offer compelling rival hypotheses. There are few areas of science as poor in evidence or experiment as evolutionary biology: our record of the evolutionary processes responsible for the genotypical and phenotypical traits we see today is remarkably paltry; our experimental evidence for evolutionary processes, beyond the artificial selection of animal breeders, is almost nonexistent (Lewontin 1984, 243; Rosenberg 1985, 169ff). In the absence of much data, the temptation to Panglossian speculation about the optimal adaptiveness of any imaginable aspect of behavior or morphology is often irresistible. An especially remarkable example comes from the sociobiology of homosexuality. Since the homosexual act is not optimally reproductive (at a minimum), the existence of homosexual tendencies has long been thought to be a quandary for evolutionary theory. However, since all apparent anomalies are mere puzzles for equilibrium theorists, a solution had to be found. Armed with the theorem of inclusive fitness, sociobiologists hypothesized that homosexuals must have played the role of maiden aunts, promoting the maximal reproduction of their close kin by caring for their children— even though there is no evidence that homosexuals have fewer children than heterosexuals, now or in the past (see Kitcher 1985, 243–52). As with legislative cycling, the theory explains phenomena we have no reason to believe actually exist.

Critics of optimization theories in biology, such as Stephen Jay Gould and Richard Lewontin, may have some useful lessons to teach critics of rational choice theory. Instead of focusing on the peripheral assumptions of equilibrium, they go directly to the core assumptions: that equilibria are optimal solutions to some problem, and that explanation and prediction can proceed without reference to historical processes. Like Green and Shapiro, Gould and Lewontin (1984) suggest that middle-level theories about phyletic inertia, genetic drift, and developmental constraints in embryology should supplant universalist theories of evolution. Their detailed factual knowledge of natural history, population genetics, zoology, and embryology enables them to show that there are many features of evolution that are non- or suboptimally adaptive, and that many of these phenomena can be explained only by reference to the historical processes of phyletic inertia, genetic drift, random catastrophe, preadaptation, and so forth. If the first question to be asked of optimization theory is whether the phenomenon to be explained (such as legislative cycles) is a real problem or an artifact of the theory, the second is whether the trait selected as the locus of optimization (for example, a decision rule) is in reality isolatable from its context; the human chin, for example, turns out to be not a distinct structure but a byproduct of the interaction of the alveolar and mandibular growth fields (Gould and Lewontin 1984). The third question is whether the trait in question (for example, a committee system) maximizes some function or is simply a result of changes in scale. For example, between species of primates, tooth size increases more slowly than does body size, so that large primates have proportionately smaller teeth than small primates—not because of adaptation, but merely because of the laws of allometry (Lewontin 1984). The fourth question is whether a trait that has been shown to be optimally adaptive in its current environment (e.g., a seniority system) can be explained by its current utility, or whether it is the product of an historical inheritance that fortuitously preadapted it to its current function.

It is ironic that equilibrium theorists in microeconomics (Alchian 1950; Friedman 1953b) and in rational choice theory (Satz and Ferejohn 1994) appeal to adaptationist evolutionary biology in the attempt to bolster their own research programs. The poor predictive power of equilibrium analysis in economics and political science will hardly be remedied by appeal to evolutionary biology, which "is itself bereft of strong predictive power. . . . Evolutionary biology has no striking retrodiction to its credit"(Rosenberg 1994, 384, 388). It is noteworthy that equilibrium theorists almost never appeal to *nonadaptationist* biological theories, such as Gould's—doubtless because they look more like history than physics. Instead, economists and rational choice theorists inevitably gravitate toward what is "scientific," even if dysfunctional.

By invoking biology, a social physics can easily dispense with psychology and with individualism. Thus Friedman (1953b) uses natural selection to explain why individual firms must maximize their returns regardless of the actual psychological motivation of the firm's decision makers—just as the psychological states of organisms play no role in their survival. Alchian (1950) paralleled the development of physics from classical to statistical mechanics in abandoning neoclassical methodological individualism, in recognition of the fact that Darwinian theory is most useful when focused "on populations large enough that statistical regularities in responses to environmental changes can be discerned" (Rosenberg 1994, 392). Abstracting from individual behavior entirely, Alchian developed a population replacement theorem that sought to explain fitness purely in terms of the statistical survival ratios of different firms.

Satz and Ferejohn's recent version of rational choice theory similarly appeals to natural selection so as to justify dropping psychology and methodological individualism (1994, 81). Natural selection, they contend, will provide the predictive success that eludes other versions of rational choice theory: "We can predict the behavior of an organism by assuming that, within constraints, it will behave in ways that will maximize its expected reproductive output" (81). It is worth noting, first, that Satz and Ferejohn do not successfully rise above methodological individualism. The statistical study of gene frequencies in population genetics does not, in fact, tell us how any individual organism will behave. More importantly, to have predictive power, evolutionary theory would have to draw on knowledge of all the environmental problems that impinge upon the reproductive success of an organism, since each environmental problem will be a constraint on the solution to every other problem. Such a knowledge of initial conditions surpasses even the dreams of Laplace. Moreover, "even if we can identify an adaptational problem and most of the constraints against which a solution can be found, it is unlikely that we will be able to narrow the range of equally adaptive solutions down to just the one that animals actually evince" (Rosenberg 1994, 390). There is always more than one way to skin a cat; no possible set of constraints eliminates all degrees of freedom. According to Rosenberg, these problems have hobbled optimality analysis in evolutionary theory and equilibrium analysis in economics. "What we want to know," he writes, "is which features of organisms increase their fitness, and which strategies of economic agents increase their returns" (1994, 391). Yet neither biologists nor economists have been able to identify the necessary or sufficient requisites for survival within a given environment (even assuming a stable environment); and even if they had, one wonders how one could usefully distinguish among the many different equally adaptive features and strategies.

The Future of Equilibrium Analysis in Political Science

At bottom, Green and Shapiro accuse rational choice theory of hypocrisy: with indignation and occasional sarcasm they seem to delight in pointing out the yawning chasm between the ambitious claims to the virtues of science and the vices of actual research practices. Since hypocrisy is the homage vice pays to virtue, Green and Shapiro seem confident that some rational choice theorists, now chastened, will mend their hypotheses and confront empirical data honestly and without subterfuge (196–202). Indeed, they point out that some recent empirical applications of rational choice theory seem to promise a higher standard of methodological behavior by framing hypotheses that admit of disconfirmation and by making serious efforts at data collection and measurement. Accordingly, Green and Shapiro offer recommendations designed to promote methodological pluralism and a scaling back of universalist ambitions.

From a global perspective, however, Green and Shapiro's hopes for a pluralistic, cooperative, and problem-driven equilibrium research agenda in political science appear unduly optimistic. For such a perspective suggests that the pathologies Green and Shapiro describe, rather than being "rooted in the ambition to come up with a universal theory of politics" (202), stem from the Laplacian ambition to achieve a universal explanation of *everything*. In the words of two historians of physics:

> There is the fascination always associated with a closed system capable of posing all problems, provided it does not define them as meaningless. Dynamics is such a language; being complete, it is by definition coextensive with the world it is describing. It assumes that all problems, whether simple or complex, resemble one another since it can always pose them in the same general form. Thus the temptation to conclude that all problems resemble one another from the point of view of their solutions as well, and that nothing new can appear as the result of the greater or lesser complexity of the integration procedure. (Prigogine and Stengers, cited in Mirowski 1989, 73)

The universalist aspirations of rational choice theory are not merely the personal aspirations of various theorists; rather, rational choice theory's universalism is driven by the long-term historical project of the unification of the sciences. Admonitions to surrender such vaulting ambition will not alter the objective hierarchy of the sciences—a hierarchy that inexorably inspires all sciences to mold themselves in the image and likeness of physics.

What about Green and Shapiro's hope that equilibrium analysts will "resist the theory-saving impulses that result in method-driven research" (203)? What about the hope, in short, that we can rid equilibrium analysis of its characteristic pathologies? Based on the empirical evidence of the deployment of this theory in physics, economics, and biology, these pathologies seem virtually inescapable. According to Rosenberg, rational choice theorists, by employing theory-saving strategies to resist falsification, "are only doing what every rational scientist who embraces a theory must do: They are attempting to apply it and are treating its problems as puzzles to be solved, not anomalies that refute the approach" (Rosenberg

1985, 238). Indeed, the pathologies of rational choice theory are deeply and inescapably rooted in the fundamental logic of all extremal theories: for instance, like rational choice theory,

> the theory of natural selection treats the objects in its domain as behaving in such a way as to maximize and/or minimize the values of certain variables. This strategy is especially apparent in Newtonian mechanics when that theory is expressed in so-called extremal principles, according to which the development of a system always minimizes or maximizes variables that reflect the physically possible configurations of the system. . . . Thus, we hold that a system always acts to maximize the value of a mechanical variable. If our measurements of the value of that variable in an experimental or observational setting diverge from the predictions of the theory and initial conditions, we never infer that the system is failing to minimize the value of the variable in question. Rather, we assume that our specification of the constraints under which it is operating is incomplete. (Rosenberg 1985, 238)

Given the way economics and biology have manifested the logic of extremal theories, it seems likely that rational choice theorists will forge ahead, continuing to exhibit all the disdain for apparent disconfirmation attacked by Green and Shapiro. But if Green and Shapiro's dicta are unlikely to produce a falsification of equilibrium analysis, they may help us to discern where or when it is in trouble. What Green and Shapiro call pathologies might better be called symptoms; they are signals that something is amiss. Whether the underlying illness is chronic or merely acute, only time will tell. But similar symptoms of equilibrium theory in distress have spurred biologists and economists to look for and to discover important nonadaptive and path-dependent historical processes.

Green and Shapiro conclude by urging a hybrid theorizing that combines elements of rational choice theory with other modes of explanation. "The question would change from 'Whether or not rational choice theory?' to something more fruitful: 'How does rationality interact with other facets of human nature and organization to produce the politics that we seek to understand?'" (204). This is a very attractive vision of a cooperative pluralism; but it seems to contradict the totalizing logic and mathematics of every extremal theory. Other "facets of human nature or organization" modify such an extremal theory only by imposing further constraints on the maximization of the value of the variable in question. What this means is not modification but merely recalibration. Extremal theories are uniquely resistant to modification and hybridization:

> Now all theories are strictly unfalsifiable, simply because testing them involves the employment of auxiliary hypotheses. But extremal theories are

not only insulated against strict falsification, they are also insulated against the sort of falsification that usually leads to modification of theories instead of auxiliary hypotheses. . . . With these theories, the choice is always between rejecting the auxiliary hypotheses—the description of test conditions—or rejecting the theory altogether. For the only change that can be made to the theory is to deny that its subjects invariably maximize or minimize its chosen variable. This, of course, explains why high-level extremal theories like Newtonian mechanics are left untouched by apparent counterinstances. (Rosenberg 1985, 239)

Attempts to modify equilibrium analysis in rational choice theories have been largely comic: if we find that people are ignorant, then ignorance is optimally rational, given the costs of information; if we find that people are impulsive and passionate, then passion and impulse are optimally rational, given the costs of deliberation; if we find that people act out of habit, then habits are optimal decision strategies, given the costs of thought; and so on. These auxiliary theorems modify rational choice theory in the sense that a cat is modified by the mouse it eats. Given the totalizing logic of extremal theories, perhaps the best that can be hoped for is a competitive, rather than a cooperative, pluralism. After all, the dogmatic and method-driven program of equilibrium analysis in economics and biology has not suppressed—indeed it may have greatly stimulated—a wealth of counter-equilibrium research. What this means is that rational choice theory is not likely to be deployed over many domains in conjunction with other theories, enacting what Green and Shapiro call "partial universalism"; rather, it is more likely to be hermetically sealed in a particular domain of political behavior, leading to what Green and Shapiro call "segmented universalism" (26–27). One plausible kind of segmented universalism is that outlined by Satz and Ferejohn (1994), in which rational choice theory becomes a statistical mechanics that explains the behavior of populations but not of individuals.

Because of their disciplinary focus on political science, Green and Shapiro pay more attention to the peripheral assumptions and auxiliary hypotheses of rational choice theory than to the core mathematical and theoretical logic of equilibrium analysis. Yet rational choice theory is evolving before our very eyes; already some versions are shedding their references to individuals, to reason, and to choice. What equilibrium analysis in political science will be called in the future cannot be guessed; but its evolution will be driven more by its core logic than by its optional claims about human nature, motivation, or reason. Nor is it possible to guess what research program might eventually replace equilibrium analysis.

But it is safe to assume that so long as the study of politics aspires to be a science, it will aspire to a political physics.

NOTES

1. Green and Shapiro speak of "the embryonic rational choice arguments of Hobbes (who assumed that individuals maximize power) and Bentham (who assumed that they maximize pleasure)" (18). It is true that Hobbes attempted to ground his political analysis in the physics of his day, but that was a Cartesian mechanics that lacked the extremal principles of equilibrium; Bentham was a chemist who never mastered Newtonian mechanics. Thus the claim that they were maximizers is anachronistic: I know of no place where Hobbes says that individuals maximize power; and Bentham says that the legislator *ought* to maximize utility, not that individuals *do* maximize utility.

2. The story of Benoit Mandelbrot's fractal geometry is fascinating in light of the inescapable social logic of physics envy. Although Mandelbrot's study of fractals grew out of his work in economics, economists showed no interest in his theories or techniques until they had been deployed by physicists. As one eminent economist explained to him: "*No* mathematical technique ever becomes prominent in orthodox [read, neoclassical] economic theory without having first proved itself in physics." (Cited in Mirowski 1989, 387.)

3. Satz and Ferejohn (1994, 75n) claim that a behavioral theory may be able to dispense with the consistency conditions of preference ordering, undermining even a "thin" conception of rationality.

4. The core mathematics of the analysis of equilibrium in dynamics is the calculus of variational principles. Beginning with some quantity or conserved function of a quantity, we ask: Where does the first variation (often the first derivative) equal zero? The answer tells us where the quantity or function is at a local maximum or minimum, that is, where the function is stationary, which is crucial for identifying equilibria. An extremal principle is a special case of a variational principle and uses the second variation of the quantity or function to test whether the maximum or minimum is global or merely local. The use of extremal principles in physics evolved from the law of least action, to Lagrangian multipliers, to Hamiltonian dynamics. For technical details, see Mirowski 1989, 11–98.

5. A leading neoclassical theorist (Koopmans) first describes mathematics as a conceptually neutral formalism, and then goes on to observe: "A utility function of a consumer looks quite similar to a potential function in the theory of gravitation" (Mirowski 1986, 185). So the differential calculus of neoclassical analysis gives us an accurate description of utility insofar as utility resembles potential energy.

6. Critics of the Leibnizian assumption that this is the best of all possible

worlds often refer to his teleology as "Panglossian," after Voltaire's famous satirical attack on Leibnizian theodicy. I do not use this pejorative term to refer to the assumption that an equilibrium state is optimal out of respect for the religious convictions of equilibrium analysts in economics, biology, and political science.

Peter C. Ordeshook

ENGINEERING OR SCIENCE:
WHAT IS THE STUDY OF POLITICS?

Green and Shapiro's argument that rational choice theory is too inattentive to substantive matters is well taken. However, their suggestions for future research are unlikely to generate what they seek: an empirically relevant, coherent theory of political processes and a rational choice paradigm that accommodates other perspectives. To achieve this end, we require a clearer understanding of the practical objectives of our discipline and of the difference between modelling and theorizing about politics, and between science and engineering. Until the "engineering" component of the discipline assumes a more central role, research—whether theoretical, empirical, or any combination of the two—will continue to generate an incoherent accumulation of theorems, lemmas, correlations, and "facts."

In *Pathologies of Rational Choice Theory* Donald Green and Ian Shapiro have issued an important challenge to rational choice theorists: produce more substantively relevant work, or move aside and make room for other paradigms. Any number of responses are possible, including arguing that the research they criticize is already driven by substantive concerns. Certainly we can anticipate the rejoinder, "Show us a viable alternative!"

My argument here is different. Green and Shapiro's critique, although sometimes incomplete and inaccurate, nevertheless seems to me largely correct: the substantive relevance of much formal rational choice analysis

---

Peter C. Ordeshook, Professor of Political Science, Division of the Humanities and Social Sciences, California Institute of Technology, Pasadena, CA 91125, telephone (818) 395–4478, telefax (818) 405–9841, is most recently the author of *Game Theory and Political Theory* (1986), *A Political Theory Primer* (1993), and *Lessons for Citizens of a New Democracy* (1995).

is tenuous, and its empirical content lacks coherence. Even the treatment of such basic matters as voting, committee agendas, and spatial conceptualizations of preferences are confounded by dubious assumptions and often wholly irrelevant analyses. However, the remedies Green and Shapiro offer are no more likely to move us toward a useful understanding of politics than is the vast majority of research found in the current political science literature, regardless of the paradigm to which that literature corresponds.

The core of my argument is this: Green and Shapiro, rational choice analysts, and most other political scientists fail to distinguish between science and engineering—that is, between the discovery of first principles and the identification of the empirical generalities to which they pertain, on the one hand; and, on the other, the resolution of practical issues. Too many rational choice researchers try to do science when "engineering" better describes their goal. The failure to make this distinction leads to research that does not identify first principles, isolate empirical phenomena that warrant empirical generalization, delineate phenomena that are manifestations of complex interdependent processes, develop expertise that has practical relevance, or refine our ability to predict something other than gross or trivial events.

There are exceptions to our assertion. Donald Horowitz's (1991) use of what we know about parties and electoral rules shows the practical application of some macro-political ideas to ethnically divided states. William Riker's (1982) discussion of populist democracy provides both a warning about naive political "reforms" and insights into the practical side of social choice theory. Steven Brams's advocacy (e.g., 1980) of approval voting, although sometimes tinged with ideological excess, has compelled dissenters from his view to advance our understanding of electoral systems other than simple majoritarian ones. And Elinor Ostrom's (1990, 1992) analyses of the different ways people solve specific "commons" problems points to a research agenda in which public choice theory, game theory, and hard field research interact to deepen our understanding of the design of political institutions. For the most part, though, rational choice fails to do much more than refine theoretical results of dubious import or, when it is explicitly empirical, merely report regression coefficients or other statistical relationships consistent with the unsurprising idea that people act in their self-interest when it is important for them to do so.

My discussion has three parts. First, I show that both science and engineering are essential to the development of worthwhile theories. Second, I illustrate the problems of rational choice research and Green and Shapiro's misperceptions of its most fruitful avenues by reconsidering two of the topics they assess: voting and spatial models of elections. Finally, I consider why, in political science at least, there are few incentives to proceed in a more useful way; and I offer some suggestions about alternative research agendas that might move us closer to a science of politics.

Science vs. Engineering

Judging by the frequent use of the word, it would seem that political science suffers from too much, not too little "theory." Innumerable texts refer to theories of international affairs, political development, democratic transition, elections, voting, party formation, cooperation, federalism, and war. Notwithstanding our willingness to attach the word *theory* to vague frameworks, ad hoc hypotheses, and journalistic interpretations of events, it is silly to suppose either that theory in any rigorous sense can be formulated in the near future, or that each subfield warrants separate theoretical treatment.

Developing theoretical principles in the social sciences, as elsewhere, begins with the identification of empirical regularities that require explanation. Unfortunately, few regularities describe international affairs, political development, comparative politics, or elections. Are the regularities that concern us the fact that nations sometimes go to war and sometimes do not; that some nations are stable democracies and others are not; that some people vote and others do not; that coalitions in some parliaments are stable while in others they are not; that variable X explains Y percent of the variance of Z, or that X and W explain a bit more?

Despite our propensity to characterize our efforts as tests of some theoretical hypothesis, most of the empirical research that fills our journals is a search for regularities that warrant theoretical treatment. Is there a correspondence between the number of political parties and elections in single-member plurality-rule districts? Is there a correlation between turnout and the competitiveness of elections? Can the preferences of voters and legislators be usefully described by a spatial construction? What relationship exists between domestic politics and the likelihood that nations will go to war? Is there a relationship between the relative power of states and the character of alliances? Are presidential systems more stable than parliamentary ones? Is there a pattern to when legislators vote strategically? What characterizes federal states that survive, as opposed to those that do not? How does the internal organizational structure of a legislature relate to electoral and constitutional environments?

If research into these questions constitutes theory testing, then what propositions are we subjecting to refutation? Aside from particular hypotheses, the natural rational choice candidate is the hypothesis that people act, consciously or unconsciously, to ensure that Nash equilibrium outcomes (or equilibrium outcomes of some other type) prevail. After all, game-theoretic notions of equilibria lie at the heart of any rational choice explanation: they define what we mean by rational. But nearly all empirical studies can be criticized as providing too crude a test of this hypothesis to allow for definitive conclusions. Few if any studies control or measure the relevant parameters—the prior beliefs of subjects about other people's preferences, their perceptions about the game people are playing, and their beliefs about beliefs and perceptions. And few rational choice models encompass even a small fraction of the factors we believe influence strategic choice and the content of equilibria.

Without a consensus about the regularities that warrant theoretical treatment, theorizing too easily becomes an exercise in curve fitting—of structuring variables in mathematical form to fit some empirical fact, real or imagined. The flexibility afforded by our ability to offer a game-theoretic model consistent with nearly any stylized "fact"—to construct deductive models that render nearly any outcome an equilibrium of some type—results in a plethora of alternative mathematical models. Thus, as Green and Shapiro note, candidates are predicted to converge under one set of assumptions, to diverge under another set, and for yet another set we cannot say whether convergence or divergence will result, since no equilibria of the usual sort exist. Since these structures too often exceed our ability to discriminate among them empirically, we cannot say whether one class of assumptions is better than another, and the discipline of political science bases its evaluation of them on their mathematical elegance, the complexity of their notation, the journals in which they appear, or simply the reputations of those who design them.

This is not to say that formal theorists have not been successful in isolating important parts of political processes and providing us with useful findings about them. We know, for instance, how certain types of agendas can induce different outcomes, how strategic voting can mute the influence of agendas, and why models that assume complete information are a theoretical discontinuity compared to their incomplete-information variants. We can abstractly characterize the circumstances under which coalitions are stable and unstable, legislative vote trading is profitable, or the precise form of a winning coalition is immaterial to final policy. Abstract analysis has also allowed us to learn how information and beliefs can influence strategic decisions, how planning horizons influence short-term strategic considerations, how reputations are formed, how constitutional provisions can be self-enforcing, and the circumstances under which deception is and is not a viable strategy.

However, driven by the demand for empirical relevance, we too quickly try to convert nearly any abstract result into an empirically meaningful *model*. Although we should legitimately be impatient with analyses that include such statements as, "Assuming an infinite sequence of elections," or "We offer here a model in which there exists an equilibrium such that," it is also incorrect to insist that our analytic explorations should have an immediate empirical payoff. Consider Richard D. McKelvey's (1976, 1979) proof that if preferences are spatial and the restrictive conditions for a Condorcet outcome are not satisfied, then the social preference ordering is wholly intransitive. Although this result only establishes the properties of the majority relationship under one abstract circumstance, treating it as a *model* leads to the common misinterpretation that agenda setters can do whatever they want, that anything can happen under majority rule, or that there is an inherent uncertainty in majoritarian processes. It is as though researchers have deliberately ignored McKelvey's (1979) own admonition that "attempts to construct a positive descriptive theory of political processes based on majority rule . . . must take account of particular institutional features of these systems" (1979, 1106).

This rush to judgment occasions a second problem. Just as we fail to distinguish the identification of generalizable empirical phenomena from the estimation of parameters in particular contexts, we too often fail to distinguish between model and theory, and between a model's particular implications and more general theoretical propositions. Many essays list a dozen or so highly limiting assumptions, but label each implication a "theorem"—as though such labeling can resurrect lost generality. Models are not theories; they are abstract recreations of some specific, real situation or process, and by themselves they cannot uncover or even represent general theoretical propositions. Their mathematical manifestations are often merely playful exercises designed either to check the implications of some assumption, or to see if some new concept can generate an unanticipated result. To the extent that we incorrectly label models "theories," we deprive ourselves of the full benefits of both. Conflating "theory" with a model devised to fit some fact diverts us from following up on the modelling exercise by producing generalizations and discovering fundamental theoretical propositions.

Although the absence of this follow-up is the basis of their critique, Green and Shapiro sometimes participate in the confusion of models with theories. But even if this confusion is resolved, we next encounter the problem that the empirical contexts of our research are vastly more complicated than are those of even the most daunting engineering task. Analysis of even "simple" things like a legislature's action on some bill should, in principle, take account of strategic manipulations of the agenda, the perceived consequences of the bill's details, each legislator's beliefs about the votes of others and the responses of constituents, the efforts of party leaders within the legislature, and expectations about the response of the president and the bureaucracy. Election processes, democratic transitions, and international affairs are more complex still.

In the face of such complexity, how do we proceed without a delineation of generalized phenomena and a clear demarcation between theory and model? The answer must begin with the realization that, despite its theoretical pretensions, political science is a practical field. We seek not only to understand political things, but also to improve the operation of political processes and institutions. We seek to understand how democracy works, for instance, so we can try to make it work better or make it work in previously authoritarian states. We study international affairs not because war amuses us, but because we want to learn how to avert conflict. This is why, as James L. Sundquist (1988) put it, "informed judgments are needed based on the best methods of analysis that are available, as rough as those methods may be." Once this admonition is extended to all fields, the importance of policy analysis to the development of theory becomes evident.

A practical orientation suggests that we should not search for singular "theories" of specific political processes, or even for some all-encompassing theory of such processes. Nor can we test general principles by focusing on these processes. Just as, say, aeronautical or environmental engineers know that their efforts must be informed by research in more basic fields like physics, chemistry, and biology, and that the use of the principles that make up those fields relies as much on experience and artfulness as anything else, students of politics must encourage more interaction between theoretical and applied enterprises.

More often than not, this interaction will not require a strictly mathematical, deductive structure. Deductive analysis has its limits. Developing more comprehensive models that treat the full complexity of politics will necessarily require long strings of ad hoc assumptions and qualitative analysis. If we try to maintain deductive rigor, the requirements of tractability will draw us away from comprehensive reasoning. Moreover, regardless of the mathematical rigor of our models, we need to drop the view of science as an enterprise directed by academics armed with theorems and lemmas or by experimentalists scurrying about in white smocks. Science proceeds less coherently, through induction and inference, informed by attempts to be practical and to manipulate real things, where those manipulations rely as much on experience, intuition, and creative insight as on theory. Out of such a process come ideas about what is generalizable, what is best understood by existent theory, and what is an anomaly that warrants further investigation.

When an engineer designs a bridge, he draws on multiple layers of substantive knowledge about the strengths of materials, how forces distribute themselves in accord with elementary Newtonian theory, and which approximations are critical and which are not. No one derives or deduces that design. It is impossible to put all the theoretical "pieces" together into one theoretical analysis (although computer-assisted design can augment the engineer's skill with complex models specific to the task at hand). The design of a bridge emerges as much from the inventiveness and skill with which the engineer combines his expertise as anything else. And if the bridge falls into the river, post mortems search for the things that were not fully anticipated so as to refine subsequent designs and, if necessary, to inform later scientists and engineers about what was not anticipated.

Bridge-building has been a human preoccupation for so long that it no longer feeds the development of basic science. But it did once. Today, that role is played by other practical enterprises, such as developing new drugs, computer chips, and even children's games. But whether the subject matter is bridges or computer chips, the process is the same: the practical application of theory and experience feeds back on our awareness of theoretical inadequacies and on our identification of phenomena that warrant generalization and theoretical understanding. The imperatives of practicality compel engineers and scientists to develop classifications of phenomena into the general and the anomalous, to learn how general ideas can be combined to contend with a complex reality, and to chip away at the anomalies through intuition, ad hoc models, approximations, and unexplained correlations. This process of discovery and application engenders an understanding of the differences between the rigorous testing of theory, the identification of empirical generalizations, and the simple estimation of empirical relations.

If the lessons of the engineer and the natural scientist seem too remote, we can look at our sister discipline, economics, which in board rooms, banking centers, parliaments, and ministries has had to confront its applied domain with greater consistency than has political science. More than any econometric test of some model or "theory," such confrontations—especially debates over economic reform, and failures to account for such things as speculative bubbles, lags in investment, and unanticipated inflation and unemployment—have instigated innumerable theoretical insights and advances in basic macro- and microeconomic formulations, and have made the economist more appreciative of the things that lie beyond the formal domain of economic theory. In contrast, the failure of political science to connect its practical objectives to its theoretical and methodological ones results in confusion about the phenomena that warrant theoretical treatment, the distinction between theory and model, and, ultimately, the methods whereby we make scientific advances.

Two Cases of Rational Choice Modelling

Among the things for which Green and Shapiro take rational choice theorists to task, the treatment of voting in mass elections and models of those elections stand out. These two topics illustrate both Green and Shapiro's critique of rational choice analysis and how alternative remedies would be more productive than the ones they suggest.

Green and Shapiro's critique of rational choice approaches to voting in mass democracies focuses on the apparent inability of rational choice theorists to account for voting by saying anything more than that people vote if they are socialized to do so. Certainly, this "explanation" does not illuminate trends in turnout or rates of voting among subsets of the population or for different offices.

Two critiques of their discussion are possible, however. First, most research—theoretical and empirical—focuses on two-candidate contests. In such elections, if p_{ij} denotes the probability that a person's vote is decisive between candidates i and j, and if u_i and u_j denote the utilities of candidates i and j, then, according to rational choice assumptions, the person in question should vote if and only if

$$|u_i - u_j| p_{ij} + A > 0 \tag{1}$$

where $||$ denotes absolute value, and A the net costs and benefits from voting that are independent of the influence a vote has on who wins or loses. In addition, once in the voting booth, a person should vote for i over j if and only if

$$u_i - u_j > 0 \tag{2}$$

Before we discuss whether these two formulae can contribute anything to our understanding of voting, suppose we add a third candidate for office, k. Ignoring three-way ties, the generalization of expression (1) becomes:

$$|u_i - u_j| p_{ij} + |u_i - u_k| p_{ik} + |u_j - u_k| p_{jk} + A' > 0 \tag{3}$$

and the generalization of expression (2), for a voter who prefers i to j to k, is

$$2\left|u_i - u_j\right| p_{ij} + \left|u_i - u_k\right| p_{ik} - \left|u_j - u_k\right| p_{jk} > 0 \qquad (4)$$

Each expression is derived from a standard decision-theoretic model of choice in plurality-rule contests. Each seems unexceptional, and, in particular, the two expressions specifying when a person should vote, (1) and (3), highlight the importance of ad hoc terms such as A and A'. Specifically, since the ps in both of them are presumed to be quite small, the A-terms must dominate, in which case it seems that all we can do is create stories about the sources of variation in A and A'—the things that might influence voting costs and a person's sense of citizen duty.

But before we conclude that the preceding expected utility calculations add little to our understanding of things, notice the difference between expressions (2) and (4). Expression (2) says only that voters vote for their preferred candidate—an unremarkable idea. Expression (4), on the other hand, is more complex and formalizes the idea that in a three-way contest, a voter might prefer to vote for a second-ranked alternative if the first-ranked candidate is uncompetitive. Thus, even if we admit that all of the ps in expressions (1) – (4) are small, we have a more complex hypothesis than that people vote if they are socialized to do so. More precisely, we infer that in two-candidate plurality rule contests, if objective and subjective probabilities do not differ much, then the closeness of the contest will not affect the decision to vote or the decision about whom to vote; but even if the decision to vote is determined by the same things that influence choice when there are only two candidates, measures of competitiveness in three-candidate contests influence ultimate choices, where those measures can have positive or negative influences, depending on a voter's ranking of the candidates (for elaboration of this argument see Ordeshook and Zeng 1994). Put differently, a plurality-rule election's competitiveness is unlikely to influence either turnout generally or candidate choice in two-candidate contests, but it should influence candidate choice in multicandidate elections, where the separate components of competitiveness will have different effects, depending on a voter's preferences.

Of course, rational choice theory and its attendant expected utility calculations may be unnecessary to remind us that it is best to vote for an acceptable second choice if a first-ranked candidate is uncompetitive. But those calculations do predict that measures of competitiveness will be relevant in certain types of contests and not in others; they tell us how to specify the relationships among variables in a statistical model in the event that we want to estimate the relative importance of different parameters; and they predict which parameters will have positive coefficients and which will have negative ones. It is true that we have not "explained" voting in two-candidate contests or added much to our understanding of preferences or perception. Nevertheless, we see here how a small bit of rational choice analysis yields empirical implications.

Should these implications be tested? Obviously the answer is "yes," but in doing so we need to realize that refutation would only lead us to question the adequacy of our measures, our confidence in asserting a relationship between objective and subjective probabilities, or the need to add new ad hoc terms to expressions (2) and (4). We are unprepared to reject rationality and, thus, we are not "testing" rational choice theory as much as we are estimating its parameters, refining our formulations of it, and adding to our intuition. Even if we find support for the predictions we derive from expressions (1) – (4) in some electorate, it is not necessarily the case that the same parameters influence things in the same way in other electorates or in other historical periods (before, say, the secret ballot). Certainly research should proceed to consider the effects of other electoral arrangements—party-list proportional representation, preferential voting, or majority rule with runoffs. In addition, we can suppose that the likelihood of strategic voting will vary with the availability of public opinion polls (the publication of which is banned in some countries before balloting) and the existence of interest groups that might try to inform voters about their strategic options. Each context may occasion a different calculus of voting, different parameter values, and different conclusions about the role of competitiveness as opposed to more psychological variables. Notice, moreover, that expressions (1) – (4) can be applied to other forms of political participation. Is it unreasonable to suppose that (1) and (3), in particular, can be consistent with these decisions? What do we conclude if we find that terms like A and A' are required to "explain" one type of decision but not another? If we can imagine that such terms might be relevant to some but not all decisions, then no hypothesis about the rationality of voters has been subjected to refutation. Since we are not positioned to test a critical hypothesis, it becomes unclear where our research into the determinants of choice leads or what directions our follow-up research should take.

By building a literature around expressions (1) – (4), we can only change our confidence that the idea of expected utility maximization has application in political science. But we cannot test definitive hypotheses. If we find that some system of expected utility equations labeled a "calculus of participation" is useful in one context but not another, or for some types of decisions but not for others, then our attempts at estimation and hypothesis testing have no definitive end. Because it is likely to be true that "the influence of strategic considerations is likely to vary across people and decision contexts" (69), the product of our research can only be different estimates of parameters for different circumstances, data sets, and decisions. That is, our research cannot be much more than mere cataloguing and description.

As with the interaction between science and engineering, our research can be productive only if we have a practical objective that organizes research around something other than the false belief that we are testing fundamental theoretical principles. That objective, and the thing that provides the ultimate assessment of substantive relevance, is the extent to which we can use it to guide our construction of democratic institutions (in this case, electoral rules) so as to achieve such goals as the encouragement of a stable party system. Since no one is prepared to assert that our regressions are estimating universal constants, only when given a practical focus can we say that a coefficient of, say, .0433 in country X versus .103 in country Y is any more meaningful than the facts we learn when playing "Trivial Pursuit." This is how we should interpret Green and Shapiro's contention that rational choice theorists should be "weaned away from ethereal speculation about why rational citizens vote and refocused on questions of a more down-to-earth nature" (71).

The need to give our research a more explicitly practical objective is clearer still when we consider election models. It is here that Green and Shapiro's discussion approximates my view of how empirical research and theory interact most productively—despite their call for incorporating even greater complexity into our formal analyses. Their argument that "what is lacking from rational choice narratives is an underlying foundation of systematic empirical inquiry" (174) is essentially correct. Yet little of any consequence will result if we proceed as though the requisite research fits into some simplistic mold of "pure science."

Our differences can be construed as matters of emphasis. Green and Shapiro prefer to find features of specific models that allow for rigorous and critical empirical assessment. For example, when commenting on the "theoretical" conclusion that candidate incentives can influence the likelihood that policy platforms converge, they suggest "tests that track a panel of candidates as they adjust their strategies to accommodate a new system of incentives" (176). Suppose, though, that we find no such relationship. What hypothesis do we reject? Do we reject rationality, our methodology and operationalization of variables, or the utility of the particular model under consideration? Do we reject the proposition that incentives in general do not operate as hypothesized or that they do not operate that way only in the particular circumstances considered? What have we learned when we find that some parameter is relevant in one election and irrelevant in another?

When studying complex processes it is unlikely that we can formulate critical hypotheses that, depending on our findings, would discernably change the direction of research or the paradigms to which we adhere. Estimating parameters is only that—estimation. It is not critical hypothesis testing of the sort that occurs when we cast one theoretical paradigm against another. Despite the application of well-structured statistical methods, testing a model is an informal act of refinement—of adding to our ability to grapple with increased complexity, of securing a better understanding of the problem at hand, and of ascertaining whether the predictions of a specific model known to be inaccurate have practical value. If we approach the empirical assessment of models of processes that most interest us in the same way that we approach abstract theory, we are unlikely to do much more than create an insurmountable bookkeeping problem. As we begin to uncover the true complexity of those processes, as the list of potentially relevant variables grows, and as the ad hoc hypotheses required to make formal analysis tractable increase, we need to ask: Do we ever reach a point of being able to reject our approach as inadequate or to accept it as superior to all competitors? Naive views of science tell us that we stop only when a better (i.e., more general and parsimonious) paradigm appears. But what if no such paradigm is evident? Or, worse still, what if there are several paradigms, each promising to make a different contribution to our understanding?

Green and Shapiro lament the fact that formal models of elections present the reader with a vast array of contingent predictions and that no coherent accounting exists for the multiplicity of models, assumptions, and hypotheses. With some analyses seemingly directed at explicit empirical phenomena and others being mere mathematical refinements, and with different models making different assumptions about the same things—about preferences, information, beliefs, available strategies, and so on—the field seems wholly incoherent. In fact, models of elections do constitute an incoherent whole. But identifying testable propositions of the sort called for by Green and Shapiro is unlikely to resolve matters or lead to definitive conclusions, if only because there are no definitive conclusions to be reached. The field is not and cannot be headed in the direction of some all-encompassing theoretical structure that accommodates all elections at all times in all contexts. In the complex world of real elections, it is unlikely that we will ever develop theoretical propositions that are more general than, say, the median voter theorem. We may find it useful to discover such theoretical possibilities as that polls can inform voters, that strategic voting alone can account for the long-term equilibrium number of parties that compete in elections, and that redistributive politics occasions no simple equilibrium in candidate platforms. But none of the "models" that generate such conclusions can be usefully tested in any rigorous scientific sense, both because they are inherently too incomplete as models and because reality is too complex to allow us to interpret them as theories.

Thus, rather than approach the construction and assessment of models as though we were *scientists* discovering basic laws of the universe, we should try to solve specific problems in specific contexts with an understanding that different models may be best suited for different situations. Every bridge is a special problem in engineering. We also need to appreciate that certain aspects of reality cannot yet be subjected to abstract theoretical analysis, or even to fully coherent empirical analysis. Crude rules of thumb, intuition based on experience, simple insight, and "mindless statistical analysis" will be an essential part of our enterprise. It also follows—as Green and Shapiro suggest—that spinning out an endless series of models, each designed to explore some as-yet-unexplored relationship, demonstrate the application of the latest theoretical fad, or provide an alternative explanation for some new fact, is worthwhile only if we have a definite purpose in mind. What Green and Shapiro do not emphasize is that the purpose must be to build something better than what already exists.

Disincentives to Learning

In 1984, Samuel Huntington asserted that "the substantial power of antidemocratic governments (particularly the Soviet Union), the unreceptivity to democracy of several major cultural traditions . . . and the prevalence of high levels of polarization and violence in many societies all suggest that, with few exceptions, the limits of democratic development in the world may well have been reached." Huntington was not alone in his pessimism; he is but one example of an engineer whose bridge has fallen into the river. It is a mistake, though, to attribute such errors to the greater complexity of political science phenomena compared to natural ones or to the phenomena confronting engineers. The essential problem concerns incentives: in social science, there are fewer consequences of being wrong than in natural science or engineering. In political science, if a model is found to be empirically inadequate, we simply publish a more elaborate or general version. If a journalistic account proves inaccurate, then one can always write with greater profundity later. If our empirical analyses are revealed to be deceptive because of some flaw in method or measurement, then we have merely opened the door to a revised manuscript. And if following our advice produces perverse results, we can always excuse ourselves by referring to the inherent uncertainties of social processes.

Unfortunately, there are profoundly important problems that require our attention: designing a stable democratic federalism for Russia or

Ukraine, understanding the nature of strategic threats in Central Europe, and formulating viable political constitutions nearly everywhere. Such matters are, at present, mostly the purview of politicians and pundits. With some notable exceptions, political scientists have reserved for themselves the role of bystanders who merely describe or offer after-the-fact explanations. Of course, one might object to this characterization by noting that, as political scientists, our job is merely to develop theoretical propositions and methodologies that can assist those who act. But we cannot do the job if we are unwilling to take the bits and pieces of theory and methodology available to us and propose alternative institutional designs and constitutional structures as solutions to specific problems.

Thus, Green and Shapiro's demand for "relevance" will fall on deaf ears until incentives change. Indeed, rational choice theory itself tells us that behavior does not change unless incentives change, which requires that the basis of our professional rewards—tenure, salary, and prestige—must change first. This is a tall order, and requires among other things that journal editors become less tolerant of manuscripts that merely mimic some naive view of scientific inquiry and more tolerant of those that propose solutions to specific problems. Such proposals should not be relegated to the op-ed pages or CNN. They need to appear in traditional academic journals and be subject to the same academic refinement now devoted to purely mathematical and methodological treatises.

Norman Schofield

RATIONAL CHOICE AND
POLITICAL ECONOMY

The purpose of rational choice is to provide a grand theoretical framework for designing human institutions. Once theoretical work had shown how markets optimally aggregated preferences, attempts were made to extend the theory from markets to politics. Attempts by Downs and Olson to describe elections and collective action produced relatively poor predictions, but impelled game theorists to generalize preference-based theories to include belief formation. A consequence of this change is that the theory is no longer purely axiomatic, but draws on insights about human behavior from other disciplines and empirical analysis of the role institutions play in determining beliefs.

In *Pathologies of Rational Choice Theory* Don Green and Ian Shapiro contend that it is pathological for rational choice theory to attempt to provide a grand theory of political behavior. An aspect of this alleged pathology is the inattention paid by rational choice theorists to empirical falsification or confirmation of their theories. The assumption underlying this critique is that political science is fundamentally an empirical discipline. If this assumption is accepted, then practitioners of political science have reason to ignore rational choice theory.

Norman Schofield, the William Taussig Professor of Political Economy and Director of the Center in Political Economy at Washington University, St. Louis, Missouri 63130, telephone (314) 935–4774, e-mail Schofld@wuecon.wustl.ed., is the author of *Social Choice and Democracy* (Springer, 1985) and coauthor of *Advanced Statistical Methods in Economics* (Holt, Rinehart, Winston, 1986) and *Multiparty Government* (Oxford, 1990). He is grateful for the support of National Science Foundation Grant SES-88-208405, and thanks Marcus Berliant, Kenneth Binmore, John Nachbar, and Douglass North for helpful discussions about this paper, and Jeffrey Friedman for his comments.

Green and Shapiro assume that rational choice theory has its roots in economic theory, and they suggest that, for this reason, it is method-driven rather than problem-driven. Moreover, they question whether a theoretical framework "designed for the different purpose of explaining the behavior of market prices" (194) need have any relevance for the understanding of political behavior. I infer that Green and Shapiro view the development of rational choice theory in political science as an act of colonization by economists.

In my view what gives rational choice theory coherence is precisely that it *is* an attempt to construct a grand theory of human behavior. That is to say, the theory is a conceptual framework through which to analyze the interplay and consequences of human incentives within institutions. This may explain why, long before rational choice theory migrated from economics into political science, it had been used by the Marquis de Condorcet in late-eighteenth-century France to provide a framework for the design of "good" government *and society*.[1] A universal theory of human behavior should equally be applicable in either politics or economics. To assess the merits of rational choice theory, then, requires an understanding of how it has evolved, regardless of which discipline served as the site of the various stages of its evolution.

I shall argue that the primary motivation for practitioners of rational choice theory, in the course of its evolution since the 1950s, has been to create an integrated, empirical theory of market and polity that would serve the normative purpose of designing "good" institutions. It has become increasingly obvious that to create such a theory, it is necessary to understand how individuals form beliefs about empirical reality and how they act in response both to their normative preferences and their beliefs. As this theory evolved, it led to changes in our understanding of how to devise "good" political and economic institutions, inasmuch as the economists' equation of "good" with "Pareto optimal" no longer appeared adequate. Given that people's beliefs—their empirical models of the world, their private information, and so on—vary so much, the aggregation of people's preferences (or values) so as to achieve Pareto optimality could no longer be the normative basis for design. This realization has led to a return to Condorcet's original desire to evaluate human institutions as devices *both* to aggregate preferences and integrate beliefs.

Green and Shapiro's critique has little weight when rational choice theory is seen as primarily normative, not empirical. Even concentrating on applications within political science, I feel their critique is misdirected. Most of the works that command Green and Shapiro's attention have their origin in the attempts by two economists, namely Anthony Downs (1957) and Mancur Olson (1965), to deal with questions of preference aggregation in the political economy. In my view, this work should be seen as part of the effort, originating in economics, to gauge whether the theoretical optimality of the market could be extended to the political economy. However, the early work in the research tradition represented by Downs and Olson was never intended to be a substantive analysis of political systems. On the contrary, the conceptual framework underlying these models was designed to be compatible with economic theory. I shall discuss in some detail below how only one component of Condorcet's concern, namely preference aggregation, was developed by economists, and particularly Kenneth Arrow (1951), in laying the foundation for a rational choice theory of political economy. Whereas the work in the Downs-Olson tradition had the virtue of simplicity in construction and prediction, the more recent efforts have shown that the predictions of these preference-based models were not corroborated, in general, in the behavior of real polities.

In the main body of the essay I shall consider the various attempts to construct a closed (or consistent) preference-based theory of human behavior in both economics and politics and show, in each case, why there were logical reasons to extend the theory beyond preferences to beliefs. As the discussion proceeds, I hope to make it clear why the normative economic criterion of Pareto optimality began to appear less appropriate than the "Condorcetian" criterion of truth. I use "truth" as a shorthand for the property of a human institution to "efficiently" aggregate the dispersed information held by its individual members. The earliest effort in this direction was Condorcet's demonstration that, among a jury judging the innocence or guilt of a defendant, a majority vote will more often be correct than the response of an average juror. As the size of the jury, or society, becomes very large, the probability that the majority will be right approaches unity. This theorem seems to justify democratic procedures for belief aggregation (of a certain kind) as optimal.[2] Below I shall mention attempts to derive analogous results for markets.

As rational choice theory has evolved, it has been obliged to become less axiomatic in structure. Indeed, the increasing emphasis on beliefs suggests that it will, of necessity, have to draw on insights from other behavioral sciences, including anthropology, linguistics, and psychology. Since the theory also includes the role of institutions in determining human choice, it is likely that there will be continuing interaction between empirical and theoretical research on this topic.

From Economics to Public Choice and Political Science

Let me amplify these introductory remarks by briefly discussing how the rational actor theory employed by economists in the 1950s was later obliged to address larger questions of social choice that were anticipated by Condorcet.

Neoclassical economic theory can be viewed as the analysis of human incentives in a particular restricted context of fixed resources, private goods, and a given technology. As such, it is a theory of preference aggregation. Contrary to Green and Shapiro's assertion (quoted previously), the theory does *not* explain the behavior of market prices. The work of Kenneth Arrow and Gerard Debreu (1954) and of Lionel McKenzie (1959) did assert, however, that, in this restricted context, the competitive price equilibrium would be Pareto optimal. In discussions of market behavior, economists often go on to assert (a claim that, as far as I know, is unproven) that *only* a competitive market can "efficiently" aggregate the diverse *beliefs* of the members of a heterogeneous economy. If this were true, then nonmarket, planned economies would be inadequate to the task of integrating the dispersed information that underlies these divergent beliefs.[3]

Since the difference between preferences and beliefs is important, but subtle, it is worthwhile briefly discussing how market institutions do aggregate beliefs. Foreign exchange markets, futures markets, financial markets, and so forth may seem to be driven by the *preferences* of buyers or sellers, but in truth the motivations of the agents are derived from their own private information and their expectations of commodity price movements. Rational expectations, or the convergence of agents' expectational beliefs, can be thought of as the appropriate type of "truth" in markets. However, this convergence need not occur.[4]

Thus, in an attempt to develop the analysis of human incentives, "rational actor theory" has been forced to go well beyond the preference-based study of private-goods markets. The intimate connection between preferences and beliefs has necessitated an attempt to reconstitute a general theory of rationality; this is exactly what "game theory" is about. Second, some goods are jointly produced and consumed. Certain of these public goods, such as technological innovation, may be produced and consumed within the economic system, but others, such as national defense and domestic security, are more traditionally created through the political system. Since one method of political choice is by some form of democracy, the need to extend the theory to public goods translates into a requirement to analyze democratic polities to determine not only preferences for such goods, but the incentives to produce them, given people's beliefs about others' willingness to pay for them. It should be noted here that the distinguishing feature of rational choice theory in its market-based form was its emphasis on the connection between preferences, "equilibrium," and "optimality." The attempt to enlarge the domain of the theory from economics to "political economy" retained these key concepts. Moreover, the nonmarket institutions that constrain human behavior are obviously important for the way individuals construct their preferences and beliefs, and for the methods by which these are aggregated. The need to examine this question has become more important in the last few years, as research has attempted to model different political institutions. The general theme underlying this research has been, I believe, a desire to determine whether or not democratic political institutions are compatible, in some sense, with "market efficiency."

A very extensive public choice literature, particularly in the 1970s and 1980s, argued that democratic politics was not compatible with market efficiency. The various arguments are too numerous to list here, but in general they asserted that democratic polities created the context for political "rent-seeking" that constrained economic growth. Indeed, political representatives were viewed as creating rents for themselves, with the consequence that government growth was accompanied by deleterious economic consequences. The debate is, of course, still being carried on in the United States, and its resolution will have quite important effects on all of us. The public choice literature, while influenced by theoretical, rational choice models, was also directed at explaining empirical facts (such as stagflation). This mix of theoretical and empirical reasoning I shall term "positive." Since positive reasoning attempts to explain facts of the world, it must address questions of empirical corroboration or falsification.

Early positive attempts to apply economic theory were based on a model of market behavior which assumed that agents are completely characterized by their preferences, and that they respond nonstrategically to prices. To some degree the inferences of this model have been corroborated in relatively simple situations. However, this preference-based theory has had little success in modelling choice under either strong uncertainty (Denzau and North 1994) or large-scale economic change over time.[5] More importantly, the attempt to use rational actor theory as a basis for macroeconomics has not been particularly successful (Weintraub 1979). Although macroeconomics purports to describe the real economic world, it often appears to be a tower of Babel, populated by Keynesians, monetarists, supply-siders, etc. On the other hand, most macroeconomists would accept, in general terms, the postulates of microeconomic theory, and the notion of rationality in particular. The empirical weakness of microeconomics has not led economists to reject this principle, but rather has led them to attempt to develop more complex models of rationality. As I suggested above, the imperative for game theory has been to extend simple models based on preferences so that agents' beliefs are made more explicit.

Is political science more like macroeconomics or microeconomics? Green and Shapiro assert that, like macroeconomics, it is fundamentally a "problem-driven" rather than a "method-driven" discipline, and on this basis they attack the rational choice recourse to formal modelling rather than empirical research. I accept that political science is problem-driven, but do not agree that, like macroeconomics, this makes it necessarily dependent on empirical analysis. Political science is driven by the age-old problem of how we are to be governed. Shapiro himself is the author of two books in this tradition (Shapiro 1986, 1990). The Founding Fathers, too, and particularly the authors of *The Federalist Papers*, were concerned precisely with the normative *problematique* of the proper form of government. I would go so far as to suggest that Hamilton and the other Federalists were rational choice theorists of a kind. To substantiate this I might mention the recent observation of Gordon Wood that the Federalist notion of government rested completely "on the assumption that most people were self-interested and absorbed in their private affairs" (Wood 1991, 264). Of course, the Founding Fathers did not engage in empirical political science, as we would understand the term "empirical" today. Nonetheless, they were men of practical reason who made intelligent guesses about the way self-interested individuals were likely to behave under different systems of government. Some of the clearest rational choice theory I have ever read can be found in Madison's argument in *Federalist* X: "the greater number of citizens and extent of territory may be brought within the compass of Republican, than of Democratic Government; and it is this circumstance principally which renders factious combinations less to be dreaded in the former, than in the latter." Not only does Madison essentially apply a Condorcetian[6] form of argument in *Federalist* X, but he distinguishes between "opinions" (i.e., beliefs) and "passions" (i.e., preferences).

However, if we distinguish the normative political theory of the Founders from the current study of American, comparative, and international politics, and if we call the latter "political science" as opposed to "political theory," then it is true that political science is now predominantly empirical, just as macroeconomics is.[7] This by no means entails that empirical political science is epistemologically superior in any way to political theory (whether normative or rational choice). My own view is that if political science focuses principally on empirical relationships rather than on the evaluation and design of government, then it is seriously wanting.[8] (An attempt within "social choice" theory to construct a normative basis for evaluation based on Pareto optimality will be discussed in the next section.)[9] Moreover, although rational choice theory is predominantly a theoretical discipline, there have been attempts at empirical corroboration.[10] I believe that the mix of problem-based concerns and empirical testing displayed by rational choice theory has contributed significantly to its increasing importance in political science.[11] It might also be mentioned that rational choice theory has had an impact on, or has at least excited the in-terest of, sociologists, philosophers, and mathematicians, as well as econo-mists and political scientists. Although Green and Shapiro emphasize the significance of rational choice theory for the study of U.S. politics, the theory has been applied in most of the substantive subdisciplines of politi-cal science.[12]

The progenitors of these attempts at positive reasoning, the seminal works in rational choice theory by Downs and Olson, on which Green and Shapiro focus, were certainly predominantly theoretical. While Arrow (1951) was concerned with the normative task of aggregating preferences, the problem addressed by both Downs and Olson was to use "microeco-nomic" tools to explore the provision of public goods through voting and collective action. Neither Downs's prediction that, in two-party competi-tion, the parties will tend to converge, nor Olson's claim about the failure of collective action when private incentives are absent, have been empiri-cally substantiated. The reason is that while both Downs and Olson fo-cused on preferences, it is evident that elections and collective problems are "games" that cannot be fully described without modelling the beliefs of the participants.

In particular, it is important to model the way agents form beliefs about other agents' beliefs, and thus their behavior. This is often described as the "common knowledge problem." In my view, it is at the heart of an under-standing of economic as well as political behavior, and indeed all collective action (see Schofield 1985a; Hinich and Munger 1994).

Preference-based models, whether of markets or elections, are relatively simple, with fairly clear predictions. Beliefs, on the other hand, are any-thing but simple: they involve, at the very least, some description of how people learn, "update," and model the world they live in. Condorcet, known both for his work on the aggregation of beliefs (the so-called Con-dorcet Jury Theorem) *and* for work on the aggregation of preferences, was unable to combine these two modes of analysis. In his honor, I shall call the venture of developing an integrated model of politics that includes both preferences and beliefs the "Condorcetian" research program. In the next sections of the paper I shall present my view of the evolution of the preference-based models (what I call the "Arrovian" research program, in honor of Kenneth Arrow) to incorporate beliefs.

Economics, Social Choice, and the Arrovian Research Program

Table 1 sets out my view of the relationships between the various branches of economics, political economy, and politics. As the table suggests, rational

196

Table 1: A Classification of Economic and Political Theories

	Economics	Political Economy	Politics
Normative	welfare economics	social choice	normative political theory
Theoretical	market (equilibrium) theory	game theory	rational choice theory
Positive	public economics	public choice	theory of institutions
Empirical	macroeconomics	institutional political economy	political science

choice theory as applied to politics is only one among a number of different research activities, all characterized by their varying degrees of emphasis on the normative, the theoretical, the empirical, or the positive (i.e., theoretical arguments that make assertions about the world). The table is also meant to emphasize the close connections between game theory and the adjacent theoretical and positive subfields.

Market theory utilizes the idea of equilibrium to relate economic parameters (resources, preferences, technology) to an outcome or choice. Welfare economics and public economics, research fields that are subsidiary to market theory, are designed to address normative and positive aspects of the relationship between government behavior and the economy. Public economics deals with the appropriate relationship between government and the economy, while macroeconomics covers the empirical aspect of this relationship.

In an attempt to provide a formal basis for public finance and government, the economist must determine whether the domain of market theory can be enlarged to include *nonmarket* phenomena, such as preferences for public goods. Arrow took the first step in this program by asking if the preferences of the individuals making up a society could by aggregated to construct a measure of social welfare. Although his social choice theory addresses certain concerns that economists regard as essential, including the compatibility of the market and democracy, nothing about that theory restricts it to either welfare economics or political theory. Still, for an economist, the question of the compatibility of the market and democracy must be expressed in a formal language that is general enough to include economic theory.

Economic theory *circa* 1954 derived, from the simple preferences and resources of individuals, the existence of a market equilibrium. To enlarge its theoretical language so as to answer the question of democracy, the nature of preferences was extended from private goods to public goods, but the concept of preference had to be retained. And since the question involved the degree to which the market equilibrium result could be generalized, it was necessary to pose it in terms of the existence (or otherwise) of the "equilibrium."

Microeconomics adopts the postulate that individual preferences are consistent. However, a variety of consistency axioms can be adopted. The most restrictive one, common in microeconomics, is that each individual's preference can be represented by a (numerical) utility function. This strong assumption implies that both strict preference and indifference are transitive: if A and B are equally preferable, as are B and C, then so are A and C. The standard example of nontransitive indifference is a cup of coffee with no sugar, which is "indifferent" compared to a cup with a single grain of sugar, to one with two grains, and so on, but not to one with a thousand grains. A weaker consistency assumption is that of the transitivity of strict preference, but not of indifference. Even weaker is the assumption of acyclicity: if A is strictly preferred to B, B is strictly preferred to C, C to D, and so on to X, then X cannot be strictly preferred to A. Acyclicity guarantees that an individual may always make a "choice," that is, select an alternative, such that if he chooses A, he must strictly prefer none of the unchosen alternatives to A.

While economic theory concentrates on preferences, it usually adopts the postulate that individuals' *behavior* will be given by their choices (if such exist). Where the outcomes are uncertain, or involve risk, behavioral predictions may associate a list of probabilities with the final eventualities. Theorists often assume that preferences under risk behave as if they were weighted by these probabilities (for discussion see Eatwell, Milgate, and Newman 1987). Yet it is entirely possible that real individual preferences in the presence of risk may fail acyclicity, leading to apparently "irrational" or inconsistent behavior (Kahneman and Tversky 1979). In my view the postulate of acyclical consistency is reasonable in the absence of risk, but is less tenable in its presence.

Rationality postulates combine with various structural assumptions about the nature of the economic system to yield an economic equilibrium that is Pareto optimal: no other allocation of resources is preferred unanimously (McKenzie 1959; Arrow and Debreu 1954). In the absence of a price mechanism, however—as in politics—rational choice theorists utilized the notion of the "core." An outcome is in the core if no coalition of agents is able and willing to bring about a different state. The concept of a core was devised, in part, to cover situations involving public goods.

Green and Shapiro seem to assume that Arrow's Impossibility Theorem is simply concerned with democratic rules of collective decision (7). But in truth, the genius of Arrow's result is that it suggests that, in general, a social utility function cannot be defined, negating the assumption that individual preferences could be aggregated so as to describe an optimal provision of public goods. In a sense, Arrow showed that the assumptions economists typically employ in modelling individual behavior are unlikely to hold where public goods are concerned. For while it is reasonable to assume that individuals prefer more rather than less of a private good, it is entirely possible that among them, individuals can have extremely complex preferences in the public domain. More of my public good may be your public bad. While I may want extensive military expenditure, you may loathe the military and prefer good schools, parks, environmental protection, and so forth. Since there is no obvious a priori restriction on the possible set of public preferences that individuals may have, Arrow adopted the "unrestricted domain assumption." That is, each individual may have any preference at all, as long as it satisfies transitivity of both strict preference and indifference. Under this assumption, the only social utility that satisfies the unanimity condition must be dictatorial. More generally, any social utility that can be used to make social choices based on individual preferences must necessarily be dictatorial.

If preferences could be equated with utilities, then social utility could be obtained simply by summing individual utilities. But economists believe in general that interpersonal comparisons of utility are scientifically meaningless, since it is impossible to "extract" the information required to construct such comparisons. Certainly markets and voting mechanisms, when viewed as methods of preference aggregation, do not provide the means of obtaining such information. However, if markets and polities are modelled as devices for aggregating both preferences and beliefs, then it is possible that the negative inferences of the Arrow impossibility theorem can be avoided. As Arrow (1987) himself observed, however, before this could be attempted, it would be necessary to deal with the question of "common knowledge," that is the foundation of our beliefs about the beliefs of others.

From Preferences to Beliefs

Duncan Black (1958) reintroduced Condorcet's work to a modern audience, and thus contributed, to some degree, to the extension of preference-based theory to include the analysis of beliefs. Although Green and Shapiro devote little attention to Black, almost all the elements of what has come to be known as spatial voting theory are present in Black's 1958 book, *The Theory of Committees and Elections.* Just as Arrow had investigated whether individual preferences could be aggregated into a social utility function, Black investigated the possibility of equilibrium in voting systems. In this context an equilibrium is a point or outcome that is unbeaten (although it need not beat every other conceivable point). Suppose that three voters have distinct preferred points on a left-right political continuum, and that each voter has single-peaked preferences (preferences that are maximized at a single point). Then the middle (or median) voter's preferred point cannot be beaten under majority rule, where a majority requires two out of three. Black called this equilibrium a "majority motion" in his book; in more recent work, the voting equilibrium is known as the core.

Suppose now that the decision problem involves more than a single continuum; for example, preferences for social liberalism or conservatism might be independent from preferences for economic liberalism or conservatism. Under such conditions, even with single-peaked individual preferences, the likelihood of the existence of an equilibrium is negligible. As Black writes, "the conditions that must be satisfied before there can be any majority motion are highly restrictive. The frequency of occurrence as a fraction of the total number of cases possible . . . is infinitesimally small or 'practically zero' " (Black 1956, 139). Earlier in the book Black seemed to equate cases without an equilibrium with the occurrence of "cycles," so he apparently took it for granted that when there is more than one dimension to voters' preferences, voting cycles will occur. Economics postulates that any observed behavior must express an actor's preference. A voting equilibrium, therefore, would be expected to manifest collective preferences. If there is no equilibrium, however, the economist can make no behavioral predictions. The term "instability" is used for this situation. Green and Shapiro object to the "vagueness with which instability is conceptualized" (135).

In one sense there is no formal ambiguity about the meaning of instability, since it is defined as an empty core or equilibrium. Over two decades of theoretical work have made it clear, however, that, in general, democratic procedures of the kind examined by Black possess no core.[13] In the absence of a behavioral prediction based on preference theory, the natural step was to account for observed outcomes by modelling the way *beliefs* caused behavior. To be more specific, it appeared plausible that the outcome would depend on the expectations of agents, their ability to "logroll" by guessing about other agents' behavior, and so on. One of the important results in the purely preference-based theory of voting was that voting cycles could, in principle, go everywhere in the policy space (McKelvey 1976; Schofield 1978a). Yet this occurrence of theoretical indeterminacy or "chaos" did not necessarily imply "behavioral chaos," since there existed no belief-based model of what voters would actually do in the context of theoretical chaos. Indeed, experimental work by Morris Fiorina and Charles R. Plott (1978) and by James Laing and Scott Olmsted (1978) demonstrated "that coreless games do not produce markedly more unstable outcomes than do games with cores" (Green and Shapiro 135).

Green and Shapiro infer that this empirical work vitiated the logic of preference-based voting theory. In my view, the empirical work suggested instead that a rational choice theory that incorporates beliefs should smooth out the difference between games with cores and coreless ones. Thus, the "local cycle set" (Schofield 1978b) seemed a good predictor of the available experimental observations. A later model of how agents might plausibly behave in the absence of equilibirum, called the "heart" (Schofield 1993, 1995a), accounts for nearly all the outcomes observed in experimental voting games conducted up to 1986.[14]

The work on theoretical voting chaos during the late 1970s induced a period of intense debate within rational choice political theory. As Green and Shapiro observe, two of the protagonists in this debate, William Riker (1980, 1982, 1986) and Gordon Tullock (1981), drew quite different conclusions concerning the significance of chaos results for the study of legislatures (see also the essays in Ordeshook and Shepsle 1982). Because Green and Shapiro view politics as an empirical science, they fault both Riker and Tullock for the inadequate empirical basis of their respective arguments about the relevance or irrelevance of the chaos theorems. My own criticism of Riker and Tullock is more fundamental. Formally, the chaos theorems on which they drew apply only to committees, where there is some foundation for supposing the voters have well-specified preferences. It is not at all clear that representatives in a legislature can be assumed to have "preferences" that are similar in kind to the members of a committee. It may be intuitively plausible that each legislator seeks to provide certain kinds of "goods" to constituency members. But until the voter-legislator connection is modelled in detail, there is no formal rational choice basis for the study of a U.S.-style legislature.

I have argued (Schofield 1995b), however, that it is plausible that the models of committee voting are applicable to European-style legislatures involving well-disciplined parties. In particular, it appears reasonable to me to assume that party leaders in such legislatures do have preferred policy outcomes, and that they attempt to construct legislative majorities to implement these policies. There is an extensive empirical literature on coalition formation in European legislatures (see the references in Laver and Schofield 1990), and recent attempts to use rational choice theory in this context do produce empirical predictions that have been substantiated. One insight that comes out of this work concerns the possibility that a large nonmajority party may form a minority government when its preferred point is at the core or equilibrium position in the policy space.[15]

Rational choice theory also provides a logical framework within which to make some sense out of some well-established empirical relationships that have been noted in multiparty political systems. For example, the fragmentation of parliamentary systems into many small parties is highly correlated with government brevity in the European systems (Dodd 1976). It should be obvious that in the absence of a core or policy equilibrium, any government that does form may be defeated by another majority coalition with a counter-policy proposal. Thus a connection between political fragmentation and the remote probability of a core would give insight into "macropolitical" relationships.[16] Recent events in Russia, Italy, and Japan suggest, to me at least, that such insights would be helpful in understanding how different democratic systems operate.

In my view, the United States Congress is fundamentally different from European multiparty systems for a number of reasons. It would be worthwhile to develop a general theory of comparative politics that would make clear how different institutional or electoral rules affect political behavior. In the next section I shall address some of these issues in the context of the observations by Green and Shapiro on rational choice theories of elections.

Rational Choice and Elections

There is a venerable tradition on the connection between proportional representation and political fragmentation (Duverger 1954). The recent empirical work by Rein Taagepera and Matthew Schugart (1989), for example, provides a detailed examination of this connection. European polities in general use proportional representation and typically have more than two parties. Maurice Duverger (1954) and Karl Popper (1945) argued that this tends to result in weak government. By the same token, there is some evidence that (plurality) systems based on single-member constituencies tend to produce two parties and thus a clearer electoral choice. The British electoral system, for example, which clearly is a plurality, or first-past-the-post arrangement, has always tended toward two dominant parties. While this is consistent with some rational choice models of elections, Duverger's argument, that small parties will wither away under plurality, is confounded by the continued presence of small British parties such as the "centrist" SDLP. On the other hand, although the United States is usually regarded as having a two-party system, its "parties" appear less disciplined, in general, than European-style parties. In particular, members of Congress are generally more heterogeneous in their voting behavior than one would expect within a European-style party. The political science literature, from Duverger onwards, is even more inadequate in terms of the theoretical (rather than empirical) analysis of these relationships.[17] My own view is that the formal analysis of elections should start with a general conception of electoral laws and *deduce* facts about the number and nature of political parties. Perhaps because the most influential election theorist, Downs (1957), was American, almost all formal work on elections has concentrated on plurality, two-party (or two-candidate) elections in single-member constituencies.[18] Since Green and Shapiro restrict their attention to applications of rational choice theory in U.S. politics, I shall follow the convention and suppose that U.S. elections are fundamentally two-candidate affairs.[19]

There are two distinct classes of models of electoral competition. The first class assumes that voting is deterministic. That is, the candidates make "promises" and each voter picks a candidate depending on which promise the voter prefers. Within this class of models, "policy blind" models assume that the candidates gain no utility except from winning, and that they attempt, therefore, to gain the maximum number of votes. Green and Shapiro (Chapter 7) refer to such candidates as "purely election-seeking." Just as in the committee model examined by Black, if the space of possible promises is one-dimensional, then two rational candidates will make the same promise, attempting to occupy the point at the median voter position.

As an economist, Downs (1957) could be justified in viewing this as a solution to the equilibrium problem in political economy. From the perspective of public finance, two-party competition could be assumed to provide a "median" tax schedule which could then be used to cover the provision of the public good in question. Obviously, however, government provides more than one public good, so individual voter preferences must be described in more than one dimension. The results from the committee voting model imply that, in such cases, there will be no core. In other words, no matter what one candidate promises, an opponent can promise something else that will obtain a majority. From the perspective of noncooperative game theory, the nonexistence of a core means there is no pure strategy Nash equilibrium (PSNE) in the two-candidate game. For public economics, this is a serious problem.

The obvious theoretical response is to develop a more general notion than the core. Gerald Kramer (1978) showed that there will be a mixed strategy Nash equilibrium (MSNE) where candidates make ambiguous promises. The nice feature of the uncovered set, mentioned earlier, is that the MSNE will belong to it. Thus, the political economist can assert that actual political outcomes will lie in the uncovered set. To some extent, at least, the theoretical problem of equilibrium is thus solved.

However, the motivation for this modelling strategy comes from economics, not political science. Its sole purpose is to solve the formal requirements of public economics, *not* to describe actual politics. Indeed, any model that "predicts" that candidates will make *identical* promises cannot be considered to have made any effort to characterize real politics. My guess is that it was this realization that led Donald Wittman (1983) to observe that "the research on formal models has been almost devoid of empirical content" (quoted in Green and Shapiro, 148).

Wittman, and others, have attempted to inject some political reality into the model by assuming the candidates are "policy motivated," in the sense that the candidates' own policy preferences are reflected in the promises they make. A candidate may, for example, "contract" with a group of supporters to constrain his or her personal policy objectives in a certain way in return for campaign contributions. Green and Shapiro observe that "a policy-motivated candidate is at a disadvantage when confronted by a pure election-seeking opponent" (107). This observation is not at all self-evident and may, indeed, be false. A policy-motivated candidate may find a way to be more *credibly* committed to supporters' objectives, and thus raise much greater campaign contributions, than a pure election-seeking candidate. In any case, the possibility of a tradeoff between contributions and voting suggests that a PSNE can exist where the candidates make quite different promises.

The second class of electoral models assumes that voters are "probabilistic" rather than "deterministic." Once the candidate promises are made, a voter in the deterministic model chooses one of the candidates with certainty (except when the two candidates are identical in all respects). In the probabilistic model, on the other hand, the voter's behavior, after the candidate promises are known, is a random variable which is based on the voter's beliefs about the likely consequences of the choice. In particular, such beliefs should deal with the estimates each voter makes concerning the likelihood that the candidates will deliver on their promises.

The advantages of the probabilistic model are two-fold. First, if voter preferences and candidate promises (or positions) are known, than it is possible to model the voter response econometrically. The early empirical work concentrated on two-candidate models (Enelow and Hinich 1984), but recent research has modelled multicandidate (or multiparty) situations (Nixon et al. 1995). Second, the probabilistic model is "continuous" in voter and candidate positions, and the chaos theorems (mentioned above) do not apply. Because the total vote for each candidate is a random variable, it can be characterized by its expectation and variance. Probabilistic models typically assume "pure-election seeking" candidates who make promises to maximize their expected vote. The usual result in models of two-candidate competition is that there exists a PSNE where both candidates propose the mean rather than the median position (Enelow and Hinich 1984; Coughlin 1992). This result solves the equilibrium problem of public economics very neatly.

However, there are a number of theoretical and substantive problems with this probabilistic model. Even policy-blind candidates make promises under risk, and the degree of risk depends not just on the expectation of voter response, but on the variance of this response. The models implicitly assume that the variance is independent of candidate positions, and this is untenable in the absence of a clear model of the formation of voter beliefs. Secondly, the models assume that each voter's behavior is statistically independent of the others'. This is unwarranted for the same reason. (I shall discuss this difficulty below.) More importantly, however, the conclusions of the model are not empirically substantiated. Our analysis (Nixon et al. 1995) of voting data from Israel in a multiparty situation showed the existence of a PSNE where the parties cluster into two groups. In fact, all the parties maintained separate identities and declared quite different policies to the electorate.

I infer that a more realistic variant of the probabilistic model must assume that candidates, or parties, are "policy motivated," at least to the extent of choosing positions that balance their policy and and electoral objectives. As one would expect, the Nash equilibrium (if it exists) may allow candidates to make very different promises (Cox 1984).

My observations about these models are intended to highlight the differences in the requirements of public finance and formal political theory. For public finance, the motivation is to extract predictions about political choice that can be used to evaluate the optimality of public decisions concerning taxation and public goods provision. The need to add greater political verisimilitude has obliged political theorists to address questions of belief formation (particularly regarding what voters believe the winning candidate will do after the election) and candidate commitment. From the perspective of public finance, the more refined model appears untidy and less parsimonious. The political theorist, however, faces the quite difficult task not just of comparing predictions with reality, but of evaluating how reasonable the assumptions about belief formation are. It is only recently that these belief-based models have been developed to a degree sufficient to offer plausible predictions.[20]

I have tried to suggest, in this brief section on elections, why the simple unidimensional two-candidate model of electoral competition is both theoretically and empirically inadequate. On the theoretical side, the attempt to base the analysis purely on techniques of preference aggregation proved to be unsatisfactory. As I have implied above, Downs paid considerable attention to questions of risk or uncertainty in elections, but the formal techniques to address those problems were not available at that time. The observation that these simple models were also empirically unsatisfactory gave greater weight to the theoretical attempt to model both preferences and beliefs. In the next section, I shall attempt to enlarge the discussion about the nature of beliefs, and show the connection with Condorcet's Jury Theorem.

The Importance of Beliefs and the Condorcetian Research Program

From the point of view of pluralistic political theory, no individual preference can be privileged over another. This could be taken to imply that no fundamental agreement may be reached among individuals who differ in their preferences. A Nash equilibrium in a game, or a voting equilibrium in a committee, specifies the nature of the compromise (rather than agreement) that individuals will accept given that they attempt to maximize what they prefer. In contrast to preferences, people with differing empirical beliefs about how the world works may come to agree with each other if they communicate and share information. Economists have recently attempted to model this process when beliefs are uncontaminated by preferences (Aumann 1976; McKelvey and Page 1986).

To some extent, political decision making is a matter of aggregating beliefs. Thus, while people may disagree about what action to take, debate may lead to an agreed solution. When two candidates offer differing courses of action (based on their own beliefs about the world), it is perfectly reasonable to suppose that the probability that a given voter chooses one candidate over the other is determined by the relative degree to which (s)he agrees with the two candidates' beliefs. From this point of view, the paradox of voter turnout (discussed by Green and Shapiro in Chapter 4) does not exist, since voting is not based on the desire to implement one's preferences but on the attempt to ascertain the truth.[21] Moreover, convergence of candidates to the same (Nash equilibrium) position is no longer a problem but a virtue, inasmuch as the equilibrium position is the one that has the highest probability of being "correct," given the distribution of beliefs in the society. Thus the Nash equilibrium result solves the optimality problem for political-economic theory.

This argument, admittedly, depends on the validity of the Condorcet Jury Theorem, which in turn depends on the assumption of the statistical independence of voter behavior (see Ladha and Miller 1995). This assumption may not be warranted when votes are determined by voters' beliefs. Moreover, if the candidates or voters are policy motivated, their policy concerns will "contaminate" the process of belief aggregation. Similarly, parties strong enough to impose policy objectives on candidates will also contaminate this process.[22] Nonetheless, since the empirical evidence suggests that party discipline in the U.S. Congress is weak, there may be a basis for inferring that successful congressional candidates at least approximate the "belief optimum" of their constituents.

The Jury Theorem depends on beliefs that are, in turn, dependent on the pattern of factions in the political economy. It should be possible, therefore, to use a more complex version of the theorem to resolve some of the questions raised by the Founding Fathers about the relationship between factions, institutional rules, and "good" government.[23] On the other hand, the "optimality" question that formal democratic theory may now pose is whether institutional rules and voters' and legislators' private preferences will intrude on the formation of the outcome that best represents the diverse beliefs of the members of the society.

Pursuing these issues will require the development of rationality models that incorporate both preferences and beliefs,[24] and it is obvious that the interrelation between beliefs and preferences is fundamental in the context of "social dilemmas" (discussed by Green and Shapiro in Chapter 5). Olson's (1965) attempt to analyze the problem of collective action (including voluntary provision of public goods and voter turnout) adopted the simpler perspective of preference aggregation. In this context it is traditional to use game theory to model the situation, and indeed to describe it as a prisoner's dilemma (Hardin 1971, 1982; Taylor 1976; Axelrod 1980; etc.).

The paradox of the n-person prisoners' dilemma, of course, is that the dominant or best strategy for each individual is to defect rather than cooperate. This inference was used as the basis for the argument that public goods would not be provided, or that interest groups would collapse in the absence of private incentives. Green and Shapiro point out that this argument flies in the face of reality. But they make no reference to the last decade of theoretical work on the prisoner's dilemma. This work has suggested that it is far too simplistic to infer that defection will always occur. One possibility is that a dominant player may bribe or persuade the other members of a group to form a cooperative coalition. It seems to me that these theoretical observations provide the basis for the "positive" literature on hegemony in international relations (e.g., Gilpin 1987). However, the possibility that cooperative coalitions can form entails that they may also collapse. Indeed, Diana Richards (1990) has recently demonstrated the occurrence of chaos, or unpredictability, in the experimental prisoner's dilemma. More recent analysis by David Kreps, Paul Milgrom, John Roberts, and Robert Wilson (1982), Robert Sugden (1986), Reinhard Selten and Rolf Stroecker (1986), Peyton Young (1993), and others has emphasized the importance of modelling the beliefs agents hold about the beliefs of others. Because the analysis of an agent's choice necessarily requires a model of what the agent thinks others will do and *why* they will do it, analysis of the relationship between beliefs and preferences must deal with the common knowledge problem.

While capitalism and democracy were initially viewed by rational choice theorists simply as methods of preference aggregation, all the current work has had to view rational agents not simply as preference maximizers, but as rational modellers of other agents and the world in which they live. To model another agent means modelling how that agent models others. The problem of common knowledge is whether there can be a formal basis for this hierarchy of individual knowledge. Although the question of why voters vote or why soldiers fight may seem very similar from the point of view of preference-based game theory, no plausible understanding of their behavior can ignore voters' or soldiers' beliefs. In these two cases, the relationship between beliefs and preferences could, in principle, be very different.

As the Arrovian and Condorcetian programs have intermingled over the last 50 years, two aspects of the resulting research program have been become increasingly obvious. First, the attempt to extend closed, preference-based economic theory to the political economy has failed. The motivation of this economistic program seems very similar in a sense to that of the "Hilbert program" of logically closing mathematics. Just as Gödel (1931) showed the Hilbert program to be impossible,[25] so, I believe, did Arrow demonstrate the inadequacy of the preference-based rational choice program.[25] A theory of rationality based on both preference and belief is likely to be "open," both in the sense that it is not completely mathematized[26] and also in the sense that it incorporates "nonrationalist," or at least "nonlogical," aspects of thought.[27]

Indeed, the recent book by Roger Penrose (1994) makes a strong case that the Gödel-Turing problem forbids any purely formalistic or computational account of self-awareness. I believe Penrose's argument implies that there must be fundamental constraints on our ability to model our own behavior. However, I feel these constraints apply not only to theoretical work, but even more importantly to all empirical accounts of behavior.

As the inadequacy of the formalism of "pure" preference-based game theory is increasingly appreciated, I predict that the flow of ideas between the theoretical and empirical aspects of political economy will increase. This is already evident in attempts to relate the positive theory of institutions to empirical work in political economy. For example, while Douglass North's (1990) ideas on institutions and economic performance grew out of his earlier empirical work in economic history (North 1981), they were also informed by the developments in game theory that I have mentioned above. Researchers on the positive aspects of political economy are increasingly aware of the way different institutions, whether economic or political, determine the "rules of the game" and thus the formation and maintenance of beliefs. This, in turn, can create the context for work of a predominantly empirical nature, but situated in political economies very unlike those of developed societies (e.g., Ensminger 1994). Thus while political economy will retain the normative and theoretical focus of the Condorcetian and Arrovian research programs, it will also increasingly sustain empirical work of a truly comparative nature.

Because Green and Shapiro consider only the applications of rational choice theory to American politics, they have presented an incomplete description of the current status of the theory and its empirical significance. Even so, their criticism will have served a useful purpose if it induces scholars to think about the nature of rationality in political economy.

I hope this essay will have served a similar purpose in reminding the reader that our ability to juxtapose theoretical and empirical analysis of human behavior is limited by the fundamental Gödel-Turing constraints on the consistency and completeness of self-knowledge.

NOTES

1. Of course the period 1759 to 1788 saw the publication of major works on "social design" in Britain and the United States as well as France. These include the *Theory of Moral Sentiments* (1759) and *The Wealth of Nations* (1776), by Adam Smith, and *The Federalist Papers* (1787 to 1788). See Muller 1993 for the notion of "social design" and Lasch 1991 for the notion of "progress" in Adam Smith. See also Commager 1977 for the influence of the French *philosophes* and Beer 1993 for the influence of Harrington and other British and European writers on the debate in the United States. I emphasize the importance of Condorcet's *Essai* of 1785 partly because his influence is less well known (perhaps due to its highly technical nature), but principally because Condorcet's insights are increasingly understood to be theoretically powerful. (See Urken n.d., forthcoming, for a

recent translation of Condorcet's *Essai* and McLean 1995 for a review of Condorcet's importance.)

2. It is necessary to assume in the theorem that the average juror probability of being correct exceeds one-half, and that the jurors' choices are made independently (see Grofman and Owen 1986). Recent results by Krishna Ladha (1992, 1993) indicate that the independence condition may be weakened, yet still preserve the Condorcet Jury Theorem.

3. See for example the "calculation" argument of F. A. Hayek (1976). It should be noted that the recent collapse of the economic system of the USSR may be viewed as corroboration that such a system is, in the long run, not well adapted to the generation of technological innovation, one key aspect of information aggregation. The reader may note that this theoretical argument concerning markets is identical in form to the Condorcetian argument concerning democracy. Thus the underlying question is how, exactly, different polities aggregate information.

4. Brian Arthur (1995) has recently shown the failure of models of rational expectations. Although Frank Page and Myrna Wooders (1995) have obtained a *sufficient* condition for "belief equilibrium" or "truth" in a market, it is possible for certain markets to exhibit a form of "chaos." I elaborate on this below.

5. Douglass North (1994) has emphasized how important it is to restructure economics to take account of dynamic effects: learning, innovation, the transformation of institutions, and so on. I refer to some of these effects below.

6. It is interesting that Jefferson and Condorcet are known to have been intimate friends in France (Randall 1993) in 1786 (the year before the publication of the first *Federalist Papers*). Jefferson and Madison corresponded regularly at that time. However, there is disagreement over the extent to which Jefferson and Madison were persuaded by Condorcet's views about the normative basis for government. In fact, since Condorcet argued for a unicameral assembly, there appears to have been some difference of opinion (see McLean and Urken 1992 and Urken 1991).

7. I have no objection to empirical testing, but it should be noted that the development of quantitative methods of analysis is essentially a recent phenomenon, dating from the 1950s. I suggest below that the various subfields of political economy are characterized by differing balances between normative, theoretical and empirical considerations. This implies differing roles for empirical falsification.

8. For example, empirical research might suggest that there is a correlation between political fragmentation and inflation. While this may be mildly interesting, if there is no effort to say why the correlation occurs, or to draw out inferences for the design of good government, then the result would be without theoretical or normative interest.

9. Important work in normative political theory by John Rawls (1972), David

Gauthier (1986), etc., is influenced, to some degree, by social choice theory. See also Binmore 1994 for an attempt to base normative political theory in game theory.

10. On the extent to which political science, as opposed to rational choice theory, involves empirical work, a recent analysis by Larry Grossbeck, a graduate student at Washington University, suggests that 68 percent of the non-RCT (rational choice theory) articles in the *American Political Science Review* during 1980–1993 had empirical content. Of the 22 percent of the articles classified as RCT, 29 percent had empirical content.

11. The extent of this importance is somewhat overemphasized by Green and Shapiro. In 1980–1982, about 10 percent of all *APSR* articles had some RCT content, while in 1990–92 the figure had increased to 26 percent.

12. For example, Grossbeck estimates that out of 145 RCT articles in the *APSR* between 1980 and 1993, about 20 percent were on comparative politics, 18 percent on international relations, 5 percent on normative political theory, and 14 percent on methodology. In my view, comparative politics has seen some of the most interesting applications of RCT, and the majority of these have been heavily empirical.

13. Work by Charles Plott (1967), Gerald Kramer (1973), Richard McKelvey (1976), Norman Schofield (1978a, 1984, 1985b), Linda Cohen (1979), Joseph Greenberg (1979), Steve Matthews (1982), Jeff Strnad (1985), McKelvey and Schofield (1986), and others elaborated the full structure of the spatial voting model. Essentially Black's intuition was shown to be generally true for any democratic voting procedure. That is, for each procedure, a voting equilibrium can only be guaranteed if the dimension is "low enough" (for majority rule, "low enough" means one). If the dimension is "high enough," the probability of an equilibrium is infinitesimal (for majority rule, "high enough" means two or three, depending on whether there is an odd or an even number of voters). In other words, instability is "generic."

14. A review essay by Richard McKelvey and Peter Ordeshook (1990) presents the data from over 30 different experiments carried out in the period 1978–1986. Out of many hundreds of observations, only 13 were outside the Pareto set, so these games were clearly nonchaotic. For the noncore games, I estimate that 80–90 percent of the observations were in the heart. Another model, the uncovered set, was developed during 1980-1986 (Miller 1980; Shepsle and Weingast 1984; McKelvey 1986). However this set is very difficult to compute, so I am unable to determine its predictive success based on the data presented by McKelvey and Ordeshook.

15. There is strong evidence that European polities can be assumed to have two-dimensional policy spaces (Schofield 1995b). Because of the unequal distribution of party strengths, a core party position can exist. Hence the chaos theorems do not apply.

16. In principle this could provide a "theoretical" explanation of the political "causes" of inflation. See n8 above.

17. See Poole and Rosenthal 1991 for empirical evidence on voting heterogeneity in the United States Congress. A recent anomaly is the Euopean-style Republican Contract With America, for whose measures Republican representatives appear to be voting as a bloc (as of April 1995).

18. Almost all the later election theories were implicit, to some degree, in Downs's book, including multiparty (coalition) competition and two-party competition. Only recently has this aspect of his work had much influence. (See Cox 1990 and Shepsle 1991, and the references therein.)

19. Most election theorists have been primarily interested in two-party competition. However, it is not obvious that theories of two-candidate elections in a single constituency have a lot to say about two-party competition across many constituencies.

20. A number of models of this type are presented in the volume edited by William Barnett et al. (1993). In any case, the rigorous empirical work I have mentioned seems to refute Green and Shapiro's assertion that rational choice theory is method-driven rather than problem-driven.

21. The "preference-based" problem of voter turnout is due to the fact that the "cost" of voting exceeds any likely effect from actually voting. This need not be the case for belief aggregation. A single juror may sway the remaining jurors and change the entire verdict.

22. To illustrate, whether a given bill should be interpreted as a compromise or as an agreement depends on whether votes are the result of preferences or beliefs. Note also that, under certain conditions, supermajority rule may be an optimal method of "belief aggregation" given the balance of the costs of different kinds of errors. See Schofield 1972.

23. In this connection, Madison's argument in *Federalist* X (mentioned above) can be interpreted to imply that heterogeneity and size in a polity weaken belief dependence, and so enchance the optimality of voting in the Republic.

24. See recent work by Yaw Nyarko (1993) and Cristina Bicchieri (1994).

25. See Wang 1987 for a discussion of Gödel's work.

26. See Binmore 1993 and Schofield 1995c for discussion of connections between rational choice theory and the work of Gödel 1931 and Turing 1937. In fact, both the game-theoretic assumption that agents learn about their opponents and that they choose their best response have recently been shown to be incompatible because of the Turing "halting problem" or *Entscheidungsproblem* (Nachbar 1995).

27. See Margolis 1994 for some interesting views on such a possibility.

Kenneth A. Shepsle

STATISTICAL POLITICAL PHILOSPHY
AND POSITIVE POLITICAL THEORY

Green and Shapiro's tour de force fails as a convincing critique of rational choice applications in political science because it locks itself into a statistical form of assessment. Rather than seeing the constructive side of rational choice theory, both as an engine of theoretical development and as a source of non-obvious empirical insights about politics, Green and Shapiro depart from the procedure in most sciences, comparing rational choice against an ideal rather than some concrete alternative. Finally, they fail to note the recent emphasis on sophisticated empirical testing of rational choice hypotheses.

Rational choice theory in political science is experiencing a mid-life crisis. Partly this is because many of its practitioners have reached middle age. But it is also because this body of theory has now reached maturity—in terms both of its evolution as science and its impact on political science. Twenty-five years ago a special issue of a journal like the present one would probably not have been possible; surely its contributors would have threatened to outnumber its readers.

Theoretical mid-life crisis is the subject of the recently published book by Donald Green and Ian Shapiro. In *Pathologies of Rational Choice Theory*, they have joined a bandwagon of recent reaction against the rational choice paradigm in political science.[1] Indeed, their book is likely to move

Kenneth A. Shepsle, Department of Government, Harvard University, Cambridge, MA 02138, telephone (617) 495–4928, telefax (617) 496–5149, is the author, most recently, of *Making and Breaking Governments: Cabinets and Legislatures in Parliamentary Democracies* (Cambridge, forthcoming).

right up to the front of the queue, becoming something of a bible for rational-choice bashers of all stripes.

There are several reasons to believe this volume will exert significant influence. First, the two authors, a political statistician and a political philosopher respectively, are smart fellows with important scholarly accomplishments; their critique flows from a credible source. Second, their book is full of insights about how to do better political science than has been practiced in the past. Third, they are especially strong in focusing both their critique and their suggestions for new research on the empirical side of things, striking a chord that will likely resonate with those impatient with, if not explicitly hostile to, formal (and often formidable) theory. Fourth, the book is written in a straightforward, accessible manner; the authors avoid superficiality or taking cheap shots most of the time, but also shun mathematical subtleties and nuances of argument over which the less-than-dedicated reader is likely to stumble. In short, the Yale Press has, in all probability, a hit on its hands.

But I did not like *Pathologies* very much. It is most assuredly provocative,[2] but it is unfriendly to the rational choice enterprise at the outset, confrontational, and ultimately unconstructive. Although it certainly does not contain inflammatory language, emotional rhetoric, or unsubstantiated charges, it is based (in this reader's opinion) on an immature account of how to do science—a statistical view that is rigid and mechanical. I will develop this theme in the pages to follow. This brief essay is not a wide-ranging review of *Pathologies*; it is a point-of-view piece, focusing on a small number of facets of the book that, in my opinion, detract from Green and Shapiro's broader project and weaken some of the strong empirical points they make.

Why Critique? Why Now?

The plethora of essays and edited volumes expressing concern about rational choice theory is reminiscent of the anguish caused in an earlier era by the growing dominance of behavioral studies in political research. Indeed, in a fashion strikingly parallel to the behavioral experience, many major political science departments at first refused to hire anyone in the rational choice tradition—"It's not political science; it's mathematics"—then consented to hire "just one" (at the junior level), and now have reached the point of worrying that the vandals are at the gates and that it will be difficult to avoid being overrun by rat choicers, regardless of the field in which a personnel search is under way.[3] This experience parallels the general movement of rational choice scholarship from research conducted by scholars at a handful of frontier outposts (Rochester, Carnegie-Mellon, Caltech, Washington University, Michigan State, Indiana, VPI), to the situation today, where rational choice scholars are found in the ranks of the most prestigious departments and their work is represented in the pages of the best journals and on the programs of the most important conferences.

With the foundations of rational choice fleshed out for well over a quarter-century now, and its penetration into substantive subfields in American politics (legislatures, voting and elections, bureaucracy, interest groups), comparative politics (parliamentary institutions, electoral systems, mass participation, democratization, economic development), and international relations (institutions, strategy, political economy) proceeding apace,[4] it has become a paradigm, a scientific regime, a target worthy of worthy adversaries. Somewhere out there, in a metaphor from the old West, is a graduate student's bullet with "rational choice" chiseled on it! In many respects, Green and Shapiro offer themselves as the intellectual gunslingers available to rid Dodge of the Riker Gang.

Rational choice theory is now a well-established technology for doing political science. It has had time to elaborate not only its foundations but applications as well. Its impact has flowed from minor tributary to mainstream, from back alley to main street, in political science. While it has had to jostle with other approaches, avoiding the sharp elbows of sociological and psychological paradigms, it has won a place at the intellectual table. Given the successes of recent years, today it no longer sits "below the salt." Its success, however, is not because of its mathematical elegance, but because rational choicers have moved out from foundational arguments (which, like debates within any church, are arcane and generally of interest only to those on the inside) to substantive concerns. This is especially evident in the field of legislative politics, where Fenno-style soakers and pokers, various sorts of quantitatively oriented observers, and rational choice modelers quite comfortably break bread together. They are all interested in the many facets of legislative life and consider their alternative approaches, with their respective strengths and weaknesses, as wholly compatible and complementary enterprises. So, too, is it in other fields, if not as dramatically and comprehensively as among the Congress jocks.

In sum, in a discipline noted for its lack of intellectual commitments, conventions, or party lines (or, what amounts to the same thing, its abundance of these things), rationality approaches, in all their polyglot forms, have become something of a focal point in late-twentieth-century political science. Having achieved this status, they have generated, at one and the same time, the comfortable environs in which normal science proceeds, and the constraining boundaries against which rebellious thinkers push. Taking on so substantial and increasingly established a paradigm now be-

216

comes something worth the effort; if successful, one could establish one's mark. This is "why critique," and it is "why now."

In the remaining pages of this essay, I want to focus on two methodological foundations of Green and Shapiro's *Pathologies*. First, they take what is in my view a rather unproductive statistical orientation toward science; second, they are disturbed by the "universalist aspiration" of rational choice theory, an aspiration that seeks to squeeze a vast heterogeneity of phenomena into the confines of a common framework. Each of these perspectives possesses some validity, but Green and Shapiro, I believe, push their analysis beyond the point of usefulness.

In concentrating on several methodological failings of *Pathologies*, and in not wandering very far from these moorings in my critique, I will say little about what I like in this book. So let me briefly do that here. Green and Shapiro are concerned with the empirical consequences of rational choice arguments. Their claim, one that they substantiate with a wide-ranging (though selective)[5] review of the empirical rational choice literature, is that formal theorists have not been very attentive to empirical implications, on the one hand, and have, on the other, been methodologically unsophisticated even when they have sought to test their theories. I could not agree more with the spirit of these sentiments, though I do so with the empathy of one who has at times been disdainful of the empirical consequences of formal arguments and has, at other times, tried (undoubtedly in an unsophisticated fashion) to deal systematically with real-world data.[6] *Pathologies* hammers home the fact that, for too long, positive political theory has been primarily a series of modeling exercises for which the excuse that its results are not yet ready for prime-time empirical testing is becoming increasingly lame. Despite the qualms about the thrust of their argument that I develop in the next section, I believe the impatience expressed by Green and Shapiro is defensible. Moreover, they scatter throughout *Pathologies* highly creative critiques of extant empirical work, accompanied by equally highly original suggestions for how to do it better. In this mode they are at their constructive best.

Green, Shapiro, and Statistical Philosophy

Although the strength of *Pathologies* resides in its dogged interrogation of formal models for empirical content, this interrogation is conducted in what I regard as a highly idiosyncratic manner. Green and Shapiro subscribe to the "tryout" philosophy of theory assessment. They invite a theory in for a reading, so to speak: an occasion on which the theory can be judged against data on the real-world phenomena it purports to explain.

Sitting out in the audience as judges, Green, Shapiro, and other empirical friends determine whether the tryout has been successful or not. Failure (and most, but not all, of the rational choice theories reviewed in *Pathologies* fail) ends that theory's prospects, and the judges wait for the next candidate to appear on stage.

I have two problems with the tryout philosophy of theory assessment, in particular, and two more general concerns. First, Green and Shapiro are not consistent about specifying a null against which a theory is compared. Indeed, in practice they examine theory X against no theory at all. Second, there is no middle ground in their statistical hypothesis-testing perspective; the theory (or some specific theoretical proposition) is either accepted or rejected, right or wrong, up or down. Third, their criticism of rational choice theory for its general empirical shortcomings is dated. Finally, they are dismissive of empirical methods that are not as systematic as a political statistician might demand. Let me take up each of these criticisms briefly.

Unspecified null. A long time ago, when I took philosophy of science courses in graduate school, I remember reading or hearing (though I cannot now remember where) about the First Law of Wing Walking. Simply stated, it advises, "Don't let go of something until you have something else to hold on to." In this view, theories are compared against alternative theories. In relatively undeveloped fields of inquiry, a theory may remain a live prospect, even though it is not a very good theory, because it trumps alternatives. It is imprudent to let go of it, since nothing more secure is available. (Because of this, theorists ought to remain modest at all times, and those of us who employ rational choice theory have occasionally displayed a hubris that has been self-damaging.) In more sophisticated fields the test will be sterner, because the alternatives are more rigorous and elaborate.

This is not as easy a theory-assessment regimen as it may first appear, for it requires the proponent of a novel theory to "nest" the relevant alternative theories into the assessment. Using a multivariate statistical instrument like ordinary least squares or logit as an assessment tool, for example, one would want to include variables not only from the novel theory but also from its strongest competitor; appropriate joint hypothesis tests permit assessments of the performance of the novel theory relative to its competitor. This allows the novel theory to subsume the alternatives, leading to cumulativeness in the theory-building enterprise. It also explicitly underscores the comparative nature of theory assessment.

Green and Shapiro claim to have provided alternative theoretical accounts—"normative, cultural, psychological, and institutional" (83–85)—throughout their critique. But these alternatives, first of all, are half-formed and half-baked. Second, the authors do not in any way, shape, or form actually compare the relative performance of these so-called alternatives. They are unhappy with rational choice, so they award the prize to some untested contender. In doing so, they commit the fallacy described next.

Updating theoretical beliefs. At the time I learned of the First Law of Wing Walking, I also was exposed to George Stigler's Parable of the Opera Singers. According to this story, two opera singers auditioned for a part. After the first candidate performed, the judges instantly awarded the part to the second! Green and Shapiro, finding a rational choice theory of, say, political participation wanting empirically, award the prize to a sociological alternative (without necessarily testing the latter). This approach is rigid and mechanical: rational choice is either valuable or it is not. If it is inadequate, then throw it away and either go back to the blank sheet on the drawing board (despite the First Law of Wing Walking) or embrace an alternative theory (despite the lesson of the Parable of the Opera Singers). In practice, it seems to me, this approach discards a lot of useful information. The life and death of a theoretical idea surely cannot, and should not, hinge on any specific empirical test. The theorist, instead, updates his or her beliefs about a theory on the basis of evidence, develops hunches about which bits of it should be retained and which jettisoned, and on that basis formulates views on what steps should be taken next. Science is not a horse race or an election in which a winner is declared once and for all. Science is a belief system, always in flux, in which more or less weight is placed on competing theoretical ideas in light of both new arguments and new evidence.

The recent generation of rational choice theory. It seems to me that in assessing a field of study in terms of its empirical persuasiveness, one should not look at the field as a whole, nor at average or representative pieces of research, and certainly not at the weaker empirical efforts. Rather, a field should be assessed according to its most refined arguments and its most sophisticated empirical evaluations. In reading *Pathologies*, I was struck by the degree to which some of the stronger work was not given its due. I cited some in the electoral realm in note 5 above. In the legislative realm, an area in which I have greater familiarity with the literature, there has been a tremendous outpouring of extremely sophisticated theory combined with equally sophisticated empirical examination: Krehbiel 1991 on information and legislative structure, Kiewiet and McCubbins 1991 on legislative delegation, and Cox and McCubbins 1993 on legislative parties, to name but three, develop rationality-based theories in which, on the basis of sophisticated data analysis, a lively debate within the subfield continues to this day, a debate informed by both analytical argument and empirical assessments.[7] These books are mentioned by Green and Shapiro in passing in their discussion of legislative research, and treated more extensively and lauditorily in their concluding chapter. They do not, however, modify their strictures against "pathological" rational choice models despite these exemplary pieces of empirical scholarship.

Hard theory, soft assessment. I concur with Green and Shapiro that rational choice theorists tend to be much more rigorous in their theorizing than in assessing the results. There are exceptions, and I have tried to point some out and argue that judgments about a field should concentrate on these superior products. On the whole, though, the comparative advantage of rational choice theorists lies in deriving theoretical propositions and advancing theoretical arguments; empirical assessment is a secondary matter, and we are often content to point to some stylized facts or anecdotes as sufficient to keep a theory plausible. Even though this has begun to change quite substantially, as more and more theorists hold themselves to high empirical standards, it is incontrovertible that more systematic empirical assessment is to be preferred—who could argue with that?

But political statisticians are often contemptuous of anything short of hard assessment—systematic, comprehensive, and sophisticated data analysis. Formal theories don't always lend themselves to these high-powered forms of analysis. Indeed, precisely because such theories employ carefully specified concepts and often draw subtle distinctions, the normal sorts of data problems that plague all the social sciences are magnified. How, for example, does one estimate whether a game-theoretic forecast obtains when it implies the use of mixed strategies? It is not impossible, but the subtlety required is often overwhelmed by the crudeness of our technology of measurement. In light of this, I am much more charitable toward relatively soft assessments—for example, assessments drawing on the participant-observations of the behavior of senators, gathered from one of Fenno's "soaking and poking" exercises—even though such observations may entail selection biases and other (unknown) departures from representative sampling of the universe in question. These softer assessments clearly convey less (and less reliable) information than would a design that took *ex ante* account of statistical requirements. But they are not useless, since they force even the most abstract of theorists to confront his or her arguments with other than make-believe worlds, thereby—albeit in a subjective sort of way—enhancing or diminishing one's confidence in a given theory.

While rational choice theory and its applications tend toward hard theory and soft assessment, much of the truly sophisticated statistical work in political science combines soft (or no) theory with hard assessment. It is not apparent to me that a reasonable person could defend a preference for the one or the other. My hunch, however, is that the world of hard theory and soft assessments provides a much firmer foundation for scientific progress—precisely by following some of the advice on measurement and data analysis proferred by Green and Shapiro—than is provided by the more sophisticated empirical enterprises that are only weakly grounded in theory; at best, it seems to me, the latter can only provide more and more refined regularities that might serve as grist for someone's (including the rational choice theorist's) mill.

The Universal Aspirations of Rational Choice

Green and Shapiro believe that one of the root causes of the methodological failing of rational choice theory is its insistence on being a universal theory, a theory that applies always and everywhere. Surely they are right if, by rational choice theory, they mean an incredibly stripped-down and simplified version. It is implausible that a highly simplified theory could be applicable in a wide range of circumstances; such a theory is likely to be serviceable only where the suppression of texture and detail does minimal damage.

But how could any theory that is more than a recapitulation of observations not aspire, at the very least, to "conditional universality"? By this I mean the applicability of theoretical claims to all circumstances demarcated by a stipulated set of conditions. Thus, Duncan Black's famous theorem asserts: *If* alternatives are unidimensional, *if* preferences over them are single-peaked, and *if* decisions are made by majority rule, *then* the median alternative will be chosen. A rational choice theorist would claim that this assertion holds in all circumstances that satisfy the well-defined conditions appearing in the statement of the theorem. In principle, laboratory experiments can determine the empirical validity of this theorem's claim so that, once established, departures from its predictions in a natural, non-experimental setting lead one to explore which of the premises failed to hold.

Green and Shapiro, however, probably have something slightly different in mind. They implicitly argue that while rational choice theory may be suitable in some realms, alternative theories—cultural, psychological, or whatever—are more appropriate in others. This is not, in my view, a very satisfactory approach, since it fails to provide a theoretical basis for establishing which type of theory is appropriate to which realm. To do so would require theoretical arguments as to why rationality fails as a theoretical engine in some particular context.

The real problem, of course, is that Green and Shapiro believe that cultural, psychological, or institutional explanations really are alternatives to rational choice explanations, a belief that most rational choice theorists would reject. Indeed, rational choice theorists in recent years have rescued institutional explanations from the behavioral graveyard to which they had been relegated for a quarter-century or more; incorporated cultural explanations into their framework by acknowledging dynamic features, repeat-play, and intertemporal properties of social phenomena; and generalized their "models of man" to accommodate both hard-wired limitations in human computing capabilities and the very real costs of information acquisition and processing. In short, rational choice theorists have been admirably attentive to their theoretical critics, accommodating and subsuming alleged anomalies. That we will be attentive to our empirical critics, such as Green and Shapiro, is indicated by the fact that, contrary to the impression left by *Pathologies*, rational choice theorists of the last decade have vigorously pursued precisely the sort of empirical agenda urged by Green and Shapiro.

Mid-life crisis or not, the rational choice paradigm has not shied away from extending its reach to new areas of political structure and behavior. In the years that have passed since the first rational-choice analyses of arms races, American elections, and congressional politics, the paradigm has been extended to include theories of presidential and judicial action; multiparty electoral competition; parliamentary politics and coalition governments; the design of party systems, electoral institutions, and whole constitutions; debate, deliberation, and other forms of information acquisition and dissemination; ethnic conflict; and delegation and other principal-agent intergovernmental relationships. The full list, of which this is only a partial selection, is very long indeed.

The empirical assessment of rational choice theories now proceeds in a more sophisticated manner, as well. But rational choice is mainly a theoretical beacon—a firm foundation for scientific understandings of politics. The more constructive bits of Green and Shapiro's critique deserve attention, and are already receiving it. But I doubt the main thrust of *Pathologies* will deter many political scientists from proceeding with our work.

NOTES

1. I use the term "against" advisedly, since the entries in this literature range from the gently chiding, to the constructively critical, to the thoroughly hostile. They include Cook and Levi 1990; Elster 1986, 1989c; Mansbridge 1990; Monroe 1991; Slote 1989; and, of course, Barry 1970.

2. The book's impact is suggested by roundtables specially designated to discuss it at successive annual meetings of the American Political Science Association, as well as long stories about it in *The Chronicle of Higher Education*, *Lingua Franca*, and the (London) *Times Higher Education Supplement*.

3. Ironically, Yale's department, in which both Green and Shapiro reside, is a

significant exception to this pattern, landing one of the preeminent positive political theorists, Gerald Kramer, in the late 1960s, hosting important visitors like Norman Schofield and Michael Taylor in the 1970s, and continuously seeking to expand its rational-choice stable throughout this period.

4. I have left political philosophy off the list since, from time immemorial, the philosophers have often regarded man and the state as rational, interest-pursuing entities. There's nothing new about which some early modern, such as Machiavelli or Hobbes or Hume, didn't write—if it hadn't already been anticipated by an ancient.

5. For example, I was rather surprised that in their treatment of voting and elections, Green and Shapiro do not even mention Fiorina (1981) and the literature on retrospective voting spawned by his work; nor do they discuss the continuing series of books by Paul Abramson, John Aldrich, and David Rohde on change and continuity in elections.

6. These latter efforts include Shepsle 1978 on committee assignments and Laver and Shepsle 1996 on government formation in parliamentary regimes.

7. These debates are summarized in Shepsle and Weingast 1994, which introduces a special issue of the *Legislative Studies Quarterly* devoted to theoretical and empirical controversies. These essays will appear as a collection in Shepsle and Weingast 1995.

Michael Taylor

WHEN RATIONALITY FAILS

Pathologies of Rational Choice Theory *is a largely valid critique of the rational choice approach to politics. Rational choice theory may be useful under some conditions, but a general characterization of these suggests that American political behavior is unpromising terrain. Some forms of behavior cannot without strain be treated as instrumental; some sources of behavior cannot be accomodated by any theory built wholly out of preferences and beliefs. Explaining cooperation, in particular, requires attention to normative, expressive, and intrinsic motivations and social identification, and to the conditions in which they are mobilized.*

As I'm sure most rational choice theorists and practitioners know, there is a great deal of real prejudice about their work: it is rejected and despised by people who know very little about it—sometimes, as I have learned at first hand, by people who have no understanding of it whatsoever. So it is refreshing to read a detailed critique of the rational choice approach by two authors who have taken the trouble to inform themselves about what they are criticizing—who have, in fact, read a substantial part of the literature of rational choice in political science, understood most of what they've read, and produced a measured and constructive response to it. This makes Green and Shapiro's *Pathologies of Rational Choice Theory* a unique book, and a valuable one.

They criticize rational choice theorists on their own terrain. They are not anti-science, do not object to mathematical modelling, and are agnos-

---

Michael Taylor, Department of Political Science, University of Washington, Seattle, WA 98195, telephone (206) 543–2766, telefax (206) 685–2146, is the author of *Community, Anarchy and Liberty* (1982) and *The Possibility of Cooperation* (1987) and the editor of *Rationality and Revolution* (1988), all published by Cambridge University Press.

tic about the premise of instrumental rationality as a foundation for explaining political behavior. Their criticism of rational choice theorists—of those, at least, who aspire to develop empirically supported explanations—is that they fail to live up to their own ideals. Their focus is on the ability of rational choice theory (RCT)—or rational actor models (RAMs)—to explain certain political phenomena in the United States, namely voter turnout, contributions to collective political causes (especially interest groups), legislative behavior, and party competition. Their claim is that, at least in these domains, "to date few theoretical insights derived from rational choice theory have been sujected to serious empirical scrutiny and survived" (9). Rational choice theorists have done much splendid theorizing, but often with little reference to the real world (a criticism which of course has long been levelled, in my view with justification, against the economic theory from which RCT is derived); and when they have been interested in the evidence they have often uncovered it, and used it, selectively.

It has to be said that this criticism can fairly be directed against other kinds of theorizing in the social sciences, some of which make no contact at all with any facts, if indeed they allow for the existence of such things. Yet this should not be used as an excuse by rational choice theorists. *Pathologies* will no doubt give comfort to the many who already prejudicially loathe RCT and encourage others to dismiss the approach entirely without having to do their own homework. But it should be welcomed by rational choice theorists anyway. Taking its lessons to heart, they might do better.

Would Green and Shapiro's judgment of RCT have been less unfavorable if their book's scope had been wider? After all, rational choice theories of collective action alone have been applied to not only voting and interest groups but social movements, rebellions, and revolutions; cooperation amongst capitalists, workers, peasants, hunter-gatherers, nation-states, and nonhuman animals; collective action problems amongst users of a wide range of common-pool resources (from local fisheries to the planetary atmosphere); and more.

My view is that Green and Shapiro's judgment could fairly apply to the whole body of rational choice social science. RCT typically does not approach the evidence in an open-minded way; it never seriously considers and rarely even countenances the possibility of alternative explanations based on non-rational choice premises. Rational choice students of collective action, in particular, standardly ignore a range of motivations that can give rise to cooperation, or else treat them in a limited form in which they can be accomodated artificially within the rational choice framework. (I'll discuss some of these motivations later). This is an aspect of a very general and very large failing of rational choice work, including economics: its programmatic blindness to the rich diversity of ways in which humans value things (its insistence on reducing them all to preferences). Unfortunately this failing is not remediable within the rational choice framework, in part because it is unable to deal with influences on behavior which do not work through preferences and beliefs—the only materials used in the whole rational choice edifice.

Before proceeding, I should make it clear that I do not want my comments to be understood as a complete rejection of the rational choice approach. Pareto (writing of Kepler) said: "Give me a fruitful error any time, full of seeds, bursting with its own corrections." Perhaps this is how we should think of RCT, for the time being. And though the Final Theory, which we'll never have, is unlikely to be a merely corrected and amended RCT, I am convinced that rational choice would have a nontrivial part to play in it.

When Rational Choice Should Work

The response of several rational choice practitioners to the mixed explanatory performance of their approach is to withdraw to the position that the approach has explanatory power in some domains but not in others. If this just means abandoning domains ad hoc as they are found to be refractory to rational choice theorizing, then Green and Shapiro are right to call this position "arbitrary domain restriction." It would be less arbitrary (and of great practical interest) if we had a good predictive theory which told us when and why a rational choice account would and would not work.

Consider the following attempt at such a theory: rational choice explanations are most likely to work where (i) the courses of action available to the actor are limited; (ii) the costs and benefits attached to the alternative courses of action are, to the agent in question, well defined and clearly apparent; and (iii) much, for the agent, turns on his or her choice.[1]

On one reading this argument seems to be, or to come close to being, a tautology: a rational choice explanation—which is to say, an explanation of action in terms of certain specified incentives, or benefits and costs—works well when the postulated incentives are the most (or only) important motivators for the actor (or: when other motivators, other sources of action, are absent or relatively unimportant). But what might be the contingent truth intended here? One possibility is that incentives of the kind usually assumed by rational choice theorists (economic or material incentives supplemented, perhaps, by a desire for social approbation or acceptance) are, as a matter of fact, the most powerful motivators for most people, and if *these* costs and benefits are big enough, *other* motivators and sources of action, although often present, will tend to be outweighed. I'll return to this thought later.

A second possibility is that, because so much is at stake—because so much turns on choosing with reference exclusively to the specified incentives—only those who so choose will survive or prosper, and the differently motivated will tend to be eliminated or to learn how to act rationally. In other words, there are processes at work by which nonrational behaviors (or their carriers) are *selected* out, or *filtered* out (by social learning and cultural inheritance), or both in combination.

We might therefore add to the first three conditions for the applicability of RCT a fourth condition: (iv) "repetition": prior to the choice situation in question, there have been many similar or analogous occasions. Perhaps we need also a fifth condition, which further specifies what is conducive to learning, or working out, how to make rational choices: (v) the connections between the means and the ends (which themselves are well defined) are transparent; i.e., the actors can understand the effects of what they do on the outcomes.[2]

I think there is something to this line of reasoning about the applicability of RCT; but we have to proceed very cautiously. The one area where we can have some confidence that observed behavior has been molded by selection pressures in the direction of optimality is, of course, the behavior of nonhuman animals shaped by *natural* selection. An instructive example is the behavior of Great tits (*Parus major*) as revealed in experiments done by John Krebs and others (1978). Two perches delivered food to the birds on different random schedules. One of the perches delivered more food on average; an optimal "strategy" would require a bird to devote a certain definite proportion of its fixed time in the apparatus to discovering which of the two it was. Elaborate calculations, informed by some advanced mathematics, are required for humans to solve this problem. The birds' behavior comes very close to the correct solution. Thus, they behave *as if* they were clever rational actors. We have good reason (an empirically well-supported general theory of evolution) to suppose that this ability is the product of natural selection. And we have good reason to suppose that *much* (but not all) nonhuman animal behavior is "rational" in the sense that it solves optimization problems.

Now, in cases like this, even though the animal is not a rational actor, RCT contributes something to the explanation of its behavior—it sheds light at least on what the animal is doing, what problem it is "solving"—and that is why biologists and ethologists are now finding good use for decision theory and game theory. (Perhaps this is the only domain where RCT is truly appropriate!) But no biologist or ethologist would say that

RCT *was* the explanation of the behavior of *Parus major*. There is indeed a sense in which it is doing no explanatory work at all, but is merely helping to show what has to be explained.

In the sphere of *human* behavior, a mechanism analogous to that of natural selection—namely, selection by market competition—has been proposed as an explanation of profit maximizing (or satisficing) by firms (Alchian 1950; Nelson and Winter 1982; and see the critical discussion in Elster 1983). The managers of firms may not understand how to maximize profit, may not even consciously try to do so, but those firms using procedures which don't in fact maximize profit, or at least return a satisfactory profit, will be (blindly) selected out. Therefore (most of) the firms we observe should be profit maximizers.

One problem with this argument (there are others) is that, while we can be fairly confident that giraffes have long necks because, over an extended period, long necks gave their possessors an advantage in getting food, we do not know what it is that enables firms to make enough money to survive. At any rate, there is much disagreement about this—about how firms should be run internally, how they should relate to other firms, and so on.

There are, however, cases—which satisfy all five criteria for the applicability of RCT—where it could plausibly be argued that selection *and*, more importantly, filtering (e.g., *cultural* evolution) have produced patterns of human behavior which are rational or optimal, given their environments. In these cases there is a more transparent connection between means and ends than exists between the choices of managers and their firms' bottom lines. The production choices made by hunter-gatherers, tribal cultivators, and peasants are plausible candidates. Individual peasants, choosing seed varieties, sowing times, or techniques of cultivation, may or may not consciously make optimizing calculations, but over time, through obvious selection and filtering mechanisms—provided that conditions and the available options have been relatively stable—they are collectively likely to arrive at optimal choices. These are actions that a rational choice theory could adequately explain, even though those who make the choices think they are following custom or looking to magical signs for guidance; as sometimes they do. The same argument should apply to the foraging strategies of hunter-gathers, or the form of their arrangements for reciprocal access to food resources.[3] (Although hunter-gatherers often have plenty of time on their hands, their subsistence practices have to be such as to meet the real constraints of periodical scarcity).

So there *are* "domains" (though not, perhaps, in the sense intended by Green and Shapiro) where, it seems to me, we can have some confidence in the suitability of RCT—though, again, it will be only a *part* of a full explanation, or only *facilitate* a good explanation. These "domains" are indicated by the five conditions I've suggested for the applicability of RCT, if we interpret them as producing rational behavior through selection and especially filtering processes.

Rational Choice vs. Expressive Behavior

But notice how far my examples in the last section are from the sphere of interest to Green and Shapiro: political behavior in the United States. RCT cannot explain such behavior—and much other behavior; or it does not explain it well. To explore why this is so, I want to add my own constructive criticisms of RCT to, and amplify, those advanced by Green and Shapiro.

In strikes, protests, and rebellions, a certain sequence is sometimes observed. A small number of people ("the leaders") initiate action, often risking substantial penalties (loss of livelihood, or liberty, or even life). Then, and only then, others ("the followers") join in, though not all at once. Still others do not participate at all. If the collective action succeeds, members of all three groups benefit. Suppose that there are no direct, material, selective incentives for participation. How does RCT cope with the diversity of action here? Not too well, I fear.

The RCT of collective action as presented by Olson—which is where the theory is stuck in some people's minds—might say that at least it explains the behavior of those in the third group, the non-joiners. Its defenders might also argue that the followers are an example of what Olson called an intermediate group, and could therefore somehow overcome the free-rider problem. Or if the RCT of collective action encompasses the theory of repeated games, it could claim to explain the behavior of those in the second group (as rational conditional cooperators) as well as those in the third (whose thresholds for conditional cooperation are too high).

This leaves the first group, the leaders. Here, rational choice theorists might say that rational actors are concerned not only with material incentives, or not only with the benefits brought by successful collective action[4] and the costs of contributing, but also with what are sometimes called *solidary* incentives, especially reputation and social (dis-)approbation. If, with Harsanyi (1969), we believe that "people's behavior can be largely explained in terms of two dominant interests: economic gain and social acceptance," we could draw the line here and *assume* these two interests to explain the behavior of the leaders; then at least we would have an explanation that could, in principle, be refuted. For if we can add any incentives we like, ad hoc, to "explain" this or that action, then the hypothesis of rational action is a tautology (as Barry 1970 warned us long ago) and RCT is not distinct from the ordinary exercise of *interpreting* action, in which we all engage and which some "theorists" believe to be the best we can do. As Green and Shapiro note, rational choice theorists have often been tempted down this path of "*post hoc* embellishment."

But if the theory admits only these two (or any two) classes of incentives, it will often be wrong. Leaders of strikes, protests, and the like, seem sometimes to be motivated not by a concern for their reputation, but by their normative (including ideological) beliefs or commitments. To call these all indiscriminately *incentives* ("purposive incentives"), as some writers do—to treat them as just another set of benefits and costs that motivate people instrumentally or consequentially—is, I think, a gross error. (This is, to repeat, what RCT *has to* do: reduce every source of action and behavior to preferences and beliefs). Moreover, to reduce the effects of social relationships on action and behavior to nothing more than incentives ("social sanctions")—as many, including I, have done—is also a mistake. (I'll return to this below).

Some of the ways in which our normative beliefs give rise to or enter into motivation can be accomodated by the model of instrumental rationality—but only by adding incentives to the standard model: a desire to maintain one's self-respect, to do the right thing, to avoid unpleasant feelings like guilt, and so on. Others cannot, as where they are part of an attitude or complex of attitudes I call *commitment*.

We can be committed to norms and to practices (or we can say that to be committed to a practice is just to be committed to the norms that constitute it). There is not room here to explain fully what I have in mind, but very briefly: to be committed to something is, first, to view competing or conflicting alternatives to it as *incommensurable* with it, to refuse in thought or deed to exchange its value for competing ones. Second, a commitment functions as an *exclusionary reason* (in the sense developed by Joseph Raz), that is, a (second-order) reason to refrain from acting on some particular (first-order) reason or reasons. And third, to have a commitment is to have certain (usually tacit) normative beliefs which are included in or entailed by incommensurability and exclusion, and to have a (usually backgrounded) desire for one or more internal goods.

I am not suggesting that those who initiate protests and rebellions are generally people with commitments, but I do believe this is sometimes the case. In another context, a clear illustration of commitment and how it "motivates" is provided by the behavior of those who, at enormous risk to themselves and their families, rescued Jews during World War II. One thing that emerges very clearly from many of the interviews that have been conducted with surviving rescuers[5] is that, although they were aware at some level of the very great risks, they did not take them into account, did not weigh costs and benefits; they say *they could not have done otherwise, that not offering shelter would have been unthinkable.* In other words, other considerations, in particular the very great costs that would normally have mattered for them a great deal, were in this context excluded, or silenced.

We can say that commitment-derived behavior is *expressive* of a *self* constituted by commitments. Expressive behavior in this sense cannot be accomodated by any version of RCT. The best that economists and rational choice theorists can do (if they do not simply deny that there are incommensurable values) is to reduce this complex of attitudes to lexicographic preferences. But incommensurability and the excluding or silencing of reasons are not captured by such preferences (which, in any case, would make serious trouble for utility-maximizing models).

Our attitudes to norms are various—commitment, in the strong sense I've just defined, is one, possibly not very common form—and they therefore affect our behavior in different ways that are not well understood. But there is much evidence—from experiments, surveys, and other sources—that certain norms, especially norms of reciprocity and fairness, are widely endorsed and motivate (or in some way give rise to) behavior—most commonly, perhaps, via emotions of self-assessment, such as guilt and shame.

If RCT either neglects normative and expressive motivations altogether or incorporates them in ways that fail to do them justice, we are not for that reason thrown into the arms of those sociologists who see norms (or identities) behind every action—who see people in groups necessarily generating norms, everyone endorsing those norms or properly socialized to accept them, such endorsement or socialization infallibly giving rise to motivation to act in accordance with them, and, most heroically of all, such motivation being sufficient for action.[6]

Identificatory and Intrinsic Motivation

There are (at least) two other sources of action and behavior that are highly relevant to the study of cooperation and collective action, but that are both ignored by RCT, despite the substantial experimental literature establishing their significance. The first is "social identification." Briefly: if a person defines herself as a member of a group, or if her membership in a group (even a group defined by some trivial or arbitrary criterion) is made cognitively salient, then she is more likely to observe the group's norms and to cooperate with group members in "social dilemmas." This is a very robust finding of many experiments done by social psychologists. (Turner 1984 provides a convenient introduction.)

The second is intrinsic motivation.[7] Intrinsically motivated action is done for its own sake; the "reward" is the activity itself. Psychologists have shown—again a very robust finding—that extrinsic rewards (like money) *weaken* intrinsic motivation if the extrinsic reward is made contingent on doing well at an intrinsically interesting activity. A person's enjoyment of and interest in an intrinsically interesting activity *diminishes* when the extrinsic reward is introduced, and she is likely to be less resourceful and creative in her approach to it. Of course, the extrinsic reward can itself be a powerful motivator (though not good at inducing creative effort), but it nevertheless tends to reduce, not to augment, intrinsic motivation. This is the effect of an extrinsic *reward*; obviously, extrinsic punishment, or coercion, is not good for intrinsic motivation either.

How social identification works—the causal paths to the behavior to which it gives rise—is unclear. But it seems not to operate through any sort of instrumental rationality, and it is not describable in the standard folk-psychological terms of RCT. In any case, the reality of social identification and its ability to overcome the free-rider problem, even amongst total strangers who will never meet again, must, I think, be accepted.

The significance of intrinsic motivation for the RCT of collective action is obvious. Many (but not all) of the activities that are standardly treated by economists and other rational choice theorists as costs—interesting work, some political activities, but not (e.g.) mailing checks to your favorite causes—may, in fact, be rewards. (Since work may be its own reward, the phenomenon of intrinsic motivation can play havoc with some economic theories, too). We should note in passing the dangers of treating policy prescription and institutional design purely as exercises in manipulating incentives (as many economists and rational choice theorists in political science have urged us to do), given that extrinsic rewards and penalties can undermine intrinsic motivation.

Explaining Cooperation: Two Stories

Normative motivation, expressive motivation, intrinsic motivation, social identification . . . RCT ignores them all. Its excuse may be that we cannot have theory without simplification; besides, we do not have a clear understanding of how these other motivations interact with instrumental rationality and with each other. This is true; but it is not a good excuse. It would be a better excuse if the simplifications actually assumed by RCT had yielded empirically successful explanations. Since, as Green and Shapiro show, they have not (yet), we should be more open-minded about the sources of collective action and of other social behavior.

Consider, for example, an argument about collective action which is now, I believe, empirically well supported: that cooperation is facilitated by community, by social networks, by repeated interaction in a stable group, by ongoing social relationships—the argument takes different forms, which there is not space here to lay out carefully. *How* do such social relations facilitate cooperation? The answer given by rational choice theorists is, of course, that such relations provide (or just are) a set of *incentives* which make it *rational* to cooperate. Continuing interaction facilitates rational conditional cooperation, and if that is not enough, then a community makes available a range of positive and negative sanctions sufficiently powerful to overcome free riding and bring about cooperation.[8]

We can, however, tell a quite different story about the role of community (etc.) in collective action: that *a community provides the conditions in which normative motivation, social identification, and in some cases intrinsic motivation are mobilized*. In stable groups, where people have continuing social ties, certain norms are likely to emerge, or certain universal norms to be seen as applicable. Norms of reciprocity and fairness—requirements that everyone in the group do his or her fair share for the collective good—are widely endorsed, but are seen as applicable only in certain conditions: normative motivation is not mobilized in coercive, inegalitarian conditions lacking trust. Continuing interaction with others in stable groups is also likely to give rise to social identification; community is especially conducive to this. And finally, as we have seen, intrinsic motivation is undermined by coercion, by the use of extrinsic rewards and punishments. Insofar as social ties, interactions in networks, and so on, are uncoercive, trusting, respectful, and relatively egalitarian (which is certainly not the case in *all* communities), and so long as the collective action requires contributions of effort that are intrinsically interesting, intrinsic motivation will also contribute to cooperation.

The only role rational choice theorists have found for norms in explaining cooperation is that of coordinating the expectations of players in a repeated game so that they may converge on an equilibrium. This is the line that has been taken by political economist Gary Miller (1992) in his notable recent effort to understand why there is more *hierarchical* cooperation—cooperation between superiors and subordinates—in some firms than in others. Norms are here wheeled out to save noncooperative game theory from the indeterminacy arising from the existence of multiple equilibria. The role of such norms is, in effect, to guide the beliefs of rational egoists, enabling them to achieve their best outcomes, given their preferences. On this account, norms have no motivating power of their own. Faced with conditional cooperation, rational choice theorists simply *assume* that it is the behavior of rational actors responding to social sanctions, or of players in a repeated game who may, at most, need a little help from social norms to select an equilibrium.

I submit that there are alternative explanations of why people cooperate in some conditions and not in others, explanations which have as much plausibility and are built on premises with much empirical support. It is as reasonable to begin from the premise, for example, that people in a group cooperate because they identify with the group and are disposed to respect its norms (and may even be committed to them). In the case of hierarchy, cooperation (when it occurs) might be explained not as the rational conditional cooperation of purely self-interested actors, but in terms of normative (and perhaps expressive) and intrinsic motivations that can be mobilized or activated if (and only if) hierarchical subordinates are treated by their superiors in the right way.[9]

I am not arguing that people never behave like rational egoists (this is obvious nonsense), or that the rational choice account of cooperation is no part of the truth and should be put aside. And I am not arguing that the sociologists and psychologists, individually or collectively, have a good alternative *theory*: they do not. The work that has been done on normative, expressive and intrinsic motivation and social identification does not amount to a unified, complete theory; far from it. Indeed, some of the work making use of these ideas—especially that of certain sociologists who see norms or identities unproblematically behind all collective action—is built on assumptions every bit as heroic as those of RCT. I argue, rather, that we should not *assume* that cooperative (and other) behavior must rest on rational choice. We should instead at least consider the possibility that, though we sometimes act in an instrumentally rational fashion, we are also capable of acting from normative, expressive, and intrinsic motivations and from a sense of social identification; that in *some* conditions one or more of these are engaged or mobilized; and that *this* is what explains at least some cooperative behavior.

In the final sentence of their book, Green and Shapiro tell us that instead of answering the question, "Whether or not rational choice theory?" (Them or Us?), we should be asking, "How does rationality interact with other facets of human nature and organization to produce the politics that we seek to understand?" What I have attempted here is to sketch one partial answer, in one particular context, to just that question.

NOTES

1. These three conditions constituted my attempt, in Taylor 1988, to characterize the proper domain of RCT. This was extended in Taylor 1989, with the

addition of condition (iv) below. Versions of some of these conditions had been suggested earlier by several writers, and have been proposed again in the last two or three years by several rational choice theorists cited by Green and Shapiro, 27–28. I do not claim that the five conditions are either necessary or collectively sufficient; only that, *ceteris paribus*, the more any one of them is satisfied, the more successful an RCT is likely to be.

2. See Ernest Gellner, "The Gaffe-Avoiding Animal," in Gellner 1985. To RAM-bashers generally, especially those impressed by "culture," I recommend Gellner's collected works, especially this volume.

3. For examples of recent work bearing on these claims, see Smith and Winterhalder 1992 and Cashdan 1990.

4. According to Green and Shapiro's reading of the RCT of collective action, collective benefits are irrelevant to an individual's decision. This is wrong. Whether or not any particular theorist believes this, the correct rational-choice formulation must be that free riding occurs if the costs to the individual of making a contribution exceed *the benefits to him of the increased amount of the non-excludable good which results (directly or indirectly) from his contribution*, plus the selective benefits contingent on his contribution, if there are any. There are other flaws in Green and Shapiro's account in Chapter 5 of the RCT of collective action: interpersonal communication *is* recognized as important when the game is not a one-shot Prisoners' Dilemma; the expectation of a finite number of repetitions *does* make a difference under some circumstances; and decentralized incentives are *not* deemed necessarily ineffectual. These errors stem from the authors' incomplete picture of the RCT of collective action.

5. See for example Monroe, Barton, and Klingemann 1990 and Fogelman 1994.

6. Goldstone 1994 is a good example, though I agree, of course, with most of what he says about the role of community, etc., in revolutionary collective action.

7. See Deci and Ryan 1985 and Lane 1991, Part VI.

8. For some different versions, see Taylor 1982, Granovetter 1985, and Ellickson 1991.

9. See Taylor n.d., forthcoming.

Donald P. Green and Ian Shapiro

PATHOLOGIES REVISITED:
REFLECTIONS ON OUR CRITICS

More than three decades after its advent in political science, rational choice theory has yet to add appreciably to the stock of knowledge about politics. In Pathologies of Rational Choice Theory *we traced this failure to methodological defects rooted in the aspiration to come up with universal theories of politics. After responding to criticisms of our argument, we elaborate on our earlier recommendations about how to improve the quality of rational choice applications. Building on suggestions of contributors to this volume, we lay out an empirically based research program designed to delineate the conditions under which rational choice explanations are likely to be useful.*

I. INTRODUCTION

The social sciences were founded amid high expectations about what could be learned through the systematic study of human affairs, and perhaps as a result social scientists are periodically beset by intellectual crises. Each generation of scholars expresses disappointment with the rate at which knowledge accumulates and yearns for a new, more promising form of social science. The complexity of most social phenomena, the crudeness

---

Donald P. Green, e-mail gogreen@yalevm.cis.yale.edu, and Ian Shapiro, e-mail ianshap@minerva.cis.yale.edu, both of the Department of Political Science, Yale University, New Haven, CT 06520–8301, thank Eric Schickler and Ian Hurd for invaluable research assistance, while absolving them of remaining defects. Financial support was provided by Yale's Institution for Social and Policy Studies and National Science Foundation grant SBR-935937.

with which explanatory variables can be measured, and the inability to perform controlled experiments may severely constrain what *any* form of social science can deliver. Nevertheless, nostrums that seem to put social science on the same path as the natural and physical sciences have great appeal. One can scarcely attend an academic conference in the social sciences without hearing someone, young or old, wax eloquent about the need for more linguistic precision, analytic refinement, and rigorous theorizing.

Into the breach steps rational choice theory, the essence of which is that people maximize utility in formally specifiable ways. As we point out in *Pathologies of Rational Choice Theory* (17–30), variants of rational choice theory impose different assumptions about the sorts of utilities people maximize, the nature of the beliefs they possess, and the manner in which they acquire and process information. All share in common, however, a concern with the existence and nature of equilibria resulting from strategic interaction. A given work of rational choice scholarship may be more or less formal in presentation, but its claims about social equilibria must in principle be deducible from a logic of instrumental behavior.

Only by dint of *hautes mathématiques* snobbery or technical aversion could one fail to be impressed by the analytic achievements of rational choice theory in political science. Each passing year witnesses some new extension or refinement in what has become a vast web of interconnected logical propositions. To all appearances, this immense deductive system would seem to furnish the rigorous, cumulative theory that has long been the El Dorado of social science.

But what has this theoretical apparatus contributed to the stock of knowledge about politics? The central claim of our book is that very little has been learned by way of nonobvious propositions that withstand empirical scrutiny. One encounters arresting propositions that are not sustainable (e.g., that changes in collective incentives have little effect on rates of participation in large groups; or that majority rule engenders voting cycles over redistributive questions). And one encounters sustainable propositions that are not arresting (e.g., that rising selective incentives increase participation in collective action; or that supermajoritarian voting rules limit opportunities for policy change). But seldom does one encounter applications of rational choice theory that are at once arresting and sustainable.

It is customary for proponents of rational choice theory to meet this charge by shifting the burden of persuasion. They will defy the critic to show that rational behavior plays no role whatsoever in politics or, in the case of particular anomalies, to establish that no conceivable rational choice logic could account for the phenomenon in question. Neither rejoinder suffices to vindicate rational choice theory. Alternatively, defenders of rational choice theory will lay claim to intuitions that are widely shared by non-rational choice theorists, reminding us that behaviors like voting become less frequent as they become more costly. The idea that human action is to some degree price elastic, though important and empirically sustainable, nonetheless runs afoul of what Robyn Dawes calls the Grandmother Test: Is the sustainable proposition one of which Robyn's grandmother is unaware? As noted in *Pathologies* (147), virtually all students of politics, past and present, harbor causal intuitions consistent with rational choice theory. The question is whether the advent of rational choice scholarship has *added* to the existing stock of knowledge.

Of course, as Bernard Grofman (1993) points out in an essay entitled "The Gentle Art of Rational Choice Bashing," it is one thing to assert that little has been learned, another to build a case based on a careful inspection of existing literature. We therefore set ourselves the task of reviewing what are widely regarded as the most well-developed and sophisticated literatures, those concerning mass collective action, legislative behavior, and party competition. These literatures contain many works that claim to furnish theoretically advanced and empirically supported propositions. But the vaunted reputation of rational choice applications fades when these works are subjected to the kind of close reading they receive in Chapters 4–7 of *Pathologies*. After one cuts through the tendentious and uninformative empirical work, post hoc theoretical embellishments, and clever attempts to sidestep discordant facts, what remains does not warrant the fanfare with which rational choice contributions are so often advertised.

One would hardly expect proponents of rational choice theory to accept this claim without putting up a fight, and several contributors to this volume allege that *Pathologies* fails to acknowledge legitimate empirical contributions. We respond to this charge, and its accompanying bill of particulars, in the next section. At this juncture we wish to reiterate that, while contending that rational choice has added little to the stock of nonobvious, empirically sustainable propositions about politics, our book did not address the extent to which traditional forms of political science have done so.[1] One of the most frequent reactions to our book among those with whom we have spoken is, "Why isn't this book *Pathologies of Social Science*? Why pick on rational choice?" The answer is twofold. It is our impression, first, that traditional research in political science, while often trivial, uninspired, and ill-conceived, is more flatfooted than tendentious. Examples of the kinds of theory-saving biases described in Chapter 3 of *Pathologies* can be found in traditional political science, but for the most part its shortcomings are what we describe as pedestrian (33). Tellingly, pathological research tends to turn up in precincts of political science inhabited by those who cling to theories comparable in scope and ambition to rational choice theory: classical Marxism, elite theory, systems theory, structural-functionalism, and the like. Second, traditional political science, for all its defects, is not similarly bereft of empirical accomplishments. Key's (1949) encyclopedic account of how the racial hierarchy of the South shaped its political institutions, Stouffer's (1955) pathbreaking demonstration that intolerance of the Left had more to do with insulation from cosmopolitan ideas than fears of the threat posed by international communism, and Campbell et al.'s (1960) account of the central role that social-psychological attachments play in shaping political perceptions and evaluations—these represent but a small sample of works unknown to the growing cadre of political scientists who lack graduate or undergraduate degrees in political science. *Pathologies* does not purport to contrast the accomplishments of rational choice and traditional political science, but that should not be taken to mean that we believe no contrast exists.

What explains the gap between rational choice theory's formidable analytic advances and its lackluster empirical applications? Our view is that empirical progress has been retarded by what may be termed method-driven, as opposed to problem-driven, research. Rather than ask "What causes X?" method-driven research begins with the question "How might my preferred theoretical or methodological approach account for X?" Framing the research endeavor in this way sets in motion the methodological biases to which *Pathologies* calls attention, such as the tendency to ignore alternative explanations, make slippery predictions, or dwell on confirming illustrations.

The method-driven proclivities of rational choice scholars may, in turn, be accounted for by their universalistic aspirations: to construct a unified, deductively based theory from which propositions about politics—or, indeed, all human behavior—may be derived. One of our central objections to the way in which rational choice is applied in political science concerns its proponents' drive to show that *some* variant of rational choice theory can accommodate every fact, an impulse that is not accompanied by an equally strong drive to test the proposed account against new phenomena. The rational choice approach inspires great commitment among its adherents, and too often this leads to scientific practices seemingly designed to insulate rational choice theories from untoward encounters with evidence.

Our book ascribes the methodological deficiencies of rational choice scholarship to universalism and the method-driven science it engenders, but an abundant supply of alternative hypotheses exists. Flawed empirical research could be the product of inadequate training: unfamiliarity with the principles of research methodology, insufficient knowledge of the day-to-day workings of politics, lack of exposure to non-rational choice literatures and explanations. Alternatively, one could attribute the empirical track record of rational choice theory to problems more basic than methodological miscues. It could be, as Abelson, Lane, Lohmann, and Ferejohn and Satz all suggest in this volume, that the psychology of choice presupposed by rational choice models cannot adequately characterize decision-making within a political context. It could be that strategic interaction of the sort found in politics gives rise to multiple equilibria and that rational choice theory will remain at an impasse until these theoretical indeterminacies are worked out. It could be that the laws that govern human conduct do not accord with the rules of deductive logic, or that no such laws exist.

None of these hypotheses can be ruled out a priori, and only time will tell whether our diagnosis stands up. Ours is an optimistic view. We do not suppose that every rational choice proposition is doomed to fail, nor do we regard the methodological deficiencies we identify as inevitable features of rational choice theorizing. Furthermore, we believe that applied scholarship can be improved in the short run by greater attentiveness to the methodological concerns we raise. The long-term question is whether these problems can be corrected without attending to what we suppose to be the root cause: the tenacious *commitment* rational choice theorists seem to have to their preferred method of political analysis. Various authors in this volume assure us that universalism is less evident among younger generations of rational choice scholars, who are doing correspondingly better empirical work. This upward trajectory would be consistent with our thesis, and we hope it continues. On the other hand, if we should look back 20 years hence only to discover that little had been learned despite the move away from universalism, we would conclude that the causes of failure run deeper than we supposed.

Our essay is structured as follows. After responding in detail, in the next section, to the charge that *Pathologies* fails to acknowledge important empirical achievements of rational choice scholarship, in Section III we rebut the charges put forward by Lohmann, Fiorina, Taylor, and Chong that we get the rational choice literature on collective action wrong in ways that lead us to undervalue its theoretical and empirical achievements. In Section IV we meet the charge that our ignorance of "modern philosophy of science" (Diermeier, 60) causes us to criticize unfairly the achievements of rational choice scholarship. We respond that neither Lakatos nor Kuhn supplies the conceptual resources to salvage the rational choice enterprise as it is construed by our critics who appeal to their views. In Section V we revisit the distinction between problem-driven and method-driven research in the course of responding to various criticisms of what we say about universalism in *Pathologies*. Building on our earlier discussions of partial and segmented universalism, as well as on the arguments of Fiorina and Taylor in the present volume, we describe five types of domain restriction that, we hypothesize, are likely to delimit the range of successful rational choice applications. In Section VI we briefly take up Ordeshook's call for an engineering-based conception of political science. We hesitate to follow his advice, which in any case begs important questions that are thrown into sharp relief by Abelson's discussion of the effects of rational choice experimental research on the subjects studied. In a concluding section we sum up the reasons for our conviction that advances in political science should be expected to come at the level of the hypothesis or the middle-level generalization rather than that of the architectonic theory or paradigm.

II. WHAT HAS BEEN LEARNED

A basic objection to our argument is that, through oversight or thickheadedness, we fail to acknowledge the legitimate empirical accomplishments of rational choice scholarship in political science. As against our claim that little has been learned from rational choice theorizing that is both nonobvious and empirically sustainable, Chong, Ferejohn and Satz, Fiorina, Lohmann, Schofield, and Shepsle praise a list of rational choice applications or at least wave approvingly in the direction of certain literatures. Our critics tend not to spell out precisely what has been learned from the works they laud.[2] Indeed, they at times seem satisfied merely to call attention to the existence of empirical research, without commenting on its quality (e.g., Schofield 210nn10, 12; Lohmann, 130).[3] Nevertheless, upon reading a dozen or so references to putative accomplishments, the fairminded reader might well begin to wonder whether *Pathologies* gave short shrift to a body of carefully executed empirical work grounded in formal analysis of instrumental behavior.

This impression is quickly dispelled once the elements of this body of work are evaluated seriatim. Although they may be said to include empirically sound, substantively significant, and formally rigorous applications of rational choice theory, no one piece of scholarship meets all of these criteria. Consider first Donald Horowitz's *A Democratic South Africa?*, which Ordeshook (176) praises as an exception to the rule that rational choice scholarship tends to be empirically uninformative. Like Ordeshook, we think this an excellent book, but it contains no empirical test of any theory (nor does it purport to), and in any case Horowitz's is not a rational choice argument (nor does it purport to be). True, he believes that the design of electoral systems should be based on the assumption that aspiring politicians will try to win elections. No minimally literate political scientist would ever have suggested differently, and if that were Horowitz's contribution, it would run afoul of the Grandmother Test. But it is not. On the contrary, his contribution is to propose an electoral system for South Africa premised on the idea that variables other than the strategic calculations of politicians, most importantly the depth of ethnic antipathies, determine the viability of electoral institutions.[4] Whether or not Horowitz is right about South Africa, his argument does not draw discernibly upon the insights of rational choice theory.

By the same token, Jane Mansbridge's (1986, ch. 10) analysis of the campaigns for and against the Equal Rights Amendment, which Fiorina (91) regards as an insightful application of Mancur Olson's *Logic of Collective Action*, can only with some imagination be called a piece of rational choice scholarship.[5] Granted, Mansbridge prefaces her discussion by arguing that the logic of collective action may explain why involvement in these campaigns tended to be sporadic and largely the province of those with deep ideological commitments. But this thought is neither the subject of empirical analysis nor central to the thrust of Mansbridge's argument, which is that the pro-ERA movement lost as a result of lapses in leadership, tactical problems in coordinating a fractious coalition of backers, and the difficulty of formulating persuasive reasons why lawmakers should back the amendment. Why one mass movement should lose to another in this instance cannot readily be explained by reference to Olson, particularly since these two groups did not, by Mansbridge's account, differ appreciably with regard to selective incentives. Like Horowitz, Mansbridge makes no attempt to link the relevant actors' tastes, beliefs, and strategic options to game-theoretic propositions. Indeed, passages in which Mansbridge highlights the strategic blunders that resulted from ideological rigidity and self-deception (136–37) lead one to question whether she regards political behavior as the product of utility maximization.

William Riker's *Liberalism Against Populism* (1982) is at least billed by its author as an application of rational choice theory. Ordeshook (176) calls this work a "discussion of populist democracy [that] provides both a warning about naive political 'reforms' and insights into the practical side of social choice theory." The empirical basis for Riker's "warning" is a collection of historical narratives about the cycle-prone and manipulated character of majoritarian politics. As we document at some length in *Pathologies* (44, 107–13), however, these narratives are not only tendentious but fraught with factual inaccuracies. Ordeshook makes no mention of these difficulties. If Riker (1982) is an example of the empirical successes of rational choice theory, one shudders to think of what Ordeshook would regard as its failures.

A self-conscious attempt to apply rational choice analysis to American politics not discussed in *Pathologies* is Fiorina's (1981) memorable work, *Retrospective Voting in American National Elections*. Shepsle wonders why we fail to discuss this justly acclaimed book, implying that we tiptoe around an uncomfortable example of an empirical success. Apart from the fact that the subject matter of Fiorina's book—the effects of retrospective performance evaluations on electoral choice and partisan identification—is tangential to the four broad literatures we review, our reasons were twofold.[6] First, it is unclear whether Fiorina's is a rational choice model (see Achen 1992, 192). Fiorina himself seems at times apologetic about the ways in which his model departs from what he calls "rational choice, narrowly interpreted" (1981, 77), conceding that "whether or not the model is rational, it is realistic" and "if not completely 'rational,' the model at least attempts to be highly reasonable" (78). Second, without in any way denying the extent to which Fiorina's work contributed to conceptual debates, introduced methodological innovations, and stimulated subsequent empirical inquiry, his central empirical claim has not, in our view, survived subsequent challenges. As against the social-psychological perspectives on partisanship and voting behavior advanced in *The American Voter* (Campbell et al. 1960), Fiorina claims to have provided "a great deal of evidence on the side of voter rationality," noting that "undoubtedly, the most important set of findings concerns the accommodation of a voter's party identification to political reality" (199). Green and Palmquist 1990 and Green 1990 have called into question the empirical basis for the claim that party identification represents a running tally of retrospective performance evaluations, and we did not see the point in rehashing the arcane statistical issues that form the basis of this critique in *Pathologies*. The bottom line is that traditional accounts of partisanship seem to fare better empirically than the one offered by Fiorina.

Like Fiorina's analysis of survey data, Elinor Ostrom's (1990) discussion of how a variety of small communities have dealt with common-pool resource problems is thoughtful and engaging. This work, which draws praise from Ordeshook (176) and Fiorina (91), is largely an inductive empirical inquiry into the conditions under which people can "organize and govern themselves to obtain continuing joint benefits when all face temptations to free-ride, shirk, or otherwise act opportunistically" (1990, 29). Ostrom uses her collection of case studies to identify a set of "design principles" or "essential elements or conditions that help to account for the success of these institutions in sustaining [common pool resources] and gaining the compliance of generation after generation of appropriators to the rules in use" (90). This exploratory approach seems a sensible way to develop hypotheses; indeed, it illustrates the kind of close-to-the-ground theorizing that we advocate in *Pathologies*. But what is the connection with rational choice theory? Are rational choice hypotheses tested and shown to be persuasive? To be sure, the inquiry is inspired by longstanding theoretical interest in the so-called tragedy of the commons and in the logic of collective action, yet the connection between the resulting "framework" of eight design principles and rational choice theory is tenuous. In this vein, Paul Sabatier (1992) notes that certain key components of Ostrom's analysis correspond more closely to functional than rational choice analysis, while Michael Taylor (1992) takes Ostrom to task for relying on an informal analysis that makes no use of recent currents in game theory. As for hypothesis testing, Ostrom herself balks at the idea of calling her design principles causes of successful resource management (90), a reluctance that seems fitting on conceptual grounds and in light of the inductive manner in which these principles were derived. Whatever its merits, this work cannot be regarded as a successful test of empirical propositions derived from rational choice theory.[7]

Ostrom's subject matter is rather exotic by the standards of American political science. Kiewiet and McCubbins 1991, Cox and McCubbins 1993, and Krehbiel 1991, on the other hand, apply rational choice theories to the U.S. Congress. We discussed these works at length in *Pathologies* (134, 197–202), characterizing them as praiseworthy attempts to theorize in closer proximity to data. Although these works are well-informed and innovative, their (informal) models of Congressional politics have certain basic theoretical flaws, and the central hypotheses they generate do not make a strong showing empirically. Nonetheless, Shepsle (218) lavishes praise on them, applauding the way in which they combine "extremely sophisticated theory" with "equally sophisticated empirical examination."[8] Yet Shepsle neither tells us what has been learned from them nor grapples with the specific criticisms we advance. The careful reader will have noted that, like Shepsle, neither Fiorina nor Diermeier—who also praise these works—explain why they find their central arguments persuasive. A different approach is taken by Ferejohn and Satz, who do not dispute our empirical evaluation of the works in question but try to circumvent it by arguing that they offer *interpretive* insights:

> A wide range of congressional actions can be understood as instances of underlying general causal mechanisms. Even if none of these studies had provided an improved statistical account of any specific behavioral phenomenon, they would remain outstanding additions to our understanding of congressional behavior and organization (76).

To be sure, congressional behavior *can* be understood in terms of utility maximization. But why should we believe these particular interpretations?

244

We come finally to three venerable pieces of congressional scholarship, Fenno 1973, Mayhew 1974, and Dodd 1977, which resemble rational choice scholarship insofar as they interpret congressional politics by reference to the ways in which purposive actors negotiate their strategic environments. Notice, however, that they contain no theorems, no game-theoretic models, and no formal exposition of any kind. The contrast between the spartan stylizations of contemporary rational choice scholarship (e.g., Baron and Ferejohn 1989; Weingast and Marshall 1988) and the descriptive richness of *Congressmen and Committees* and *Congress: The Electoral Connection* calls to mind Ordeshook's Dilemma (180): "comprehensive models that treat the full complexity of politics will necessarily require long strings of ad hoc assumptions and qualitative analysis. If we try to maintain deductive rigor, the requirements of tractability will draw us away from comprehensive reasoning." It is doubtful that even the most technically proficient rational choice theorists could fashion a formal rendering of Dodd's oscillating equilibria of legislative-executive balance, Mayhew's depiction of multifaceted and continually evolving reelection strategies, or Fenno's account of how reelection-influence-policy seekers come to adhere to the endogenous and often self-contradictory "strategic premises" of the committees on which they sit. To frame these works as examples of rational choice is to abandon the very features of rational choice scholarship—parsimony, formal precision, deductive rigor—that are so often touted as its principal selling points.

Two conclusions emerge from this brief review of the successes our critics attribute to rational choice theory. First, one cannot but be impressed by the paucity of sustainable empirical analysis flowing from rational choice theory, particularly in relation to the vast corpus of analytic rational choice scholarship that has developed over the past three decades. That our critics should have to resort to examples such as Mansbridge 1986 and Horowitz 1991 attests to the dearth of empirical accomplishment; all the more so, references to Fenno 1973 and Mayhew 1974, which antedate many of the most important analytic developments within rational choice theory. And, of course, it is far from clear that these authors would characterize their own work as examples of rational choice. Like patients undergoing psychoanalysis, these authors learn that they harbor rational choice proclivities of which they are unaware.[9]

Second, the list of exemplars contains no instances in which rigorous formal modeling combines with careful and insightful empirical work. On the contrary, the handful of empirical successes that turn up tend to exhibit weak connections, at best, with rational choice theory. It is no small irony that after one peels away the claims that are made on behalf of the formal precision and theoretical depth of rational choice analysis, the putative accomplishments turn out to be works like Dodd 1977 or Ostrom 1990. We regret that rational choice scholars have not aspired to produce the sort of meticulously researched, inductively based political science characteristic of Fenno 1973 or Mayhew 1974. Had they done so, there would have been no need to write *Pathologies*.

What of Fiorina's charge, echoed by Diermeier, that our standards for evaluating scholarship are so stringent that even works like *Congressmen in Committees* cannot meet them?

> Fenno's book is highly empirical, but it is not based on random samples of committees or members, contains no multivariate equations or even signifi-cance tests, and doesn't explicitly consider and reject alternative explana-tions. Moreover, the theoretical account is built on the same data that it is used to explain. By the standards used in *Pathologies*, it is pretty clear that Fenno's study makes no empirical contribution. (90)

Only a superficial reading of both books can sustain this conclusion. The main empirical contribution of Fenno's work is to establish a correla-tion between the dispositions of Congressional representatives and the character of the committees on which they serve. It is not necessary to draw a random sample in order to sustain this claim. And far from failing to consider alternatives, Fenno grapples repeatedly with the issue of whether committee differences may be attributable to policy content, rather than goals, norms, and external environment. It is true that Fenno derives his hypotheses inductively, and he is careful to point out (280–81) that the transformations afoot at the time of his writing will subject his analysis to a more demanding test.

Nor would we take Fenno to task for conducting qualitative research or failing to conduct statistical tests. Both Fiorina (90) and Shepsle (219) seem to believe that we advocate the exclusive use of quantitative methods in political science, despite the fact that this position is nowhere expressed in *Pathologies*. Our objection to method-driven political science extends to categorical recommendations of quantitative over qualitative methods. Some political phenomena will be more amenable to statistical analysis than others, and the decision about how to study politics should follow the choice of which problem to study. Like Fiorina and Shepsle, we sense that method-driven insistence upon the use of quantitative techniques leads to inferior political science. Our injunction is that empirical research in po-litical science be systematic, whether the mode of inquiry be ethnographic or statistical. At a minimum, systematic inquiry requires attentiveness to the manner in which cases are selected, constructs measured, and infer-ences drawn.[10]

III. COLLECTIVE ACTION

We cannot be said to be in a position to evaluate rational choice scholarship if we fail to understand rational choice theory or to appreciate its implications for collective action in politics. This charge, advanced in various forms by Lohmann, Taylor, and Chong, is directed at Chapters 4 and 5 of *Pathologies*, which address the adequacy of rational choice explanations of mass political participation.

The premise of these chapters is as follows. Each year millions of Americans are asked to contribute money to political parties, candidates, or interest groups. Millions are invited to participate in the policy-making process at some level, whether by attending city council meetings, contacting elected officials, or voting. And, in a given year, large numbers of people engage in one or more such forms of collective action (Rosenstone and Hansen 1993, 42, 51). Doubtless, some proportion of those considering whether to devote time or money find political participation exciting or personally rewarding. A larger proportion, one suspects, regard hours spent attending meetings or dollars given away to political causes as a sacrifice, in the sense that they can easily imagine more gratifying uses for this time and money.

The problem of creating and sustaining voluntary public participation in democratic institutions has long been a concern among political philosophers. More than a century before Downs, Hegel ([1821] 1942, 202–3) predicted the collapse of voter turnout in large democracies, where no individual's ballot is likely to make a difference. Rational choice theorists like Olson extended this logic to a wide variety of situations in which large groups of people are asked to make sacrifices for collective causes but have only a vanishingly small probability of making a pivotal contribution.[11] As Chong (40) explains:

> Instead of assuming, as in earlier group theories, that individuals will naturally take action that is in their collective interest, rational choice theory implied that, paradoxically, individuals will refrain from contributing even if they stand to benefit from the collective good. Since people can potentially receive the benefits of such goods without paying for them, they will not readily contribute to their provision.

An equally arresting implication is that in large groups potential participants cannot be stirred to action by blandishments that take the form of collective incentives; only incentives that flow solely to those who participate are predicted to work.

As game theory has become increasingly sophisticated, this underlying argument has been embellished in ways that take into account repeated in teraction over time, various beliefs about the expected behavior of others, and so forth. From an analytic standpoint, Fiorina (90) might be right to assert that "the working out of the prisoner's dilemma/collective action logic has as strong a claim as any to being the most important political science contribution of the twentieth century." But as an empirical matter, rational choice theorists have been unable to resolve a broad array of anomalies without reformulating rational choice propositions in ways that make them empirically banal. The conclusion we draw in *Pathologies* (47-97) is that rational choice models of collective action have yet to deliver nonobvious, empirically sustainable predictions. This conclusion does not sit well with some of our critics.

Paradox? What Paradox?

As may be inferred from the title of her paper, Lohmann objects strenuously to our discussion of rational choice models of voter turnout and collective action. The central objective of her essay is to dispel the impression that rational choice theory is incapable of accounting for high levels of political participation by showing that it is *logically possible* to craft models that make this prediction. Lohmann believes that demonstrating the existence of just one such model—regardless of how ludicrous its underlying assumptions— enables her to pronounce high levels of collective action "qualitatively consistent" with rational choice theory. This gambit culminates in a series of snappy rejoinders to our work: we do not understand rational choice theory; we present a logically flawed account of collective action; we foolishly render examples of anomalies that are in fact consistent with some variant of rational choice theory.

We do not deny for a moment that it is logically possible to formulate a rational choice model that implies large-scale collective action among self-interested actors. *Pathologies* summarizes an assortment of such models. Some presuppose that citizens engage in collective action because they each expect to cast the decisive vote in a national election or throw the decisive fist in the air during a political demonstration; others, that citizens are enticed or blackmailed into political participation by local officials, interest groups, or nosy neighbors (see Lohmann, 146). And this by no means exhausts the range of logical possibilities. The constraints of logic in no way prevent one from imputing to voters the belief that their failure to cast ballots will dislodge the earth from its orbit. We cannot be criticized for failing to recognize that *some* rational choice model can be constructed to explain mass collective action, as well as every other form of human conduct; no one appreciates more than we the rational choice theorist's capacity for mercurial theoretical invention.

The question is whether to take seriously any proposed model that rests on preposterous assumptions, such as the notion that each eligible voter possesses complete information about the tastes and beliefs of the rest of the electorate. As Lohmann (146) herself concedes, "under incomplete information, voter turnout is vanishingly low if the electorate is large," and since "incomplete information about voter preferences or voting costs is a closer approximation to reality than is the complete information assumption," this result trumps the very models she lays out. In the end, her survey has done nothing more than to "establish the empirical irrelevance of rational choice theory (defined narrowly as a theory that does not allow for noninstrumental motivations) as an explanation of high voter turnout" (ibid.). Notwithstanding the sharp rhetoric that infuses her essay, the bottom line to Lohmann's exegesis of formal theories of collective action is the same as ours: rational choice models that account for high levels of mass participation strain credulity.

The refrain throughout Lohmann's essay is the *logical* error of likening problems of collective action to an n-person prisoner's dilemma. Analogies of this sort are variously denounced as "erroneous" or "false," as though the proper way to model an empirical phenomenon were an analytic rather than synthetic question. "Many rational choice theorists share the view that rational choice theory predicts no voluntary contributions to public goods," Lohmann (138) reminds us, "but this only demonstrates that rational choice scholars can be wrong about their theory. What rational choice theory implies is a matter of logic, not of what claims well-known political scientists at high-status research departments have made in leading political science journals." It should be obvious that this characterization begs the question of what substantive premises will undergird rational choice logic. Modeling social phenomena inevitably means focusing attention on certain causal factors rather than others. The question of which factors go farthest in explaining the phenomenon under study is an empirical one. Why should a model that fails to incorporate any number of plausible influences upon the turnout decision necessarily concern itself with the tiny existential possibility that a voter could cast the decisive ballot in a national election?[12]

Lohmann avoids entirely the issue of how to achieve verisimilitude between rational choice models and actual cases of collective action. Each of the examples she supplies is artificial and concededly unrealistic (141, 144-45). And rather than take up any of the real instances of political action described in *Pathologies*, Lohmann dwells instead on an ancient fable that we use to introduce Chapter 5.[13] The only point during which Lohmann's essay intersects with the realm of observable phenomena occurs when she takes up some of the experimental evidence we discuss in that chapter. But there, Lohmann offers up a series of misinterpretations that can only be ascribed to the pathology we dub "projecting evidence from theory."

First, Lohmann (140) charges that we draw the "false conclusion" that experimental evidence of prosocial behavior is at variance with rational choice theory due to our "erroneous belief that defection is necessarily a dominant strategy on the part of rational, self-interested individuals in a collective dilemma." So determined is Lohmann to emphasize the rational choice insight that cooperation may be a rational strategy when players have the potential to make a pivotal contribution, she fails to realize that the conclusions we draw are supported by evidence from experiments in which, *by design, each player has no opportunity whatsoever to make a pivotal contribution* (see Dawes et al. 1977; McDaniel and Sistrunk 1991; Orbell et al. 1988, 1991; Van de Kragt et al. 1986). The fact that defection constitutes a dominant strategy in such games renders Lohmann's criticisms entirely irrelevant. Next, Lohmann turns her attention to the effects of communication in social dilemma games. "Rational choice theory," she explains, "implies that pre-play communication cannot affect the outcome of a prisoner's dilemma game, in which each player's dominant strategy is to defect" (140). But noting that "there are many social dilemma situations in which communication can further cooperation," Lohmann questions our interpretation of one experiment (Dawes et al. 1977), apparently not realizing that *this study presented players with incentives that made defection a dominant strategy* (see also Orbell et al. 1988, 1991; Schwartz-Shea and Simmons 1990; Van de Kragt et al. 1986). Again, Lohmann launches into a theoretical exegesis designed to show that we fail to appreciate the subtleties of game theory, when in fact none of her arguments speak to the anomalies we cite or in any way undermine our interpretation of them.[14]

One senses that grappling with the complex array of empirical phenomena charted in Chapters 4 and 5 is a motivation of secondary importance for Lohmann, who, like Schofield (206), is animated primarily by indignation at the notion that we "make no reference to the last decade of theoretical work on the prisoner's dilemma." One need not be a rational choice theorist to understand why Lohmann and Schofield would prefer to see more credit assigned to the latest currents in game theory. However, the purpose of *Pathologies* was to assess the empirical performance of rational choice theory, not chart its analytic refinements. This objective led us to say relatively little about the kinds of models Lohmann describes, which generate multiple equilibria and therefore diffuse empirical predictions (see, e.g., the test Lohmann proposes on 137 above). It should be clear from the myriad of studies cited on pages 89–93 of *Pathologies* that the models

Lohmann proposes do not even begin to accommodate the range of anomalies that turn up in the laboratory. Rather than wheel out ever more elaborate analytic structures, rational choice scholars should strive to understand the conditions under which rational choice models tend to work empirically. Absent evidence that these conditions are far reaching, it is not obvious to the empirically minded why the models Lohmann summarizes should be termed "important" or "powerful."

The Motive Power of Collective Incentives

Michael Taylor is on the whole sympathetic to the claims made in *Pathologies* but, like Lohmann, believes we misunderstand rational choice theories of collective action.

> According to Green and Shapiro's reading of the RCT of collective action, collective benefits are irrelevant to an individual's decision. This is wrong. Whether or not any particular theorist believes this, the correct rational-choice formulation must be that free-riding occurs if the costs to the individual of making a contribution exceed *the benefits to him of the increased amount of the non-excludable good which results (directly or indirectly) from his contribution*, plus the selective benefits contingent on his contribution, if there are any (234n4, Taylor's italics) .

This corrected decision rule turns out to be the same one that we discuss at length in Chapters 4 and 5. Taylor is evidently not thinking, as we do, about mass-based collective action, where the expected collective benefits flowing from any one person's contribution are likely to be minute. Even if an individual would in principle trade $10,000 to determine unilaterally the outcome of a presidential election, the likelihood that she will cast the decisive vote in an actual election is vanishingly small. If we were to post odds of such an occurrence at one in a million, the *expected value* of the collective good in question is a penny. Expected values are not mentioned in Taylor's formulation, and this obscures what rational choice theories imply about how changes in the value of collective goods are likely to influence decisions to participate.

As the odds of influencing collective outcomes become infinitesimal, the motive force of collective incentives becomes severely attenuated. Consider again the case in which the probability that one's participation will be decisive is .000001. Increase the personal value of an election or social cause from $100 to $100,000, and one has merely increased the expected benefit from one-tenth of a mil to a dime. Since it is difficult to imagine that a dime's worth of incentive would stimulate any appreciable increase in collective action, it follows that even implausibly large changes in collective incentives will have little effect on behavior. Indeed, it is this comparative statics proposition that makes rational choice theories of collective action interesting and testable. As it happens, these tests have not tended to concord with theoretical expectations (see *Pathologies*, 62–65, 84–85).

Comparative Statics and a Bit of Revisionism

Olson's (1965) account of mass-based collective action is best remembered for its grim prediction that such efforts can be sustained only through coercion or selective benefits. At least, that is how everyone but Fiorina remembers it. He categorically denies that Olson makes any such point prediction, so to refresh memories, let's hear from Olson himself:

> Unless the number of individuals in a group is quite small, or unless there is coercion or some other special device to make individuals act in their common interest, *rational, self-interested individuals will not act to achieve their common or group interests.* In other words, even if all of the individuals in a large group are rational and self-interested, and would gain if, as a group, they acted to achieve their common interest or objective, they will still not voluntarily act to achieve that common or group interest. (1965, 2, Olson's emphasis)

> In a large group in which no single individual's contribution makes a perceptible difference to the group as a whole, or the burden or benefit of any single member of the group, it is certain that a collective good will *not* be provided unless there is coercion or some outside inducements that will lead the members of the large group to act in their common interests. (44)

> The rational individual in the large group in a socio-political context will not be willing to make any sacrifices to achieve the objectives he shares with others. There is accordingly no presumption that large groups will organize to act in their common interest. Only when groups are small, or when they are fortunate enough to have an independent source of selective incentives, will they organize to act to achieve their objectives. (166–67)

Fiorina resists the notion that conventional rational choice analysis predicts the collapse of mass-based collective action. But unlike Lohmann, who seeks refuge in the empirical indeterminacy of multiple equilibria, Fiorina's instincts are to recast Olson's empirical propositions in ways that are amenable to the experimental or quasi-experimental research methods of social science. Out with equilibrium results; in with comparative statics. Forget about point predictions, and focus on predictions about how rates

252

of mass political participation *change* as a consequence of exogenous shifts in the strategic environment. Far from disagreeing with this prescription, we would lay claim to it as a recurrent theme in *Pathologies*. Our disagreement with Fiorina concerns the extent to which rational choice theorists follow this prescription. Perhaps he ought to spread the word among rational choice theorists who, like Lohmann, attach great theoretical and empirical importance to absolute rates of mass political participation. Notice, however, that the retreat to comparative statics robs rational choice theory of much of its cachet. Would *The Logic of Collective Action* have made the same splash if its central prediction had been merely, "other things being equal, the level of collective action within large latent groups ebbs and flows with selective incentives"?[15] Similarly, much of the air goes out of rational choice big-think when its question, "Why do people vote?" changes to "What factors increase or decrease turnout?"

Having made the move to what we term partial universalism, Fiorina nonetheless fails to take up the empirical questions that naturally follow. To what extent does the level of collective action respond to changes in the incentives identified by rational choice theories, and to what extent do other factors account for changes in turnout? Furthermore, Fiorina has little to say about the comparative statics findings reviewed in *Pathologies*, which, among other things, underscore the anomaly, pointed out by Ferejohn and Fiorina 1975, that collective incentives attract voters to the polls even when they do not foresee a close election.[16] In an apparent retreat from this more nuanced form of hypothesis testing, Fiorina (89) at one point proposes to require of rational choice propositions only that they make predictions of proper sign, reminiscent of Lohmann's notion that predictions of positive turnout are "qualitatively consistent" with the observation that millions vote in national elections.

The Pathologies of Pathologies

Like most of the other contributors to this volume, Chong seems to concede the basic thrust of our critique concerning collective action. He does not dispute our claim that much of the empirical evidence gathered to date poses problems for non-banal variants of rational choice theory. His critique focuses instead on three interrelated concerns. First, he charges us with overlooking the fact that rational choice theory "is valuable for specifying a causal mechanism behind the phenomenon in question" (41). Second, he takes us to task for failing to offer alternatives to rational choice explanations of collective action, arguing that, in the absence of alternative explanations, empirical setbacks ought to be classified as rational choice theory's "unsolved problems" rather than its "anomalies." Finally, he is troubled by what he sees as our attempt to "impose arbitrary rules about the limits of rational choice theory" (46). We address these concerns as they apply to theories of collective action here, saving a more general discussion of them for subsequent sections.

It is ironic that Chong lauds rational choice for its capacity to furnish a causal mechanism by which social action emanates from individual choice, when during the course of his essay he lists not one but several mechanisms alleged to fall within the penumbra of rational choice explanation (cf. *Pathologies*, 20-23). Initially, Chong suggests that the mechanism is a cognitive one, in which decision makers determine which of the many courses of action available to them furnishes maximum utility. Putting stock in this mechanism, however, immediately raises the question whether it is plausible to believe that ordinary people can solve the kinds of complex strategic puzzles that may stymie game theorists for months. Recognizing that "no individual has the resources to evaluate thoroughly all the choices he must make" (56), Chong offers another mechanism: "conformity" to the actions advocated by "community leaders" or the "cumulative wisdom of the community." Why conformity, and why "such strong emotional attachments to the patterns of behavior [developed] through socialization"? To answer this requires yet another mechanism, this one structural-functional or evolutionary, by which "blind conformity is adaptive early in life because it improves the rate of information transmission from parents to their offspring." It is far from apparent why this mélange of causal mechanisms should inspire confidence in the claims of rational choice theory.

As for the charge that *Pathologies* makes only "half-hearted" reference to alternative theories, our views concerning architectonic theory (*Pathologies*, 183-88) bear repeating. The fact that there are no alternative theories of comparable scope and generality implies nothing about the empirical serviceability of rational choice theory; it is equally compatible with the view that no single theory can account for the recalcitrant complexity of politics. If pressed to come up with an alternative to rational choice theory, our immediate inclination is to ask: What is the phenomenon to be explained? Presumably, one must have a clear sense of the object of inquiry before one can canvass the relevant explanations, some of which may involve utility maximization while others stress the role of habit, impulse, or cognitive biases. The formulation of alternative explanations, in other words, should be a problem-driven activity.

It is certainly incorrect to say that *at the level of specific empirical claims* we propose no alternatives. As against the claim that collective action is stimulated by selective incentives or the opportunity to make pivotal contributions, we suggest that mass political behavior may be shaped by enthusiasm for the collective objectives, attitudes toward leaders and prominent symbolic figures in the movement, and feelings of personal adequacy and obligation to participate.[17] Granted, these propositions neither stem from broad-gauge theories nor presuppose that individual action need be irrational; thus, they seem to fall short of Chong's requirement that critics of rational choice theory must show that strategic behavior plays no part whatsoever (52, 56). Moreover, since Chong seems to believe that everything from conscious calculation to "cultural inertia" (56) may be squared with some variant of rational choice logic, he may regard these alternatives as indistinct from rational choice theory. But then our disagreement becomes largely semantic, and rational choice theory is nothing but an everexpanding tent in which to house every plausible proposition advanced by anthropology, sociology, or social psychology.

Chong (45) defends post hoc embellishment of rational choice theories on the grounds that such modification "increases the empirical power of a theory and therefore is a progressive development," noting, however, that "ad hoc modification should generate additional tests of the theory." For us, the question of whether ad hoc modifications are in fact progressive (since they necessarily imply a tradeoff between predictive accuracy and theoretical parsimony) hinges on the *outcome* of such tests. This point warrants emphasis, because our critics often take us to be categorically opposed to post hoc modification, or they sense a contradiction between our call for inductive theory-building and our criticism of post hoc theorymodification. Both criticisms are mistaken. Inductive theorizing draws on existing evidence and attempts to understand it; meaningful empirical assessment therefore comes when the reformulated predictions confront new data. Wood and McLean (1995, 3) take us to task for "ridicul[ing]the way in which rational choice articles end with calls for more empirical work"; what we object to are disingenuous calls. This criticism has special force as applied to rational choice theories of collective action, where meaningful empirical testing seldom materializes.

Is it surprising that rational choice theories should encounter difficulty when applied to mass political participation? Each of our critics furnishes reasons to believe that the answer is no. Fiorina (88) speculates that "RC models are most useful where stakes are high and numbers low, in recognition that it is not rational to go to the trouble to maximize if the consequences are trivial and/or your actions make no difference"; Lohmann (131), that "the rational choice approach is bound to be more useful when applied in domains with high-powered incentives, where a 'rational' response has high payoffs, than in domains . . . where learning effects or selection pressures are weak"; Taylor (225), that "rational choice explanations are most likely to work where . . . much, for the agent, turns on his or her choice"; and Chong (46), citing Harsanyi, that "acts of altruism or morality are likely to occur when the costs of doing so are small." Nonetheless, Chong is right to oppose the imposition of "arbitrary rules about the limits of rational choice theory." As we make clear in our discussion of arbitrary domain restriction in *Pathologies* (44–46), our position is that propositions about the conditions under which rational choice theories offer powerful explanations must themselves be testable and tested. Indeed, one of the central purposes of *Pathologies* is to open up a research agenda in which such middle-range hypotheses are developed and evaluated empirically.

Note, however, that this line of inquiry is undone by the kind of post hoc theorizing in which Chong engages. To the extent that "values and dispositions that are not acquired through conscious calculation and may even be unresponsive to changes in opportunity costs" (56) are absorbed into rational choice theory, its boundaries become so murky that it becomes difficult, if not impossible, to assess when rational choice theories succeed and when they fail. This problem becomes especially acute when those who advance post hoc theories are content merely "to show that it is not obvious that social norms and values lie entirely outside of rational choice theory" (57). The universalistic impulse to explain everything by reference to "the operation of interests and more-or-less conscious strategic calculation," often justified in the name of theoretical parsimony and "backed up" by reference to multiple equilibria, is in tension with efforts to understand the circumstances in which interests hold sway or in which calculation conforms to the logic of formal models.

IV. WHY A LITTLE PHILOSOPHY OF SCIENCE IS A DANGEROUS THING

Several critics take us to task for misunderstanding the rational choice enterprise for reasons having to do with the philosophy of science. Different critics make different points in this regard. However, all seem to think that, our earlier discussion of these issues notwithstanding, we are flatfooted positivists whose ignorance about philosophy of science blinds us to the contributions of rational choice theory.

Wingwalking with Lakatos

Ferejohn and Satz, Chong, Fiorina, and Shepsle all take us to task for naively assuming that theories are accepted or rejected as a result of a confrontation with the relevant evidence, rather than—as Lakatos argued—by comparison with alternative theories. Their arguments boil down to two connected claims: You can't beat something with nothing, and What's your alternative to rational choice theory? These are both arguments to which we attended in *Pathologies* (180-85), but since what we said there appears not to have persuaded our critics, we take up their claims more fully here.

The Lakatosian argument that theories are not rejected until something better comes along resurfaces now as Shepsle's "First Law of Wingwalking" ("Don't let go of something until you have something else to hold on to" (217). We advanced two considerations as pertinent to thinking about this claim in the context of the empirical achievements of rational choice theory. First, given that the alleged achievements of the theory are so difficult to identify, a whiff of hubris inevitably accompanies the suggestion that the rational choice paradigm occupies a position in political science analogous to that of Newtonian physics before the Einsteinian revolution. Shepsle's appeal to the First Law of Wingwalking might be easier to take seriously if one could develop a degree of confidence that the aircraft in question were in fact airborne. It is doubtful, after all, that any of the contributors to this volume—ourselves included—would be engaged in the present debate if rational choice theorists could point to a track record of noteworthy empirical achievements.

In *Pathologies* we also insisted that the Lakatosian position be advanced consistently or not at all. Although rational choice theorists are sometimes quick to criticize others by reference to Lakatosian reasoning, it is rare that they live up to it themselves. One of our central complaints concerns the skimpy attention to extant alternative explanations in the rational choice literature. As a result, rational choice theorists are less than well placed to fault others for failing to evaluate rational choice explanations by comparing them with an alternative that can be shown to do better. Far too often, as we showed (*Pathologies*, 37, 84, 88, 121-22, 126, 180-85), the standard rational choice modus operandi is to adduce sufficient accounts of political phenomena by reference to rational choice models, with reference either to no alternatives or to trivial ones. Some (such as Elster [1986]) think that rational choice accounts should be presumptively privileged; some (such as Diermeier) think it unnecessary to consider alternatives; and some (such as Chong) propose recasting the alternatives as rational choice explanations.

Critics like Chong find the preceding criticism unpersuasive. They believe that, in evaluating the rational choice enterprise, *we* should shoulder the burden of supplying an alternative to it. This criticism misses the mark for two reasons. First, we argued in *Pathologies* that there are good reasons for skepticism that there is any such alternative general theory to be found, so disparate in kind are the phenomena that political scientists study. Even a question of the form: "What explains collective action?" seems to us likely to be too general to get very far empirically. The causal variables that explain why some people contribute money to environmental interest groups while others don't, why some people join the White Aryan Resistance and others don't, and why some people attend school board meetings and others don't, may well differ from one another. Better to ask more finely honed questions about the circumstances in which certain types of actors engage, or fail to engage, in different sorts of collective action. Our concern is not to reject rational choice theory *in toto* in favor of embracing some alternative *in toto*, but rather to suggest that there are better ways of doing social science. Indeed, as we say repeatedly (and elaborate in Section V below), we believe that some rational choice hypotheses can reasonably be expected to do well in certain types of political contexts.

Second, it bears reiterating that, at the level of evaluating particular hypotheses, Chong's argument reflects a misunderstanding of where burdens of persuasion appropriately rest. Someone who points out that a theory has failed to deliver on its claims no more adopts the burden of supplying an alternative than would a mechanic who points out that a car has a broken engine be obliged to have a working engine in his possession. Like Shepsle's charge that we are "not consistent about specifying a null against which a theory is compared" (217), Chong's complaint that the alternatives to rational choice explanations mentioned in *Pathologies* are "vague" (39) misses the point. Our aim was not to propose and defend alternatives. Rather, we sought to point out to those who invoke Lakatos that, in case after case, proponents of rational choice explanations have not tried to show that their accounts do better than alternatives, and to indicate the kinds of alternatives we think they might want to consider.

Now a theory need not triumph over an alternative in order to be considered plausible; indeed, some of the work we praised in *Pathologies* (189-90) is not victorious in this way. However, a proposed explanation will be unpersuasive to the extent that no effort is made to demonstrate that it does better than credible extant alternatives. Consider Chong's (41) discussion of the observation that "collective action piggybacks on existing community organizations. People who were affiliated with churches and fraternal organizations . . . were more likely to be active in the civil rights movement." Chong attributes this relationship to the fact that, within a small-group context, cooperative behavior can be "monitored" and "rewarded and punished." But one could hardly come away from the immense literature on political participation without envisioning an alternative hypothesis: that individual differences in proclivities (tastes, senses of obligation, feelings of personal competence) for small-group membership might account for both organizational participation and political activism.

This is not to deny that there may be circumstances in which an explanation might prove illuminating even if no alternative is considered, particularly when the phenomenon in question has not previously been studied or the proposed explanation seems counterintuitive. However, explanations of this sort must be conceded to be speculative in a stronger sense than that in which all well-tested explanations are provisional: accepted as the best available account until something better comes along. One might usefully think about the process of considering alternative explanations in a quasi-Bayesian fashion: the more credible the existing explanations of a particular phenomenon, the heavier the comparative burden to be shouldered by someone who proposes a new one. Our complaint in *Pathologies* (181-83) was that, all too often, proponents of rational choice models seem uninterested in—even unaware of—bodies of established scholarship that offer pertinent competing explanations.

Similar misunderstandings infuse Shepsle's parable of the opera, which leads him to the assertion that because we are "unhappy" with rational choice, we "award the prize to some untested contender" (218). The analogy is misleading, however, because in science the prize does not have to be awarded to anyone. Before the discovery of chlorophyll scientists did not know why grass is green, but scientifically minded people could nonetheless have good grounds for rejecting a theory that accounted for it on the grounds that the moon is made of green cheese.[18] Likewise, if someone advances a theory that purports to explain the relatively poor performance of blacks in certain fields by reference to alleged genetic inferiority, one does not have to have in one's possession an alternative theory that does account for their poor performance in order to conclude that there is not a shred of credible evidence to support the genetic inferiority view. Of course one has to know *something* to dismiss these theories as implausible, but it does not have to be much, and certainly one does not have to have an explanation that does account for the phenomenon in question. Often in political science, perhaps typically, no one knows the correct answer. Proponents of particular hypotheses properly adopt the burden of demonstrating that they triumph over the most credible extant alternative. One who is skeptical of their claims properly adopts no analogous burden; after all, a hallmark of the scientific outlook is the presumption it accords to skepticism. To suggest that the burden of providing an alternative should be shouldered by the skeptic would make it possible for theories routinely to appear to be more credible than they really are, and for scholars to claim that they know things when they do not. What more dangerous barrier to the growth of knowledge could there be?

A different variant of the Lakatosian claim is put forward by Ferejohn and Satz, who insist that successful theories in other sciences do not always yield unique predictions. The example they give is of evolutionary theory, which does not predict "a unique evolutionary path" (75). Indeed this is so, not least because most versions of evolutionary theory assume that evolutionary outcomes are critically influenced by random events. But in biology, as we noted in *Pathologies* (22-23), evolutionary theory can and does produce testable predictions. For instance, a variant of evolutionary theory might generate the hypothesis that there was a gradual expansion of the cranial capacities of a given species during a particular period. This, in turn, would issue in predictions that could be falsified if larger skulls were subsequently discovered that could be shown (by independent dating methods) to be older than smaller, younger skulls from the specified period.[19] If evolutionary theory produced no falsifiable predictions of this kind, there would be little reason to take it any more seriously than creationism.

Kuhn to the Rescue?

Diermeier adopts a Kuhnian point of view, thereby placing himself at odds with our Lakatosian critics. On his view, the "normal" science of rational choice legitimately involves "puzzle-solving" within an established paradigm. Diermeier insists that according to "Kuhn's concept of paradigms," what we describe as pathologies "are perfectly acceptable and indeed consistent with characteristic behavior in the most successful natural science." They are "standard" features of "normal research, i.e. research guided by a paradigm" (68, 61). Diermeier's argument boils down to two central contentions, one concerning the relations between theories and tests, the other concerning the appropriate interpretation of empirical anomalies. With regard to the first, Diermeier devotes considerable attention (61-63) to establishing something we never sought to deny: that assumptions on which theories are built are seldom, if ever, directly tested empirically. To this he adds that since unobservables are by their nature unmeasurable, theories incorporating them cannot be tested.[20] But we no more objected to the use of unobservables than we did to the use of untested assumptions. Diermeier seems not to realize that we agree with his contention that the empirical failings of rational choice applications do not necessarily invalidate the rational actor assumption (see *Pathologies*, 21, 39). We did insist, however, that there must be *some* form of empirical evaluation, a view Diermeier appears to accept in his essay's opening sentence. Typically, testing focuses not on a theory's core assumptions but on the propositions

260

generated by a proposed model. When, for instance, voting is explained on the grounds that people expect to cast the pivotal vote, the belief itself is unobservable, but it presumably has observable consequences. Interviews or other measurement techniques (e.g., wagers) might be employed to determine the degree to which people in fact believe that they will cast decisive ballots.[21] The message in *Pathologies* is not, as Diermeier contends, that latent terms render a theory unscientific (64–65); it is that rational choice theorists have been too little concerned with assessing the empirical ramifications of the latent phenomena they so readily envision.

Of course, even if the rational actor assumption is not tested directly, one might still ask whether it has provided the foundation upon which noteworthy empirical propositions have been built. Here, Diermeier qualifies his comparisons between Newtonian physics and rational choice theory by noting that it would be "absurd" (60) to claim that the latter has been as successful as the former, although he never tells us the yardstick by which he judges their relative achievements. Still, Diermeier is sanguine about rational choice theory's prospects. His counsel to those who may be troubled by the anomalies confronting rational choice theory is: Stay the course; successful theories often continue to be maintained in the face of particular anomalies. Before the discovery of Einsteinian relativity theory, Newton's theory failed to account for the nature of Mercury's orbit, but "it would have been foolish," he notes, "to give up Newton's theory, which worked so well in most areas, just because of one anomaly" (66). We took up this claim in *Pathologies* (180–81). Indeed, we discussed Diermeier's much-debated example of the implications of inexplicable planetary "misbehavior" for Newtonian physics, pointing out that it was the accumulated successes of Newtonian theory that made scientists understandably reluctant to give it up in the face of a small number of anomalies. Diermeier's reliance on the analogy assumes just what is in dispute here: that rational choice *is* a successful theory.[22]

As we note in *Pathologies* (182–83), would-be defenders of this view confront a substantial challenge. To begin with, they must come to grips with Lakatos's (1970, 91–196) critique of Kuhn, in which he pointed out that if demonstrably superior empirical performance to the going alternatives is not a criterion for the scientific evaluation of theories, it is impossible to distinguish advancing research agendas, where the puzzle-solving is contributing to better understanding, from decaying ones, where it consists of endless post hoc modifications whose sole function is to rescue a worthless paradigm. That Diermeier never speaks to this question is particularly striking in view of the fact that he fails to adduce a single empirical proposition about politics that he takes to have been established by rational choice theory. One can scarcely enter a debate as to whether or not an anomaly should lead us to abandon a successful theory absent some evidence of the theory's success. Rather than how to cope with this or that "single" anomaly, the question here is: What is there besides anomalies that passes the Grandmother Test?

Perhaps Diermeier would do better to follow his philosophical mentor a little further. Unlike Diermeier, Kuhn (1970, 244-45) realized that there is no established body of theoretical knowledge on which hypotheses in the social sciences can be shown to depend, even though they do "generate testable conclusions." Consequently, he described the social sciences as "proto-sciences" in which "incessant criticism and continual striving for a fresh start are primary forces, and need to be." So far as we have been able to tell, the only evidence so far adduced that rational choice *is* the established paradigm (and entitled to all the special privileges of established paradigms everywhere) is the assertions of its proponents. Furthermore, if the range of opinion among the authors in the present volume is anything to go by, there seem to be close to as many characterizations of the rational choice paradigm as there are rational choice theorists. Whereas Lohmann (130) distances herself from universalist ambitions, characterizing rational choice as little more than a method or approach, for Schofield "what gives rational choice theory coherence is precisely that it *is* an attempt to construct a grand theory of human behavior" (190, Schofield's italics). Chong (41-43) declares that rational choice's inherent advantage over other theories is that it supplies us with causal mechanisms, while Satz and Ferejohn (1994) insist that rational choice explanations are "external." Shepsle (216-18) conceives of rational choice as the best available theory for the moment, to be jettisoned when something better comes along. For Fiorina, by contrast, it is a badge of honor that he is rational choice "down to my DNA" (85), suggesting that its hold over him is rather more profound. To this Diermeier might respond that such disagreements about the nature of the enterprise are not indigenous to rational choice; they pervade the social sciences. This is readily conceded, but the effect is surely to buttress Kuhn's view of them as preparadigmatic.[23]

V. METHOD-DRIVEN VS. PROBLEM-DRIVEN RESEARCH

The argument in *Pathologies* is that rational choice theorists share a propensity to engage in method-driven research, and that this propensity is characteristic of the drive for universalism. To be sure, a commitment to universalism might stem from beliefs about the philosophy of science, in particular the view that unless one's hypotheses are deduced from equilibrium results that are validated by theorems, there can be no science.[24] But it might just as easily stem from other sources. Some rational choice theorists are universalists because they believe that utility maximization is the wellspring from which all human behavior emanates.[25] Others seem to be universalists almost by default: their lack of interest in, or awareness of, competing explanations lead them to embrace the rational choice approach. Universalist aspirations may also result from plain intellectual ambition, or—its flipside—ennui with what are seen as the more mundane findings of conventional political science. One has only to attend a rational choice conference to realize that the ambitious pursuit of general theoretical results is more highly prized than empirical research—a status hierarchy that, as we argue in *Pathologies*, has the pernicious effect of reinforcing the division of labor between those engaged in theory building and theory testing.

The drive for universalism can thus reflect impatience with the journalistic quality of much descriptive political science, or with the less-than-arresting nature of many of the propositions of behavioral political science that do withstand empirical scrutiny. As Charles Taylor (1967, 57) pointed out long ago, knowing that Catholics in Detroit tend to vote Democratic (or at least that they did when he wrote) scarcely adds much of profundity to one's knowledge about politics. Leaving aside the fact that the empirically sustainable insights of rational choice theory are not notably more impressive, as in the breathless proclamation that rational choice models have now been developed which predict "positive" voter turnout, it should be said that we have nothing against theoretical ambition. We think it prudent, however, to construct theories in ways that offer some prospect of being empirically sustainable. Otherwise one runs the risk of sounding like the Monty Python figure who insists *ad nauseam* to all the world that "this is my theory, and mine alone"—without ever indicating why anyone should care. The aim of science, after all, is not to produce theories but rather to accumulate knowledge. Theories are more or less valuable to the degree that they contribute to that endeavor.

Now one can, of course, be method-driven without being an aspiring universalist; one might be unreflectively so inclined, or motivated by a desire to cash in on the technical virtuosity one has achieved as a formal modeler, or aesthetically attached to mathematical argumentation.[26] Nonetheless, the drive for universalism should be expected to foster method-driven research, because it all too easily transforms the social-scientific enterprise from a dispassionate search for the causes of political outcomes into brief-writing on behalf of one's preferred theory. If one is committed—in advance of empirical research—to a certain theory of politics, then apparent empirical anomalies will seem threatening to it and stand in need of explaining away. Lawyers may properly be committed to vindicating their clients' points of view. For scientists, by contrast, the appropriate professional commitment is to getting at the truth regardless of its theoretical implications.

Kelley is thus mistaken (102-3) if he takes it to be our view that the pathologies are the necessary result of employing rational choice models. They are, rather, the characteristic result of universalist ambition, and for that reason should be expected to afflict other equally ambitious theoretical constructions.[27] Fiorina is right when he says that theories of comparable scope and range would likely run into similar difficulties; indeed we made this point ourselves in relation to Marxism, elite theory, systems theory, and structural-functionalism (*Pathologies*, 189-90). As Fiorina seems to concede, this is scarcely a reason to emulate them.[28] We have never contended that anything in the maximization postulate itself leads to the pathologies we described. They are generated, rather, by the conviction that some manner of utility maximization must account for all political outcomes or else the enterprise of political science is dead.

A possible response to the preceding argument is that rational choice explanations are no more or less universalistic than other explanations in the social sciences. In the present volume, this view is most forcefully stated by Fiorina. Implicitly or explicitly, he notes, the applicability of all explanations is limited by *ceteris paribus* clauses. Critics of rational choice accounts "often assume that a monocausal explanation is being offered" as a result of their failure to recognize that rational choice propositions "typically are stated with a *ceteris paribus* condition. Such an assumption is *always* made whenever there is an attempt to apply a model empirically" (Fiorina 88, Fiorina's italics). Like any other explanations, rational choice explanations are intended to zero in on a particular part of the causal terrain only. Their proponents have never sought, or, at any rate, they should not seek, to deny that other causal factors are covered by *ceteris paribus* conditions.

We have no difficulty with this formulation; in effect, it is a version of what we described in *Pathologies* as partial universalism. Our worry is that if one approaches explanation in a method-driven way (designed to vindicate *some* rational choice explanation), for all one knows one might be dealing with one percent of the problem. Even if true, rational choice explanations may be rendered utterly trivial by the variables that are embedded in the relevant *ceteris paribus* clauses—tall men being more likely, *ceteris paribus*, to bump their heads against the moon (*Pathologies* 61, 193). This difficulty can be compounded by the fact that failure to attend to other independent variables may throw off inferences that one draws from the data. Once the world of monocausal explanation has been eschewed, it makes little sense to zero in on one variable and model it, without trying first to get a sense of how important it is in relation to other variables and how it interacts with them. This is why we press the question, What seems most likely to account for X?, as superior to: How can a rational choice model be developed that accounts for X?[29]

It is not surprising that those rational choice theorists who have grappled with empirical questions seriously have also distanced themselves from aggressively universalist formulations. For example, Fiorina insists that rational choice theorists share nothing more than a commitment to viewing human action as purposive. He proposes that different models be applied to different types of problem as appropriate (though he says nothing about the criteria for determining appropriateness); he embraces variants of what we describe as partial and segmented universalism in *Pathologies* (88-89), and—unlike Jon Elster (1986) and Gary Becker (1986)—he does not think there should be any presumptive preference for rational choice explanations. True, at times Fiorina cannot restrain himself from such extravagant assertions as that "in terms of empirical contributions" rational choice theories "are a significant improvement on the so-called theories that have held sway in the past" (91) without disclosing what has been learned from these contributions. But most of his discussion is more circumspect.[30]

Ordeshook is even more explicit than is Fiorina in backing away from both universalism and the deductive formulation of hypotheses. "Science proceeds less coherently" than the deductive model presupposes, he argues,

> through induction and inference, informed by attempts to be practical and to manipulate real things, where those manipulations rely as much on experience, intuition, and creative insight as on theory. Out of such a process comes ideas about what is generalizable, what is best understood by existent theory, and what is an anomaly that warrants further investigation (180).

Although, for reasons spelled out below, we disagree with Ordeshook's engineering-based conception of political science, nothing he says here is incompatible with the view we are advocating.

Ferejohn and Satz do not go as far as Ordeshook in distancing themselves from universalism. However, in different places Ferejohn has embraced both partial universalism, where rationality is assumed to account for an outcome in conjunction with other independent variables, and segmented universalism, where rational choice models are assumed to apply in some types of circumstances but not in others.[31] Rechristening them in the present volume (77–78) as two kinds of partial universalism, Ferejohn and Satz appear to embrace both.[32] In addition, they now register their endorsement (80-83) of what we described in *Pathologies* (28-30, 193-94) as the family-of-theories view. This amounts to saying, in effect, that some type of rationality explains some of what happens in politics some of the time. Who could possibly object to that? Certainly not us, but three points follow from adopting this stance. It is evident, first, that if defenders of the rational choice enterprise back away from universalism to the degree that Ferejohn and Satz, Ordeshook, and Fiorina do in these essays, the claim that others should be faulted for not offering an alternative universal theory of politics is not sustainable. A corollary of this, second, is that once these moves have been made, there is nothing left of the proposition that rational choice theorists are engaged in an enterprise that is qualitatively different from—let alone superior to—conventional empirical political science. Third, from the standpoint of these stripped-down universalisms, the merits of deductive hypothesis-generation are far from self-evident. Once it has been conceded *de facto* that there is no universal theory to be found, why continue to generate hypotheses as though this were not the case?

Ferejohn and Satz (76–78) make heavy weather of the proposition that both partial and segmented universalism are, nonetheless, forms of universalism, and that putative explanations cannot deserve the name unless they include a claim to be valid across a range of like phenomena. We agree. Where we part company concerns how one goes about determining the range of application of particular explanations, or of the interactions among independent variables in multicausal explanations. Like Shepsle (219), Ferejohn and Satz seem to think that it is worthwhile to go about this deductively. We remain skeptical. The decisions one has to make in plotting the range of application of a particular theory, determining the interactions among independent variables, and deciding which types of rationality might be germane to different types of circumstance are, in part, empirical decisions. Unless one goes about making these choices from a problem-driven standpoint, it is difficult to know how to think intelligently about the interactions among explanatory variables or why the domain should be restricted to one class of phenomena rather than another. It was this observation that supplied the basis for our discussion of arbitrary domain restriction in *Pathologies* (44–46). None of our critics in the present volume disputes it, and some, such as Fiorina (87), endorse it.[33]

It might be contended that our distinction between problem-driven and method-driven research is misleadingly simple-minded. For example, Ferejohn and Satz (72) assert that the "very notion of explanatory success depends on a prior (theoretical) characterization of what exactly needs to be explained." Thus, they state that before the advent of the collective action literature, nonvoting was thought by political scientists to stand in need of explanation; Olson and Downs suggested that, on the contrary, it was voting that needed to be explained. No one would dispute Ferejohn and Satz's contention that Olson and Downs had a big impact on the study of turnout, but this begs the question whether this impact was for the good. As we note in *Pathologies* (67-68), researchers had indeed studied which factors make it more or less likely that people will vote before the advent of the rational choice literature, and this comparative-statics question receded into the background after the rational choice reconceptualization of the problem. The effects on turnout of perceived closeness of elections had been assessed by writers such as Gosnell (1927, 3) and Campbell et al. (1960, 99-100), as had those of civic duty (Campbell, Gurin and Miller 1954, 199). Particularly in view of the fact that, like Fiorina in this volume, Ferejohn and Satz 1994 appear to concede that rational choice models cannot account for turnout without repackaging such findings, the question arises whether Olson and Downs picked out a problem or a pseudo-problem.[34] Ferejohn and Satz point out that different theoretical frameworks can be expected to identify different problems, but for just this reason committing oneself to a single theoretical perspective is shortsighted. In the face of *ex ante* uncertainty as to which perspective is likely to pay the best dividends, diversifying one's theoretical portfolio seems the more prudent course.

We do not deny that rational choice might be useful in generating research questions and hypotheses. Working within the rational-actor framework might be helpful, or it might send researchers on the sort of wild goose chase that the turnout literature became. On the other hand, alternative means of identifying problems and generating research questions might have similar results, so that it is not clear a priori which approach will prove most fruitful. Nor do we have a difficulty with the further contention that what one perceives to be a problem will, to some degree, be a function of one's theoretical preconceptions. But there is a world of difference between agreeing with this and signing onto a method-driven research program. The manner in which one arrives at a research question is separable from the manner in which one studies it. Regardless of how one got to the question to be addressed, from a problem-driven perspective the researcher should begin with the following three questions: First, what are the existing attempts to account for the phenomenon in question, and how, if at all, are they defective? Second, if the existing accounts are defective, what alternatives are likely to account for the phenomenon, and why? Third, given that any proposed explanation might be wrong, what datum or data should persuade the researcher that this is so? It is because method-driven researchers are not guided by these questions—asking instead: How might my approach account for this or that phenomenon?—that the pathologies we described arise.

This is not to say that theorizing about the conditions under which certain types of explanations are likely to do better than others is a waste of time. It should be emphasized, however, that such theorizing should itself be tested empirically. For instance, Satz and Ferejohn 1994 conjectured that rational choice explanations are likely to do best when individual action is severely constrained. Just as in economics, where rational-actor models account better for the behavior of firms than that of consumers, in politics they should be expected to do better with parties than with voters. This was a reasonable conjecture, but as we noted in *Pathologies* (Ch. 7), rational choice models have not been shown to account for the behavior of political parties in general, suggesting that more refined constraints on the domain may be in order.

Satz and Ferejohn are clearly on the right track, however. If segmented universalism is to be freed of the pathology of arbitrary domain restriction, researchers interested in the applicability of rational choice models should begin systematically to examine the conditions under which they can be expected to account for political outcomes better than the going alternatives. In this respect we applaud Kelley's (101) attempt to specify the conditions under which rational choice explanations should be expected to apply: When goals are uncomplicated, pertinent knowledge is widely available, interaction is iterated, stakes are high, and agents are rewarded for rational behavior. Likewise, Taylor's (225-28) exploration of the threefold requirement that the number of options be limited, their costs and benefits clear to the agents, and the stakes high, seems to us another move in the right direction. Our own conjecture builds on these suggestions. Rational choice explanations should be expected, *prima facie*, to perform well to the extent that the following five conditions are met: (i) the stakes are high and the players are self-conscious optimizers; (ii) preferences are well ordered and relatively fixed (which in turn may require actors to be individuals or homogeneous corporate agents); (iii) actors are presented with a clear range of options and little opportunity for strategic innovation, (iv) the strategic complexity of the situation is not overwhelmingly great for the actors, nor are there significant differences in their strategic capacities, and (v) the actors have the capacity to learn from feedback in the environment and adapt. Like those of Kelley and Taylor, our conjecture is at bottom empirical, rooted in our best judgment concerning why rational choice models have failed in the literatures we have examined. As Lane (108) suggests, we might be wrong about one or more of these constraints; only the progress of empirical inquiry will tell.[35]

Some have accused us of being antitheoretical, but skepticism about rational choice theorists' claims is no more indicative of one's being against theory than is skepticism about a particular political party's claims evidence that one is against politics. We are all for the development of more rather than less general theory in the social sciences, but any theoretical proposition worth having must be empirically sustainable. Given the current condition of theoretical knowledge in political science, our sense is that the most fruitful theory building will remain in relatively close proximity both to the data and—in the quasi-Bayesian sense mentioned in the preceding section—to the existing knowledge about the phenomenon under study. This is a pragmatic point rather than an epistemological one; it leaves as an open question whether or not there are general laws about politics to be discovered. But our view has the advantage that if there are no general laws about politics, or if valid general laws turn out to lie in some direction other than that currently being explored by rational choice theorists, it might nonetheless be possible, in the meantime, to increase the stock of empirical knowledge about politics.

It is possible that deductive modelling might produce empirical successes in political science. In that case the gamble will turn out to have been worth taking, despite what we have said about the odds. It might be worth pointing out, however, that—if the history of political science is anything to go by—highly ambitious attempts at theory building are likely to fail, whatever their origins. The difference between inductive and deductive approaches comes down, then, to what one is left with in the likely event that one's hypothesis proves empirically inadequate: a rich supply of information about politics and a grasp of the going attempts to understand it, or a bunch of algebra that is unlikely to impress anyone in the math department.

VI. COLLAPSING BRIDGES AND SELF-FULFILLING PROPHECIES

In *Pathologies*, we do not comment on the normative debates that have motivated, or arisen from, rational choice theory. Our central concern is with the extent to which rational choice models might succeed in advancing the understanding of politics, and the ways in which empirical research might be improved. Because rational choice theorists have sometimes pressed dubious or unsubstantiated empirical claims into the service of prescriptive arguments, we do note (*Pathologies*, 11-12) that our venture is not without normative significance. Beyond this we avoid normative debates, restricting our attention to assessing the so-called "positive" rational choice program on its own terms. In the present volume, however, two normative considerations have emerged which seem to merit comment, the first arising out of Ordeshook's engineering-based conception of the social-scientific enterprise, the second out of Abelson's survey of studies dealing with the effects of rational choice-inspired experimental work on the subjects studied.

Ordeshook calls for rational choice theorists to think about their tasks by analogy to engineers. Bridge-building engineers, he contends, generally intend to build better bridges than have been built in the past. Trying to understand why a particular bridge fell into the river motivates the enterprise of designing better bridges, and generates criteria for assessing the merits of particular efforts. The failure of political science "to connect its practical objectives to its theoretical and methodological ones results in confusion about the phenomena that warrant theoretical treatment, the distinction between theory and model, and, ultimately, the methods whereby we make scientific advances" (181–82). Thus, Ordeshook argues that political science should become a practical field in which we "seek not only to understand political things, but also to improve the operation of political processes and institutions" (180). Political scientists try to understand how democracy works, he insists, "so we can try to make it work better or make it work in previously authoritarian states. We study international affairs not because war amuses us, but because we want to learn how to avert conflict" (180).

Although we share Ordeshook's concerns about the quality of rational choice applications, his perspective assumes a degree of agreement on engineering objectives that cannot be taken for granted in the study of politics. People will generally agree on the purposes for which bridges should be designed, even if some in the construction business might have a pecuniary interest in bridges periodically falling into rivers. Ordeshook's account fails to come to grips with the fact that motives for studying politics vary widely. Some study war not in order to avert it, but to try to ensure that their country wins the next one. Likewise, as Ordeshook asserts, some may indeed study democracy to try to make it more stable or viable. But others, including some of those whom Ordeshook praises for having advanced our understanding of it, seem to have had a different agenda: to delegitimate democracy and limit political interference with property rights and market relations.[36] Thus, although we agree with Ordeshook's preference for problem-driven research and with his skepticism that it will ever be possible in political science "to put all the theoretical 'pieces' together into one theoretical analysis" (181), we are doubtful that the goals can ever be self-evident in the ways the engineering analogy suggests.

This point is worth emphasizing in light of Abelson's (29–31) discussion of what might usefully be described as the performative dimension of rational choice scholarship: in some circumstances rational choice theorists might actually produce the behavior in people that they believe they have discovered. Studies suggesting that the propensity for strategic behavior increases with the study of economics, or that the introduction of selective incentives into children's games can make continued play dependent on those incentives where previously it was not, raises potentially worrisome possibilities. It may be that agency problems can be created, where previously they did not exist, simply by drawing people's attention to their possibility. Likewise with agenda manipulation and free riding: researchers may help create the monster they describe by pointing out and legitimating as "rational" certain forms of strategic behavior. This is not to settle the question of whether instrumental behavior is necessarily "bad"; normative questions of this sort cannot themselves be settled by political science. It is to insist, however, that they are genuine questions. This can all too easily slip from view if it is assumed, in advance of research and whatever its results, that strategic behavior is ubiquitous.

VII. CONCLUDING REMARKS

Rational choice theorists are not the first to believe that the way to place the study of politics on the secure path of a science is to embrace a new paradigm, outlook, approach, or general theory. At different times, systems theorists, structural-functionalists, and Marxists, among others, have all harbored comparable theoretical ambitions. Although it is always possible that an architectonic effort of this sort will bear fruit, the history of accumulated failures leaves us skeptical. In our view, advances in political science are more likely to come at the level of the hypothesis or middle-level generalization than at that of the grand theory or paradigmatic innovation, and the energy that is poured into developing new theories and paradigms, translating the existing stock of knowledge into them, and defending them against all comers would be better spent on problem-driven research. As we have sought to establish in the preceding pages, this stance is not borne of any particular animus toward theorizing. Rather, it rests on the pragmatic judgment that empirically sustainable general theories about politics are unlikely to be formulated in any other way.

Nor does this stance place us at odds with the interdisciplinary outlook with which rational choice scholarship is often advertised. Problem-driven research pays no particular heed to existing disciplinary divisions. Whether the tools of economics, psychology, sociology, or some other discipline should be brought to bear in the study of a given problem is always an open question, depending on the nature of the problem and the prior history of attempts to study it in these and other disciplines. Unlike many of our critics, we see no more reason to suppose that economic models will be successful across the board than those drawn from psychology or sociology. To assume the contrary is to clothe what is actually a parochial, not to say myopic, outlook in an interdisciplinary garb. This observation may go some way toward explaining why what rational choice theorists often take to be their open-minded and interdisciplinary spirit is seen by others as intellectual imperialism. Rational choice theorists will encounter less resistance when they supply a satisfactory answer to the question, What has been learned from rational choice theory? The present response, that its empirical accomplishments will be judged "eventually," (Diermeier, 59), while true, is not enough.

NOTES

1. Diermeier proposes that we sample articles at random from leading journals in an effort to compare the quality of rational choice and other forms of political science. This research design changes the inquiry to: What is the likelihood that a given RC article advanced our stock of knowledge, and how does this compare to the likelihoods for non-RC scholarship? First, the evaluative criterion should properly be what has been learned *in toto*, not article-for-article efficiency. Second, literatures represent a more defensible sampling unit than articles. Besides leading to a critique that would have been scattered and disjointed, random sampling of articles along the lines he suggests would surely have opened us to the charge that we had managed to miss the best work. As it happens, despite Diermeier's qualms about our literature review, he does not believe rational choice to be "empirically more successful than the collection of mutually inconsistent middle-level approaches that had dominated political science before the advent of rational choice theory" (68).
2. Fiorina (91), for example, refers to Frohlich et al. 1971, Moe 1980, and Walker 1991 merely as instances in which scholars were led to "think harder about the importance of leadership or entrepreneurship in the formation of groups" in the wake of Olson 1965. Similarly, Diermeier (68n12) chides us for failing to discuss Snyder 1990, 1991, which he describes only as "important." The prize for the most opaque reference goes to Shepsle (222n5), who questions why we did not discuss "the continuing series of books by Paul Abramson, John Aldrich, and David Rohde on change and continuity in elections."
3. Not to mention the converse tactic of applauding findings that are unobservable for the reason that they do not yet exist in print (e.g., Schofield, 203–4, 210n15, Fiorina, 91).
4. Specifically, Horowitz thinks that winner-take-all electoral systems that might be expected to work in pluralist political cultures (where cleavages are cross-cutting) will not work in "deeply divided" cultures such as he takes South Africa's to be, and he proposes a different system that is designed to take account of the ethnic divisions there.

5. By citing this work, Fiorina attempts to catch us coming and going. At one point (94n3) he takes us to task for criticizing the work of Carole Uhlaner (who attempts to apply rational choice propositions) on the grounds that she is not a rational choice theorist. However, here he chides us for not taking up the work of Jane Mansbridge, who is no more a rational choice theorist than Uhlaner.

6. There is some disagreement among rational choice theorists about the theoretical coherence of propositions about electoral choice, be they Fiorina's claims about retrospective voting or Ordeshook's assertions (182–83) about strategic voting in multicandidate elections. As Ferejohn and Fiorina (1993) and Brennan and Buchanan (1984) point out, it is unclear how rational actors should choose among candidates when their ballots have no plausible chance of influencing the election outcome.

7. Like Ostrom, Steven Brams (1980) is interested in the crafting of institutions, in this case voting rules. He argues on behalf of a system of "approval voting" based on a formal analysis suggesting that this voting rule encourages voters to cast "sincere" ballots. The empirical question concerns the extent to which voters in fact respond to these incentives. Brams, to his credit, has made a concerted effort to engage this question but has to date been hampered by the dearth of approval voting systems currently in place at the national and subnational level. It remains to be seen, therefore, whether Brams's work will precipitate an "advance [in] our understanding of electoral systems," as Ordeshook (176) contends.

8. Fiorina seems equally enthusiastic but does not spell out what has been learned from these works. Drawing instead upon what would appear to be the labor theory of value, Fiorina (93) exclaims: "Who in the legislative subfield has put together a wider array of data on the congressional parties than RC scholars Cox and McCubbins, and who in the legislative subfield is a more painstaking empirical worker than RC scholar Keith Krehbiel?"

9. On reading Satz and Ferejohn 1994, 80, one might add Jim Scott to the list of scholars alleged to be suffering from this particular disorder.

10. Lane and Murphy both implicitly criticize us on the "What has been learned?" question for failing, as a result of restricting ourselves to political science, to discover that even less has been learned than we claim. As we say in *Pathologies* (179-80), we are agnostic about this matter, though it should be plain from our discussion in Section V below that we think it is the type of problem under study, rather than anything to do with disciplinary divisions, that determines what sort of explanations are appropriate. In economics no less than in politics, rational choice explanations should be expected to do better in some circumstances than others.

11. Granted, the probability that one will cast the decisive vote in a national election, alter the course of history through one's participation in a mass demonstration, or tip the scales in a policy dispute through one's volunteer work on behalf of a political cause is not precisely zero. The odds, howev-

er, are long—arguably longer than the odds of sustaining injury or financial loss as a result of one's political involvement.

12. To put it another way, why should "logic" necessarily dictate an analogy between voter turnout and contributions to a collective cause? One could liken political participation instead to rooting for sports teams or to acts of religious piety, and indeed rational choice theorists have, from time to time, trotted out these very analogies.

13. Lohmann wanders off into an extended formal analysis of the barge parable without ever taking notice of the tenuous link between her algebra and the subject matter of Chapters 4 and 5. Repeatedly in these chapters we advise readers that the political phenomena under discussion are cases in which large numbers of people must independently and under conditions of imperfect information decide whether to sacrifice valued resources on behalf of a collective undertaking that their contributions are unlikely to influence to any appreciable degree. As applied to the case of mass politics, the barge parable ought to have conjured up in Lohmann's mind an image of a supertanker being pulled against the current of a mighty river through the efforts of millions of citizens each tugging a line.

14. Likewise, Taylor (234n4) believes he has found a "flaw" in our discussion of interpersonal communication, noting that it can be important when the game is not a one-shot prisoner's dilemma. We never claim otherwise and in fact attempt to forestall this very criticism on p. 89.

15. Fiorina mentions Olson's other important proposition concerning the differential organizing capabilities of large and small latent groups. For reasons given by Taylor 1987, this proposition is difficult to test empirically.

16. Lohmann, relying on the word of Grofman 1994, seems to think that the comparative statics predictions of rational choice theory fare well empirically. It is not clear what Lohmann makes of the evidence to the contrary cited in *Pathologies*. Her sole discussion of the subject concerns the findings of Hansen et al. 1987, but she ignores the methodological concerns we advance (see *Pathologies*, 64). Hansen et al. find turnout in Oregon school district elections to be higher in smaller districts, in which voters are more likely to cast pivotal votes. The authors do not, however, examine whether the same pattern of turnout holds for state and national elections, where such interdistrict variation should be absent.

17. The category of alternative hypotheses properly includes methodological objections as well. Chong, for example, alludes to the survey-based finding purporting to show that participants in large-scale collective action perceive their own contributions as pivotal to the success of the cause. An alternative (and testable) view is that *claiming* to be pivotal is part of the ideological discourse of activism and that a more refined survey questionnaire would discern that people do not actually believe that the movement would fail if they were suddenly to become incapacitated. Chong believes this hypothesis commits us to a full-scale indictment of survey research,

but advancing a methodological criticism of this sort no more obliges us to embrace this broader critique than does reference to economic class oblige one to embrace Marxism.

18. We are indebted to Brian Barry for this example.

19. Murphy (167ff) might be right that evolutionary theory has done best empirically when proponents have detached particular evolutionary hypotheses from the method-driven search for equilibrium results. For reasons that are spelled out in the next section, we would, however, dispute what appears to be his concluding claim: that abandoning the search for equilibria is tantamount to abandoning science.

20. "A general form of Green and Shapiro's argument concerning problems with unobservables goes as follows: By definition, unobservables cannot be measured. Thus, theories that contain unobservables cannot be tested empirically. Since rational choice theories contain unobservables, they cannot be tested empirically. Therefore they are unscientific" (63). As indicated in the text, we never contend any such thing. Furthermore, this formulation betrays Diermeier's idiosyncratic view that theories must be dubbed scientific or unscientific. Theories are true or false; it is methods of assessing them that are scientific or unscientific.

21. Diermeier claims to be "baffled" at our observation that problems associated with unobservables become more severe as the ratio of unobservable terms to observable indicators increases, but this principle is basic to the standard "identification problem" in the statistical analysis of latent variables (see *Pathologies*, 40–41).

22. Diermeier (66) makes much of the fact that our example of red apples (*Pathologies*, 44) is a single anomaly. Apart from our response in the text, it should be said that it differs from Mercury's "misbehavior" in that the latter did not matter much, given its peripheral nature to scientists' concerns at the time. Had they been planning to fly to Mercury they would have been forced to grapple with the reasons for their inability to understand its orbital behavior.

23. Kuhn also warned that "I claim no therapy to assist the transformation of a proto-science to a science, nor do I suppose that anything of the sort is to be had." Apparently with the likes of Diermeier in mind, he elaborated as follows: "If . . . some social scientists take from me the view that they can improve the status of their field by first legislating agreement on fundamentals and then turning to puzzle-solving, they are badly misconstruing my point. A sentence I once used when discussing the special efficacy of mathematical theories applies equally here: 'As in individual development, so in the scientific group, maturity comes most surely to those who know how to wait.'" (Kuhn 1970, 244–45).

24. We did note the curious fact that the covering-law model of science referred to in the text also requires that the assumptions on which models rest be realistic, a feature that, as Moe (1979) pointed out over 15 years ago,

is lacking in rational choice models. Unrealistic models are usually justified, by contrast, on the grounds of their predictive success, which we argued is notably lacking in the case of rational choice theories of politics.
In any case, such instrumental views place no stock in the development of
covering laws (*Pathologies*, 30-32).

25. See Elster 1986. As we note in *Pathologies*, it is not clear what the defensible basis for this view is. In the present volume, Ferejohn and Satz appear
to think that in the social sciences the merits of rational choice explanations—as a point of departure, at least—are self-evident. The reason for
this seems to be that social-scientific explanations must be intentional.
Granting this, *arguendo*, it is irrelevant to the issue at hand because, unlike
Riker (whose views on this subject are dealt with in *Pathologies*, 185-86),
Ferejohn and Satz concede that rational choice explanations are only one
of several types of intentional explanation (79-80).

26. One wonders, in this connection, about how to interpret appellations like
"elegant" or "beautiful" that can sometimes be heard at rational choice
conferences in reference to an impressive proof or deductive argument.

27. This was evident to at least some readers of *Pathologies*. In the present volume, see Ferejohn and Satz (71), who characterize our argument on this
point accurately.

28. Noting that Parsons, Truman, and Easton "were not exactly modest" with
respect to grand theoretical ambition, Fiorina asserts that "not every scholar who found a structural-functionalist, a groups, or a systems perspective
useful shared the universalist ambitions of these theorists" (87).

29. Wood and McLean (1995) point out that, even within one set of *ceteris
paribus* conditions, virtually any outcome can typically be retrodicted as an
equilibrium result. Like Ferejohn 1991 and Schofield, they think that our
preoccupation with empirical testability misses rational choice theory's
most profound problems. What they appear not to realize is that even if
this theoretical difficulty were resolved the pathologies that flow from
method-driven science would remain.

30. Indeed, by embracing the family-of-theories view Fiorina goes farther
than we propose in backing away from universalism. Against this approach,
in Chapter 5 of *Pathologies* (97) we argue for sticking to one definition of
rationality in order to keep rational choice explanations analytically distinct from other accounts.

31. Partial universalism is embraced in Ferejohn 1991 and segmented universalism in Satz and Ferejohn 1994.

32. To avoid confusion we stick to our original terms, *partial* and *segmented*, in
the following discussion.

33. It should also be said, *contra* Chong (46), that it is at best an open question
whether the different partial and segmented universalist accounts that
apply to different domains can be strung together into a general theoretical
account.

34. Fiorina (91) nonetheless insists that "every empirically based modification, generalization or even rejection of Olson is an empirical contribution stimulated by his work. . . . Even seeming counterexamples that lead people to see matters in a new light are empirical contributions." This is a bit like insisting that Robert Dahl's *Who Governs?* represents an accomplishment of elite theory.

35. It should be added that even when political phenomena meet our five criteria, they may nonetheless be so complex as to be intractable from the standpoint of formal modeling. For instance, in working on the impact on constitutional settlements reached through negotiations over the transition from authoritarianism to democracy, Jung and Shapiro 1995 noticed that this problem did seem to meet the five criteria just enumerated. When they asked several game theorists for help in modeling the process, however, the universal response was that the number of players, variables, constraints, and interactions made the problem too difficult to model. Problem-driven research agendas may often run into this difficulty.

36. See Shapiro 1990.

REFERENCES

Abelson, Robert P. 1976. "Social Psychology's Rational Man." In *Rationality and the Social Sciences*, ed. S. I. Benn and G. W. Mortimore. London: Routledge & Kegan Paul.

Abelson, Robert P., and Ariel Levi. 1985. "Decision Making and Decision Theory." In *Handbook of Social Psychology*, 3rd ed., vol. 1, ed. Gardner Lindzey and Elliot Aronson. New York: Random House.

Abramson, Paul R., John H. Aldrich, and David W. Rohde. 1995. *Change and Continuity in the 1992 Elections*. Washington: CQ.

Alchian, Armen. 1950. "Uncertainty, Evolution and Economic Theory." *Journal of Political Economy* 58: 211–22.

Aldrich, John. 1980. *Before the Convention: Strategies and Choices in Presidential Nominating Campaigns*. Chicago: University of Chicago Press.

Aronson, Elliot. 1968. "The Theory of Cognitive Dissonance: A Current Perspective." In *Advances in Experimental Social Psychology*, vol. 4, ed. Leonard Berkowitz. New York: Academic Press.

Arrow, Kenneth J. 1951. *Social Values and Individual Values*. New York: John Wiley & Sons.

Arrow, Kenneth J. 1987. "Rationality of Self and Others in an Economic System." In *Rational Choice: The Contrast between Economics and Psychology*, ed. Robin M. Hogarth and Melvin W. Reder. Chicago: University of Chicago Press.

Arrow, Kenneth J. 1989. "The State of Economic Science." Presented at the annual meeting of the American Economics Association. Reported by Leonard Silk, *New York Times*, 29 December 1989.

Arrow, Kenneth, and Gerard Debreu. 1954. "Existence of an Equilibrium for a Competitive Economy." *Econometrica* 22: 265–90.

Arthur, Brian. 1995. "Self Reinforcing Beliefs: Path Dependence and Human Learning." Stanford University. Unpublished manuscript.

Aumann, Robert. 1976. "Agreeing to Disagree." *Annals of Statistics* 4: 1236–39.

Axelrod, Robert M. 1984. *The Evolution of Cooperation*. New York: Basic Books.

Balzer, Wolfgang. 1982. *Empirische Theorien: Modelle-Strukturen-Beispiele*. Braunschweig: Vieweg.

278

Balzer, Wolfgang, Caesar U. Moulines, and Joseph D. Sneed. 1987. *An Architectonic for Science*. Dordrecht: Reidel.

Barnett, William, Melvin Hinich, and Norman Schofield, eds. 1993. *Political Economy: Institutions, Competition and Representation*. Cambridge: Cambridge University Press.

Baron, David P., and John Ferejohn. 1989. "Bargaining in Legislatures." *American Political Science Review* 83: 1181–1206.

Barry, Brian. [1970] 1978. *Sociologists, Economists and Democracy*. Chicago: University of Chicago Press.

Bartels, Larry M. 1988. *Presidential Primaries and the Dynamics of Public Choice*. Princeton: Princeton University Press.

Bates, Robert. 1995. *The International Economics and Domestic Politics of Coffee*. Unpublished manuscript.

Becker, Gary S. 1976. *The Economic Approach to Human Behavior*. Chicago: University of Chicago Press.

Becker, Gary S. 1986. "The Economic Approach to Human Behavior." In *Rational Choice*, ed. Jon Elster. New York: New York University Press.

Becker, Gary S., Michael Grossman, and Kevin M. Murphy. 1993. "Rational Addiction and the Effect of Price on Consumption." In *Choice Over Time*, ed. George Loewenstein and Jon Elster. New York: Russell Sage Foundation.

Beer, Samuel. 1993. *To Make a Nation*. Cambridge, Mass.: Harvard University Press.

Bell, David E. 1982. "Regret in Decision Making under Uncertainty." *Operations Research* 30: 961–81.

Bem, Daryl J., and David C. Funder. 1978. "Predicting More of the People More of the Time: Assessing the Personality of Situations." *Psychological Review* 85: 485–501.

Benn, Stanley I. 1979. "The Problematic Rationality of Political Participation." In *Philosophy, Politics and Society*, 5th series, ed. Peter Laslett and James Fishkin. New Haven: Yale University Press.

Berelson, Bernard R., Paul F. Lazarsfeld, and William N. McPhee. 1954. *Voting*. Chicago: University of Chicago Press.

Berk, R. A., and S. F. Berk. 1983. "Supply Side Sociology of the Family: Challenge of the New Home Economics." *Annual Review of Sociology* 9: 375–95.

Bicchieri, Christina. 1993. *Rationality and Coordination*. Cambridge: Cambridge University Press.

Binmore, Kenneth. 1993. "De-Bayesing Game Theory." In *Frontiers of Game Theory*, ed. Kenneth Binmore, Alan Kirman, and Piero Toni. Cambridge, Mass.: MIT Press.

Binmore, Kenneth. 1994. *Game Theory and the Social Contract: Playing Fair*. Cambridge, Mass.: MIT Press.

Black, Duncan. 1958. *The Theory of Committees and Elections*. Cambridge: Cambridge University Press.

Blais, André, and Stéphane Dion, eds. 1991. *The Budget-Maximizing Bureaucrat*. Pittsburgh: University of Pittsburgh Press.

Blaug, Mark. 1980. *The Methodology of Economics*. Cambridge: Cambridge University Press.

Bliss, Christopher, and Barry Nalebuff. 1984. "Dragon-Slaying and Ballroom Dancing: The Private Supply of a Public Good." *Journal of Public Economics* 25: 1–12.

Borcherding, Thomas E., Werner Pommerehne, and Friedrich Schneider. 1982. *Comparing the Efficiency of Private and Public Production: The Evidence from Five Countries*. Zurich: Institute for Empirical Research in Economics, University of Zurich.

Brams, Steven. 1980. "Approval Voting in Multicandidate Elections." *Policy Studies Journal* 9: 102–8.

Buchanan, James M. [1979] 1984. "Politics without Romance." In *The Theory of Public Choice—II*, ed. James M. Buchanan and Robert D. Tollison. Ann Arbor: University of Michigan Press.

Buchanan, James M., and Gordon Tullock. 1962. *The Calculus of Consent*. Ann Arbor: University of Michigan Press.

Cain, Michael J. G. 1993. Review of Lewin 1991. *Public Choice* 76: 378–80.

Caldwell, Bruce J. 1982. *Beyond Positivism*. London: George Allen & Unwin.

Caldwell, Bruce J. 1992. "Friedman's Predictive Instrumentalism—A Modification." *Research in the History of Economic Thought and Methodology* 10: 119–28.

Calvert, Randall L. 1985. "Robustness of Multidimensional Voting Models: Candidate Motivations, Uncertainty, and Convergence." *American Journal of Political Science* 29: 69–95.

Campbell, Angus, Philip Converse, Warren Miller, and Donald Stokes. 1960. *The American Voter*. New York: John Wiley & Sons.

Campbell, Angus, Gerald Gurin, and Warren E. Miller. 1954. *The Voter Decides*. Evanston Ill.: Row, Peterson.

Campbell, Donald T. 1975. "On the Conflicts between Biological and Social Evolution and between Psychology and Moral Tradition." *American Psychologist*. December: 1103–26.

Carnap, Rudolf. 1979. *Der Logische Aufbau der Welt*. Frankfurt/Main: Ullstein.

Cashdan, Elizabeth, ed. 1990. *Risk and Uncertainty in Tribal and Peasant Economies*. Boulder, Colo.: Westview .

Chong, Dennis. 1991. *Collective Action and the Civil Rights Movement*. Chicago: University of Chicago Press.

Clark, Margaret S., and Judson Mills. 1979. "Interpersonal Attraction in Exchange and Communal Relationships." *Journal of Personality and Social Psychology* 37: 414–25.

Clark, Margaret, and Sherri P. Pataki. 1995. "Interpersonal Processes Influencing Attraction and Relationships." In *Advanced Social Psychology,* ed. Abraham Tesser. New York: McGraw-Hill.

Coase, R. H. [1937] 1988. *The Firm, the Market, and the Law.* Chicago: University of Chicago Press.

Cohen, Linda. 1979. "Cyclic Sets in Multidimensional Voting Models." *Journal of Economic Theory* 20: 1–12.

Collard, D. 1978. *Altruism and Economy: A Study in Non-Selfish Economics.* Oxford: Martin Robertson.

Commager, Henry Steele. 1977. *The Empire of Reason.* Garden City, N.Y.: Doubleday.

Condorcet, Marquis de. [1785] 1972. *Essai sur l'application de l'analyse à la probabilité des voix.* New York: Chelsea.

Converse, Philip E. 1964. "The Nature of Belief Systems in Mass Publics." In David Apter, ed., *Ideology and Discontent.* New York: Free Press.

Cook, Karen Schweers, and Margaret Levi, eds. 1990. *The Limits of Rationality.* Chicago: University of Chicago Press.

Cosmides, Leda, and John Tooby. 1992. "Are Humans Good Intuitive Statisticians after All? Rethinking Some Conclusions from the Literature on Judgment under Uncertainty." University of California at Santa Barbara. Mimeograph.

Coughlin, Peter J. 1992. *Probabilistic Voting Theory.* Cambridge: Cambridge University Press.

Cox, Gary. 1984. "An Expected-Utility Model of Electoral Competition." *Quality and Quantity* 18: 337–49.

Cox, Gary. 1990. "Centripetal and Centrifugal Incentives in Electoral Systems." *American Journal of Political Science* 34: 903–35.

Cox, Gary, and Mathew McCubbins. 1993. *Legislative Leviathan.* Berkeley: University of California Press.

Crawford, Vincent, and Joel Sobel. 1982. "Strategic Information Transmission." *Econometrica* 50: 1431–51.

Cyert, R. M., and James G. March. 1961. *A Behavioral Theory of the Firm.* Englewood Cliffs, N. J.: Prentice-Hall.

Darley, John M., and Bibb Latané. 1968. "Bystander Intervention in Emergencies: Diffusion of Responsibility." *Journal of Personality and Social Psychology* 8: 377–83.

Davidson, Donald. 1984. "Truth and Meaning." *Inquiries into Truth and Interpretation.* Oxford: Oxford University Press.

Davis, Kingsley, and Wilbert Moore. 1945. "Some Principles of Stratification." *American Sociological Review* 10: 242–49.

Dawes, Robyn M., Jeanne McTavish, and Harriet Shaklee. 1977. "Behavior, Communication, and Assumptions about Other People's Behavior in a Commons Dilemma Situation." *Journal of Personality and Social Psychology* 35: 1–11.

Deci, Edward L., and Richard M. Ryan. 1985. *Intrinsic Motivation and Self-Determination in Human Behavior.* New York: Plenum.

DeNardo, James. 1995. *The Amateur Strategist: Intuitive Deterrence Theories and the Politics of the Nuclear Arms Race.* Cambridge: Cambridge University Press.

Denzau, Arthur, and Douglass North. 1994. "Shared Mental Models: Ideologies and Institutions." *Kyklos* 47: 1–31.

Dodd, Larry. 1976. *Coalitions in Parliamentary Governments.* Princeton: Princeton University Press.

Dodd, Lawrence C. 1977. "Congress and the Quest for Power." In *Congress Reconsidered,* ed. Lawrence C. Dodd and Bruce I. Oppenheimer. New York: Praeger.

Dollard, John, and Neil E. Miller. 1941. *Social Learning and Imitation.* New Haven: Yale University Press.

Dowding, K. H. 1991. *Rational Choice and Political Power.* London: Edward Elgar.

Downs, Anthony. 1957. *An Economic Theory of Democracy.* New York: Harper & Row.

Dreier, Volker. 1993. *Zur Logik politikwissenschaftlicher Theorien.* Frankfurt/Main: Lang.

Duesenberry, James. 1952. *Income, Saving and the Theory of Consumer Behavior.* Cambridge, Mass.: Harvard University Press.

Dupre, John. 1993. *The Disorder of Things.* Cambridge, Mass.: Harvard University Press.

Duverger, Maurice. 1954. *Political Parties.* New York: Wiley.

Earl, Peter. 1983. *The Economic Imagination: Towards a Behavioral Analysis of Choice.* Armonk, N. Y.: Sharpe.

Easton, David, and Jack Dennis. 1969. *Children in the Political System: Origins of Political Legitimacy.* New York: McGraw-Hill.

Eatwell, John, Murray Milgate, and Peter Newman. 1987. *Utility and Probability.* New York: Norton.

Einhorn, Hillel J., and Robin M. Hogarth. 1978. "Confidence in Judgment: Persistence of the Illusion of Validity." *Psychological Review* 85: 395–416.

Einhorn, Hillel J., and Robin M. Hogarth. 1987. "Decision Making Under Ambiguity." In *Rational Choice: The Contrast between Economics and Psychology,* ed. Robin M. Hogarth and Melvin W. Reder. Chicago: University of Chicago Press.

Ellickson, Robert C. 1989. "Bringing Culture and Human Frailty to Rational Actors: A Critique of Classical Law and Economics." *Chicago-Kent Law Review* 65: 23–55.

Ellickson, Robert C. 1991. *Order without Law: How Neighbors Settle Disputes.* Cambridge, Mass.: Harvard University Press.

Elster, Jon. 1975. *Leibniz et la formation de l'esprit capitaliste.* Paris: Aubier Montaigne.

Elster, Jon. 1976. "A Note on Hysteresis in the Social Sciences." *Synthese* 33: 371–91.

Elster, Jon. 1983. *Explaining Technical Change.* Cambridge: Cambridge University Press.

Elster, Jon. 1986. Introduction. In idem, ed., *Rational Choice.* New York: New York University Press.

Elster, Jon. 1989a. *The Cement of Society.* Cambridge: Cambridge University Press.

Elster, Jon. 1989b. *Nuts and Bolts for the Social Sciences.* Cambridge: Cambridge University Press.

Elster, Jon. 1989c. *Solomonic Judgements: Studies in the Limitations of Rationality.* Cambridge: Cambridge University Press.

Enelow, James, and Melvin J. Hinich. 1984. *The Spatial Theory of Voting: An Introduction.* Cambridge: Cambridge University Press.

Engel, James F., Roger D. Blackwell, and David T. Kollat. 1978. *Consumer Behavior,* 3rd ed. Hinsdale, Ill.: Dryden Press.

Ensminger, Jean. 1994. "Transaction Costs through Time: The Case of the Orma Pastoralists in East Africa." In *Anthropology and Institutional Economics,* ed. James Acheson. Lanham, Md.: University Press of America.

Etzioni, Amitai. 1988. *The Moral Dimension.* New York: Free Press.

Farmer, James. 1985. *Lay Bare the Heart: An Autobiography of the Civil Rights Movement.* New York: New American Library.

Farrell, James. 1988. "Meaning and Credibility in Cheap Talk Games." In *Mathematical Models in Economics,* ed. M. Dempster. Oxford: Oxford University Press.

Feddersen, Timothy J. 1992. "A Voting Model Implying Duverger's Law and Positive Turnout." *American Journal of Political Science* 36: 939–62.

Fenno, Richard F., Jr. 1973. *Congressmen in Committees.* Boston: Little, Brown.

Ferejohn, John. 1991. "Rationality and Interpretation: Parliamentary Elections in Early Stuart England." In *The Economic Approach to Politics,* ed. Kristin Monroe. New York: Harper-Collins.

Ferejohn, John, and Morris Fiorina. 1974. "The Paradox of Not Voting." *American Political Science Review* 68: 525–36.

Ferejohn, John, and Morris P. Fiorina. 1975. "Closeness Only Counts in Horseshoes and Dancing." *American Political Science Review* 69: 920–25.

Ferejohn, John, and Morris P. Fiorina. 1993. "To P or Not to P? Still Asking after All These Years." Stanford University. Typescript.

Ferejohn, John, and Debra Satz. 1994. "Rational Choice Theory and Folk Psychology." Stanford University. Working Paper.

Festinger, Leon. 1957. *A Theory of Cognitive Dissonance.* Evanston, Ill.: Row-Peterson.

Fiorina, Morris P. 1979. Comments on Gordon Tullock's "Public Choice in Practice." In *Collective Decision Making,* ed. Clifford S. Russel. Baltimore: Johns Hopkins University Press.

Fiorina, Morris P. 1981. *Retrospective Voting in American National Elections.* New Haven: Yale University Press.

Fiorina, Morris P. 1989. *Congress: Keystone of the Washington Establishment.* New Haven: Yale University Press.

Fiorina, Morris P. 1990. "Information and Rationality in Elections." In *Information and Democratic Processes,* ed. John A. Ferejohn and James H. Kuklinski. Urbana: University of Illinois Press.

Fiorina, Morris P. 1994. "Divided Government in the American States: A By-Product of Legislative Professionalism." *American Political Science Review* 88: 304–16.

Fiorina, Morris P. 1995. "Rational Choice and the New (?) Institutionalism." *Polity,* forthcoming.

Fiorina, Morris P., and Charles R. Plott. 1978. "Committee Decisions under Majority Rule: An Experimental Study." *American Political Science Review* 72: 575–98.

Fogelman, Eva. 1994. *Conscience and Courage: Rescuers of Jews during the Holocaust.* New York: Doubleday.

Frank, Robert H. 1988. *Passions within Reason: The Strategic Role of the Emotions.* New York: Norton.

Frank, Robert H., Thomas Gilovich, and Dennis T. Regan. 1993. "Does Studying Economics Inhibit Cooperation?" *Journal of Economic Perspectives* 7 (2): 159–71.

Friedman, Milton. 1953a. *Essays in Positive Economics.* Chicago: University of Chicago Press.

Friedman, Milton. 1953b. "Methodology of Positive Economics." In idem, 1953a.

Frohlich, Norman, Joseph Oppenheimer and Oran Young. 1971. *Political Leadership and Collective Goods.* Princeton: Princeton University Press.

Gaehde, Ulrich. 1993. *T-Theoretizitä und Holismus.* Frankfurt/Main: Lang.

Gauthier, David. 1986. *Morals by Agreements.* Oxford: Clarendon Press.

Gellner, Ernest. 1985. *Relativism and the Social Sciences.* Cambridge: Cambridge University Press.

Gibson, Quentin. 1960. *The Logic of Social Enquiry.* London: Routledge & Kegan Paul.

Gilpin, Robert. 1987. *The Political Economy of International Relations.* Princeton: Princeton University Press.

Gödel, Kurt [1931] 1962. *On Formally Undecidable Propositions.* New York: Basic Books.

Goldstone, Jack A. 1994. "Is Revolution Individually Rational?" *Rationality and Society* 6: 139–66.

Gosnell, Harold F. 1927. *Getting Out the Vote: An Experiment in the Simulation of Voting.* Chicago: University of Chicago Press.

Gould, Stephen Jay, and Richard Lewontin. 1984. "The Spandrels of San Marco and the Panglossian Paradigm: A Critique of the Adaptationist Pro-

284

gramme." In *Conceptual Issues in Evolutionary Biology,* ed. Elliott Sober. Cambridge, Mass.: MIT Press.

Granovetter, Mark. 1985. "Economic Action and Social Structure: The Problem of Embeddedness." *American Journal of Sociology* 91: 481–510.

Green, Donald Philip. 1990. "The Effects of Measurement Error on Two-Stage Least-Squares Estimates." *Political Analysis* 2: 57–74.

Green, Donald Philip. 1992. "The Price Elasticity of Mass Preferences." *American Political Science Review* 86: 128-48.

Green, Donald, and John Cowden. 1992. "Who Protests: Self-Interest and White Opposition to Busing." *Journal of Politics* 54: 471–96.

Green, Donald Philip, and Bradley L. Palmquist. 1990. "Of Artifacts and Partisan Instability." *American Journal of Political Science* 32: 884–907.

Greenberg, Joseph. 1979. "Consistent Majority Rule over Compact Sets of Alternatives." *Econometrica* 47: 627–36.

Grether, David, and Charles Plott. 1979. "Economic Theory of Choice and the Preference Reversal Phenomenon." *American Economic Review* 69: 623–38.

Grofman, Bernard. 1993. "On the Gentle Art of Rational Choice Bashing." In *Information, Participation and Choice,* ed. Bernard Grofman. Ann Arbor: University of Michigan Press.

Grofman, Bernard. 1994. "Downsian Political Economy and the Neo-Downsian Agenda." University of California at Irvine. Mimeograph.

Grofman, Bernard, and Guillermo Owen, eds. 1986. "Information Pooling and Group Decisionmaking." Greenwich, Conn.: JAI.

Hansen, Stephen, Thomas R. Palfrey, and Howard Rosenthal. 1987. "The Downsian Model of Electoral Participation: Formal Theory and Empirical Analysis of the Constituency Size Effect." *Public Choice* 52: 15–33.

Hardin, Russell. 1971. "Collective Action as an Agreeable N-Person Prisoner's Dilemma." *Behavioral Science* 16: 472–81.

Hardin, Russell. 1982. *Collective Action.* Baltimore: Johns Hopkins University Press.

Harsanyi, John C. 1966. "A Bargaining Model for Social Status in Informal Groups and Formal Organizations." *Behavioral Science* 11: 357–69.

Harsanyi, John C. 1969. "Rational-Choice Models of Political Behavior vs. Functionalist and Conformist Theories." *World Politics* 21: 513–38.

Hausman, Daniel M. 1992a. *Essays in Philosophy and Economic Methodology.* Cambridge: Cambridge University Press.

Hausman, Daniel M. 1992b. *The Inexact and Separate Science of Economics.* Cambridge: Cambridge University Press.

Hayek, Friedrich. 1976. *Individualism and Economic Order.* London: Routledge & Kegan Paul.

Hegel, G.W.F. [1821] 1942. *Philosophy of Right.* Trans. T. M. Knox. Oxford: Oxford University Press.

Hempel, Carl G. 1965. *Aspects of Scientific Explanation and Other Essays in the Philosophy of Science.* New York: Free Press.

Hempel, Carl G. 1966. *Philosophy of Natural Science.* Englewood Cliffs, N. J.: Prentice Hall.

Herrnstein, Richard J. 1990. "Rational Choice Theory." *American Psychologist* 45: 356–67.

Herrnstein, Richard J. 1993. "Behavior, Reinforcement, and Utility." In *The Origin of Values,* ed. Michael Hechter, Lynn Nadel, and Richard E. Michod. New York: Aldine de Gruyter.

Hinich, Melvin, and Michael Munger. 1994. *Ideology and the Theory of Political Choice.* Ann Arbor: University of Michigan Press.

Hirschman, Albert O. 1982. *Shifting Involvements.* Princeton: Princeton University Press.

Hirshleifer, Jack. 1983. "From Weakest-Link to Best-Shot: The Voluntary Provision of Public Goods." *Public Choice* 41: 371–86.

Hirshleifer, Jack. 1985. "The Expanding Domain of Economics." *American Economic Review* 75. 53–68.

Hogarth, Robin M., and Melvin W. Reder. 1987 "Introduction: Perspectives from Economics and Psychology." In *Rational Choice: The Contrast between Economics and Psychology,* ed. Robin M. Hogarth and Melvin W. Reder. Chicago: University of Chicago Press.

Holsti, O. R. 1979. "Theories of Crisis Decision Making." In *Diplomacy: New Approaches in History, Theory, and Policy,* ed. P. G. Lauren. New York: Free Press.

Horowitz, Donald L. 1985. *Ethnic Groups in Conflict.* Berkeley: University of California Press.

Horowitz, Donald. 1991. *A Democratic South Africa?* Berkeley: University of California Press.

Hotelling, Harold. 1929. "Stability in Competition." *Economic Journal* 39: 41–57.

Hsee, Christopher K. In press. "Elastic Justification: How Task-Irrelevant Yet Affectively Tempting Factors Influence Decisions." *Organizational Behavior and Human Decision Processes.*

Huntington, Samuel P. 1984. "Will More Countries Become Democratic?" *Political Science Quarterly* 99 (2): 193–218.

Hurley, Susan. 1989. *Natural Reasons.* Cambridge, Mass.: Harvard University Press.

Hutchison, Terence. 1938. *The Significance and Basic Postulates of Economic Theory.* London: Macmillan.

Hutchison, Terence. 1994. *The Uses and Abuses of Economics.* New York: Routledge.

Isen, Alice M., and Robert Patrick. 1983. "The Effect of Positive Feelings on Risk Taking: When the Chips are Down." *Organizational Behavior & Human Performance* 31: 194–202.

286

Janis, Irving L., and Leon Mann. 1977. *Decision Making: A Psychological Analysis of Choice, Conflict, and Commitment.* New York: Free Press.

Jung, Courtney, and Ian Shapiro. 1995. "South Africa's Negotiated Transition: Democracy, Opposition, and the New Constitutional Order." *Politics and Society* 23, forthcoming.

Kahneman, Daniel, Jack L. Knetsch, and Richard Thaler. 1987. "Fairness and the Assumptions of Economics." In *Rational Choice: The Contrast between Economics and Psychology,* ed. Robin W. Hogarth and Melvin W. Reder. Chicago: University of Chicago Press.

Kahneman, Daniel, Jack L. Knetsch, and Richard Thaler. 1991. "The Endowment Effect, Loss Aversion, and the Status Quo Bias." *Journal of Economic Perspectives* 5: 193–206.

Kahneman, Daniel, Paul Slovic, and Amos Tversky, eds. 1982. *Judgment under Uncertainty: Heuristics and Biases.* Cambridge: Cambridge University Press.

Kahneman, Daniel, and Amos Tversky. 1979. "Prospect Theory: An Analysis of Decision under Risk." *Econometrica* 47: 263–91.

Kahneman, Daniel, and Amos Tversky. 1984. "Choices, Values and Frames." *American Psychologist* 39: 341–50.

Kamenka, Eugene. 1985. "Revisionist Marxism and Materialist Interpretation of History." Lectures at Australian National University, Canberra.

Katona, George. 1975. *Psychological Economics.* New York: Elsevier.

Kelman, Mark. 1988. "On Democracy-Bashing: A Skeptical Look at the Theoretical and 'Empirical' Practice of the Public Choice Movement." *Virginia Law Review* 74: 199–273.

Kelman, Steven. 1987. *Making Public Policy.* New York: Basic Books.

Key, V. O. 1949. *Southern Politics in State and Nation.* New York: Knopf.

Keynes, John Maynard. 1936. *The General Theory of Employment, Interest, and Money.* London: Macmillan.

Kiewiet, D. Roderick. 1983. *Macroeconomics and Micropolitics.* Chicago: University of Chicago Press.

Kiewiet, D. Roderick, and Mathew D. McCubbins. 1991. *The Logic of Delegation.* Chicago: University of Chicago Press.

Kinder, Donald R., and Kiewiet, D. Roderick. 1981. "Sociotropic Politics: The American Case." *British Journal of Political Science* 11: 129-61.

Kinder, Donald R., and David O. Sears. 1985. "Public Opinion and Political Action." In *Handbook of Social Psychology,* 3rd ed., vol. 2, ed. Gardner Lindzey and Elliott Aronson. New York: Random House.

Kinder, Donald R., and Lynn M. Sanders. 1994. *Divided by Color: Racial Politics and Democratic Ideals in the American Republic.* University of Michigan. Unpublished manuscript.

Kitcher, Philip. 1985. *Vaulting Ambition.* Cambridge, Mass.: MIT Press.

Kramer, Gerald. 1973. "On a Class of Equilibrium Conditions for Majority Rule." *Econometrica* 41: 285–97.

Kramer, Gerald. 1978. "Existence of Electoral Equilibrium." In *Game Theory and Political Science,* ed. Peter Ordeshook. New York: New York University Press.

Krebs, John R., A. Kacelnik, and P. Taylor. 1978. "Test of Optimal Sampling by Foraging Great Tits." *Nature* 275: 27–31.

Krehbiel, Keith. 1988. "Spatial Models of Legislative Choice." *Legislative Studies Quarterly* 13: 259–319.

Krehbiel, Keith. 1991. *Information and Legislative Organization.* Ann Arbor: University of Michigan Press.

Kreps, David, Paul Milgrom, John Roberts, and Robert Wilson. 1982. "Rational Cooperation in the Finitely Repeated Prisoner's Dilemma." *Journal of Economic Theory* 27: 245–52.

Kristof, Nicholas D. "Lamas Seek the Holy Child, but Politics Intrude." *New York Times,* 1 October 1990.

Kuhn, Thomas S. 1962. *The Structure of Scientific Revolutions.* Chicago: University of Chicago.

Kuhn, Thomas S. 1970. "Reflections on My Critics." In *Criticism and the Growth of Knowledge,* ed. Imre Lakatos and Alan Musgrave. Cambridge: Cambridge University Press.

Ladha, Krishna. 1992. "Condorcet's Jury Theorem, Free Speech and Correlated Votes." *American Journal of Political Science* 36: 617–34.

Ladha, Krishna. 1993. "Condorcet's Jury Theorem in the Light of de Finetti's Theorem: Majority Rule with Correlated Votes." *Social Choice and Welfare* 10: 69–86.

Ladha, Krishna, and Gary Miller. 1995. "Political Discourse, Factions, and the General Will: Correlated Voting and Condorcet's Jury Theorem." In *Social Choice and Political Economy,* ed. Norman Schofield. Boston: Kluwer.

Laing, James, and Scott Olmsted. 1978. "An Experimental and Game-Theoretic Study of Committees." In *Game Theory and Political Science,* ed. Peter C. Ordeshook. New York: New York University Press.

Lakatos, Imre. 1970. "Falsification and the Methodology of Scientific Research Programmes." In *Criticism and the Growth of Knowledge,* ed. Imre Lakatos and Alan Musgrave. Cambridge: Cambridge University Press.

Lane, Robert E. 1991. *The Market Experience.* Cambridge: Cambridge University Press.

Langer, Ellen J. 1983. *The Psychology of Control.* Beverly Hills, Cal.: Sage.

Larrick, Richard P., James N. Morgan, and Richard E. Nisbett. 1990. "Teaching the Use of Cost-Benefit Reasoning in Everyday Life." *Psychological Science* 1 (6): 362–70.

Lasch, Christopher. 1991. *The True and Only Heaven.* New York: Norton.

Lau, Richard R., David Sears, and R. Centers. 1979. "The 'Positivity Bias' in Evaluations of Public Figures: Evidence against Instrumental Artefacts." *Public Opinion Quarterly* 43: 347–58.

Laudan, Larry. 1977. *Progress and Its Problems.* Berkeley: University of California Press.

Laver, Michael. 1980. "Political Solutions to the Collective Action Problem." *Political Studies* 28: 195–209.

Laver, Michael, and Norman Schofield. 1990. *Multiparty Government.* Oxford: Oxford University Press.

Laver, Michael, and Kenneth A. Shepsle. 1996. *Making and Breaking Governments: Cabinets and Legislatures in Parliamentary Democracies.* Cambridge: Cambridge University Press.

Lea, Stephen E. G., Roger M. Tarpy, and Paul Webley. 1987. *The Individual in the Economy.* Cambridge: Cambridge University Press.

Ledyard, John O. 1984. "The Pure Theory of Large Two-Candidate Elections." *Public Choice* 44: 7–41.

Leontief, Wassily. 1982. "Academic Economics." *Science* 217: 104, 107.

Lepper, Mark R., D. Greene, and Richard E. Nisbett. 1973. "Undermining Children's Intrinsic Interest with Extrinsic Reward: A Test of the 'Overjustification Hypothesis.'" *Journal of Personality and Social Psychology* 28: 129–37.

Lewin, Leif. 1991. *Self-Interest and Public Interest in Western Politics.* New York: Oxford University Press.

Lewontin, Richard. 1984. "Adaptation." In *Conceptual Issues in Evolutionary Biology,* ed. Elliott Sober. Cambridge, Mass.: MIT Press.

Lichtenstein, Sarah, and Paul Slovic. 1971. "Reversal of Preferences between Bids and Choices in Gambling Decisions." *Journal of Experimental Psychology* 89: 46–55.

Linder, Darwyn E. 1981. "Social Trap Analogs: The Tragedy of the Commons in the Laboratory." In *Cooperation and Helping Behavior: Theories and Research,* ed. Valerian J. Derlage and Janusz Grzlak. New York: Academic Press.

Lipnowski, Irwin, and Shlomo Maital. 1983. "Voluntary Provision of a Pure Public Good as the Game of Chicken." *Journal of Public Economics* 20: 381–86.

Lipset, Seymour M., Paul F. Lazarsfeld, Allen H. Barton, and Juan Linz. 1954. "The Psychology of Voting: An Analysis of Political Behavior." In *Handbook of Social Psychology,* vol. 2, ed. Gardner Lindzey. Reading, Mass.: Addison-Wesley.

Little, Daniel. 1991. *Varieties of Social Explanation.* Boulder, Colo.: Westview.

Little, Daniel. 1993. "On the Scope and Limits of Generalizations in the Social Sciences." *Synthese* 97: 183–207.

Loewenstein, George, and Jon Elster, eds. 1992. *Choice over Time.* New York: Russell Sage.

Lohmann, Susanne. 1993. "A Signaling Model of Informative and Manipulative Political Action." *American Political Science Review* 88: 319–30.

Londregan, John, and James Snyder, Jr. 1995. "Comparing Committee and

Floor Preferences." In *Positive Theories of Congressional Institutions,* ed. Kenneth Shepsle and Barry Weingast. Ann Arbor: University of Michigan Press.

Loomes, Graham, and Robert Sugden. 1982. "Regret Theory: An Alternative Theory of Rational Choice under Uncertainty." *Economic Journal* 92: 805–24.

Luce, R. Duncan. 1959. "Analyzing the Social Process Underlying Group Voting Patterns." In *American Voting Behavior,* ed. Eugene Burdick and Arthur J. Brodbeck. New York: Free Press.

McAdam, Doug. 1982. *Political Process and the Development of Black Insurgency, 1930–1970.* Chicago: University of Chicago Press.

McAdam, Doug. 1988. "Social Movements." In *Handbook of Sociology,* ed. Neil J. Smelser. Beverly Hills, Cal.: Sage.

McDaniel, William C., and Frances Sistrunck. 1991. "Management Dilemmas and Decisions." *Journal of Conflict Resolution* 35: 21–42.

Machlup, Fritz. 1956. "Terence Hutchison's Reluctant Ultra-Empiricism." *Southern Economic Journal* 22: 483–93.

MacIntyre, Alasdair. 1972. "Is a Science of Comparative Politics Possible?" In *Philosophy, Politics, and Society,* 4th series, ed. Peter Laslett, W. G. Runciman, and Quentin Skinner. Oxford: Basil Blackwell.

McKelvey, Richard D. 1976. "Intransitivities in Multidimensional Voting Models and Some Implications for Agenda Control." *Journal of Economic Theory* 12: 472–82.

McKelvey, Richard D. 1979. "General Conditions of Global Intransitivities in Formal Voting Models." *Econometrica* 47 (5): 1085–1112.

McKelvey, Richard D. 1986. "Covering, Dominance, and Institution Free Properties of Social Choice." *American Journal of Political Science* 30: 283–315.

McKelvey, Richard, and Peter Ordeshook. 1990. "A Decade of Experimental Research on Spatial Models of Elections and Committees." In *Advances in the Spatial Theory of Voting,* ed. James Enelow and Melvin Hinich. Cambridge: Cambridge University Press.

McKelvey, Richard, and Toby Page. 1986. "Common Knowledge, Consensus, and Aggregate Information." *Econometrica* 54: 109–27.

McKelvey, Richard, and Norman Schofield. 1986. "Structural Instability of the Core." *Econometrica* 15: 179–88.

McKenzie, Lionel. 1959. "On the Existence of General Equilibrium for a Competitive Economy." *Econometrica* 27: 54–71.

McKinsey, James C. C., A. C. Sugar, and Patrick C. Suppes. 1953. "Axiomatic Foundations of Classical Particle Mechanics." *Journal of Rational Mechanics and Analysis* 2: 253–72.

McLean, Iain. 1995. "The First Golden Age of Social Choice, 1784–1803." In *Social Choice, Welfare and Ethics,* ed. William Barnett et al. Cambridge: Cambridge University Press.

McLean, Iain, and Arnold Urken. 1992. "Did Jefferson or Madison Understand Condorcet's Theory of Social Choice?" *Public Choice* 73: 445–57.

Magnusson, David, ed. 1981. *Towards a Psychology of Situations.* Hillsdale, N. J.: Erlbaum.

Mandler, George. 1982. "The Structure of Value: Accounting for Taste." In *Affect and Cognition: The Seventeenth Annual Carnegie Symposium on Cognition,* ed. Margaret S. Clark and S. T. Fiske. Hillsdale, N. J.: Erlbaum.

Mansbridge, Jane J. 1986. *Why We Lost the ERA.* Chicago: University of Chicago Press.

Mansbridge, Jane J. 1990. *Beyond Self-Interest.* Chicago: University of Chicago Press.

Margolis, Howard. 1982. *Selfishness, Altruism, and Rationality: A Theory of Social Choice.* Cambridge: Cambridge University Press.

Margolis, Howard. 1993. *Paradigms and Barriers.* Chicago: University of Chicago Press.

Marshall, Alfred. 1938. *Principles of Economics,* 8th ed. London: Macmillan.

Matthews, Steve. 1982. "Local Simple Games in Public Choice Mechanisms." *International Economic Review* 23: 623–45.

Maupertuis, P.L.M. [1744] 1964. *Maupertuis.* Ed. Emile Callot. Paris: Marcel Riviere.

Mayer, Thomas. 1993. *Truth versus Precision in Economics.* London: Edward Elgar.

Mayhew, David. 1974. *Congress: The Electoral Connection.* New Haven: Yale University Press.

Meehl, Paul E. 1977. "The Selfish Citizen Argument and the Throw Away Vote Argument." *American Journal of Political Science* 71: 11–30.

Miller, Dale T., and Rebecca K. Ratner. 1995. "The Power of the Myth of Self-Interest." *Current Societal Issues in Justice,* ed. L. Montada and Michael J. Lerner. New York: Plenum.

Miller, Gary J. 1992. *Managerial Dilemmas: The Political Economy of Hierarchy.* Cambridge: Cambridge University Press.

Miller, George A. 1967. *The Psychology of Communication:* Seven Essays. Hardmondsworth, U. K.: Penguin.

Miller, Nicholas R. 1980. "A New Solution Set for Tournaments and Majority Voting." *American Journal of Political Science* 21: 769–809.

Mirowski, Philip. 1986. "Mathematical Formalism and Economic Explanation." In *The Reconstruction of Economic Theory,* ed. Philip Mirowski. Boston: Kluwer Nijhoff.

Mirowski, Philip. 1989. *More Heat than Light: Economics as Social Physics, Physics as Nature's Economics.* Cambridge: Cambridge University Press.

Mischel, Walter. 1968. *Personality Assessment.* New York: Wiley.

Mitchell, Robert C. 1979. "National Environmental Lobbies and the Apparent Illogic of Collective Action." In *Collective Decision-Making,* ed. C. Russell. Baltimore: Johns Hopkins University Press.

Moe, Terry. 1979. "On the Scientific Status of Rational Choice Theory." *American Journal of Political Science* 23: 215–43.

Moe, Terry. 1980. *The Organization of Interests*. Chicago: University of Chicago Press.

Monroe, Kristen Renwick, ed. 1991. *The Economic Approach to Politics*. New York: Harper-Collins.

Monroe, Kristen R., Michael C. Barton, and Ute Klingemann. 1990. "Altruism and the Theory of Rational Action: Rescuers of Jews in Nazi Europe." *Ethics* 101: 103–22.

Morris, Aldon. 1984. *The Origin of the Civil Rights Movement*. New York: Free Press.

Morton, Rebecca. 1991. "Groups in Rational Turnout Models." *American Journal of Political Science* 35: 758–76.

Mueller, Dennis C.. 1989. *Public Choice II*. Cambridge: Cambridge University Press.

Mullen, Brian, and Craig Johnson. 1990. *The Psychology of Consumer Behavior*. Hillsdale, N. J.: Erlbaum.

Muller, Jerry. 1993. *Adam Smith in His Time and Ours*. New York: Free Press.

Nachbar, John. 1995. "Prediction, Optimization, and Rational Learning in Games." Washington University Center in Political Economy.

Nagel, Ernest. 1979. *The Structure of Science*. Indianapolis: Hackett.

Nannestad, Peter, and Martin Paldam. 1994. "The Egotropic Welfare Man: A Pooled Cross-Section Study of Economic Voting in Denmark, 1986–92." Institute of Economics, University of Aarhus. Memo.

Neale, Margaret A., and Max Bazerman. 1991. *Cognition and Rationality in Negotiation*. New York: Free Press.

Nelson, Richard R., and Sidney G. Winter. 1992. *An Evolutionary Theory of Economic Change*. Cambridge, Mass.: Harvard University Press.

Newcomb, Theodore M., Kathryn E. Koenig, Richard Flacks, and Donald P. Warwick. 1967. *Persistence and Change*. New York: Wiley.

Nisbett, Richard E., and Lee Ross. 1980. *Human Inference: Strategies and Shortcomings in Social Judgment*. Englewood Cliffs, N. J.: Prentice-Hall.

Nisbett, Richard E., and Timothy D. Wilson. 1977. "Telling More than We Can Know: Verbal Reports on Mental Processes." *Psychological Review* 84: 231–59.

Niskanen, William A. 1993. "The Reflections of a Grump." *Public Choice* 77: 151-58.

Nixon, David, Dganit Olomoki, Norman Schofield, and Itai Sened. 1995. "Probabilistic Multiparty Spatial Competition among Voters." Washington University Center in Political Economy.

North, Douglass. 1981. *Structure and Change in Economic History*. New York: Norton.

North, Douglass. 1990. *Institutions, Institutional Change and Economic Performance*. Cambridge: Cambridge University Press.

North, Douglass. 1994. "Economic Performance through Time." *American Economic Review* 84: 359–68.

Nozick, Robert. 1993. *The Nature of Rationality.* Princeton: Princeton University Press.

Nyarko, Yaw. 1993. "Convergence in Economic Models with Bayesian Hierarchies of Beliefs." New York University. Mimeo.

Olson, Mancur, Jr. [1965] 1971. *The Logic of Collective Action.* Cambridge, Mass.: Harvard University Press.

Olson, Mancur, Jr. 1982. *The Rise and Decline of Nations.* New Haven: Yale University Press.

Opp, Karl-Dieter. 1989. *The Rationality of Political Protest.* Boulder, Colo.: Westview.

Orbell, John M., Alphons J. C. Van de Kragt, and Robyn M. Dawes. 1988. "Explaining Discussion-Induced Cooperation." *Journal of Personality and Social Psychology* 54: 811–19.

Orbell, John N., Alphons J. C. Van de Kragt, and Robyn M. Dawes. 1991. "Covenants without the Sword: The Role of Promises in Social Dilemmas." In *Social Norms and Economic Institutions,* ed. Kenneth Koford and Jeffrey Miller. Ann Arbor: University of Michigan Press.

Ordeshook, Peter C., and Kenneth A. Shepsle, eds. 1982. *Political Equilibrium.* Boston: Kluwer-Nijhoff.

Ordeshook, Peter C., and Langche Zeng. 1994. "Rational Voters and Strategic Voting: Evidence from the 1968, 1980, and 1992 Elections." California Institute of Technology. Working paper.

O'Shaughnessy, John. 1992. *Explaining Buyer Behavior.* Oxford: Oxford University Press.

Oster, George F., and Edward O. Wilson. 1984. "A Critique of Optimization Theory in Evolutionary Biology." In *Conceptual Issues in Evolutionary Biology,* ed. Elliott Sober. Cambridge, Mass.: MIT Press.

Ostrom, Elinor. 1990. *Governing the Commons: The Evolution of Institutions for Collective Action.* Cambridge: Cambridge University Press.

Ostrom, Elinor. 1992. *Crafting Institutions for Self-Governing Irrigation Systems.* San Francisco: ICS.

Page, Frank, and Myrna Wooders. 1995. "Arbitrage with Price-Dependent Preferences and Unbounded Consumption Sets." University of Alabama.

Palfrey, Thomas R., and Howard Rosenthal. 1983. "A Strategic Calculus of Voting." *Public Choice* 41: 7–53.

Palfrey, Thomas R., and Howard Rosenthal. 1984. "Participation and the Provision of Discrete Public Goods: A Strategic Analysis." *Journal of Public Economics* 24: 171–93.

Palfrey, Thomas R., and Howard Rosenthal. 1985. "Voter Participation and Strategic Uncertainty." *American Political Science Review* 79: 62–78.

Palfrey, Thomas R., and Howard Rosenthal. 1988. "Private Incentives and So-

cial Dilemmas: The Effects of Incomplete Information and Altruism."
Journal of Public Economics 28: 309–32.

Palfrey, Thomas R., and Howard Rosenthal. 1991a. "Testing for Effects of
Cheap Talk in a Public Goods Game with Private Information." *Games
and Economic Behavior* 3: 183–220.

Palfrey, Thomas R., and Howard Rosenthal. 1991b. "Testing Game-Theoretic
Models of Free Riding: New Evidence on Probability Bias and Learn-
ing." In *Laboratory Research in Political Economy,* ed. Thomas R. Palfrey.
Ann Arbor: University of Michigan Press.

Penrose, Roger. 1994. *Shadows of the Mind.* Oxford: Oxford University Press.

Plott, Charles R. 1967. "A Notion of Equilibrium and Its Possibility under
Majority Rule." *American Economic Review* 57: 787–806.

Poole, Keith, and Howard Rosenthal. 1991. "Patterns of Congressional Voting."
American Journal of Political Science 35: 228–78.

Popper, Karl. 1945. *The Open Society and Its Enemies.* London: Routledge.

Popper, Karl R. 1961. *The Poverty of Historicism.* New York: Harper & Row.

Popper, Karl R. 1963. *Conjectures and Refutations: The Growth of Scientific Knowledge.* London: Routledge & Kegan Paul.

Popper, Karl. 1970. *Logik der Forschung.* Tübingen: Mohr.

Posner, Michael I. 1973. *Cognition: An Introduction.* Glenview, Ill.: Scott, Foresman.

Prentice, Deborah. 1987. "Psychological Correspondence of Possessions, Attitudes, and Values." *Journal of Personality and Social Psychology* 53:
993–1003.

Prisching, Manfred. 1995. "The Limited Rationality of Democracy: Joseph
Schumpeter as the Founder of Irrational Choice Theory." *Critical Review*
9, no. 3 (Summer), forthcoming.

Putnam, Hilary. 1962. "What Theories Are Not." In *Logic, Methodology, and Philosophy of Science,* ed. Ernest Nagel, Patrick Suppes, and Alfred Tarski.
Stanford: Stanford University Press.

Quattrone, George A., and Amos Tversky. 1984. "Causal vs. Diagnostic Contingencies: On Self-Deception and the Voter's Illusion." *Journal of Personality and Social Psychology* 46: 237–48.

Quine, Willard van Ormand. 1953. "Two Dogmas of Empiricism." In *From a
Logical Point of View,* ed. Willard van Ormand Quine. Cambridge: Cambridge University Press.

Quine, Willard van Ormand, and J. S. Ullian. 1978. *The Web of Belief,* 2nd ed.
New York: Random House.

Ramsey, Frank P. 1960. "Theories." In *The Foundations of Mathematics,* ed. Frank
P. Ramsey. Totowa, N. J.: Rowman & Littlefield.

Randall, William Sterne. 1993. *Thomas Jefferson: A Life.* New York: Holt.

Rapoport, Amnon. 1985. "Public Goods and the MCS Experimental Paradigm." *American Political Science Review* 79: 148–55.

Rawls, John. 1972. *A Theory of Justice.* Cambridge, Mass.: Harvard University Press.

Richards, Diana. 1990. "Is Strategic Decision Making Chaotic?" *Behavioral Science* 35: 219–32.

Riker, William H. 1980. "Implications from the Disequilibrium of Majority Rule for the Study of Institutions." *American Political Science Review* 74: 432–47.

Riker, William H. 1982. *Liberalism against Populism.* San Francisco: Freeman.

Riker, William H. 1986. *The Art of Political Manipulation.* New Haven: Yale University Press.

Riker, William H., and Peter C. Ordeshook. 1968. "A Theory of the Calculus of Voting." *American Political Science Review* 62: 25–42.

Robbins, Lionel. 1935. *An Essay on the Nature and Significance of Economic Science,* 2nd ed. London: Macmillan.

Robinson, Joan. 1964. *Economic Philosophy.* Harmondsworth, U. K.: Penguin.

Rosch, Eleanor, and Carol B. Mervis. 1975. "Family Resemblances: Studies in the Internal Structure of Categories." *Cognitive Psychology* 7: 573–605.

Rosenberg, Alexander. 1985. *The Structure of Biological Science.* Cambridge: Cambridge University Press.

Rosenberg, Alexander. 1992. *Economics—Mathematical Politics or Science of Diminishing Returns?* Chicago: University of Chicago Press.

Rosenberg, Alexander. 1994. "Does Evolutionary Theory Give Comfort of Inspiration to Economics?" In *Natural Images in Economic Thought,* ed. Philip Mirowski. Cambridge: Cambridge University Press.

Rosenstone, Steven J., and John Mark Hansen. 1993. *Mobilization, Participation, and Democracy in America.* New York: Macmillan.

Russell, T., and Richard H. Thaler. 1985. "The Relevance of Quasi-Rationality and Competitive Markets." *American Economic Review* 75: 1071–82.

Sabatier, Paul A. 1992. Review of Ostrom 1990. *American Political Science Review* 86: 248–49.

Salancik, Gerald. 1974. "Inference of One's Attitude from Behavior Recalled under Linguistically Manipulated Cognitive Sets." *Journal of Experimental Social Psychology* 10: 415–27.

Samuelson, Paul A. 1954. "The Pure Theory of Public Expenditure." *Review of Economics and Statistics* 36: 386–89.

Satz, Debra, and John Ferejohn. 1994. "Rational Choice and Social Theory." *Journal of Philosophy* 91: 71–87.

Schattschneider, E. E. 1975. *The Semisovereign People.* Hinsdale, Ill.: Dryden.

Schelling, Thomas. 1960. *The Strategy of Conflict.* Cambridge, Mass.: Harvard University Press.

Schofield, Norman. 1972. "Is Majority Rule Special?" In *Probability Models of Collective Decision Making,* ed. Richard Niemi and Herbert Weisberg. Columbus, O.: Merrill.

Schofield, Norman. 1978a. "Instability of Simple Dynamic Games." *Review of*

Economic Studies 45: 475–94.

Schofield, Norman. 1978b. "The Theory of Dynamic Games." In *Game Theory and Political Science*, ed. Peter C. Ordeshook. New York: New York University Press.

Schofield, Norman. 1984. "Social Equilibrium and Cycles on Compact Sets." *Journal of Economic Theory* 33: 59–71.

Schofield, Norman. 1985a. "Anarchy, Altruism and Cooperation." *Social Choice and Welfare* 2: 207–19.

Schofield, Norman. 1985b. *Social Choice and Democracy.* Berlin: Springer.

Schofield, Norman. 1993. "Political Competition in Multiparty Coalition Governments." *European Journal of Political Research* 23: 1–33.

Schofield, Norman. 1995a. "Existence of a Smooth Social Choice Functor." In *Social Choice, Welfare and Ethics*, ed. William Barnett, et al. Cambridge: Cambridge University Press.

Schofield, Norman. 1995b. "Coalition Politics: A Formal Model and Empirical Analysis." *Journal of Theoretical Politics.*

Schofield, Norman. 1995c. "Research Programs in Preference and Belief Aggregation." In *Social Choice and Political Economy*, ed. Norman Schofield Boston: Kluwer.

Schram, Arthur J.H.C. 1991. *Voter Behavior in Economic Perspective.* Berlin: Springer .

Schroder, Harold M., and Peter Suedfeld, eds. 1971. *Personality Theory and Information Processing.* New York: Ronald.

Schumpeter, Joseph A. 1950. *Capitalism, Socialism, and Democracy*, 3rd ed. London: George Allen & Unwin.

Schumpeter, Joseph A. 1954. *History of Economic Analysis.* Oxford: Oxford University Press.

Schwartz-Shea, Peregrine, and Randy T. Simmons. 1990. "The Layered Prisoners' Dilemma: Ingroup versus Macro-Efficiency." *Public Choice* 65: 61–83.

Scitovsky, Tibor. 1976. *The Joyless Economy.* Oxford: Oxford University Press.

Scriven, Michael. 1988. "Explanations, Predictions, and Laws." In *Theories of Explanation*, ed. Joseph Pitt. Oxford: Oxford University Press.

Sears, David O. 1983. "The Persistence of Early Political Predispositions." In *Review of Personality and Social Psychology*, vol. 4., ed. Ladd Wheeler and Philip Shaver. Beverly Hills, Cal.: Sage.

Sears, David O., and Carolyn L. Funk. 1990. "Self-Interest in Americans' Political Opinions." In *Beyond Self-Interest*, ed. Jane Mansbridge. Chicago: University of Chicago Press.

Sears, David O., and Carolyn L. Funk. 1991. "The Role of Self-Interest in Social and Political Attitudes." In *Advances in Experimental Social Psychology*, vol. 24, ed. Mark P. Zanna. New York: Academic Press.

Selten, Reinhard. 1989. "Evolution, Learning, and Economic Behavior." Nancy L. Schwartz Memorial Lecture. Kellogg Graduate School of Management, Northwestern University.

Selten, Reinhard, and Rolf Stroecker. 1986. "End Behavior in Sequences of Finite Prisoner's Dilemma Super-Games." *Journal of Economic Behavior and Organization* 7: 47–70.

Sen, Amartya K. 1970. *Collective Choice and Social Welfare.* San Francisco: Holden Day.

Sen, Amartya K. 1977. "Rational Fools: A Critique of the Behavioral Foundations of Economic Theory." *Philosophy and Public Affairs* 6: 317–44.

Shafir, Eldar, Itamar Simonson, and Amos Tversky. 1993. "Reason-Based Choice." *Cognition* 49: 11–36.

Shapiro, Ian. 1986. *The Evolution of Rights in Liberal Theory.* Cambridge: Cambridge University Press.

Shapiro, Ian. 1990. "Three Fallacies Concerning Majorities, Minorities, and Democratic Politics." In *Nomos XXXII: Majorities and Minorities,* ed. John Chapman and Alan Hertheimer. New York: New York University Press.

Shapiro, Ian. 1990. *Political Criticism.* Berkeley: University of California Press.

Shavitt, Sharon. 1989. "Operationalizing Functional Theories of Attitudes." In *Attitude Structure and Function,* ed. Anthony R. Pratkanis, Stephen J. Breckler, and Anthony G. Greenwald. Hillsdale, N. J.: Lawrence Erlbaum Associates.

Shepsle, Kenneth A. 1978. *The Giant Jigsaw Puzzle: Democratic Committee Assignments in the Modern House.* Chicago: University of Chicago Press.

Shepsle, Kenneth A. 1991. *Models of Multiparty Electoral Competition.* Chur, Switzerland: Harwood.

Shepsle, Kenneth A., and Barry R. Weingast. 1984. "Uncovered Sets and Sophisticated Voting Outcomes with Implications for Agenda Institutions." *American Journal of Political Science* 28: 49–74.

Shepsle, Kenneth A., and Barry R. Weingast. 1994. "Positive Theories of Congressional Institutions." *Legislative Studies Quarterly* 19: 149–80.

Shepsle, Kenneth A., and Barry R. Weingast. 1995. *Positive Theories of Congressional Institutions.* Ann Arbor: University of Michigan Press.

Simon, Herbert A. 1967. "Motivational and Emotional Controls of Cognition." *Psychological Review* 74: 29–39.

Simon, Herbert A. 1979. *Models of Thought.* New Haven: Yale University Press.

Simon, Herbert A. 1982. *Behavioral Economics and Business Organization.* Vol. 2 of Models of Bounded Rationality. Cambridge, Mass.: MIT Press.

Simon, Herbert A. 1986. "Decision Making and Problem Solving." In *Decision Making: Alternatives to Rational Choice Models,* ed. Mary Zey. Newbury Park, Cal.: Sage.

Sims, Verner M., and James R. Patrick. 1936. "Attitude toward the Negro of Northern and Southern College Students." *Journal of Social Psychology* 7: 192–204.

Skinner, B. F. 1972. *Beyond Freedom and Dignity.* New York: Bantam/Vintage.

Skocpol, Theda. 1979. *States and Social Revolutions.* Cambridge: Cambridge University Press.

Slote, Michael. 1989. *Beyond Optimizing: A Study of Rational Choice*. Cambridge, Mass.: Harvard University Press.

Slovic, P., and S. Lichtenstein. 1983. "Preference Reversals: A Broader Perspective." *American Economic Review* 73: 596–605.

Smelser, Neil J., and Richard Swedberg, eds. 1994. *The Handbook of Economic Sociology*. Princeton: Princeton University Press.

Smith, Adam. [1776] 1976a. *An Inquiry into the Nature and Causes of the Wealth of Nations*. Oxford: Oxford University Press.

Smith, Adam. [1759] 1976b. *The Theory of Moral Sentiments*. Oxford: Oxford University Press.

Smith, Eric Alden, and Bruce Winterhalder, eds. 1992. *Evolutionary Ecology and Human Behavior*. New York: Aldine De Gruyter.

Smith, John Maynard. 1984. "Optimization Theory in Evolution." In *Conceptual Issues in Evolutionary Biology*, ed. Elliott Sober. Cambridge, Mass.: MIT Press.

Sneed, Joseph D. 1979. *The Logical Structure of Mathematical Physics*. Dordrecht: Reidel

Snyder, James M., Jr. 1990. "Campaign Contributions as Investments: The U.S. House of Representatives, 1980–1986." *Journal of Political Economy* 98: 1195–1227.

Snyder, James M., Jr. 1991. "On Buying Legislatures." *Economics and Politics* 3: 93–109.

Sorauf, Frank J. 1988. *Money in American Elections*. Glenview, Ill.: Scott, Foresman.

Stegmüller, Wolfgang. 1986. *Theorie und Erfahrung*. Vol. 2 of *Probleme und Resultate der Analytischen Philosophie and Wissenschaftstheorie*. Berlin: Springer.

Stigler, George J. 1961. "The Economics of Information." *Journal of Political Economy* 69: 213–25.

Stinchcombe, Arthur. 1991. "The Conditions of Fruitfulness of Theorizing about Mechanisms in Social Science." *Philosophy of the Social Sciences* 21: 367–88.

Stouffer, Samuel Andrew. 1955. *Communism, Conformity, and Civil Liberties*. Garden City, N.J.: Doubleday.

Strnad, Jeff. 1985. "The Structure of Continuous-Valued Neutral Monotonic Social Functions." *Social Choice and Welfare* 2: 181–95.

Sugden, Richard. 1986. *The Economics of Rights, Cooperation and Welfare*. Oxford: Basil Blackwell.

Sundquist, James L. 1988. "Needed: A Political Theory for the New Era of Coalition Government in the United States." *Political Science Quarterly* 103 (4): 613–35.

Suppes, Patrick. 1969. *Studies in the Methodology and Foundations of Science*. Dordrecht: Reidel.

Taagepera, Rein, and Matthew Shugart. 1989. *Seats and Votes*. New Haven: Yale University Press.

Taylor, Charles. 1967. "Neutrality in Political Science." In *Philosophy, Politics and Society,* 3rd series, ed. P. Laslett and W. G. Runciman. Oxford: Blackwell.

Taylor, Michael. 1976. *Anarchy and Cooperation.* London: Wiley.

Taylor, Michael. 1982. *Community, Anarchy and Liberty.* Cambridge: Cambridge University Press.

Taylor, Michael. 1987. *The Possibility of Cooperation.* Cambridge: Cambridge University Press.

Taylor, Michael. 1988. "Rationality and Revolutionary Collective Action." In *Rationality and Revolution,* ed. Michael Taylor. Cambridge: Cambridge University Press.

Taylor, Michael. 1989. "Structure, Culture and Action in the Explanation of Social Change." *Politics and Society* 17: 115–62.

Taylor, Michael. 1992. Review of Ostrom 1990. *Natural Resources Journal* 32: 633–48.

Taylor, Michael. N.d. "Good Government: On Hierarchy, Social Capital and the Limitations of Rational Choice Theory." *The Journal of Political Philosophy.* Forthcoming.

Thaler, Richard H. 1987. "The Psychology and Economics Conference Handbook: Comments on Simon, on Einhorn and Hogarth, and on Tversky and Kahneman." In *Rational Choice: The Contrast between Economics and Psychology,* ed. Robin M. Hogarth and Melvin W. Reder. Chicago: University of Chicago Press.

Thaler, Richard. 1991. *Quasi-Rational Economics.* New York: Russell Sage.

Tsebelis, George. 1990. *Nested Games: Rational Choice in Comparative Politics.* Berkeley: University of California Press.

Tullock, Gordon. 1981. "Why So Much Stability?" *Public Choice* 37: 189–202.

Turing, Alan. 1937. "On Computable Numbers, with an Application to the Entscheidungsproblem." *Proceedings of the London Mathematical Society* 42: 230–65.

Turner, John. 1984. "Social Identification and Psychological Group Formation." In *The Social Dimension,* vol. 2, ed. Henri Tajfel. Cambridge: Cambridge University Press.

Tversky, Amos. 1969. "Intransitivity of Preferences." *Psychological Review* 76: 105–110.

Tversky, Amos. 1994. "Contrasting Rational and Psychological Principles of Choice." Stanford University. Typescript.

Tversky, Amos, and Daniel Kahneman. [1974] 1982. "Judgment under Uncertainty: Heuristics and Biases." In *Judgment under Uncertainty,* ed. D. Kahneman, P. Slovic, and A. Tversky. Cambridge: Cambridge University Press.

Urken, Arnold. 1991. "The Condorcet-Jefferson Connection and the Origins of Social Choice Theory." *Public Choice* 72: 213–36.

Urken, Arnold, ed. N.d. *Condorcet's Essai.* New Haven: Yale University Press. Forthcoming.

INDEX